The Administrative History of the Hong Kong Government Agencies, 1841–2002

T0351204

The Administrative History of the Hong Kong Government Agencies, 1841–2002

Ho Pui-yin

香港大學出版社
HONG KONG UNIVERSITY PRESS

Hong Kong University Press
14/F Hing Wai Centre
7 Tin Wan Praya Road
Aberdeen
Hong Kong

© Public Records Office, Government Records Service,
Hong Kong SAR Government 2004

ISBN 962 209 656 5 (Hardback)
ISBN 962 209 657 3 (Paperback)

British Library Cataloguing-in-Publication Data
A catalogue record for this book is available from the British Library.

Secure On-line Ordering
http://www.hkupress.org

Photographs on cover, courtesy Hong Kong Tourism Board
Printed and bound by ColorPrint Production Ltd., Hong Kong, China

Contents

Legend for Charts

· · · ·   related organizations

————   subordinate organs

➤   transformed organs

▭   abolished agencies

Foreword

As a user of the Public Records Office of Hong Kong since its creation some thirty years ago, I congratulate Dr. HO Pui Yin, the author of this book. She is to be commended for her pains-taking work in collecting and organizing the history of the complicated history of the numerous changed in the structure of the agencies of the Hong Kong government from its establishment to the present day. It is an impressive and monumental work.

Such a book has long been needed. Its appearance should save hours of digging in many sources by persons wishing to untangle the intricacies of the many changes of names and shifting connections of the Government agencies and department. I would have profited greatly if there would have been such a book when I began my research into the history of Hong Kong some forty years ago.

At first glance, the compilation of names, dates and responsibilities of the hundreds of the present agencies and their histories appears somewhat daunting, but soon the structure of the work guides you to easily find the information wanted. A scan of the index of the seven chapters of the book will locate the particular item you are hunting for.

Each chapter has the same format:
1. An introductory overview
2. A one page chart of the changes and connections of the administrative unit. At first it look like a labyrinth, but one soon finds the path to find the information needed. The layout is a masterpiece of charting within a limited space. The chart can be worked from the simplicity of the first creation of the unit, to the multiplicity of its many branches today.
3. A chronological list of the Directors of the agency from the date of its creation to the present. These lists are of great value to the historian.
4. A chronological presentation of the important changes in structure, creation of new agencies and transfer of responsibilities from one agency to another. It is all here without having to wade through many scattered sources.

This book should be on the reference shelf of anyone that wishes or needs to understand the convoluted twist and turnings in the development of our present government administration. Within the book are the answers to many questions that are asked by economists, political scientists, historians, businessmen, or anyone who has some need to relate to a government agency.

We are indebted to Dr. HO and the publishers for this invaluable easy to use and long needed resource book on the past and present administrative structure of Hong Kong.

Rev. Carl T. Smith

Honorary Vice President of the Hong Kong Branch of the Royal Asiatic Society
Consultant of the Cultural Institute of the Macau SAR
Distinguished Research Fellow of the Centre of Asian Studies, University of Hong Kong

Preface

In 2002, prior to July 1, the Government of the Hong Kong Special Administrative Region was organized into 16 administrative bureaux and 68 administrative departments. The origins of the administrative structure of the HKSAR Government can be traced back in 1841 when the Hong Kong Colonial Government was first established. From creation to expansion, transfer, fusion and abolition, the evolving experience of these government agencies was long and difficult during the past one-and-a-half centuries. The scale of the Government has grown ever bigger and its structure increasingly complicated. Thus, it is not an easy task to understand the fundamental elements that include the origins, the structure and the functions of government departments. Since the return of Hong Kong to China's sovereignty in 1997, numerous studies of the contemporary administrative structure and personnel system of the HKSAR government departments have been published to identify the advantages and weaknesses of the existing political system. However, very few of these studies have dealt with the fundamental problems facing administrative history. To overcome this lack of information, the following research is a bold effort to trace the origins and outline the evolution of each of the existing government departments since 1841.

If we look at the administrative history since the establishment of government, we find that the Colonial Government in the 1840s was directed by a group of officers from Great Britain. With the Colonial Secretary taking charge of the general administration; the Attorney General for the judicial administration; the Superintendent of Police for the maintenance of social order; the Surveyor General for the basic infrastructure; the Colonial Surgeon for the medical services; the Harbour Master for the import and export control as well as maintaining order of the Hong Kong harbours; and the Postmaster for the internal and external information services; the personal character and management skill of these high officials very often had a direct bearing on the structure and functions of their subordinate offices. Moreover, administrative offices were often named after the titles of the officials, such as the Colonial Secretary's Office, the Surveyor General's Office, etc.

In general, the activities of all government offices were supervised and co-ordinated by the Colonial Secretary's Office since the 1870s. The Colonial Secretary was deputy to the Governor and the official head of the civil service. The department heads carried out the duties laid upon them by the various ordinances and the decisions of the Executive Council. All suggestions for changing policy and requests had to be referred to the appropriate branches of the Colonial Secretariat. This basic government structure had remained the same until the end of the nineteenth century. In the twentieth century, the emphasis of the Government was shifted from the fundamental responsibilities of law and order maintenance, public and urban infrastructure construction, to social hygiene and economic development.

After the Sino-Japanese War it devoted more attention to social services, especially public housing, social welfare and medical services. The role of government agencies increased steadily as the administration became more complex and specialized. The accelerating pace of change was the predominant characteristic of Hong Kong government departments. Offices were reorganized into larger departments, and numerous independent government departments were established in response to the rapid growth of population. For example, immigration control, which was originally a responsibility of the Police Force, became a separate department in 1959. The Transport Department was established in 1968 to take over the management and planning of transportation from the Police Force. In 1982 the Trade, Industry and Customs Department was split into three separate departments, and a new Technical Education and Industrial Training Department was established from sections of the Education and Labour Departments. In 1946 there were 19 administrative departments; and the routine duties of the Government were carried out by more than 60 departments in the 1950s. Enormous increases in public expenditures to fund the modernization of Hong Kong necessarily expanded the civil service. Medical, police, public works and urban services departments represented two-thirds of the entire civil service.[1] In 1973 there were 127 service departments. The principal officials were supported by subordinates who had the required professional or technical skills.

As the earliest officials and their subordinate offices were predecessors of all government departments, my study of the existing government departments, beginning with their first appearance, is organized into seven major chapters. The study does not cover the reorganization of bureaux and departments which took place on 1 July 2002, to co-incide with the introduction of the accountability system. Nor does it cover the related organizations such as the Independent Commission Against Corruption. The development of each sector is grouped under the same chapter and is described by a chart which indicates the evolution of major departments through the establishment and the abolition dates of the departments and subdepartments concerned. The chart is conducted in chronological order by placing the earliest establishments on the upper part of the chart and the contemporary institutions at the bottom. Details of crucial changes, such as the establishment, functions, structure, as well as the abolition of departments, are then laid out following the evolution chart. An index in alphabetical order is presented at the end of the book to facilitate readers locate their special interest. A general and comprehensive view on the structure of the Government is thus given.

The materials used in this book are inevitably derived from government official records. The annual departmental administrative reports are the main study references. Other documents such as despatches, memorandums, and circulars

---

1. Ian Scott and John P. Burns, *The Hong Kong Civil Service—Personnel Policies and Practices*, Hong Kong, Oxford University Press, 1984, pp. 20-22.

between the Hong Kong Colonial Government and the British Colonial Office, between principal officials and governors, and among government departments; Hong Kong ordinances; and commemorative historical studies of individual departments; are also essential research resources. Local newspapers, and the archives of Tung Wah Hospital Group and Po Leung Kuk are valuable information sources to counterbalance the heavy reliance on government documents.

All who have to work with government records will come across the problems of inconsistent and inaccurate research materials. Owing to war or other unknown reasons, some of the annual departmental reports were not produced, some were missing; and even the departments concerned did not possess a complete collection of their own reports. The annual departmental reports were produced independently by departments. No uniform presentation format of departmental annual reports was required, and no clear guidelines were adopted among the government departments. This phenomenon has remained true to this day. In terms of the presentation of the administrative structure and functions of the departments, the official titles of the subordinate organs under different departments were not standardized. Confusion often occurred in using terms such as branch, department, division, section and unit. Sometimes the information provided was a mere repetition of previous years' reports. Most of the departments stressed on the current duties implemented and potential development plans in their annual reports. Worst of all, the information provided by different departments was at times incoherent and contradictory. Repeated comparisons and verifications of materials had to be made. Notwithstanding such work, it was difficult to verify the information for the period prior to the Sino-Japanese War. Thus, it is with a degree of uncertainty in relation to structure and functions, that this book seeks to provide a comprehensive account on the development history of the government departments.

Limited by source nature, the description on the foundation, development, function and structure of each department is highlighted by its internal characteristics in chronological order. Their individual history might not necessarily correspond to contemporary major political or social events. Nor could it lend itself to comparative analysis among government departments. Also, the information collected on the departments cannot be standardized, as the important functional changes and structural reforms took place at different times. On occasions, significant events or changes could not be followed in a continuous manner, due to inconsistent historical materials.

The presentation methodology adopted in this book is perhaps not ideal but is, in my opinion, the most practical one under the circumstances. It is my wish that it can provide a comprehensive picture of each government department by identifying the major changes such as the official title, director, basic structure and functions in chronological order. Academics from other disciplines might be of the opinion that the grouping of the departments does not reflect the existing administrative structure, when measured against the current political and economic concepts. I hope they understand that the aim of this study is to reconstruct the origins and evolution of most of the existing government departments, and to provide readers with a handy and basic reference on the administrative history of government departments and agencies. If it can assist those who wish to compare the past system with the current one, my primary objective will have been more than met.

I take this opportunity to thank the Public Records Office for initiating the publication of this book; the provision of all relevant government departmental reports and generous support during research; in particular Mr Simon Chu Fook-keung and Miss Sarah Choy Cheung-ching, who have expressed valuable opinions on my research findings and analyses. I appreciate greatly the efforts put in by Mr Hui Sung-tak and members of my research team — Miss Cheng Ling-ling, Mr Leung Koon-ting, Miss Yiu Wing-ka and Miss Ng Ka-yee. I am also grateful to the Reverend Carl Smith and Dr James Hayes who have reviewed the manuscript and given many valuable comments on the research output. Special thanks go to my husband Johnson and my daughter Fabien, for without their encouragement and support, this book would not have been completed.

In a reference work of this scale, I envisage that some of my research viewpoints and analyses require further studies. There are bound to be mistakes and errors, which remain my responsibility.

Chapter 1
General Administration

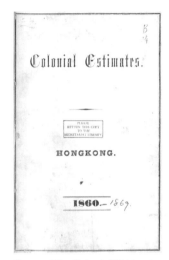

Hong Kong Gazette No. 1, 1841

Cover of the Colonial Estimate, 1869

Content of the Colonial Estimate, 1869

Photograph of Colonial Secretary Sir Thomas Southorn, 1936

Looking north from Government House, CGO westwing in foreground, 1961

Evolvement of General Administration

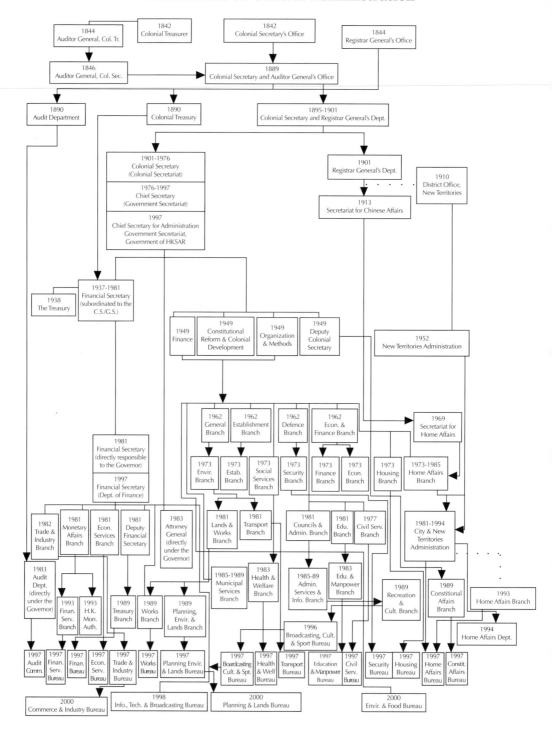

To maintain a stable government administrative structure and develop the economic prosperity of Hong Kong are the prime objectives of the present-day Government of the Hong Kong Special Administrative Region. Such emphases are demonstrated by the pre-eminence of the two principal departments of public and economic services within the government administrative structure — the Department for Adminstration (led by the Chief Secretary for Administration) and the Department of Finance (led by Financial Secretary) before 1 July 2002. However, the administrative structure of the Government, in its foundation stage, was dissimilar. In this chapter, the study explores the history of the precursor of the Department for Administration — the Colonial Secretary's Office — and the role of another leading department — the Registrar General's Office — in order to trace the expansion and transformation process of the composition of the Government's top echelons.

From the mid-nineteenth to the early twentieth centuries, the different functions of the Colonial Secretary's Office and the Registrar General's Office gave a strong impression of a governing policy that, for practical reasons of the day and age, and largely owing to cultural differences, distinguished Chinese from European citizens. Nevertheless, the services rendered by the Registrar General's Office were very different from those provided by the Colonial Secretary's Office, in that they were not limited to European citizens only. The administrative responsibilities of the Registrar General's Office were extended to the Chinese community.

The Colonial Secretary was considered the housekeeper and the principal administrator of the Colonial Government, the right-hand man of the Governor and an adviser to the Executive Council. He was characterised by his multifunctional role in the early years. Apart from undertaking advisory work to the Governor on major policies, he also had the responsibilities as the Government's principal finance overseer and public affairs director. He held the dual post of Colonial Secretary and Auditor General in 1889, and acted concurrently as Colonial Secretary and Registrar General between 1895 and 1901. The duties of the Colonial Secretary's Office were flexible and extensive. As Acting Governor, he also handled such tedious jobs as the approval of leave applications of officials, and the daily expenses of all government departments. The Colonial Secretary's Office, however, was supported only by a group of clerks. The division of duties was not precisely defined until the late 1930s. As a result, it had been criticized as being over-staffed and was downsized in 1932.

In contrast, the Registrar General's Office dealt mainly with Chinese affairs and the Registrar General had been known as the "Protector of Chinese" since his appointment in 1844. The Office was retitled Secretariat for Chinese Affairs in 1913 to reflect its close relationship with the Chinese community. Its particular Chinese characteristics remained until 1969 when the Secretariat for Chinese Affairs passed its functions to its successor — the Secretariat for Home Affairs. The existence of the Registrar General's Office for more than one hundred and twenty years reflected the early Colonial Government's administrative policy towards Chinese citizens.

In fact, the original reason for establishing the post of Registrar General, as suggested by the title, was to deal with the registration of persons, workers, gambling places and brothels etc; and his later duties also covered liaison work related to crime prevention and the preservation of social order of the Chinese community. The close co-operation with local Chinese commercial guilds, charitable associations, watchman districts; and his knowledge of Chinese culture had allowed the Registrar General to play an intermediate role between the Government and the Chinese community. The Registrar General's Office had the opportunity to extend its political powers to the New Territories in 1898 through the nomination of its high-ranking officials to serve in the New Territories. Although a separate administration was soon established there, from the 1920s onwards, the Secretariat for Chinese Affairs shifted its emphasis to resolving social problems among the Chinese. After the Sino-Japanese War, social problems among the Chinese were dealt with by other government departments. The Secretariat for Chinese Affairs was gradually integrated into the Colonial Secretariat from 1969 onwards, having passed its previous duties to various newly established departments such as the Labour Department (1946), the Social Welfare Department (1958), and the Home Affairs Department (1973). The steadily reduced role of the Secretariat for Chinese Affairs was caused by the burgeoning social needs arising from population growth, rapid economic development, and political turmoil during the 1960s.

In 1937, under the supervision of the Colonial Secretary, the Financial Secretary was nominated to supervise particularly the financial administration and direct the accounting work connected with receipts and expenditures of the Government. The Office of Financial Secretary developed quickly in the 1970s, following the transformation of Hong Kong from an export-oriented city to a financial centre. In 1981, directly responsible to the Governor, it became independent and controlled three policy branches and 13 departments working on economic development. In 2002, prior to 1 July, it directed six policy bureaux, 35 administrative departments and two independent agencies. To safeguard the fruits of economic growth, sound and comprehensive financial controls are indispensable to a healthy government. The transformation of the Financial Secretary's Office from a subdepartment of the Colonial Secretariat into a policy-making department, directly responsible to the Chief Executive of the HKSAR, has borne witness to the rapid social changes of society.

Secretariat and Policy Bureaux

Colonial Secretary's Office (1842-1889, 1890-1895)
Colonial Secretary and Auditor General's Office (1889-1890)
Colonial Secretary and Registrar General's Department (1895-1901)
Colonial Secretariat (1901-1976)
Government Secretariat (1976-1997)
Government Secretariat, Government of the Hong Kong Special Administrative Region (1997-2002)

1842	The Colonial Secretary's Office was set up to assist the Governor in administering Hong Kong and J. R. Morrison was appointed Acting Colonial Secretary.
1846	The Colonial Secretary also oversaw the overall financial administration of Hong Kong. The Auditor General was annexed to the Colonial Secretary.
1869	The Colonial Secretary was an adviser to the Executive Council. The Colonial Secretary directed the government of Hong Kong, in the event of absence or sickness of the Governor. Governor Richard MacDonnell recommended the amalgamation of the offices of the Colonial Secretary and the Auditor General, with the abolition of the Office of Colonial Treasurer.
1889	The Colonial Secretary also acted as the Auditor General and was in charge of audit work.
1890	An independent Audit Department was established.
1894	The proposed amalgamation of the offices of the Colonial Secretary and the Registrar General was passed in September, which proposed salary savings between $4,804 and $7,204.
1895	James Haldane Stewart Lockhart held the combined post of Colonial Secretary and Registrar General.
1901	The office of Colonial Secretary and Registrar General was split up and became two independent departments again.
1932	The Colonial Secretary's Office was criticized as being over-centralized and over-staffed, especially for the clerical office staff. The Colonial Secretary not only had to deal with cases where policy was involved, but also matters of a trivial nature, such as administration, approval of expenditure on ordinary items of a uniform kind, personnel matters of all government departments, issuance of permits for occupying land (duties usually performed by the Superintendent of Crown Lands and Surveys), rent allowances, housing allowances, dental treatment allowances, indents on the Crown Agents, etc. The Retrenchment Commission suggested a 20% reduction in staff. The major work of the Office was to concentrate on policies of municipal matters and governmental or political matters.

1937   The post of Financial Secretary was created in July under the Colonial Secretary.

1946   As one of the four principal officers — Attorney General, Colonial Secretary, Financial Secretary and Secretary for Chinese Affairs — the Colonial Secretary was appointed following the liberation of Hong Kong. The Colonial Secretary was the deputy to the Governor and the official head of the civil service. Government departments were placed under the supervision of the various branches of the Colonial Secretariat.

1949   In addition to the General Administration headed by the Deputy Colonial Secretary (comprised the four branches of Communications and Social Services, Defence, Establishment, and Trade and Development), the Colonial Secretariat was also supported by three major branches of Constitutional Reform and Colonial Development Branch; Finance; and Organization and Methods. The Constitutional Reform and Colonial Development Branch controlled matters relating to constitutional reform and the development of the city, and was headed by the Special Adviser. The Finance Branch, headed by the Financial Secretary, oversaw financial administration and civil defence claim matters.

1962   The Colonial Secretary was responsible for the overall direction and supervision of the activities of all administrative departments. As the right-hand man of the Governor, he looked after the general welfare and administration of Hong Kong. Next in rank to the Governor, the Colonial Secretary was a member of both the Executive Council and the Legislative Council. The Colonial Secretariat was supported by members of the civil service under the Deputy Colonial Secretary. The Secretariat was reorganized into four branches: General (consisted of the four sections of Councils, General, Lands and Building, and Political); Defence; Economic and Finance (supported by the Economic and Finance Sections) and Establishment (controlled the three sections of Appointments and Training, Conditions of Service and General Grades). The General Branch supervised the administration of Chinese affairs, education, New Territories administration, press and public relations, social welfare, telecommunications, film censorship, television and urban services. The Defence Branch advised on matters of defence, co-ordinated local forces and acted as the main channel of communication between the Hong Kong Government and British Forces stationed in Hong Kong. The Economic and Finance Branch, under the Financial Secretary, was responsible for the economic and financial policies of the Government and prepared annual budgetary estimates and the final accounts. The Establishment Branch handled the personnel matters of government employees.

1973   The Colonial Secretariat was reorganised, based on the blueprint of the McKinsey's report entitled "The Machinery of Government: A New Framework for Expanding Services", which was released in May. According to the report, the policy branches were to be responsible for policy formulation and should transfer most of their day-to-day administrative load to the departments; ensured that plans were developed for the major programmes; and that departmental objectives and activities were co-ordinated in a balanced manner. The former General Branch was disbanded. The Lands and Buildings Section of the General Branch became the Environment Branch. The Defence Branch was changed to the Security Branch. The Establishment Branch maintained its previous duties. The Economic and Finance Branch was spilt into two branches: Economic and Finance. Three other policy branches were created — Home Affairs, Housing and Social Services. The Secretariat consisted of eight branches — Economic, Environment, Establishment, Finance, Home Affairs, Housing, Security and Social Services. The Environment Branch was responsible for policy and programmes concerning land, planning, design and construction of new towns, pollution, urban services, roads, road transport, traffic, railway, mass transit (construction, engineering aspects and land) and the operational and works aspects of the airport and the harbour. The Home Affairs Branch was responsible for policy and programmes relating to information services, public relations, broadcasting, television, cultural activities, tourism, City District Offices and residual New Territories affairs. The Housing Branch was responsible for policy and programmes covering housing, resettlement, flatted factories, rent control and the co-ordination of departmental services relating to education, health, law and order in the new towns. The Security Branch dealt with policy and programmes on external security, emergencies, internal law and order, auxiliary forces immigration, prison, narcotics and fire services. The Social Services Branch handled policy and programmes covering education, medical and health services, social welfare, charities, labour and recreation.

1976   The Colonial Secretariat was renamed Government Secretariat and the Colonial Secretary was retitled Chief Secretary.

1981   The Administration and Environmental Affairs Branch, set up in September, dealt with environmental protection, public hygiene, country conservation and country parks administration policies. It was retitled Councils and Administration Branch in December. The responsibilities for environmental affairs of the former Administration and Environmental Affairs Branch were transferred to the Home Affairs Branch. The Education Branch was established to take over from the Social Services Branch responsibilities for education and industrial training. The Environment Branch was spilt into two new branches: Lands and Works Branch and Transport Branch. The Lands and Works Branch took over the duties from the Lands Division of the Environment Branch. It was responsible for the formulation of policies, co-ordination of the various activities relating to planning, development and production of lands to meet the requirements of the Government and the private sector, and to ensure the proper disposal and control of land. It supervised the administrative departments such as Buildings Development, Engineering Development, Lands, Mass Transit Office, New Territories Development and Water Supplies.

1982   The Chief Secretary directed ten branches: Civil Service, City and New Territories Administration, Councils and Administration, Education, Home

Affairs, Housing, Lands and Works, Security, Social Services, Transport. The Attorney General (directed the Legal Department) and the Political Adviser were responsible to the Chief Secretary, while the Financial Secretary was directly under the Governor.

I.   Civil Service Branch

II.   The City and New Territories Administration Branch supervised the Hong Kong and Kowloon Region and the New Territories Region.

III.   The Councils and Administration Branch was in charge of the Protocol Office, Public Records Office and Overseas Offices. It directed the overall policy of the Government Data Processing Agency, Government Laboratory, Government Land Transport Agency, Legal Aid Department and Printing Department.

IV.   The Education Branch supervised the Education Department, Technical Education and Industrial Training Department.

V.   The Home Affairs Branch oversaw the Environmental Protection Agency, Information Services Department, London Office, Radio Television Hong Kong, Recreation and Culture Department, Royal Observatory, Television and Entertainment Licensing Authority and Urban Services Department.

VI.   The Housing Branch supervised the Housing Department.

VII.   The Lands and Works Branch directed the Buildings Development Department, Engineering Development Department, Lands Department, Mass Transit Office, New Territories Development Department and Water Supplies Department.

VIII. The Security Branch controlled the Auxiliary Medical Services, Correctional Services Department, Civil Aid Services, Fire Services Department, Immigration Department, Royal Hong Kong Auxiliary Air Force, Royal Hong Kong Police Force and Royal Hong Kong Regiment.

IX.   The Social Services Branch directed the Social Welfare Department, Medical and Health Department, Labour Department and Registry of Trade Unions.

X.   The Transport Branch managed the Transport Department and the Kowloon-Canton Railway.

1983   The Attorney General became directly accountable to the Governor. The Chief Secretary, the Financial Secretary and the Attorney General were the three principal administrators of Hong Kong. With the support of the Political Adviser, the Chief Secretary directed ten branches:

I.   The Civil Service Branch oversaw the Civil Service Training Agency.

II.   New Overseas Offices were added to the Councils and Administration Branch.

III.   The City and New Territories Administration Branch was retitled District Administration Branch.

IV.   The Education Branch was renamed Education and Manpower Branch.

It was responsible for all levels and types of education, industrial training, vocational training, labour matters and rehabilitation. Apart from the Education Department and the Technical Education and Industrial Training Department, it also oversaw the Labour Department (responsibilities for labour and rehabilitation matters were transferred from the previous Social Services Branch to the Education and Manpower Branch), Secretariat of the University and Polytechnic Grants Committee (UPGC), and Registry of Trade Unions.

V. The Social Services Branch was changed to Health and Welfare Branch. In addition to the supervision of the Medical and Health Department and the Social Welfare Department, it also controlled the Environmental Protection Agency transferred from the Home Affairs Branch.

VI. Under the Home Affairs Branch, the Environmental Protection Agency was transferred to the Health and Welfare Branch.

VII. The structure of the Housing Branch remained unchanged.

VIII. The newly established Electrical and Mechanical Services Department was added to the Lands and Works Branch while the Mass Transit Office was detached from the Branch.

IX. The Royal Hong Kong Auxiliary Police Force and other auxiliary units came under the supervision of the Security Branch.

X. The Kowloon-Canton Railway was detached from the Transport Branch.

1984 The supervision of the Royal Observatory was transferred from the Home Affairs Branch to the Councils and Administration Branch.

1985 The Councils and Administration Branch and part of the Home Affairs Branch were restructured into the Administrative Services and Information Branch. The newly created Municipal Services Branch assumed responsibilities for environmental hygiene matters from the Health and Welfare Branch as well as cultural and recreation development from the Home Affairs Branch. The Councils and Administration Branch and the Home Affairs Branch ceased to exist.

1988 The Education and Manpower Branch also supervised the Student Finance Section of the University and Polytechnic Grants Committee, while matters related to rehabilitation work were transferred to the Health and Welfare Branch. The policy responsibility for environmental protection and pollution control was transferred from the Health and Welfare Branch to the Lands and Works Branch.

1989 The Deputy Chief Secretary was retitled Secretary for Constitutional Affairs and the Office of the Deputy Chief Secretary was renamed Constitutional Affairs Branch. It was responsible for maintaining liaison with the Urban Council and the Regional Council. It also supervised the Legal Aid Department, Regional Services Department and Urban Services Department. The Administrative Services and Information Branch and the Municipal

Services Branch were abolished. The Recreation and Culture Branch was set up to take over policy responsibilities for entertainment, broadcasting and censorship from the Administrative Services and Information Branch; and for culture, recreation and sports, music and country parks management from the Municipal Services Branch. The Lands and Works Branch was spilt into two branches: Planning, Environment and Lands Branch and Works Branch. The Planning, Environment and Lands Branch took over the policy responsibilities from the Economic Services Branch and the Recreation and Culture Branch in the areas such as country parks, woodlands, forest and country ordinances, marine reserves, wetlands, local wildlife conservation and the Deep Bay integrated environment. The Works Branch came under the supervision of the Financial Secretary.

1990   The Chief Secretary was supported by the Political Adviser, Director of Administration, Information Co-ordinator and the following policy branches — Constitutional Affairs; Civil Service; Education and Manpower; Health and Welfare; Housing; Planning, Environment and Lands; Recreation and Culture; Security; and Transport.

    I.   The Constitutional Affairs Branch directed the Legal Aid Department, Regional Services Department and Urban Services Department.

    II.   The Civil Service Branch supervised the Civil Service Training Centre and Senior Staff Course Centre.

    III.   The Education and Manpower Branch controlled the Education Department, Labour Department, Registry of Trade Unions, Secretariat of UPGC, and Technical Education and Industrial Training Department.

    IV.   The Health and Welfare Branch directed the Department of Health, Government Laboratory, Hospital Services Department and Social Welfare Department.

    V.   The Housing Department came directly under the Housing Authority.

    VI.   The Planning, Environment and Lands Branch directed the Buildings and Lands Department, Environmental Protection Department and Planning Department.

    VII.   The Recreation and Culture Branch supervised the Radio Television Hong Kong, and Television and Entertainment Licensing Authority.

    VIII.   The Security Branch supervised the Auxiliary Medical Services, Civil Aid Services, Correctional Services Department, Fire Services Department, Immigration Department, Royal Hong Kong Police Force, Royal Hong Kong Auxiliary Police Force and Royal Hong Kong Regiment.

    IX.   The Transport Branch controlled transport policy and highways development programmes of the Transport Department and Highways Department.

1993   Supported by the Director of Administration, Efficiency Unit, Information Co-ordinator and Political Adviser, the Government Secretariat supervised nine policy branches: Civil Service; Constitutional Affairs; Education and Manpower; Health and Welfare; Home Affairs; Planning, Environment and Lands; Recreation and Culture; Security; and Transport. Three units — Public Service Commission, Standing Commission on Civil Service Salaries and Conditions of Service, and Standing Committee on Disciplined Services Salaries and Conditions of Service — were under the supervision of the Civil Service Branch. The Land Registry was transferred to the Planning, Environment and Lands Branch. The responsibilities of the branches remained mostly unchanged.

1994   The Registration and Electoral Office, which was part of the Constitutional Affairs Branch, was separated from the Branch with effect from April 1. The Housing Branch was re-established on November 18 to assume responsibilities for development policies and strategies for the provision of housing in private and public sectors and the co-ordination of government activities in implementing housing policies and programmes.

1995   A new General Grade Office was added to the Civil Service Branch. Policy-making responsibilities for amusement games centres and miscellaneous licences, as well as liaison work with the municipal councils and legislation matters, were transferred from the Home Affairs Branch to the Recreation and Culture Branch. The Hong Kong and Kowloon Region Department and the New Territories Region Department under the Home Affairs Branch were abolished. The Home Affairs Department and the Departmental Information and Public Relations Units of the Information Services Department were set up. The Planning, Environment and Lands Branch also supervised the Lands Department. The Independent Police Complaints Council, which was set up in 1994, came under the control of the Security Branch.

1996   The Chinese Division was separated from the Office of the Director of Administration on April 1 to form the Official Language Agency. The Recreation and Culture Branch was renamed Broadcasting, Culture and Sport Branch. The Civil Service Training Centre under the direction of the Civil Service Bureau was retitled Civil Service Training and Development Institute.

1997   The Government Secretariat was renamed Government Secretariat, the Government of the Hong Kong Special Administrative Region. The Chief Secretary was retitled Chief Secretary for Administration. The policy and resource branches of the Government Secretariat were retitled bureaux. The Official Languages Agency was put under the Civil Service Bureau. The Royal Hong Kong Regiment, under the supervision of the Security Bureau, was disbanded.

1998   A Quality Education Fund Secretariat was set up within the Education and Manpower Bureau. The Broadcasting, Culture and Sport Bureau was reorganized into the Information Technology and Broadcasting Bureau and came under the supervision of the Financial Secretary. It took over from the Secretary for Economic Services and the Secretary for Treasury responsibilities for the formulation of telecommunications policies and the co-ordination of information technology applications among government bureaux and departments. It also supervised the information technology developments and promotion policies within the community.

1999   The Office of the Government of the HKSAR in Beijing was set up in March to liaise with mainland authorities and provide information about the HKSAR to the Central Government, mainland provincial/municipal authorities and non-governmental bodies. It also rendered practical assistance to Hong Kong residents, handled HKSAR immigration-related matters, liaised with Hong Kong's non-governmental bodies such as the Trade Development Council and the Hong Kong Tourist Association. Under the supervision of the Health and Welfare Bureau, the Hospital Services Department merged with the Department of Health and became the Hospital Staff Division of the Department of Health.

2000   The Environment and Food Bureau was set up in January. It was responsible for the formulation of policies on food supply, food safety, environmental hygiene, waste management, environmental protection and nature conservation. It took over duties such as food supply, animal welfare and protection of endangered species from the Economic Services Bureau; food safety and pesticides from the Health and Welfare Bureau; and the protection of environment, country and marine parks from the Planning, Environment and Lands Bureau. It led and co-ordinated the work of the Food and Environmental Hygiene Department; Agriculture, Fisheries and Conservation Department; and Environmental Protection Department. A new department — Leisure and Cultural Services Department — was created under the Home Affairs Bureau. It took over the management of cultural and recreation facilities managed by the former municipal services departments. The Planning, Environment and Lands Bureau was renamed Planning and Lands Bureau.

2002   The Chief Secretary for Administration, through the Department for Administration, controlled 33 administrative departments grouped under 10 policy bureaux: Civil Service (General Grades Office, Civil Service Training and Development Institute, Official Languages Agency, and Joint Secretariat for the Advisory Bodies on Civil Service and Judicial Salaries and Conditions of Service); Constitutional Affairs (Registration and Electoral Office); Education and Manpower (Education Department, Labour Department, University Grants Committee Secretariat, Student Financial Assistance Agency); Environment and Food (Food and Environmental Hygiene Department, Agriculture, Fisheries and Conservation Department, Environmental Protection Department); Health and Welfare (Social Welfare Department, Department of Health, Government Laboratory); Home Affairs (Home Affairs Department, Information Services Department, Leisure and Cultural Services Department); Housing; Planning and Lands (Buildings Department, Lands Department, Planning Department, Land Registry); Security (Hong Kong Police Force, Fire Services Department, Correctional Services Department, Immigration Department, Government Flying Service, Civil Aid Service, Hong Kong Auxiliary Police Force, Auxiliary Medical Service, Independent Police Complaints Council Secretariat); and Transport (Transport Department,

Highways Department). The Department for Administration also directed four other administrative units — Administration Wing (also had the responsibility for the Legal Aid Department Protocal Division, Public Records Office and others), Office of the Government of the HKSAR in Beijing, Efficiency Unit (directed the Management Services Agency), Hong Kong Guangdong Co-operation Co-ordination Unit (which also reported to the Financial Secretary).

Sources:

1. *CO129/137*, no.19 of Feb 15, 1869; April 17, 1869.
2. "General Administration", *Hong Kong Directives*, HKRS, D&S no. 2/4.
3. *Hong Kong Government Gazette*, Feb 25, 1860, p.40; June 4, 1862, p.3; Sept. 30, 1882, p.783.
4. Hsueh, S. S., *Government and Administration of Hong Kong*, Hong Kong, Winsome Printing Press, 1962, pp.56-61.
5. McKinsey & Company Inc., *The Machinery of Government — A New Framework for Expanding Services*, Hong Kong, Government Printer, 1973.
6. Miners, Norman, *The Government and Politics of Hong Kong* Hong Kong, Oxford University Press, 1991, pp.85-89.
7. Organisation and Methods Branch, Colonial Secretariat, *Report on the Organisation, Methods and Staff Survey*, Hong Kong Government, 1949, Appendix A.
8. www.info.gov.hk/cso/

Department for Administration — Changes in Names and Directors

Year	Name of Department	Title	Name of Director
1843-1844	Colonial Secretary's Office	Colonial Secretary	Malcolm, George Alexander
1844-1846	Colonial Secretary's Office	Colonial Secretary	Bruce, Frederick William Adolphus
1846-1854	Colonial Secretary's Office	Colonial Secretary	Caine, William
1854-1868	Colonial Secretary's Office	Colonial Secretary	Mercer, William Thomas
1868-1879	Colonial Secretary's Office	Colonial Secretary	Austin, John Gardiner
1879-1886	Colonial Secretary's Office	Colonial Secretary	Marsh, William Henry
1886-1889	Colonial Secretary's Office	Colonial Secretary	Stewart, Frederick
1889-1890	Colonial Secretary and Auditor General's Office	Colonial Secretary and Auditor General	Stewart, Frederick
1890-1892	Colonial Secretary's Office	Colonial Secretary	Fleming, Francis

Year	Name of Department	Title	Name of Director
1892-1895	Colonial Secretary's Office	Colonial Secretary	O' Brien, George Thomas Michael
1895-1901	Colonial Secretary and Registrar General's Department	Colonial Secretary and Registrar General	Lockhart, James Haldane Stewart
1901-1911	Colonial Secretariat	Colonial Secretary	May, Francis Henry
1911-1912	Colonial Secretariat	Colonial Secretary	Barnes, Warren Delabere
1912-1926	Colonial Secretariat	Colonial Secretary	Severn, Claud
1926-1936	Colonial Secretariat	Colonial Secretary	Southorn, Wilfred Thomas
1936-1941	Colonial Secretariat	Colonial Secretary	Smith, Norman Lockhart
1941	Colonial Secretariat	Colonial Secretary	Gimson, Franklin Charles
1946-1949	Colonial Secretariat	Colonial Secretary	MacDougall, David Mercer
1949-1952	Colonial Secretariat	Colonial Secretary	Nicoll, John Fearns
1952-1955	Colonial Secretariat	Colonial Secretary	Black, Robert Brown
1955-1958	Colonial Secretariat	Colonial Secretary	David, Edgeworth Beresford
1958-1963	Colonial Secretariat	Colonial Secretary	Burgess, Claude Bramall
1963-1965	Colonial Secretariat	Colonial Secretary	Teesdale, Edmund Brinsley
1965-1969	Colonial Secretariat	Colonial Secretary	Gass, Michael David Irving
1969-1973	Colonial Secretariat	Colonial Secretary	Norman-Walker, Hugh Selby
1973-1976	Colonial Secretariat	Colonial Secretary	Roberts, Denys Tudor Emil
1976-1978	Government Secretariat	Chief Secretary	Roberts, Denys Tudor Emil
1978-1981	Government Secretariat	Chief Secretary	Cater, Jack
1981-1985	Government Secretariat	Chief Secretary	Haddon-Cave, Charles Philip
1985-1987	Government Secretariat	Chief Secretary	Akers-Jones, David

Year	Name of Department	Title	Name of Director
1987-1993	Government Secretariat	Chief Secretary	Ford, David Robert
1993-1997	Government Secretariat	Chief Secretary	Chan Fang, Anson
1997-2001	Department for Administration	Chief Secretary for Administration	Chan Fang, Anson
2001-2002	Department for Administration	Chief Secretary for Administration	Tsang, Yam-kuen, Donald

Sources:
1. *Civil and Miscellaneous List Hong Kong Government,* Hong Kong, Government Printer, 1968-1996.
2. *Hong Kong Civil Service List,* Hong Kong Government, 1947-1958.
3. *Staff Biographies Hong Kong Government, Hong Kong,* Government Printer, 1974, 1976, 1982, 1987, 1990, 1993.
4. *Staff Biographies the Government of the Hong Kong Special Administrative Region,* Hong Kong, Government Printer, 1998, 2001.
5. *Staff List Hong Kong Government,* Hong Kong, Government Printer, 1959-1996.
6. *Staff List the Government of the Hong Kong Special Administrative Region,* Hong Kong, Government Printer, 1997-2000.
7. www.info.gov.hk/cso/

Financial Secretary (1937-1997)
Department of Finance (1997-2002)

1937   The financial administration of Hong Kong was reorganized. The post of Financial Secretary was created in July. The Financial Secretary carried out executive duties such as setting levels for certain charges and remunerations, and oversaw the accounts of certain trust funds and statutory bodies.

1938   The Financial Secretary supervised the financial administration work of the Colonial Secretariat and at his direction an Accountant General was appointed to administer the accounting work connected with receipts and expenditures. The Accounts and Stores Office of the Public Works Department, which was in charge of purchase, safekeeping and distribution of stores, was detached from the Public Works Department and became the Stores Department. It came under the authority of the Financial Secretary, under the charge of a Controller of Stores.

1962   The Financial Secretary directed the Economic and Finance Branch, which functioned under the general direction of the Colonial Secretariat. It was responsible for the economic and financial policies of the Government and prepared annual budgetary estimates and the final accounts. The Economic and Finance Branch consisted of two sections: Economic and Finance. The Economic Section was responsible for the financial aspects of public utilities; control of exchange, banking, import and export; and the development of agriculture, fisheries and forestry. The Finance Section exercised general financial control for the Government, oversaw taxation and fees, public works budgets and government purchases.

1976   The post of Secretary for Monetary Affairs was set up in October to manage the official assets and liabilities, foreign exchange operations, banking, relations with international banks, the Exchange Fund and the Coinage Security Fund.

1981   The Financial Secretary became directly accountable to the Governor, and was responsible under the Public Finance Ordinance for the fiscal and economic policies of government, as well as laying before the legislature each year the Government's estimates of revenue and expenditure. He also carried out executive duties, such as setting levels for government charges and remunerations, and oversaw the accounts of trust funds and statutory bodies. The Financial Secretary was an ex officio member of the Executive Council and the Finance Committee of the Legislative Council. The Financial Secretary supervised three branches: Deputy Financial Secretary (oversaw the Audit Department, Government Supplies Department, Inland Revenue Department, Rating and Valuation Department, The Treasury); Economic Services Branch (controlled the Agriculture and Fisheries Department; Census and Statistics Department; Civil Aviation Department; Marine Department; Post Office; Registrar General's Department; Commodities Trading Commission and Office of the Commissioner for Commodities Trading; Trade, Industry and Customs Department); Monetary Affairs Branch (contained the Office of the Commissioner of Banking and the Office of the Securities Commission).

1982   The Trade and Industry Branch was set up in August. The Trade, Industry and Customs Department was spilt into three departments of Trade Department, Industry Department, and Customs and Excise Department. They all came under the supervision of the Trade and Industry Branch. It was in charge of external commercial relations, import and export controls, copyright, trade marks, industrial product safety, provision of industrial infrastructure and facilities, and relations with government organizations.

1983   The Financial Secretary controlled four branches: Economic Services, Deputy Financial Secretary, Monetary Affairs, Trade and Industry. The major structural changes of these branches included: Economic Services (the two commissions were combined to form the Office of the Commissioner for Securities and Commodities Trading), Deputy Financial Secretary (the Audit Department became directly responsible to the Governor), Monetary Affairs, and Trade and Industry.

1989   Transferred from the previous Lands and Works Branch, the newly created Works Branch came under the supervision of the Financial Secretary. It consisted of the seven departments of Architectural Services, Civil Engineering Services, Drainage Services, Electrical and Mechanical Services, Highways (the Highways Department was responsible to the Transport Branch under the control of the Government Secretariat for transport policy and highways development programmes; while works policy and standards, contract procedures and co-ordination of the public works programmes were under the supervision of the Works Branch of the Financial Secretary), Territory

Development and Water Supplies. The Deputy Financial Secretary was renamed Treasury Branch. The Printing Department, Government Data Processing Agency and Government Land Transport Agency, previously under the Administrative Services and Information Branch of the Government Secretariat, were now under the supervision of the Treasury Branch. The Royal Observatory, formerly under the direction of the Administration Services and Information Branch, came under the control of the Economic Services Branch. The Registrar General's Department was transferred to the Monetary Affairs Branch. The Trade and Industry Branch also supervised the Overseas Offices.

1993   The Monetary Affairs Branch was restructured into two branches: Financial Services Branch and Hong Kong Monetary Authority. The Financial Services Branch supervised the two departments previously subordinated to the Registrar General's Department — Companies Registry and Official Receiver's Office — as well as the Census and Statistics Department (transferred from the Economic Services Branch), and the Office of the Commissioner of Insurance. The newly established Port Development Board was under the control of the Economic Services Branch. The Intellectual Property Department and the Travel Agents Registry came under the supervision of the Trade and Industry Branch. The Information Technology Services Department, previously under the Director of Administration of the Government Secretariat, was now under the Treasury Branch. The recently established New Airport Projects Co-ordination Office came under the direction of the Works Branch.

1995   The Office of the Telecommunications Authority came under the control of the Economic Services Branch.

1997   All policy branches were renamed bureaux. The Royal Observatory which was under the control of the Economic Services Bureau was retitled Hong Kong Observatory. The Office of the Commissioner of Insurance under the Financial Services Bureau was enlarged and became the Office of the Commissioner of Insurance and the Office of the Registrar of Occupational Retirement Schemes. The newly established Mandatory Provident Fund Office was under the direction of this bureau.

1998   The Broadcasting, Culture and Sport Bureau, previously under the Government Secretariat, was restructured into Information Technology and Broadcasting Bureau and came under the Financial Secretary. The new bureau directed four departments: Office of the Telecommunications Authority (previously under the control of the Economic Services Bureau), Information Technology Services Department, Radio Television Hong Kong, Television and Entertainment Licensing Authority. It was responsible for the formulation of policies and the supervision of information technology developments throughout the Government and in the Hong Kong community.

2000   The Trade and Industry Bureau was reorganized into Commerce and Industry Bureau. It supervised seven departments: Customs and Excise, Intellectual Property, Overseas Economic and Trade Offices (previously Overseas Offices), Trade and Industry, Innovation and Technology Commission, Invest Hong Kong, and Business and Services Promotion Unit.

2002   The Port Development Board under the Economic Services Bureau was renamed Hong Kong Port and Maritime Board. The Travel Agents Registry was transferred from the Commerce and Industry Bureau to the Economic Services Bureau. The Office of the Commissioner of Insurance and the Office of the Registrar of Occupational Retirement Schemes under the supervision of the Financial Services Bureau was renamed Office of the Commissioner of Insurance. The Mandatory Provident Fund Office under the Financial Services Bureau was abolished. The New Airport Projects Co-ordination Office under the direction of the Works Bureau was cancelled.

The Financial Secretary, through the Department of Finance, directed six bureaux and 35 departments: Commerce and Industry (Customs and Excise Department, Trade and Industry Department, Intellectual Property Department, Overseas Economic and Trade Offices, Innovation and Technology Commission, Invest Hong Kong, Business and Services Promotion Unit); Economic Services (Civil Aviation Department, Marine Department, Hongkong Post, Hong Kong Observatory, Hong Kong Port and Maritime Board, Travel Agents Registry); Finance (Government Supplies Department, Inland Revenue Department, Rating and Valuation Department, The Treasury, Printing Department, Government Land Transport Agency, Government Property Agency); Financial Services (Office of the Commissioner of Insurance, Official Receiver's Office, Census and Statistics Department, Companies Registry); Information Technology and Broadcasting (Radio Television Hong Kong, Television and Entertainment Licensing Authority, Information Technology Services Department, Office of the Telecommunications Authority); and Works (Architectural Services Department, Civil Engineering Department, Drainage Services Department, Electrical and Mechanical Services Department, Highways Department, Territory Development Department, Water Supplies Department). Two independent agencies — Hong Kong Guangdong Co-operation Co-ordination Unit (which also reported to the Chief Secretary for Administration) and Hong Kong Monetary Authority — also came under the direction of the Financial Secretary.

Sources:

1. "General Administration", *Hong Kong Directives*, Hong Kong, 1945, HKRS 211, D&S, no.2/4.
2. *Hong Kong 1999*, Hong Kong, Government Printer, 1999, p.24.
3. *Hong Kong Administration Reports*, Hong Kong Government, 1937, p.5; 1938, pp.4-5, Appendix, A. 4-5.
4. Hsueh, S. S., *Government and Administration of Hong Kong*, Winsome Printing Press, 1962, pp.60-61.
5. McKinsey & Company, Inc, *The Machinery of Government: A New Framework for Expanding Services*, Hong Kong, Government Printer, 1973.
6. Miners, Norman, *The Government and Politics of Hong Kong*, Hong Kong, Oxford University Press, 1991.
7. ww.info.gov.hk/fso/

Department of Finance — Changes in Names and Directors

Year	Name of Department	Title	Name of Director
1937-1940	Financial Secretary	Financial Secretary	Caine, Sydney
1940-1941	Financial Secretary	Financial Secretary	Butters, Henry Robert
1945-1952	Financial Secretary	Financial Secretary	Follows, Charles Geoffrey Shield
1952-1961	Financial Secretary	Financial Secretary	Clarke, Arthur Grenfell
1961-1971	Financial Secretary	Financial Secretary	Cowperthwaite, John James
1971-1981	Financial Secretary	Financial Secretary	Haddon-Cave, Charles Philip
1981-1986	Financial Secretary	Financial Secretary	Bremridge, John Henry
1986-1991	Financial Secretary	Financial Secretary	Jacobs, Piers
1991-1995	Financial Secretary	Financial Secretary	Macleod, Nathaniel William Hamish
1995-1997	Financial Secretary	Financial Secretary	Tsang, Yam-kuen, Donald
1997-2001	Department of Finance	Financial Secretary	Tsang, Yam-kuen, Donald
2001-2002	Department of Finance	Financial Secretary	Leung, Kam-chung, Antony

Sources:

1. *Civil and Miscellaneous Lists Hong Kong Government*, Hong Kong, Government Printer, 1996, p.408.
2. *The Hong Kong Civil Service List*, Hong Kong Government, 1947-1958.
3. *Staff Biographies of the Government of the Hong Kong Special Administrative Region*, Hong Kong, Government Printer, 1998-2001.
4. *Staff List Hong Kong Government*, Hong Kong, Government Printer, 1959-1996.
5. *Staff List the Government of the Hong Kong Special Administrative Region*, Hong Kong, Government Printer, 1997-2000.
6. www.info.gov.hk/fso/

Local Administration

Registrar General's Office (1844-1895)
Colonial Secretary and Registrar General's Department (1895-1901)
Registrar General's Department (1901-1913)
Secretariat for Chinese Affairs (1913-1969)
Secretariat for Home Affairs (1969-1973)
Home Affairs Department (1973-1981)

1844   The Office of Registration was established to register all male inhabitants of aged 21 and over. The Registrar General was responsible for taking census of the inhabitants of the Island of Hong Kong and the issuance of registration tickets to registered citizens.The Registrar General was also known as the Protector of Chinese.

1857   Ordinance no. 6 of 1857 for the registration of Chinese residents and for the population census was enacted. The Registrar General was a Justice of the Peace, a Joint Superintendent of Police and the Protector of Chinese Inhabitants. His major duty was to prevent the commission of crimes. He was also empowered to enter at any time, any buildings, vessels or boats within Hong Kong, and to exercise the authority of a Justice of the Peace and of a Superintendent of Police.

1860   An ordinance was enacted for the registration and regulation of boatmen and others employed in licensed cargo boats, and for the survey of such boats. The Registrar General was responsible for the registration of cargo boatmen.

1863   An ordinance to provide for the regulation of public vehicles and their drivers and bearers within Hong Kong was enacted. The Registrar General was authorized to inspect vehicles and chairs, issue licences and fix the licence fee.

1864   The cadet system was established to improve administration. The Registrar General was required to have a knowledge of the Chinese language.

1865   The Registrar General was responsible for the registration of boats, hawkers, lands not leased, emigrants, brothels, hospital, markets, cargo boats, chairs, horse carriages, drivers, and Chinese gazettes.

1866   For the purpose of registration, the City of Victoria was divided into nine districts: Bowrington, Choong Wan North and South, Ha Wan, Sai Ying Poon, Shektongtsui, Sheong Wan, So Kun Poo, Tai Ping Shan, and Wanchai. Separate registers for each district were kept at the Registrar General's Office. Registration of servants was obligatory for all employers.

1872   The Registrar General was the Chief Registrar of all births and deaths. The district registers of birth and deaths could be kept at police stations declared by the Governor to be registration offices.

1875	Ordinance no. 4 of 1875 provided for the Registrar General to be the Registrar of Marriages.
1878	The Registrar General' Office was assisted by a staff of 22, including one Deputy Registrar, clerks, interpreters, Chinese writers, notice servers and messengers.
1884	The Registrar General became an ex officio member of the Legislative Council.
1886	An ordinance was enacted to prevent adopted children and female servants from being brought up for the purpose of prostitution. The Registrar General was authorized to enforce this legislation.
1888	The Registrar General kept a record of books published in Hong Kong, and was responsible for the issuance and renewal of night passes.
1891	The Registrar General's Office performed multifarious duties which included the registration of births and deaths, marriages, books, householders; liaison with the District Watchmen Committee, Tung Wah Hospital and Po Leung Kok; translation work of Chinese and English documents; issuance of hawker licences and collection of hawker licence fees; letting of market shops and stalls and collecting rents; issuance of brothel licences; reinforcement of the Women's and Girls' Protection Ordinance; and the establishment of the Chinese recreation ground at Possession Point.
1892	The Registrar General's Office was also responsible for the regulation of emigration and the examination onshore and on board ships against contagious diseases.
1895	James Haldane Stewart Lockhart held the combined post of Colonial Secretary and Registrar General. The three principal channels of Chinese opinions were the District Watch Committee, Tung Wah Hospital and Po Leung Kuk.
1898	The Registrar General administered two funds: Market Charitable Fund and Passage Money Fund.
1901	The post of Colonial Secretary and Registrar General was separated into two.
1906	The licensing function of postmen and postal hongs was transferred to the Post Office; the issuance of boat licences was taken over by the Harbour Department.
1907	Examination of assisted emigrants was transferred from the Harbour Master's Department to the Registrar General's Department and the licensing of postal hongs was once again performed by the Department.
1909	The registration of births and deaths, collection of revenue from special fruit licences, laundries and markets were transferred to the Sanitary Department.
1910	The function of issuing hawker licences was transferred to the Police Force.
1911	The Registrar General's Department was responsible for the registration of societies in order to provide for a more effective control over Chinese societies and clubs.
1912	The Police Force took up the issuance of money changer licences.
1913	The Registrar General's Department was retitled Secretariat for Chinese Affairs.

1918   The Secretariat administered all the charitable funds in the Colonial Treasury.

1922   The Secretary for Chinese Affairs became the Protector of Juvenile Labour. One male and one female inspector were appointed. The registration of marriages was transferred to the Land Office.

1928   The Secretary became the Chairman of the Chinese Temple Committee and was responsible for the registration of all Chinese temples, with the exception of Man Mo Temple. According to Ordinance no. 7 of 1928, the Secretariat was authorized to administer charitable funds including the General Chinese Charities Fund, the Chinese Temples Fund and the Chinese Recreation Ground Fund.

1930   According to Ordinance no. 31 of 1930, the Secretariat for Chinese Affairs was responsible for the administration of Tung Wah Hospital.

1933   Registration of factories and workshops was made compulsory under the direction of the Secretary.

1937   The inspection of factories was transferred to the Urban Council. The Secretary for Chinese Affairs passed his role as Protector of Labour to the Chairman of the Urban Council. A new post of Lady Assistant to the Secretary for Chinese Affairs was established to take charge the work concerning the protection of women and girls.

1938   Under the Protection of Women and Girls Ordinance no. 5 of 1938, the Secretary for Chinese Affairs became the legal guardian of girls under 21. The Labour Office was set up within the secretariat.

1946   The Secretary resumed his pre-war functions; his office acted as a communication medium between the Government and the Chinese population; advised the Government on questions involving Chinese laws and customs; administered the charitable funds; co-ordinated with Chinese societies; acted as an unofficial court of arbitration in Chinese disputes occasionally; protected Chinese women and girls; issued permits in connection with Chinese celebrations, licences of Chinese hotels, boarding houses, restaurants, passage brokers; managed the Chinese permanent cemetery at Aberdeen; registered guilds, societies, trade unions and newspapers; and translated documents into English/Chinese.

1947   The Social Welfare Office was formally set up as a special subdepartment of the Secretariat on August 27 by the appointment of an administrative officer as Social Welfare Officer. The protection of women and girls work was transferred to the Social Welfare Office. The Social Welfare Advisory Committee was set up to advise the Government on social welfare policies and on schemes upon which such policies might be implemented.

1949   A new District Watch Force Ordinance was enacted; the maintenance of such Force, now met from public revenue, was placed under the control of the Secretary for Chinese Affairs.

1951   The Secretary for Chinese Affairs was appointed Registrar of all newspaper distributors and news agencies, under the new Control of Publications Consolidation Ordinance no. 15 of 1951.

1953   Two Tenancy Inquiry Bureaux were set up to deal with tenancy matters in July under the direction of an Assistant Secretary for Chinese Affairs.

1955   The Secretary for Chinese Affairs reassumed the management of the Trustee of the Brewin Trust Fund.

1956   The Secretary was nominated ex officio Chairman of the Licensing Justices Board which was responsible for the issuance of all liquor licences.

1957   Three Liaison Offices were established to deal with matters affecting kaifong, district and clan associations.

1958   The Social Welfare Office became an independent department. The responsibilities for the protection of women, young girls and children were transferred to the Social Welfare Department, while the duties for liaison with the community of the former Community Development Section of the Social Welfare Office were integrated with the Secretariat for Chinese Affairs. A Narcotics Advisory Committee was set up to fight the increasing trade in and consumption of narcotics in Hong Kong.

1960   The Public Health and Urban Services Ordinance Sections 90-92 provided the Urban Council with the authority to license and control boarding houses. The Secretariat ceased the licensing of the Chinese hotels.

1961   The Sir Robert Black Trust Fund was constituted by Ordinance no. 50 of 1961 with the Secretary for Chinese Affairs as ex officio Chairman to manage the fund.

1962   Two branch offices were opened in Kowloon and Kwun Tong.

1963   The Secretariat for Chinese Affairs, in conjunction with the Medical and Health Department, dealt with the implementation of the Medical Clinics Ordinance no. 27 of 1963. The Secretary was also chairman of a working party which viewed and made detailed recommendations on past and future policies with regard to squatters and the rehousing of people living in dangerously overcrowded or unsuitable conditions. The Li Po Chun Charitable Trust Fund was constituted by Ordinance no. 34 of 1963 with the Secretary as Chairman to administer the fund.

1968   The Government adopted the City District Officer Scheme to improve the quality of the administration and the general image of the Government through closer liaison with the public in the city district.

1969   The title of the Secretariat for Chinese Affairs was changed to Secretariat for Home Affairs on February 28. The head of the Secretariat was known as Secretary for Home Affairs. The District Watch Force was disbanded and its members were employed within the new organisation of the Secretariat for Home Affairs. Ten City District Offices — six in Kowloon and four in Hong Kong were set up under the direction of the Secretariat. Two City District Commissioners, one in charge of Kowloon district and the other of Hong Kong, were responsible for the overall administration of city districts in urban areas.

1971   An Information Policy Committee was set up to handle information, public relations and publicity.

1972   The Television Authority Secretariat and the Film Censorship Unit were detached from the Information Services Department, and transformed into the Television and Films Division of the Secretariat for Home Affairs. The Secretariat was designated the Authority for the implementation of government policy on the use of Chinese language in official business in January. A Commissioner for Chinese Language was appointed to assist the Secretariat on the day-to-day work of implementating the government language policy. The Chinese Language Branch was set up to establish a centralized translation service to departments, carry out research and development programmes and maintain enforcement service as regards current official policy on the use of Chinese language.

1973   The Secretariat for Home Affairs was retitled Home Affairs Department. The Secretary for Home Affairs became the head of the Home Affairs Branch of the Government Secretariat and a new post of Director of Home Affairs was created as the head of the Department. Duties for liquor licensing were transferred to the Urban Services Department. Responsibilities to deal with narcotics matters were transferred to the Security Branch of the Government Secretariat.

1974   The two Tenancy Inquiry Bureaux were transferred to the Rating and Valuation Department in April. The Television and Films Division was separated from the Department to form an independent department.

1975   The Department was organized into five divisions: Administration; City District; Community Services (consisted of the City Districts Section, Information Section, Lands Section, Trust Funds Section); Departmental Headquarters; Language, Traditional and Community Relations (comprised the Chinese Language Section, Community Relations Section, Tradition Section).

1977   The Department was reorganized into two branches: Community Relations and Chinese Language Branch, and District Services and Administration Branch.

1981   The Department merged with the New Territories Administration to form a new agency — City and New Territories Administration. The Home Affairs Branch continued to exist under the direction of the Secretary for Home Affairs. Its responsibilities altered considerably. The Secretary for Home Affairs took over some of the duties of the Information Branch and assumed responsibility for the Environmental Affairs Division from the Administration and Environmental Affairs Branch. The responsibility for the development of programmes, the implementation of policies and the co-ordination of resources for the Home Affairs and Community Building Sector was transferred to the Secretary for City and New Territories Administration.

Sources:

1.   *Hong Kong Administration Reports*, Hong Kong Government, 1931-1939.
2.   *Hong Kong Administrative Reports*, Hong Kong Government, 1909-1930.
3.   *Hong Kong Annual Report by the Secretary for Chinese Affairs*, Hong Kong, Government Printer, 1949-1969.
4.   *Hong Kong Sessional Papers*, Hong Kong, Noronha & Co., 1899, pp.302-304; 1900, p.393; 1902, pp.589, 592; 1903, p.137; 1907, p.331; 1909, pp.181, 184, 194.

5. "Report on Labour and Labour Conditions in Hong Kong" *Hong Kong Sessional Papers*, Hong Kong, Noronha & Co., 1939, pp.121-122, 125.
6. *Report of the Secretariat for Chinese Affairs and the Social Welfare Officer 1947-1948*, Hong Kong, Government Printer, 1948.
7. *Report of the Secretary for Chinese Affairs 1946-1947*, Hong Kong, Government Printer, 1947.

Home Affairs Department — Changes in Names and Directors

Year	Name of Department	Title	Name of Director
1845-1846	Registrar General's Office	Registrar General	Fearon, Samuel Turner
1846-1849	Registrar General's Office	Registrar General	Inglis, Andrew Lysaght
1849-1850	Registrar General's Office	Registrar General	Mercer, William Thomas
1850-1856	Registrar General's Office	Registrar General	May, Charles
1856-1862	Registrar General's Office	Registrar General	Caldwell, Daniel Richard
1862-1864	Registrar General's Office	Registrar General	Turner, Thomas
1864-1881	Registrar General's Office	Registrar General	Smith, Cecil Clementi
1881-1883	Registrar General's Office	Registrar General	Russell, James
1883-1887	Registrar General's Office	Registrar General	Stewart, Frederick
1887-1895	Registrar General's Office	Registrar General	Lockhart, James Haldane Stewart
1895-1901	Colonial Secretary and Registrar General's Department	Colonial Secretary and Registrar General	Lockhart, James Haldane Stewart
1901-1912	Registrar General's Department	Registrar General	Brewin, Arthur Winbolt
1912-1913	Registrar General's Department	Registrar General	Hallifax, Edwin Richard
1913-1933	Secretariat for Chinese Affairs	Secretary for Chinese Affairs	Hallifax, Edwin Richard

Year	Department	Title	Name of Director
1933-1934	Secretariat for Chinese Affairs	Secretary for Chinese Affairs	Wood, Alan Eustace
1934-1936	Secretariat for Chinese Affairs	Secretary for Chinese Affairs	Smith, Norman Lockhart
1936-1941	Secretariat for Chinese Affairs	Secretary for Chinese Affairs	North, Roland Arthur Charles
1946-1955	Secretariat for Chinese Affairs	Secretary for Chinese Affairs	Todd, Ronald Ruskin
1955-1957	Secretariat for Chinese Affairs	Secretary for Chinese Affairs	Hawkins, Brian Charles Keith
1957-1965	Secretariat for Chinese Affairs	Secretary for Chinese Affairs	McDouall, John Crichton
1966-1971	Secretariat for Chinese Affairs	Secretary for Chinese Affairs	Holmes, David Ronald
1971-1973	Secretariat for Home Affairs	Secretary for Home Affairs	Luddington, Donald Collin Cumyn
1973-1976	Home Affairs Department	Director of Home Affairs	Ho, Eric Peter
1976-1981	Home Affairs Department	Director of Home Affairs	Walden, John Charles Creasey

Sources:
1. *The Hong Kong Civil Service List*, Hong Kong Government, 1947-1958.
2. *Staff Biographies Hong Kong Government*, Hong Kong, Government Printer, 1974, 1976, 1978.
3. *Staff List Hong Kong Government*, Hong Kong, Government Printer, 1959-1981.

District Office (1910-1952)
New Territories Administration (1952-1981)
Home Affairs Department (1973-1981; 1994-2002)
City and New Territories Administration (1981-1994)
Home Affairs Branch (1973-1985; 1993-1997)
Home Affairs Bureau (1997-2002)

District Office

1899   Tai Po was the administration headquarters in the New Territories. The police force operating throughout the New Territories was controlled directly from Hong Kong.

1905   With the completion of the Crown lease schedules, the Assistant Land Officer in Southern District and the Assistant Superintendent of Police in Northern District, became collectors of revenue in addition to their normal duties.

1907   In Northern District, the offices of Police Magistrate, Assistant Superintendent of Police and Collector were amalgamated under the title of District Officer, but no separate department was created. The District Officer was subordinated to the Captain Superintendent of Police and the Treasurer as part of his duties.

1909   The Assistant Land Officer was given the title of Assistant District Officer in Northern District and was subordinated to the District Officer. The District Officer and the Assistant District Officer were both Assistant Superintendents of Police.

1910   The District Office was formally established. In Southern District, the title of the officer in charge was altered from Assistant Land Officer to Assistant District Officer. His powers were similar to those of the Assistant District Officer in Northern District.

1911   Birth registrations were introduced on July 1 in Northern District but not immediately enforced. The collection of fees for the occupation of the pile-huts at Tai O Creek was transferred from the Harbour Office to Southern District.

1912   The boundary between Northern District and Southern District was altered. The Police District of Tsuen Wan and several hill villages formerly in Au Tau were transferred from Northern District to Southern District.

1913   The post of Assistant District Officer was abolished in Northern District. The Assistant Superintendent of Police acted as Police Magistrate and Collector.

1920   The title of Assistant District Officer was changed to District Officer.

1925   In Southern District, the jurisdiction of the District Officer sitting as Police Magistrate was readjusted; cases from New Kowloon were brought before the Kowloon Magistrate, while cases from other parts of the District were brought before the District Officer.

1935   The function of issuing sand permits was transferred from Southern District to the Public Works Department.

1946   The New Territories District Office resumed its duties after the war.

1947   The geographical boundaries of Southern and Northern Districts were changed. A large part of the Sai Kung area, including the Sai Kung Market, traditionally administered by the Northern District Officer from Tai Po, was transferred to Southern District. Southern District stretched from Lantau in the south-west to Tai Long Bay in the north-east, encompassing Tai O, Cheung Chau, Tsuen Wan and Sai Kung.

1948   The New Territories Distrct Office was divided into three suboffices: District Office Tai Po, District Office Yuen Long, and District Office Southern. The head of the District Office was retitled District Commissioner.

1949   Two officers were appointed to Tai Po District because of steadily increasing volume of Police Court work and administrative duties. B. D. Wilson dealt with the general administration of the District while D. C. C. Luddington assumed duties as Magistrate and Assistant Land Officer.

1951   By amendments to the Dogs and Cats Regulations of 1951, the Director of Agriculture, Fisheries and Forestry became the licensing authority for the New Territories.

New Territories Administration

1952   The New Territories Administration was established and it was responsible for the occupation of Crown land under lease or permit for agricultural, building or other purposes. Crown rent was collected on all leased land, registers of which were maintained at each District Office. District Officers sat as Police Court Magistrates, and held Small Debts Courts and Land Courts under the New Territories Ordinance.

1954   All Police Court duties were transferred to the Legal Department. According to the Renting (Amendment) Ordinance, premises in the New Territories, other than traditional village houses, were to be assessed on the same basis as Hong Kong, Kowloon and New Kowloon.

1956   With effect from June 1, a Liquor Licensing Board was appointed, with the District Commissioner as Chairman, to issue licences for the consumption of liquor in the New Territories.

1958   The Tsuen Wan District Office which covered the mainland around Tsuen Wan, Tsing Yi, Ma Wan and part of north-east Lantau was set up.

1959   The Heung Yee Kuk Ordinance 1959 was passed. The New Territories Administration was responsible for informing the Government of local opinions and explaining government policies to local inhabitants; looking after the interests of villagers, negotiating the surrender of land, arranging payment of compensations and resettlement of persons; controlling the disposal and utilization of land and registration of private land transactions; collecting Crown rent; allocating funds for carrying out local public works; supervising government contributions towards the construction of subsidized schools;

issuing licences of food stalls, food factories, restaurants, slaughterhouses, offensive trades and other premises; arbitrating in cases of family and village disputes; dealing with public health matters; and holding Small Debts Courts.

1960   Southern District was spilt into Sai Kung District and Islands District. The responsibilities for scavenging and environmental health services, parks, playgrounds and public beaches in the New Territories were transferred to the Urban Services Department.

1961   With effect from January 1, the formal authority to approve building plans for new buildings was removed as the Buildings Ordinance was made fully applicable to all New Territories buildings. The District Officers still approved plans for certain small domestic and agricultural buildings. With the passing of the New Territories (Amendment) Ordinance 1961, the jurisdiction of the District Courts was extended to cover land and small debt cases throughout the New Territories.

1962   The New Territories Administration served as a link between the Rural Committees and the public transport authorities on matters including bus routes, bus stops, footpaths, pedestrian crossings, ferry services, ferry fares, and street lighting.

1963   Sai Kung District and Islands District were reconstituted as one district — Southern District.

1967   The original duties of the New Territories Administration, including the maintenance of law and order, judgement of criminal and civil actions, maintenance of health and sanitation, had already been passed to specialized branches of the Government. The main tasks of the Administration were now threefold: administration of Crown land, co-ordinantion with government departments; and ensuring that the interests of the indigenous people of the New Territories were considered in the formation and implementation of government policies.

1968   Southern District was spilt into two. One covered Sai Kung Peninsula and Port Shelter, and the other the southern islands of the New Territories.

1972   Following the promulgation of the Building Ordinance (Application to the New Territories) (Amendment) Regulations 1972, new rules for building small houses became effective in December.

1974   The title of the District Commissioner, New Territories was changed to Secretary for the New Territories. District Offices were set up in Sha Tin and Tuen Mun. Under the Secretary for the New Territories were District Officers in charge of the seven geographical districts in the New Territories.

1976   The post of District Officer Tsuen Wan was upgraded and retitled Town Manager and District Officer, Tsuen Wan.

1977   District Advisory Boards was set up in all New Territories Districts.

1979   Four Regional Commissioners were appointed covering the east, south, west and north. Their tasks were to co-ordinate and monitor the implementation of government policies in the regions, and to ensure that government policies were fully explained. The administrative districts of the New Territories were increased to eight: Islands, Northern, Sai Kung, Sha Tin, Tai Po, Tsuen Wan, Tuen Mun and Yuen Long.

City and New Territories Administration (CNTA)

1981   The Chief Secretary announced in the Legislative Council on November 11 that the Home Affairs Department and the New Territories Administration were to merge and became the City and New Territories Administration (CNTA) with effect from December 1. The Secretary for the New Territories became Secretary for CNTA. He was assisted by two Regional Secretaries — one for Hong Kong and Kowloon, and the other for the New Territories. The CNTA supervised the work of District Management Committees and District Boards. The Regional Secretaries of Hong Kong and Kowloon, and of the New Territories, were responsible for all aspects of district administration in the urban areas and New Territories respectively, and for the proper co-ordination of government activities within the districts and the regions. The CNTA officers monitored the demand and supply of government services, and assisted in remedying any apparent deficiencies locally, through either the relevant departments or the District Management Committees and District Boards.

1982   By March, all New Territories and City Districts had both District Management Committees and District Boards. By April and October respectively, about half of the members of each District Board were elected by constituency-based franchises in the New Territories and in the urban areas. With effect from 1 October, all nomenclature in English and Chinese of the District Offices in the New Territories and City District Offices were standardized. The Chinese name of *limin fu* or *minzheng chu* followed the district name. The District Offices in the New Territories and City District Offices in the urban areas continued to be one of the main channels of communication between the Government at the centre and the people for the feedback of public opinions on public issues, and for community building in the districts. District Officers' responsibilities for land administration were passed to the new Lands Department.

1985   The CNTA was organized into five divisions: Administration, Community, General, Headquarters, and News and Publicity. It was headed by the Secretary for District Administration. With effect from April 1, traditional and community related matters such as the collation of community information, opinion surveys, liaison with traditional Chinese organizations, management of trust funds and properties, management of Chinese temples and Chinese permanent cemeteries, advice on Chinese religion, culture and customs and co-ordination of special ceremonial functions, were transferred from the Secretary for Home Affairs to the Secretary for District Administration. District Officers were replaced as chairmen of District Boards by elected chairmen. The Home Affairs Branch ceased to function.

1988   The Special Duties Division was established.

1992   The Youth Division was set up.

1993   With effect from October 15, the Home Affairs Branch was re-established in the Government Secretariat by a redeployment of posts from the Headquarters of CNTA.

1994   The Finance Committee, at its meeting held on November 18, approved the reorganization of the CNTA into the Home Affairs Branch and a new Home Affairs Department to provide for a clear separation of functions between a conventional policy branch and an executive department.

Home Affairs Branch/Home Affairs Bureau/Home Affairs Department

1995   The CNTA was abolished at the end of 1994. Following the reorganization, the policy portfolio of the Home Affairs Branch included district administration, community building, municipal councils, traditional and rural matters, social and family laws, succession and inheritance, human rights, civic education, data protection, youth and women's matters, gambling, licensing of hotels and guesthouses, bed-space apartments, postage stamp policy, government advisory boards and committees, religious matters, Chinese temples and Chinese permanent cemeteries. The formation of the Home Affairs Department was achieved through the amalgamation of the two CNTA Regional Headquarters and 18 District Offices (nine urban districts and nine New Territories districts). The Home Affairs Department was responsible for the implementation of the District Administration Scheme, community involvement activities, rural planning and improvement strategy, local minor works and environmental improvement projects; dissemination of information relating to major government policies, strategies and development plans; collection of public opinion; operation of District Offices, public enquiry service centres and community facilities.

1997   The Home Affairs Branch changed its title to Home Affairs Bureau.

2000   With effect from January 1, 18 District Councils (nine in the urban areas and nine in the New Territories) were established to replace the Provisional District Boards. The District Councils advised the Government on district matters and monitored the municipal services provided.

2002   The Home Affairs Department was organized into Divisions I to V, Administration Division, News and Publicity Division, as well as nine Urban District Offices and nine New Territories District Offices. The 18 District Offices corresponded to the 18 District Councils.

Sources:

1. *Annual Departmental Report by the Director of Home Affairs*, Hong Kong, Government Printer, 1973-1980.
2. *Annual Report of the District Office, New Territories*, Hong Kong, Government Printer, 1946-1948; 1950-1951.

3.   *Hong Kong,* Hong Kong, Government Printer, 1979-1982.
4.   *Hong Kong Annual Departmental Report by the District Commissioner*, New Territories, Hong Kong, Government Printer, 1951-1974.
5.   *Hong Kong Annual Report of the District Commissioner*, New Territories 1948-1949, Hong Kong, Government Printer, 1949.
6.   "Report on the New Territories", *Hong Kong Administration Reports*, Hong Kong Government, 1935-1938.
7.   "Report on the New Territories", *Hong Kong Administrative Reports*, Hong Kong Government, 1909-1930.
8.   www.info.gov.hk/had/

Home Affairs Bureau — Changes in Names and Directors

Year	Name of Department	Title	Name of Director
1946-1947	District Office, New Territories	District Officer	Teesdale, Edmund Brinsley
1947-1948	District Office, New Territories	District Officer	Barrow, John
1948-1952	District Office, New Territories	District Commissioner	Barrow, John
1952-1954	New Territories Administration	District Commissioner	Teesdale, Edmund Brinsley
1954-1958	New Territories Administration	District Commissioner	Barnett, Kenneth Myer Arthur
1958-1960	New Territories Administration	District Commissioner	Holmes, David Ronald
1960-1962	New Territories Administration	District Commissioner	Walton, Arthur, St. George
1962-1964	New Territories Administration	District Commissioner	Aserappa, John Philip
1964-1965	New Territories Administration	District Commissioner	Wakefield, James Tinker
1965-1966	New Territories Administration	District Commissioner	Aserappa, John Philip
1966-1967	New Territories Administration	District Commissioner	Lightbody, Ian MacDonald
1967-1969	New Territories Administration	District Commissioner	Kinghorn, Kenneth Strathmore
1969-1971	New Territories Administration	District Commissioner	Luddington, Donald Collin Cumyn
1971-1973	New Territories Administration	District Commissioner	Bray, Denis Campbell
1973-1974	New Territories Administration	District Commissioner	Akers-Jones, David / MacPherson, Ian Francis Cluny

Year	Name of Department	Title	Name of Director
1974-1981	New Territories Administration	Secretary for the New Territories	Akers-Jones, David
1981-1983	City and New Territories Administration	Secretary for City and New Territories Administration	Akers-Jones, David
1983-1985	City and New Territories Administration	Secretary, Government Secretariat (Secretary for District Administration)	Akers-Jones, David
1985-1989	City and New Territories Administration	Secretary, Government Secretariat (Secretary for District Administration)	Liao, Poon-huai, Donald
1989-1991	City and New Territories Administration	Secretary, Government Secretariat (Secretary for Home Affairs)	Tsao, Kwang-yung, Peter
1991-1994	City and New Territories Administration	Secretary, Government Secretariat (Secretary for Home Affairs)	Suen, Ming-yeung, Michael
1994-1995	Home Affairs Department	Director of Home Affairs	Wong, Wing-ping, Joseph
1995-2002	Home Affairs Department	Director of Home Affairs	Lau Lee, Lai-kuen, Shelley
1973	Home Affairs Branch, Colonial Secretariat	Secretary for Home Affairs	Cater, Jack
1973-1976	Home Affairs Branch, Colonial Secretariat	Secretary for Home Affairs	Bray, Denis Campbell
1976-1977	Home Affairs Branch, Government Secretariat	Secretary for Home Affairs	Bray, Denis Campbell
1977-1982	Home Affairs Branch, Government Secretariat	Secretary for Home Affairs	Li, Fook-kow
1982-1985	Home Affairs Branch, Government Secretariat	Secretary for Home Affairs	Bray, Denis Campbell
1994-1997	Home Affairs Branch, Government Secretariat	Secretary, Government Secretariat (Secretary for Home Affairs)	Suen, Ming-yeung, Michael

Year	Name of Department	Title	Name of Director
1997	Home Affairs Bureau, Government Secretariat	Director of Bureau (Secretary for Home Affairs)	Suen, Ming-yeung, Michael
1997	Home Affairs Bureau, Government Secretariat	Director of Bureau (Secretary for Home Affairs)	Hung Kwok, Wai-ching, Stella
1997-2000	Home Affairs Bureau, Government Secretariat	Director of Bureau (Secretary for Home Affairs)	Lan, Hong-tsung, David
2000-2002	Home Affairs Bureau, Government Secretariat	Director of Bureau (Secretary for Home Affairs)	Lam, Woon-kwong

Sources:
1. *The Hong Kong Civil Service List*, Hong Kong Government, 1947-1958.
2. *Staff Biographies Hong Kong Government*, Hong Kong, Government Printer, 1974, 1976, 1982, 1987, 1990, 1993.
3. *Staff Biographies the Government of the Hong Kong Special Administrative Region*, Hong Kong, Government Printer, 1998, 2001.
4. *Staff List Hong Kong Government*, Hong Kong, Government Printer, 1959-1996.
5. *Staff List the Government of the Hong Kong Special Administrative Region*, Hong Kong, Government Printer, 1997-2000.
6. www.info.gov.hk/hab/index.htm

Registration and Electoral Office (1994-2002)

1994   On April 1, the Registration and Electoral Office was separated from the Constitutional Affairs Branch of the Government Secretariat and became an independent department. It comprised two major divisions: Committee and Research, Operations.

1995   The Operations Division consisted of three sections: Administration, Technical Services and Registration.

1996   The Committee and Research Division was replaced by the Administration, Committee and Research Division. It contained the Committee and Research Section and the Administration Section, of which the Administration Section was transferred from the Operations Division.

1998   The Operations Division was restructured into the Technical Services Section and the Elections Section.

1999   The Office was reorganized into four sections: Administration, Committee and Research, Voter Registration and Elections.

2000   A new section of Community Relations Section was set up.

2002   The Office, headed by the Chief Electoral Officer, comprised four major administrative units: Committee and Research/Administration Division, Operations Division, Election Division, Media Relations Unit. The Committee and Research/Administration Division was made up of the Committee and Research Section and the Administration Section. It provided the Electoral Affairs Commission with secretarial support to ensure that elections are conducted in an open, honest and fair way; and to act as the administrator of the Office. The Operations Division consisted of a Voter Registration Unit. It registered electors, and assisted in conducting and supervising elections. The Election Division conducted and supervised elections. The Media Relations Unit dealt with media relations and publicity.

Sources:

1. *Hong Kong,* Hong Kong, Government Printer, 1994-1998.
2. *Staff List Hong Kong Government*, Hong Kong, Government Printer, 1994-1996.
3. *Hong Kong Government Telephone Directory*, Hong Kong, Government Printer, 1994-1996.
4. *The Government of the Hong Kong Special Administrative Region, Telephone Directory 1998*, Hong Kong, Government Printer, 1999.
5. www.info.gov.hk/reo/index_en.htm

Registration and Electoral Office — Changes in Directors			
Year	Name of Department	Title	Name of Director
1994-1996	Registration and Electoral Office	Chief Electoral Officer, REO	Willis Yau, Sheung-mui, Carrie
1996-1997	Registration and Electoral Office	Chief Electoral Officer, REO	Cheung, Ying-choi, Venner
1997-2002	Registration and Electoral Office	Chief Electoral Officer, REO	Li, Wing

Sources:
1. *Staff Biographies the Government of the Hong Kong Special Administrative Region*, Hong Kong, Government Printer, 1998, 2001.
2. *Staff List Hong Kong Government,* Hong Kong, Government Printer, 1994-1996.
3. *Staff List the Government of the Hong Kong Special Administrative Region*, Hong Kong, Government Printer, 1997-2000.
4. www.info.gov.hk/reo/index_en.htm

External Relations

The Office of the Government of the Hong Kong Special Administrative Region in Beijing (1999-2002)

1999   The Office of the Government of the Hong Kong Special Administrative Region in Beijing was established on March 4 to strengthen communication and liaison between Hong Kong and Mainland authorities. The Office was organised into three sections: Economic Affairs, Trade and Liaison Section; Immigration Section; and Information and Office Administration Section. The major functions of the Office included the provision of information about the HKSAR to the Central People's Government, Mainland provincial/municipal authorities and non-governmental bodies; keeping the relevant bureaux and departments of the HKSAR Government informed of the latest developments on the Mainland; in charge of HKSAR immigration-related matters; liaison with HKSAR non-governmental bodies on the Mainland; provision of logistic support to visiting HKSAR delegations; provision of practical assistance to Hong Kong residents on the Mainland; and the issuance of visas for HKSAR to foreign nationals on the Mainland. In 1999, the Office received 124 requests for assistance and 110 public enquiries.

2000   The Office received 212 requests for assistance and 180 public enquires.

2001   The Office received 501 requests for assistance and 131 public enquires. Of the requests for assistance, 92 concerned commercial disputes on the Mainland, 75 were complaints about Mainland properties, 214 were complaints about Mainland's administrative, law enforcement and judicial organizations, 44 were complaints about Mainland or Hong Kong organizations, and 76 were related to miscellaneous disputes. Of the public enquires, 68 related economic and trade issues, 45 concerned the operation of the HKSAR Government and organizations in Hong Kong, and 18 were on miscellaneous matters.

2002   Apart from contact with officials, the Office also organised public activities to promote the image of Hong Kong and presented to the general public of mainland the latest developments of the HKSAR. The Office closely monitored the developments in opening up the Mainland market following China's accession to the WTO. To celebrate Hong Kong's reunification with China and the fifth anniversary of the HKSAR, the Office held an exhibition on the past, present and future of Hong Kong at the China Millennium Monument in Beijing from June 28 to July 14.

Sources:

1.   www.info.gov.hk/bjo

The Office of the Government of Hong Kong Special Administrative Region in Beijing			
Year	Name of Department	Title	Name of Director
1998-2002	The Office of the Government of the Hong Kong Special Administrative Region in Beijing	Director	Leung, Po-wing, Bowen Joseph

Sources:
1. *Staff Biographies the Government of the Hong Kong Special Administrative Region,* Hong Kong, Government Printer, 2001
2. *Staff List the Government of the Hong Kong Special Administrative Region,* Hong Kong, Government Printer, 2001.
3. www.info.gov.hk/bjo/

Civil Service

Government Training Division, Colonial Secretariat/ Government Secretariat (1967-1977)
Civil Service Training Division, Civil Service Branch (1977-1983)
Civil Service Training Centre (1983-1996)
Civil Service Training and Development Institute (1996-2002)

1952   The establishment of a central unit to investigate in greater detail gaps in departmental training programmes, to provide specialized advice, and to train general grades of officers was discussed.

1959   The Salaries Commission recommended that an organization be set up for the systematic training of staff and the co-ordination of departmental training and examinations, and to make full use of outside educational and training facilities in Hong Kong and abroad.

1961   A central Training Unit was formally established under the Establishment Branch of the Colonial Secretariat. The Training Unit was responsible for training in prosecution of government's policy of localization at the recruitment level; and to increase the general efficiency of the public service.

1967   The Unit was retitled Government Training Division. The post of the head of the Training Division was upgraded from Senior Training Officer to Principal Government Training Officer.

1977   The Civil Service Branch announced a formal civil service training policy. The Government Training Division was reorganized as Civil Service Training

Division to make more staff available to work with departments in the planning of training. The Division offered centrally-administered training, including language studies, at the staff training centre and through non-government agencies in Hong Kong and overseas.

1980   A Staff Planning Division was established under the Civil Service Branch which was in charge of the formulation and development of service-wide manpower plans to ensure adequate staff resources to meet operational needs and to implement the Government's localization policy. The administrative responsibility of the Staff Planning Division was given to the head of the Civil Service Training Division — Principal Assistant Secretary (Staff Training). In relation to the formation of the Staff Planning Division, the Training Division was recognized as a semi-autonomous unit.

1982   A new post of Civil Service Training Director was created to look after the day-to-day running of the Training Division.

1983   The Civil Service Training Centre was established as an agency with its own head of expenditure in the Estimates of Revenue and Expenditure. The Centre's head was the Assistant Principal Training Officer who was designated as Civil Service Training Director. The Centre provided language and management training for civil servants; assisted government departments with staff training and development plans; and implemented government's localisation policy through the Government Training Scholarship Scheme. The Centre was organised into four units: Administration; General Grades Training; Language Training (comprised the Chinese Section, English Section, and Police Education and Language Section); Management and Development (consisted of the Management Development Section and Management Training Section).

1984   The Development Unit was set up to review training and evaluate management practices and procedures.

1996   The Civil Service Training Centre was reorganised to form the Civil Service Training and Development Institute on April 1. The Institute, with the Director as its controlling officers, had its own expenditure. The new Director assumed responsibility for supervising and setting the strategic direction for achieving the civil service training and development long term goal, setting the strategic direction of programmes and overseeing its operation. The Institute provided training and consultancy services to all government departments. The ultimate goal of the Institute was to become a training centre of excellence for civil servants. It was organized into seven units under a Principal Training Officer and an Assistant Principal Training Officer. Units placed under the administration of the Principal Training Officer included: General Grades Training and Development Unit, Management Training Unit, Senior Management Development Unit, Training and Development Advisory Services Unit. Units supervised by the Assistant Principal Training Officer were the Administration Unit, China Studies Unit, English Communication Training Unit.

1999   The Information Technology Section under the administration of the Assistant

Principal Training Officer was set up to manage information technology training, cyber-learning and self-learning. The Leadership in the Public Sector Programme was introduced in September. The programme focused on the leadership role of the participants in public policy development, managing change and corporate and personal communication strategies.

2000   The Institute provided a variety of training activities to cope with the civil service reform, including workshops for officers serving as inquiry officers on committees; experience-sharing workshops on the new disciplinary mechanism; seminars for human resource managers on new entry pay; reinforcement training of assessment panels; workshops on managing outsourcing; training on legal aspects and the application of the Employment Ordinance; seminars on quality management.

2002   The Institute helped drive central policy initiatives through training and development; provided training and development programme and services for improving performance; advised on central and departmental human resource development. The functional units of the Institute were under the supervision of an Assistant Principal Training Officer and an Assistant Director. Units guided by the Assistant Principal Training Officer included the Administration Unit, Chinese Language Section, Chinese Studies Section, English and Communication Training Unit, and Information Technology and Learning Resource Unit. Units directed by the Assistant Director were the General Grades Training and Development Unit, Management Training Unit, Senior Management Development Unit, Training and Development Advisory Services Unit, and Training Officers in Other Departments/Bureau.

Sources:

1. *Civil Service Training and Development Institute Annual Report*, Hong Kong, Government Pritner, 1997-2001.
2. *Civil Service Training Centre, Prospectus, Hong Kong*, Government Printer, 1982-1983; 1984-1985, p.6.
3. Colonial Secretariat, *Report on Training of Government Servants 1952-1958*, Hong Kong, Establishment Branch, 1958, p.1.
4. *Government Secretariat, Civil Service Branch Circular No. 15/83*.
5. *Report on Training in the Public Service of Hong Kong* 1959-1968, Hong Kong, Government Printer.
6. www.info.gov.hk/cstdi/

Civil Service Training and Development Institute — Changes in Names and Directors			
Year	Name of Department	Title	Name of Director
1982-1983	Civil Service Training Division, Government Secretariat	Civil Service Training Director	Kitchell, Abdul Rahim Bin
1983-1989	Civil Service Training Centre	Civil Service Training Director	Kitchell, Abdul Rahim Bin
1989-1992	Civil Service Training Centre	Civil Service Training Director	Lam Wong, May-bun, Nancy
1992-1995	Civil Service Training Centre	Civil Service Training Director	Szeto Nguan, Ming-hiang, Mary
1996-2000	Civil Service Training and Development Institute	Director, Civil Service Training and Development Institute	Szeto Nguan, Ming-hiang, Mary
2000-2002	Civil Service Training and Development Institute	Director, Civil Service Training and Development Institute	Ng, Wing-cheung, William

Sources:
1. *Staff Biographies Hong Kong Government*, Hong Kong, Government Printer, 1984-1996.
2. *Staff Biographies the Government of the Hong Kong Special Administrative Region*, Hong Kong, Government Pritner, 1997-2001.
3. *Staff List Hong Kong Government*, Hong Kong, Government Printer, 1982-1996.
4. *Staff List the Government of the Hong Kong Special Administrative Region*, Hong Kong, Government Printer, 1997-2000.
5. www.info.gov.hk/cstdi/

Hong Kong Standing Commission on Civil Service Salaries and Conditions of Service (1979-2002)
Standing Committee on Judicial Salaries and Conditions of Service (1987-2002)
Standing Committee on Disciplined Service Salaries and Conditions of Service (1989-2002)
Standing Committee on Directorate Salaries and Conditions of Service (1993-2002)
Joint Secretariat for the Advisory Bodies on Civil Service and Judicial Salaries and Conditions of Service (2001-2002)

1971   The 1971 Salaries Commission, applying the occupational class system which grouped together a number of grades related to each other by occupational criteria, accepted the concept of comparison with the private sector as a primary principle. The Pay Investigation Unit started a programme of work to provide a basis for fixing civil service salaries in accordance with this principle.

1973   The Pay Investigation Unit examined each occupational class every other year by using either external comparison and/or internal relativity.

1974   The occupational class reviews were replaced by the Pay Trend Surveys to keep overall civil service pay in line with private sector pay.

1979   A Standing Commission of Civil Service Salaries and Conditions of Service was appointed to review the principles and practices governing the class, grade, rank and salary structure of the civil service and to recommend changes it considered to be necessary.

1982   The Pay Survey and Research Unit was placed under the jurisdiction of the Commission. The Unit was responsible for collecting and analyzing information related to the determination of civil service remuneration, including the annual pay trend survey.

1987   In December, the Standing Committee on Judicial Salaries and Conditions of Service was established. It advised the Governor on the pay and conditions of service of judicial officers.

1988   The Government invited the Commission to appoint a committee to review the pay and conditions of services of the disciplined services including the Royal Hong Kong Police Force, Correctional Services Department, Customs and Excise Department, Fire Services Department and Immigration Department.

1989   The Standing Committee on Disciplined Services Salaries and Conditions of Service was established in February as an independent advisory body. The Standing Committee operated through two subcommittees: Police Subcommittee and General Disciplined Services Subcommittee. The Office of the Secretary General was set up to provide secretariat support to the Standing Committee.

1990   The ICAC Subcommittee was set up to advise on the salaries and conditions of service for the ICAC.

1993   The Standing Committee on Directorate Salaries and Conditions of Service was established to advise the Governor on matters affecting the directorate of the general civil service, that is, excluding the disciplined services and the Judiciary.

2001   The Joint Secretariat for the Advisory Bodies on Civil Service and Judicial Salaries and Conditions of Service was established in December to provide support service to the following four advisory bodies: Standing Commission on Civil Service Salaries and Conditions of Service, Standing Committee on Disciplined Services Salaries and Conditions of Service, Standing Committee on Directorate Salaries and Conditions of Service, and Standing Committee on Judicial Salaries and Conditions of Service. The advisory bodies provided independent advice to the Chief Executive of the Hong Kong Special Administrative Region on the principles and practices of government pay, conditions of service and salary structure of non-directorate civil service, the disciplined services, the directorate and the judicial officers respectively.

2002   The structure and functions of the Joint Secretariat, the Standing Commission and the Standing Committees remained unchanged. The Joint Secretariat was headed by the Secretary General and was organized into: Pay Survey and Research Unit, Committee and Research Division, and Departmental Administration Division.

Sources:

1.   *Hong Kong Standing Commission on Civil Service Salaries and Conditions of Service, Report no.1, First Report on Principles and Practices Governing Civil Service Pay*, Hong Kong, Government Pritner, 1979.
2.   *Hong Kong Standing Commission on Civil Service Salaries and Conditions of Service*, Report no.3, Report on the Pay of Staff of the Independent Commission Against *Corruption*, Hong Kong, Government Printer, 1980.
3.   *Hong Kong Standing Commission on Civil Service Salaries and Conditions of Service, Report no.21, Consultative Machinery in the Civil Service*, Hong Kong, Government Printer, 1988.
4.   *Hong Kong Standing Commission on Civil Service Salaries and Conditions of Service, Report no.39, Progress Report*, Hong Kong, Government Printer, 2000.
5.   www.info.gov.hk/jsscs

Joint Secretariat for the Advisory Bodies on Civil Service and Judicial Salaries and Conditions of Service (JSSCS) — Changes in Names and Directors

Year	Name of Department	Title	Name of Director
1979-1980	Standing Commission on Civil Service Salaries and Conditions of Service	Chairman	Kan, Yuet-keung
1980-1988	Standing Commission on Civil Service Salaries and Conditions of Service	Chairman	Chung, Sze-yuen
1988-2000	Standing Commission on Civil Service Salaries and Conditions of Service	Chairman	Gordon, Sidney
1987-1996	Standing Committee on Judicial Salaries and Conditions of Service	Chairman	Ross, G. R.
1996-2002	Standing Committee on Judicial Salaries and Conditions of Service	Chairman	Lee, Hon-chiu

Year	Name of Department	Title	Name of Director
1989-1991	Standing Committee on Disciplined Services Salaries and Conditions of Service	Chairman	Swaine, John J.
1991-2000	Standing Committee on Disciplined Services Salaries and Conditions of Service	Chairman	Lau, Kin-yee, Miriam
2001-2002	Standing Committee on Disciplined Services Salaries and Conditions of Service	Chairman	Chan, Charnwut, Bernard
1993-1995	Standing Committee on Directorate Salaries and Condition of Service	Chairman	Knowles, W. C. G.
1995-1996	Standing Committee on Directorate Salaries and Condition of Service	Chairman	Ross, G. R.
1996-2002	Standing Committee on Directorate Salaries and Condition of Service	Chairman	Lee, Hon-chiu
2002	Standing Committee on Directorate Salaries and Condition of Service	Chairman	Cheng, Hoi-chuen
2000-2002	Standing Commission on Civil Service Salaries and Conditions of Service	Chairman	Yeung, Ka-sing
2002	Joint Secretariat for the Advisory Bodies on Civil Service and Judicial Salaries and Conditions of Service (JSSCS)	Secretary General, Head of the Joint Secretariat	Lee, Lap-sun

Sources:
1. Internal records from the Joint Secretariat for the Advisory Bodies on Civil Service and Judicial Salaries and Conditions of Service.
2. *Staff List Hong Kong Government*, Hong Kong, Government Printer, 1963-1996.
3. www. Info.gov.hk/jsscs

Official Language Agency (1996–1997)
Official Languages Agency (1997–2002)

1996   The Chinese Division was separated from the Office of the Director of Administration on April 1 to form the Official Language Agency. The Agency was headed by the Commissioner for Official Language who reported to the Secretary for the Civil Service. It provided translation and interpretation services to government bureaux and departments, developed the institutional arrangement for the use of official languages, including the setting of guidelines for the civil service, review of civil service language practices and the provision of advisory services to government bureaux and departments. The Agency was composed of the Bilingual Laws Advisory Committee (Secretariat), the Finance Committee and six other sections – Administration, Inspection, Putonghua Interpretation, Simultaneous Interpretation, Translation Services, and Training and Development.

2001   The Agency was restructured into seven sections. The Administration Section was responsible for providing general administrative support such as human resources, finance and office management, and word processing service. The Grade Management Section implemented and evaluated human resource management strategies; conducted manpower planning, staff deployment and postings; provided career counselling and handled staff complaints; and compiled and maintained computerized human resource management database. The Putonghua Interpretation Section dealt with communication between the HKSAR Government and the mainland authorities; and operated a Putonghua telephone enquiry service for officials. The Simultaneous Interpretation Section provided simultaneous interpretation in Cantonese/Putonghua/English for meetings of the Legislative Council and District Councils, other statutory bodies and advisory committees, briefings and press conference; and advised government departments on the planning and commissioning of simultaneous interpretation facilities. The Research and Support Services Section promoted wider use of Chinese in the civil service; updated, compiled, published English-Chinese glossaries of terms commonly used in government departments, and provided professional services on Chinese literary matters. The Training Section planned and organized training activities for Chinese Language Officers. The Translation Services Section was responsible for the translation and interpretation services; and the provision of advice on the use of Chinese and assistance to subject officers in their preparation of documents in Chinese.

2002   The structure of the Agency remained unchanged.

Sources:

1. *The Government of the Hong Kong Special Administrative Region Telephone Directory*, Hong Kong, Government Printer, 1999, p.456.
2. *Hong Kong Government Telephone Directory*, Hong Kong, Government Printer, 1996, pp.330-331.
3. www.csb.gov.hk/hkgcsb/index.jsp

Official Languages Agency — Changes in Names and Directors

Year	Name of Department	Title	Name of Director
1996-1997	Official Language Agency	Commissioner for Official Language	Choi, Ying-pik, Yvonne
1997-1999	Official Languages Agency	Commissioner for Official Languages	Lai Chan, Chi-kuen, Marion
1999-2001	Official Languages Agency	Commissioner for Official Languages	Lee, Lap-sun
2001-2002	Official Languages Agency	Commissioner for Official Languages	Allcock, Agnes

Sources:

1. *Staff Biographies the Government of the Hong Kong Special Administrative Region*, Hong Kong, Government Printer, 1998-2001.

2. *Staff List Hong Kong Government*, Hong Kong, Government Printer, 1996.

3. *Staff List the Government of the Hong Kong Special Administrative Region*, Hong Kong, Government Printer, 1997-2000.

4. www.csb.gov.hk/hkgcsb/index.jsp

Chapter 2
Judiciary and
Legal Constitution

Chief Justice, Sir Ivo Rigby, leading a judicial procession at the opening of the Assizes, 1970

Evolvement of Judiciary

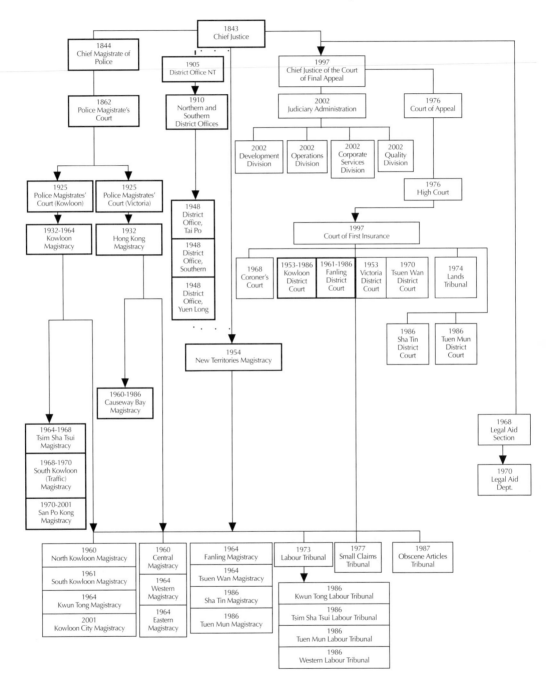

Evolvement of Department of Justice

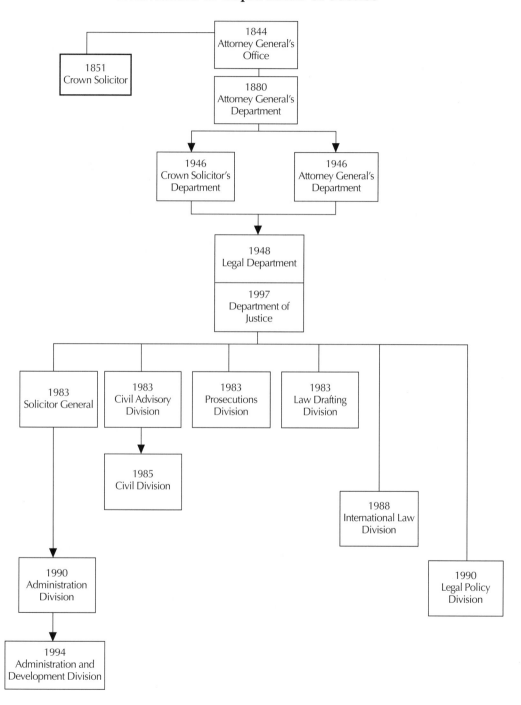

Hong Kong has endeavoured to build up the rules governing its legal process for over 160 years. Before 1997, such rules largely followed those that were developed in England. After the return to China in 1997, the most significant change in the judicial system was the establishment of the highest appellate court in the HKSAR - the Court of Final Appeal. It hears appeals on civil and criminal matters from the High Court (the Court of Appeal and the Court of First Instance). No longer can appeals be made to the Privy Council in England.

Although the establishment of British constitutional law was the first and foremost task for the Colonial Government in the mid-nineteenth century, it had to uphold traditional Chinese laws and customs in cases involving native Chinese. The implementation of British rule in Hong Kong thus faced critical challenges and hindrance in the early years. Since the early twentieth century, the British judicial and legal systems had slowly taken hold in the Chinese community in line with social and cultural changes.

The Judiciary and the Department of Justice are independent of each other. Led by the Chief Justice, the Judiciary is in charge of the administration of justice and adjudicates civil disputes as well as criminal cases. It operates on the British principle of complete independence from the executive and legislative branches of the Government. The origins of the Judiciary can be traced back to April 30 of 1841 when the Government began to publish rules and regulations for British merchant shipping. A year later, in 1842, the Office of Chief Magistrate was established to exercise magisterial and police authority over all persons who committed breaches of the peace. It detained offenders of crimes and felonies in safe custody and reported the cases to the Governor. An Office of Marine

Magistrate was set up in the same year to exercise authority according to the regulations and laws over persons resorting to or abiding in the harbours. It detained offenders who committed felonies within the harbours and waters in safe custody and reported the cases to the Governor. In 1843, a Chief Justice was nominated. A full-fledged Judicial Department was formed in 1844 and was renamed Judiciary in 1979.

The organization of the Judiciary developed rapidly from the 1950s onwards. In addition to the Hong Kong Magistracy and Kowloon Magistracy, the New Territories Magistracy was established in 1954. Numerous courts such as District Courts, Tribunals and Coroner's Court were also set up in different districts on Hong Kong Island, in Kowloon and in the New Territories. The cases were classified in a more sophisticated manner. Tribunals were categorized into labour, small claims, lands, and obscene articles. The courts have been enlarged and refined to cover the evolving social requirements.

The Attorney General's Office was the precursor of the Department of Justice. Nominated in 1844, the Attorney General was responsible for drafting and introducing laws, regulations and ordinances; processing prosecutions on behalf of the Crown in the absence of private prosecutors; and filing indictment against any person who committed crimes and offences. The Office was renamed Legal Department in 1948 and became the Department of Justice on 1 July, 1997, and the Attorney General was retitled Secretary for Justice. By 2002, the Department had developed into a substantial organization with more than 270 lawyers and 820 supporting staff. It was responsible for rendering comprehensive legal services to the

Government which included the conducting of prosecutions, legislation drafting, and the provision of legal advice.

For over one and a half centuries, continual reforms of the judicial and legal systems of Hong Kong have been implemented to develop modern and internationally recognized systems that are appropriate for Hong Kong. The Judiciary has strongly emphasized its total independence, free from interference by either the legislature or the executive branch; while the legal system protects the freedom of individuals to manage their own affairs free from arbitrary interference by the Government. The attainment of these objectives ensures the success of Hong Kong and enhances its advance towards a modern and open society.

Judicary

Office of Chief Magistrate, Office of Marine Magistrate (1842-1844)
Judicial Department (1844-1979)
Judiciary (1979-2002)

1841   William Caine of the 26th Regiment of Infantry was appointed Chief Magistrate of Hong Kong on April 30. He was required, in the case of natives, to exercise authority according to the laws, customs, and usages of China; and in the case of others, according to the customs and usages of British police law; providing at the same time a scale of punishment for offences. On the same date, rules and regulations for the British merchant shipping and for the Marine Magistrate were duly published.

1842   The Office of Chief Magistrate was established to exercise magisterial and police authority over all persons who committed breaches of peace. It detained offenders of crimes and felonies in safe custody and reported the cases to the Governor. An Office of Marine Magistrate was set up in the same year to exercise authority according to the regulations and laws over the persons resorting to or abiding in the harbours. It detained offenders who committed felonies within the harbours and waters in safe custody and reported the cases to the Governor.

1843   The Governor appointed 44 leading inhabitants as Justices of the Peace. A Chief Justice was nominated.

1844   The Judicial Department was fully formed: with the opening of a Criminal Court on March 4; the setting up of a Magistracy in May at Chuck-chu (Stanley) due to a number of daring robberies and other serious crimes committed in that area; and the formal establishment of a Supreme Court under the Chief Justice in October with civil and criminal jurisdiction and with a Registrar and interpreters. Under the Supreme Court Ordinance no.15 of 1844, Sections 25 and 27, the Chief Justice held four distinct terms of Court annually for the dispatch of the civil and criminal business, and also held occasionally a Small Debts Court for the dispatch of business on the summary side of the Court. The Chief Magistrate of Police was appointed in the same year. With the arrival of the Chief Justice in May, the Chief Magistrate of Police ceased to decide upon actions of a civil nature, restricting his Court to its duties of: exercising the authority to judge and penalize offenders who privately distilled spirits in Hong Kong; appointing persons to examine the balances, weights and measures in the market; overseeing and keeping one true copy of the declaration of printers and publishers for their periodical work as required by the Government.

1848   The Chief Magistrate of Police granted licences to persons who desired to keep more than two pounds of gunpowder.

1862   The posts of Chief Magistrate and Assistant Magistrates were abolished. The former duties of the Chief Magistrate of Police were handed over to two Police Magistrates. They heard, tried and determined general crimes, misdemeanours or offences, and the respective punishment such as imprisonment, fine or whipping; referred offences that required heavier punishment to the Supreme Court for trial; and witnessed the declaration and oath of any person who was to be appointed as police officer. Two Justices of the Peace sat together and would have the powers of a Police Magistrate. The Court of Summary Jurisdiction was established; and the post of Coroner was first set up.

1863   The jurisdiction power of the two Police Magistrates was extended to harbours and dependencies of Hong Kong.

1873   The Court of Summary Jurisdiction was abolished; with its jurisdiction handed over to the Supreme Court. The Supreme Court was supported by the Puisne Judge and the Registrar of the Supreme Court.

1889   The Police Magistrates were granted the power to allow police to forfeit illegal articles.

1890   The judiciary function was divided into two spheres: Supreme Court and Magistrates. The Supreme Court also exercised jurisdiction in admiralty cases. The Magistrates were made up of Police Magistrates, Marine Magistrate, and Justices of the Peace. As additional responsibilities, the Magistrates investigated and decided on claims for civil debts; penalized persons providing false testimonies and initiating malicious prosecution, and juvenile offenders; forfeited unlicensed articles; received appeal cases and transferred the cases to the Full Court of the Supreme Court.

1909   The Supreme Court heard, tried and determined cases related to original jurisdiction, summary jurisdiction, criminal jurisdiction, appellate jurisdiction, admiralty jurisdiction, probate jurisdiction and bankruptcy.

1925   The Police Magistrates' Court was spilt into two: Police Magistrates' Court (Victoria) and Police Magistrates' Court (Kowloon).

1931   The Police Magistrates' Court (Victoria) was renamed Police Magistrates' Court (Hong Kong).

1932   The Police Magistrates' Court (Hong Kong) and the Police Magistrates' Court (Kowloon) were renamed Hong Kong Magistracy and Kowloon Magistracy respectively.

1941   During the Japanese wartime occupation of Hong Kong (1941-45), the former functions of the Supreme Court and Magistracies to try criminal offences were taken up by the Japanese General Military Court and the Summary Military Court respectively. Civil jurisdiction was suspended during the war period.

1946   The District Officer for the New Territories was responsible for the administration of the New Territories; he also sat as Magistrate and Land Officer for small debt cases and land cases.

1948   The Supreme Court and Magistracies were separate entities. Under the Supreme Court were the Chief Justice, the Puisne Judge, the Registrar of the Supreme Court and Official Administrator. There were two magistracies — Hong Kong Magistracy and Kowloon Magistracy and three district suboffices — Yuen Long, Tai Po and Southern. The District Officers sat as Police Court Magistrates, and held Small Debts Courts and Land Courts.

1949   The Judicial Department was made up by the Supreme Court and the Magistracies. The Supreme Court was headed by the Chief Justice who was also the head of the Judicial Department; under him were the Puisne Judges, and the Registrar of the Supreme Court and Official Administrator. It heard, tried and determined cases related to original jurisdiction, summary jurisdiction, criminal jurisdiction, appellate jurisdiction, admiralty jurisdiction, probate jurisdiction, divorce jurisdiction, suitors' funds and bankruptcy. The Magistracies were under the direction of magistrates who were responsible to the Chief Justice.

1950   The Supreme Court handled also the registration of bills of sale.

1953   The Victoria District Court and the Kowloon District Court were set up to hear, try and determine cases related to criminal jurisdiction and civil jurisdiction. The Compulsory Service Tribunal was established to hear objections filed by registered British subjects who objected to their selection for service in the Royal Hong Kong Defence Force, the Special Constabulary or the Essential Services Corps.

1954   The District Courts heard appeals from the Tenancy Tribunal and determined workmen's compensation cases. The New Territories Magistracy was created to deal with offences related to criminal jurisdiction as District Officers ceased to exercise such powers.

1957   Adoption cases were heard at the Supreme Court.

1960   The Hong Kong Magistracy was spilt into Central Magistracy and Causeway Bay Magistracy. The North Kowloon Magistracy was formed. The number of magistracies was expanded to five.

1961   New Territories District Officers ceased to exercise jurisdiction on land and small debt cases. The third district court, Fanling Court, was created to handle New Territories cases. The sixth magistracy, South Kowloon Magistracy, was established. Juvenile criminal cases were tried by three newly created Juvenile Courts: at the Causeway Bay Magistracy, the North Kowloon Magistracy, and the New Territories Magistracy.

1962   The Compulsory Service Tribunal was abolished.

1963   The post of Senior Puisne Judge was created.

1964   The number of magistracies was increased from six to ten. The Western Magistracy and Eastern Magistracy were set up on Hong Kong Island. The Kowloon Magistracy was abolished, but two new magistracies — Tsim Sha Tsui Magistracy and Kwun Tong Magistracy — were created. In the New Territories, the original New Territories Magistracy was spilt into two: Fanling Magistracy and Tsuen Wan Magistracy.

1965   In addition to their original duties, distress for rent cases and rent increase applications were tried at the District Courts.

1967   A Coroner was appointed and a Coroner's Office was created at the Western Magistracy and North Kowloon Magistracy.

1968   A formal Coroner's Court was established. The Tsim Sha Tsui Magistracy was abolished. In addition to the South Kowloon Magistracy, the South Kowloon (Traffic) Magistracy was set up to handle traffic cases.

1970   The newly established organs included the San Po Kong Magistracy in Kowloon, the Anti-Litter Courts on Hong Kong Island and in Kowloon, and the fourth district court, Tsuen Wan District Court. The South Kowloon (Traffic) Magistracy was abolished.

1972   The District Courts tried divorce cases in addition to their original duties.

1973   The Labour Tribunal was formed to settle disputes between employees and employers.

1974   The Lands Tribunal was set up to determine the compensation payable by the Government to affected parties due to reclamation or development projects.

1976   The Court of Appeal and the High Court were established under the supervision of the Supreme Court. The Court of Appeal heard appeals of criminal and civil cases from the High Court, the District Courts and the Magistracies. The High Court determined cases related to criminal jurisdiction, original civil jurisdiction, adoption cases, probate jurisdiction, admiralty jurisdiction, bankruptcy and company winding up, and bills of sale registration.

1977   The Small Claims Tribunal was established to settle monetary claims of small amount not exceeding HK$3,000.

1979   Headed by the Chief Justice, the Judicial Department was reorganized into the Judiciary. The Court of Appeal and the High Court were two independent bodies directly under the Chief Justice. The Court of Appeal heard civil and criminal appeals from the High Court, the District Courts, Magistracies and Tribunals. The High Court tried cases related to civil dispute, criminal offence, lunacy, bankruptcy, company winding up, divorce, adoption and probate. The functions of the third organ, the Registrar of the Supreme Court, could be divided into two parts. The first part handled registration and administrative matters, and included ten offices: Bailiff

Section, Clerks of Court's Office, Community Relations Unit, Court Interpreters' Office, Court Reporters' Office, Library of the Supreme Court, Probate Registry, Secretary of the Judiciary, Supreme Court Accounts Office and Supreme Court Registry. The second part included: Coroner's Court, District Courts, Labour Tribunal, Lands Tribunal, Magistracies, Small Claims Tribunal and Tenancy Tribunal.

1982   The Tenancy Tribunal was abolished. and most of its functions were transferred to the Lands Tribunal.

1983   In addition to its original functions, the Lands Tribunal handled also appeals of ratable values under the Rating Ordinance and appeals against certificates of increase in rents and other determinations under the Landlord and Tenant (Consolidation) Ordinance. The Small Claims Tribunal evolved into: Hong Kong Small Claims Tribunal, Kowloon Small Claims Tribunal and Tsuen Wan Small Claims Tribunal. The Community Relations Unit was renamed Community Relations Office. The Library of the Supreme Court was renamed Supreme Court Library. The Secretary of the Judiciary was retitled Office for the Secretary of the Judiciary. The Supreme Court Accounts Office was renamed Office of the Accountant of the Judiciary.

1986   The Kowloon District Court and the Fanling District Court were abolished while the Sha Tin District Court and the Tuen Mun District Court were established. New magistracies were set up in Sha Tin and Tuen Mun, while the Causeway Bay Magistracy was dissolved. In addition to the original Labour Tribunal, four new ones were set up: Western Labour Tribunal, Tsim Sha Tsui Labour Tribunal, Kwun Tong Labour Tribunal and Tuen Mun Labour Tribunal. The Community Relations Office and Baliff Section were renamed Information Office and Bailff's Office respectively.

1987   The Obscene Articles Tribunal was created to determine whether an article referred by a court or magistrate was an obscene or indecent article and whether publicly displayed matter was indecent.

1994   The Judiciary Administrator was appointed to take over Judiciary's administration duties from the Registrar of the Supreme Court. The Registrar of the Supreme Court concentrated on judicial and statutory duties only. The Judiciary was restructured into three major functional units and six supporting offices. The three major functional unit were: Court (comprised the Court of Appeal, High Court, District Court, Magistracies, Lands Tribunal, Labour Tribunal, Small Claims Tribunal, Obscene Articles Tribunal and Coroner's Court); Judiciary Administrator's Office (included the Administration Division and Development Division); and Registries (consisted of the Clerk of Court's Office, Supreme Court Registry, Probate Registry, District Court Registry, Family Court Registry, Lands Tribunal Registry, Magistracy Registries, Labour Tribunal Registry, Small Claims Tribunal Registry, Obscene Articles Tribunal Registry and Coroner's Court Registry). The supporting offices included the Bailiff's Office, Court Interpreters' Office, Court Reporters' Office, Accounts Office, Libraries, and Press and Public Relations Office.

1997   The Court of Final Appeal of Hong Kong Special Administrative Region was established on July 1 to hear appeals on civil and criminal matters from the High Court of First Instance and the Court of Appeal.

2000   The Judiciary Administration's Office underwent extensive reforms. It was restructured into four main divisions: Development, Operations, Corporate Services and Quality. The Development Division co-ordinated and developed new initiatives in court practices as well as procedures; provided support to judicial training; and took over the functions of the former Press and Public Relations Office. Previous functions of the registries were grouped under the Operations Division. It provided essential support services to the operation of the courts and handled complaints. The Corporate Services Division dealt with human and financial resources management, planning and implementation of accommodation strategy and general administration of the judiciary. The Quality Division planned and co-ordinated with other operating units on efficiency reviews and improvement initiatives; developed and implemented information technology and management information systems.

2002   The structure of the Judiciary was divided into two parts: Court System and Judiciary Administration. The Court System, headed by the Chief Justice of the Court of Final Appeal, included the Court of Final Appeal, High Court (Court of Appeal, and Court of First Instance), District Court (the Family Court was part of it), Lands Tribunal, Magistrates' Courts (Eastern, Western, North Kowloon, Kowloon City, Kwun Tong, Tsuen Wan, Sha Tin, Fanling, Tuen Mun; the Juvenile Court was part of the Magistrates' Courts) ; Labour Tribunal, Small Claims Tribunal, Obscene Articles Tribunal and Coroner's Court. The Judiciary Administration comprised four divisions: Development Division (Legislation, Review of Court Practices and Rules, Alternative Dispute Resolution, Legal Profession Liaison, Logistical Support for Judicial Training, Public Relation); Operations Division (Court Registries, Judicial Support, Court Language, Court Orders, Mediation Service, Legal Reference, Complaints); Corporate Services Division; (Human Resources, Finance, Building, General Support); and Quality Division (Management Review, Management Information, Information Technology).

Sources:

1. *Annual Department Report on the Supreme Court and the Hong Kong and Kowloon Magistracies*, Hong Kong Government, 1950-1951.
2. *Annual Report on Hong Kong*, Hong Kong, Government, 1946-1949.
3. Cruden, C. N., *Court Standards in Hong Kong*, 5th Commonwealth Magistrates Conference, Oxford, Sept 1979, mimeo.
4. *The Friend of China, The Hong Kong Gazette*, Hong Kong Government, 5th May 1842, 2nd March 1844, 30th March 1844, 1st January 1845, 6th July 1845, 10th February 1847, 13th September 1848.
5. "General Administration" *Hong Kong Directive*, HKRS 211, D&S, no.2/4.
6. *Hong Kong*, Hong Kong, Government Printer, 1961-2003.
7. *Hong Kong Annual Departmental Report By the Registrar, Supreme Court*, Hong Kong, Government Printer, 1952-1968.
8. *Hong Kong Annual Statistics of the Judiciary Provided by the Registrar, Supreme Court*, Hong Kong, Government Printer, 1968-1979.
9. *Hong Kong Government Gazette*, 29 March 1862; 26 April 1862; 31 January 1863; 25 Aug 1866; 24 June 1871; 8 February 1873; 21 March 1874; 6 April 1878; 9 March 1889.
10. *Hong Kong Hansard, Hong Kong Daily Press*, 1908, 1910, 1912, 1914.
11. *Hong Kong Judiciary Report Prepared by the Registrar, Supreme Court*, Hong Kong, Government Printer, 1983-1990.
12. *Index to Correspondence (General Register)*, Hong Kong Government, 1899-1904.
13. Miners, Norman, *The Government and Politics of Hong Kong*, Hong Kong, Oxford University Press, 1981, p.193.

14. Norton-Kyshe, James William, *The History of the Laws and Courts of Hong Kong: From the earliest period to 1898*, Hong Kong, Noronha and Co., 1898.
15. Ordinance of Hong Kong, 1884-1890, Vol. I.
16. "Report of the Registrar of the Supreme Court", *Hong Kong Administration Reports*, Hong Kong Government, 1909-1930.
17. "Report of the Registrar of the Supreme Court", *Hong Kong Administrative Reports*, Hong Kong Government, 1931-1932.
18. "Report of the Registrar of the Supreme Court", *Hong Kong Sessional Papers*, Hong Kong, Noronha & Co., 1902, 1904.
19. "Report of the Registrar of the Supreme Court Official Trustee, Official Administrator & Registrar of Companies", *Hong Kong Administration Reports* Hong Kong Government, 1933-1939.
20. Scott, Ian, *Political Change and the Crisis of Legitimacy in Hong Kong*, Honolulu, University of Hawaii Press, 1989, p.42.
21. www.info.gov.hk/jud/eindex.htm

Judiciary — Changes in Names and Directors

Year	Name of Department	Title	Name of Director
1844-1859	Judicial Department	Chief Justice	Hulme, John Walter
1860-1866	Judicial Department	Chief Justice	Adams, William Henry
1866-1882	Judicial Department	Chief Justice	Smale, John Jackson
1882-1888	Judicial Department	Chief Justice	Phillippo, George
1888-1892	Judicial Department	Chief Justice	Russell, James
1892-1896	Judicial Department	Chief Justice	Clarke, Fielding
1896-1902	Judicial Department	Chief Justice	Carrington, John Worrell
1902-1905	Judicial Department	Chief Justice	Goodman, William Meigh
1905-1912	Judicial Department	Chief Justice	Piggott, Francis Taylor

Year	Name of Department	Title	Name of Director
1912-1924	Judicial Department	Chief Justice	Rees-Davies, William
1924-1930	Judicial Department	Chief Justice	Gollan, Henry Cowper
1930-1934	Judicial Department	Chief Justice	Kemp, Joseph Horsford
1934-1941	Judicial Department	Chief Justice	MacGregor, Alasdair Duncan Atholl
1946-1948	Judicial Department	Chief Justice	Blackall, Henry William Butler
1948-1950	Judicial Department	Chief Justice	Gibson, Leslie Bertram
1950-1951	Judicial Department	Chief Justice	Williams, Ernest Hillas
1951-1955	Judicial Department	Chief Justice	Howe, Gerard Lewis
1955-1970	Judicial Department	Chief Justice	Hogan, Michael Joseph Patrick
1970-1973	Judicial Department	Chief Justice	Rigby, Ivo Charles Clayton
1973-1979	Judicial Department	Chief Justice	Briggs, Geoffrey Gould
1979-1988	Judiciary	Chief Justice	Roberts, Denys Tudor Emil
1988-1996	Judiciary	Chief Justice	Yang, Ti-liang
1996-1997	Judiciary	Chief Justice (Acting)	Power, Noel
1997-2002	Judiciary	Chief Justice	Li, Kowk-nang, Andrew

Sources:
1. *Hong Kong Blue Book*, Hong Kong, Noronha & Co., 1844-1939.
2. *The Hong Kong Civil Service List*, Hong Kong Government, 1947-1958.
3. *Hong Kong Judiciary Report Prepared by the Registrar, Supreme Court*, Hong Kong, Government Printer, 1980-1994.
4. *Hong Kong, Judiciary Annual Report*, Hong Kong, Government Printer, 1999-2000.
5. *Staff List Hong Kong Government*, Hong Kong, Government Printer, 1960-1978.
6. www.info.gov.hk/jud/eindex.htm

Legal Aid Committee (1958-1968)
Legal Aid Section (1968-1970)
Legal Aid Department (1970-2002)

1940s   Legal aid was available in criminal cases to persons charged with capital offences and in civil cases to those litigants whose assets did not exceed HK$500 in value.

1958   A Legal Aid Committee was established to report on the feasibility of introducing a legal aid scheme for persons in civil and criminal cases who had reasonable grounds for taking or defending legal action but were lacking in means.

1962   Following the report of the Committee, legal aid became available to all eligible persons facing trials on criminal charges in the Supreme Court.

1967   A scheme of civil legal aid was introduced.

1968   The Legal Aid Section was set up to provide legal aid for the poor.

1970   The Legal Aid Department was established in July as an independent department. The Department processed applications and acted as solicitors for aided person in civil and criminal cases; obtained proper results of evidence in each trial; and to give proper instructions so as to shorten trials and appeals.

1972   The Litigation Unit was set up.

1973   The Litigation Unit handled all the solicitors' side of the work in the vast majority of cases tried in the Supreme Court, criminal appeals heard in the Full Court of the Supreme Court, as well as appeals from Magistrates' Courts to the Supreme Court.

1974   Members of the Litigation Unit conducted every aspect of certain types of proceedings, such as undefended divorces, winding up and bankruptcy matters, workmen's compensation cases, wage claims and a wide variety of miscellaneous proceedings in the District Courts.

1979   Legal aid was extended to all cases heard in the District Courts.

1984   The Department began to provide legal assistance to the sandwich class as well.

1986   Lawyers in the Department provided representation service in court, processed applications for legal aid to appeal; acted as instructing solicitors on appeal if counsel certified that there were grounds of appeal; as well as drawing the attention of the administration to proposals for reforms of legislation, codes of practice and policies.

1990   The Department was divided into four parts: Litigation Division (previously the Litigation Unit); Policy, Administration, Legal Support Services Division; Application and Processing Division; and the Official Solicitor's Office. The Litigation Division conducted litigation on behalf of aided persons and provided assistance to those engaged in the processing of applications. The Policy, Administration, Legal Support Services Division specialized in the enforcement of judgements for damages and legal costs, application for the grant of letters of administration in fatal accidents cases, preparation of itemized bills of costs, and winding up and bankruptcy proceedings against insolvent employers. The Official Solicitor's Office was set up to deal with the duties of the Official Solicitor prescribed under the Legal Aid Ordinance and to avoid the conflict of interests arising between the Director of Legal Aid's role as head of the Department and his/her role as the Official Solicitor.

1992   The Litigation Division was restructured. It comprised the Family Litigation Section; Personal Injury Litigation Section; Commercial Admiralty and Professional Negligence Section; and Insolvency, Costing and Enforcement Section.

1999   Among the 31,578 civil and 4,212 criminal legal aid applications processed by the Department in 1999, legal aid was granted in 10,075 and 2,548 cases respectively.

2001   The total number of staff was 621 in 2001.

2002   The Department provided applicants who satisfied the statutory criteria as to the financial eligibility and the merits of taking or defending legal proceedings with legal representation. It comprised the Official Solicitor's Office (a separate office directly under the Director of Legal Aid) and three divisions: Application and Processing Section, (made up of the Application and Processing Division Headquarters, Kowloon Branch Office); Policy and Administration Division (supervised the Accounts and Supplies Section, Administration Section, Computer and Statistics Section, Information Unit, Internal Audit Section, Training Unit); and Litigation Division (directed the Crime Section; Family Litigation Section; Insolvency, Costing and Enforcement Section; Personal Injury Litigation Section).

Sources:

1.   Government Information Services, *Hong Kong: The Facts, Legal System*, Hong Kong, Government Printer, 1983.
2.   *Hong Kong*, Hong Kong, Government Printer, 1983-1992.
3.   *Hong Kong Annual Departmental Report by the Director of Legal Aid*, Hong Kong Government Printer, 1972-1974.
4.   *Hong Kong Annual Report on the Judiciary by the Registrar, Supreme Court*, Hong Kong, Government Printer, 1964-1969.
5.   *Legal Aid Departmental Report*, Hong Kong, Government Printer, 1986-1998.
6.   www.info.gov.hk/lad/

Legal Aid Department — Changes in Directors

Year	Name of Department	Title	Name of Director
1970-1981	Legal Aid Department	Director of Legal Aid	Mayne, Desmond Francis O'Reilly
1981-1984	Legal Aid Department	Director of Legal Aid	Clancy, Brian Patrick
1984-1993	Legal Aid Department	Director of Legal Aid	Moss, Patrick Ronald
1993-1996	Legal Aid Department	Director of Legal Aid	Cheung Cheng, Po-lin, Pauline
1996-2002	Legal Aid Department	Director of Legal Aid	Chan, Shu-ying

Sources:
1.   *Staff List Hong Kong Government*, Hong Kong, Government Printer, 1968-1996.
2.   *Staff List the Government of the Hong Kong Special Administrative Region*, Hong Kong, Government Printer, 1997-2000.
3.   www.info.gov.hk/lad/

Legal Constitution

Attorney General's Office (1844-1880)
Attorney General's Department (1880-1948)
Legal Department (1948-1997)
Department of Justice (1997-2002)

1843   A temporary legal adviser was appointed.

1844   The Attorney General was appointed to replace the temporary legal adviser. He was responsible for drafting and introducing laws, regulations and ordinances; processing prosecution on behalf of the Crown in the absence of private prosecutors; filing indictment against any person who committed crimes and offences.

1851   A Crown Solicitor was first appointed to act as Deputy Sheriff and Coroner.

1856   The Office of Crown Solicitor was set up to exercise the functions of attorney for prosecutions which included the preparation of all information, superintending the preliminary proceedings and overseeing the witnesses and proofs when trial came in; he also provided professional advice related to periodical business of some government departments and legal assistance in land survey.

1880   The Attorney General's office was renamed Attorney General's Department.

1946   The Attorney General was reappointed following the liberation of Hong Kong. The Attorney General's Department and the Crown Solicitor's Department were two independent departments. The Attorney General's Department consisted of the Attorney General, the Solicitor General and Crown Counsel.

1948   The Legal Department was established to handle legislation, draft laws and regulations, prosecute criminal cases, advise matters related to investigation and prosecution of crimes, and represent the Government before court for civil litigation. The Attorney General, as the head of the Department, supervised the Solicitor General, Legal Officers as Crown Counsel, Crown Solicitor, Legal Officer as Legal Draftsman, and Legal Officers as Assistant Crown Solicitors.

1957   The post of Senior Crown Counsel was created.

1959   The post of Principal Crown Counsel was created.

1983   The Attorney General became directly accountable to the Governor. The Department was reorganized into four divisions. The head of the Department, the Attorney General, was responsible for all prosecutions in Hong Kong; he decided whether prosecution should be instituted in any particular case, and conducted and controlled prosecutions of particular cases. The Solicitor General oversaw the administration of the Department. The Civil Advisory Division gave legal advice in civil matters and conducted all civil litigation involving the Crown; and provided secretarial services for the Law Reform Commission through the Law Reform Commission Secretariat. The Prosecutions Division instituted prosecutions, prosecuted crimes and offences of a serious or complicated nature, provided advice to other law enforcement departments. The Law Drafting Division drafted all principal and subsidiary legislation. In addition, there was also the Law Reform Commission. It considered and reported on law topics referred to it by the Attorney General or the Chief Justice; it also proposed amendments to laws, improved laws and made them meet the needs of modern society.

1985   The Civil Advisory Division was renamed Civil Division. The Special Duties Unit was set up to handle legal work arising from the Sino-British Joint Declaration.

1986   A temporary unit, Localization and Adaptation of Laws Unit, was set up in the Law Drafting Division to study all United Kingdom laws which applied to Hong Kong and consulted policy branches on whether the laws in question would be needed in future and made preparation for local legislation to reproduce the laws found appropriate to survive after 30 June, 1997.

1988   The Special Duties Unit was renamed International Law Division. It considered treaties in which Hong Kong was a party and other international obligations in light of the Sino-British Joint Declaration.

1990   The administration function of the Solicitor General was passed on to a newly created Administration Division. A Legal Policy Division to provide secretarial services for the Law Reform Commission was created.

1992   The function of the Legal Policy Division was expanded to the provision of legal input on a wide variety of topics being considered by the Government; and to service the professional needs of the Attorney General.

1993   As principal legal adviser to the Governor and the Government, the Attorney General made decisions on the prosecution of criminal offences; represented and defended the Government in any civil actions brought against it; served as a guardian of the public interest; made applications for judicial review to enforce public legal rights; served as the Protector of Charities, Chairman of the Law Reform Commission and of the Chief Secretary's Legal Affairs Policy Group, Deputy Chairman of the Fight Crime Committee, and a member of the Operations Review Committee, Complaints Committee of the ICAC, Police Complaints Committee and the Governor's Advisory Committee on Legal Education. The Attorney General's Office directed six divisions. The Administration Division comprised the Administration Subdivision, which handled the day-to day administration such as personnel matters, staff contracts, general Chinese translation services, management of the law library, implementation of the Government's localization policy, financial and accounting services, supplies, training and computer matters. The Civil Division consisted of the Commercial Unit, Lands and Works Unit, Advisory Unit, and Civil Litigation Unit. It advised the government bureaux and departments on all aspects of commercial laws, all legal matters that had a bearing on land and public works, day-to-day operational matters in the formulation of policy and drafting instructions for proposed changes in law, all civil claims and disputes involving government before courts, tribunals and arbitrators and dealt with requests for legal assistance from overseas jurisdictions. The International

Law Division included the Joint Declaration and Basic Law Unit, Joint Liaison Group, Treaties and Negotiations Unit, and Advisory: International Law Unit. It provided legal advice on international law to the Government especially on the implementation of the Sino-British Joint Declaration on Hong Kong and on the Basic law. The Law Drafting Division comprised the English Drafting Unit, Chinese Drafting and Translation Unit, Localisation and Adaptation of Law Unit. It drafted all legislation, both ordinances and subsidiary legislation, proposed by the Government; liaised with those proposing changes, drafted the new law and steered it through the Executive and Legislative Councils; produced loose-leaf edition of the current legislative provisions. The Legal Policy Division contained the China Law Unit, Constitutional and Electoral Unit, Human Rights Unit and Legal Policy Unit. It advised the Attorney General and the Government on legal policy and assisted its formulation; advised on the law in mainland China and Basic Law and on amendments to Hong Kong's constitutional and electoral arrangements; reviewed existing legislation to ensure its consistency with the human rights provisions of the Bill of Rights and advised on amendments; carried out research and provided secretarial services for the Law Reform Commission. The Prosecutions Division was organized into the Commercial Crime Prosecutions Subdivision, General Prosecutions Subdivision, and Specialist Prosecutions Subdivision. It advised on and prepared for trial, and prosecuted commercial crime cases; specialized in trial preparation and High Court prosecutions; and prosecuted offences relating to vice, gambling, immigration, customs and excise, road traffic, labour and environmental protection.

1994   The Administration Division was retitled Administration and Development Division. Under the supervision of the Law Drafting Division, the Constitutional and Electoral Affairs Team that implemented legislative reforms in respect of constitutional and electoral matters, and the Law Revision Unit that published the loose-leaf edition of Hong Kong's latest legislation, were formed.

1997   The Legal Department was renamed Department of Justice upon the transfer of sovereignty on July 1. The Secretary for Justice assumed the former Attorney General's duties. The Attorney General's Office was renamed Secretary of Justice's Office which was made up of six divisions: Administration and Development Division (made up of the Administration Subdivision and Development Subdivision); Civil Division (consisted of the Advisory Unit, Civil Litigation Unit, Commercial Unit, Debt Collection Unit and Lands and Works Unit); International Law Division (included the Advisory: International Law Unit, Bilateral Agreements and Negotiations Unit and Multilateral Agreements Unit); Law Drafting Division (composed of the Administration Unit, Bilingual Drafting Unit, Electoral Legislation Unit, English Drafting Unit and Law Revision Unit); Legal Policy Division (comprised the China Law Unit, Basic Law Unit, Electoral Affairs Team, General Advisory Unit, Human Rights Unit and Law Reform Commission Secretariat); and Prosecutions Division (made up of the General Prosecutions Subdivision I, Specialist Prosecutions Subdivision II, and Commercial Crime Prosecutions Subdivision III).

1998   The Administration and Development Division was restructured to include the

Public Relations and Information Unit. In the Civil Division, the Litigation Unit replaced the previous Civil Litigation Unit; while the Planning, Environment, Lands and Housing Unit superseded the former Lands and Works Unit. The Law Drafting Division was divided into two subdivisions - Bilingual Drafting and Administration, and Legislation. The Legal Policy Division was restructured into three subdivisions: Advisory, Constitutional and Law Reform Commission Secretariat. The International Law Division was divided into the Treaties and Law Unit, and the Mutual Legal Assistance Unit. The Prosecutions Division was expanded from three subdivisions to four. They were Management (Subdivision I), Trial (Subdivision II), Appeals (Subdivision III) and Commercial Crime/Corruption (Subdivision IV).

2002   The Department of Justice was still made up of six divisions: Prosecutions (Subdivision I to IV, same functions as before); Civil (Advisory; Civil Litigation; Commercial; Planning, Environment, Lands and Housing); Legal Policy (Constitutional Section, General Section, Law Reform Commission Secretariat); Law Drafting (Bilingual Drafting, Law Revision, English Drafting, Electoral Legislation, Administration); International Law (Treaties and Law Unit, Mutual Legal Assistance Unit); Administration and Development (Library, Departmental Administration Unit, General Translation Unit, Information Technology Resources Unit, Finance and Accounting Unit). There was also a Secretary for Justice's Office which was made up of the Legal Adviser, Legislative Affairs; the Administrative Assistant to the Secretary of Justice; and the Public Relations and Information Unit.

Sources:

1. *CO129/603/7*, 6 May 1948.
2. *CO129/603/7*, 6 May 1948.
3. *Department of Justice*, Hong Kong, Government Printer, 1998, 2000.
4. *Friend of China and Hong Kong Government Gazette*, May 5, 1842.
5. *Hong Kong*, Hong Kong, Government Printer, 1960-1963, 1989-1993.
6. *Hong Kong Annual Report*, Hong Kong Government Printer, 1957-1960.
7. Jolly, J., "The Port of Hong Kong" in Braga, J.M. ed., *Hong Kong Business Symposium*, Hong Kong, *South China Morning Post*, 1957.
8. *Legal Department*, Hong Kong, Government Printer, 1994, 1996.
9. *The Ordinances of the Legislative Council of the Colony of Hong Kong*, Hong Kong, Noronha & Co., 1891, Vol. I.
10. www.info.gov.hk/justice

Department of Justice — Changes in Names and Directors

Year	Name of Department	Title	Name of Director
1844-1856	Attorney General's Office	Attorney General	Sterling, Paul Ivy
1856-1859	Attorney General's Office	Attorney General	Anstey, Thomas Chisholm
1859	Attorney General's Office	Attorney General	Adams, William Henry
1860	Attorney General's Office	Attorney General (Acting)	Kingsmill, Henry
1861-1866	Attorney General's Office	Attorney General	Smale, John Jackson
1866-1874	Attorney General's Office	Attorney General	Pauncefote, Julian
1874-1877	Attorney General's Office	Attorney General	Bramston, John
1877-1880	Attorney General's Office	Attorney General	Phillippo, George
1880-1890	Attorney General's Department	Attorney General	O'Malley, Edward Loughlin
1890-1902	Attorney General's Department	Attorney General	Goodman, William Meigh
1902-1906	Attorney General's Department	Attorney General	Berkeley, Henry Spencer
1906-1912	Attorney General's Department	Attorney General	Rees-Davies, William
1912-1915	Attorney General's Department	Attorney General	Bucknill, John Alexander Strachey
1915-1930	Attorney General's Department	Attorney General	Kemp, Joseph Horsford
1930-1946	Attorney General's Department	Attorney General	Alabaster, Chaloner Grenville
1946-1948	Attorney General's Department	Attorney General	Griffin, John Bowes
1948-1952	Legal Department	Attorney General	Griffin, John Bowes
1952-1962	Legal Department	Attorney General	Ridehalgh, Arthur

Year	Name of Department	Title	Name of Director
1962-1966	Legal Department	Attorney General	Heenan, Maurice
1966-1973	Legal Department	Attorney Genreal	Roberts, Denys Tudor Emil
1973-1979	Legal Department	Attorney Genreal	Hobley, John William Dixon
1979-1983	Legal Department	Attorney General	Griffths, John Calvert
1983-1988	Legal Department	Attorney General	Thomas, Michael David
1988-1997	Legal Department	Attorney General	Matthews, Jeremy Fell
1997-2002	Department of Justice	Secretary for Justice	Leung, Oi-sie, Elsie

Sources:

1. *Civil and Miscellaneous Lists Hong Kong Government*, Hong Kong, Government Printer, 1972, 1975, 1982, 1987, 1989-1990, 1996.
2. *The Hong Kong Civil Service List*, Hong Kong Government, 1947-1958.
3. *Staff Biographies Hong Kong Government*, Hong Kong, Government Printer, 1974, 1976, 1978, 1982, 1984, 1986, 1988, 1990, 1993.
4. *Staff Biographies the Government of the Hong Kong Special Administrative Region*, Hong Kong, Government Printer, 1998, 2000-2001.
5. www.info.gov.hk/justice/

Chapter 3
Disciplined Services

Indian police & Chinese police constables inside the compound of the Central Police Station, Hollywood Road, 1906

Fire Brigade on parade, 1892

Building works carried out by prisoners at Chi Ma Wan, 1964

Evolvement of Disciplined Services

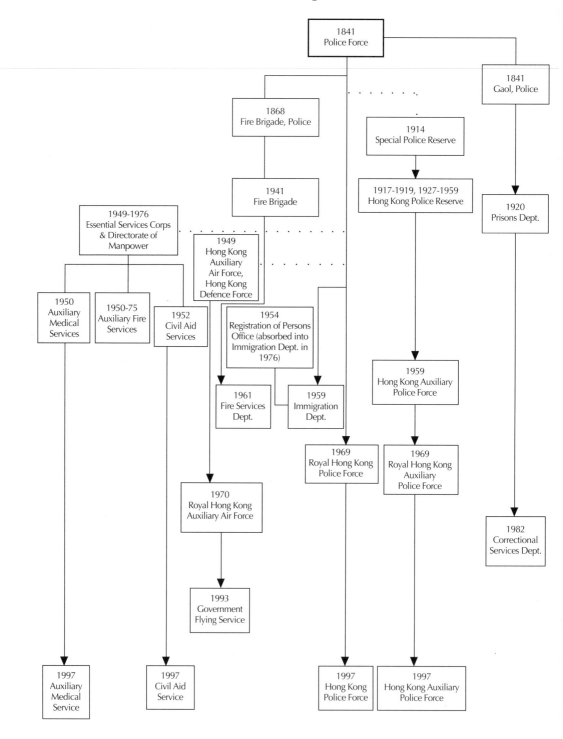

Today, the maintenance of social order relies mainly on the Hong Kong Police Force and seven other supporting disciplined services: Correctional Services Department, Fire Services Department, Immigration Department, Hong Kong Auxiliary Police Force, Auxiliary Medical Service, Civil Aid Service and Government Flying Service. The structure of the existing disciplined services, however, was not finalized until the second half of the twentieth century. Before 1945, the Police Force was the major disciplined service that handled almost every single social order problem or crisis.

In 1841, immediately after the establishment of the Colony, William Caine was appointed Chief of Police and Chief of Gaol. During that year the Police Force was led by 3 European officers who commanded 160 policemen, of which 78 (49%) were Europeans, 48 (30%) were Chinese, and 34 (21%) were Indians. Local Chinese represented only one-third of the Police Force. The Europeans were leaders and core members of the Police Force.

Since the late 1860s, the Police Force had undergone significant changes. Firstly, the proportion of European policemen had diminished. Chinese and Indian police officers played a more important role in the Force than before. The Indians represented 52% of the total force in 1868. The number of Chinese policemen increased steadily to 48% by 1909, out of a force of 1,054 men. The European policemen proportion dropped to 13% and the localization of the force was slowly taking shape. Secondly, the police had started receiving formal training since 1869 when the Police School was established. All policemen were required to attend the Police School from 1872 onwards. Lastly, the extension of police presence to the New Territories in 1903 signified the enlargement of the force.

After the Second World War, the Police Force's duties were carried out by two functional teams: Uniformed Branch and Criminal Investigation Department (CID). The Uniformed Branch covered the Hong Kong Island District, the Kowloon and New Territories District, the Traffic Branch and the Marine Police. The CID controlled the Special Branch and the Detective Branch. This organization structure formed the basic structure of the present day Police Force.

The Police Force was also the foundation of many other disciplined services. Established in 1841, the Gaol was a subdepartment of the Police Force. The government of the Gaol was prescribed by the Ordinance but was under the direction of the Police Force until 1920. In 1920, the Gaol was restructured and became the Prisons Department. It was changed to Correctional Services Department in 1982 following the introduction of new ideas in re-educating prisoners.

The Fire Services Department was also subordinated to the Police Force before 1941. The firefighting force of Hong Kong, in its formative days in 1868, consisted mainly of volunteer firemen and policemen. It became an independent department in 1941 and was organized into a Central Fire Station with four substations on Hong Kong Island, two in Kowloon, and seven in the New Territories in 1954. The Fire Brigade was renamed Fire Services Department in 1961. In 2002, the Fire Services Department was organized into eight parts: Headquarters Command, Departmental Secretariat, Ambulance Command, Fire Safety Command, Licensing and Certification Command, Hong Kong Operational Command, Kowloon Operational Command and New Territories Operational Command.

The Immigration and Passport Office and the Registration Office under the Special Branch of the Police were the precursor of the Immigration Department. The Department is not only responsible for the control of people into and out of Hong Kong; it also handles other related matters such as the issuance of passports and other travel documents, visas and identity cards; recording of nationality matters; registration of births, deaths and marriages; detection and prosecution of immigration law offenders; and removal of illegal immigrants.

The Auxiliary Police Force has been subordinated to the Police Force since its establishment in 1914. Together with the other auxiliary disciplined forces — Civil Aid Service, Auxiliary Medical Service and Government Flying Service — they provide valuable back-up assistance to the regular forces. They have served with distinction during wars, riots, natural disasters and accidents, and have helped to relieve the heavy workload of the regulars. These auxiliary forces are mainly made up of volunteers who have received formal training.

Nowadays, services provided by the disciplined forces have become increasingly professional and comprehensive, due to valuable experience gained in serving the citizens. More attention has been given to educate the general public and foster better relations with the community. Accident and crime prevention has replaced the traditional crime-fighting method and this represents the progress of society.

Maintenance of Order

Police (1841-1844)
Police Force (1844-1969)
Royal Hong Kong Police Force (1969-1997)
Hong Kong Police Force (1997-2002)

1841   A properly constituted police force was established. Three European officers commanded a total of 160 policemen: 78 Europeans, 34 Indians and 48 Chinese. The first chief officer was William Caine. The Force was modelled on the Royal Irish Constabulary and as they were dressed in rifle-green uniforms they were dubbed "the green coats" by the Chinese.

1844   Ordinance no. 5 of 1844 was enacted for the preservation of good order and cleanliness within Hong Kong and its dependencies.

1845   The size of the Force increased to three officers and 168 men. An ordinance was passed to repeal Ordinance no. 5 of 1844, and to make better provision for licensing the sale of salt, opium, bhang, ganja, betel and betel leaf, within Hong Kong, and the licensing of pawnbrokers and auctioneers, with a table of fees on official licences and signatures. The Magistrate of Police, his assistant or deputy, were authorized to summon the defaulters for selling opium without licence, and they were liable to the penalties prescribed under the new Ordinance.

1847   An ordinance for the licensing of markets and the prevention of disorders was passed to preserve peace and tranquility in the markets.

1853   An auxiliary police force was kept for the preservation of the lives and property of the inhabitants. A levy was imposed for the maintenance of the auxiliary police force.

1857   Night passes for Chinese were required to be provided, sealed and issued by the Superintendent of Police. Any Chinese found at large elsewhere other than in his/her own habitation between the hours of eight in the evening and sunrise, and not having a pass duly issued and made out in conformity with Sections 2 and 3 of Ordinance no. 9 of 1857, should be summarily punished by any Justice of the Peace for every such offence, either by a fine not exceeding 50 dollars or by imprisonment and hard labour for a term not exceeding 14 days, or by public whipping or public exposure in the stocks.

1862   The Police Force was commanded by a Captain Superintendent and consisted of Officers, Clerks, Interpreters, Subordinate Officers and Constables. The Governor could from time to time increase or diminish the strength of the Force.

1868   An ordinance amending the law relating to the granting of pensions and other allowances to the Police Force was passed on 23 May 1868. The total strength of the Police Force was 633: 113 Europeans, 328 coloured and 192 Chinese.

1869   External assistance was given to the Police Force through the continued employment of district watchmen (a District Watch Force was established in 1868), and the co-operation of informants in the pay of gambling house licensees. The former paid attention to cases of kidnapping, larceny and breaches of the peace; while the latter reported the return of any serious criminals. The British Kowloon was still left comparatively unprotected. The ratio of police to the total population of 121,000 was 1 to 191; while the proportion of foreign police officers to foreign residents was nearly 1 to 70. A Police School was established during the year.

1870   One hundred and thirty-one men attended the Police School during the year. School materials were borrowed from the Government Central School. The Police Force did not admit illiterates. All promotions in the Force were determined by the results of competitive examinations, of which educational knowledge formed a considerable part.

1871   The revenue derived from the licences was used to improve police salaries and accommodation.

1872   Attendance at the Police School was voluntary before 1872 but since 1872 it had become compulsory. Three hundred and twenty-two men attended the School that year. The School was located in the Central Barracks. Every man in the Force had to learn a second language.

1878   As a large number of Europeans possessed exemption certificates, and a considerable number left Hong Kong on the expiry of their appointment terms, attendance level at the Police School was low.

1886   According to the Opium Ordinances of 1884 and 1886, the power given to Inspectors of Police under Section 27 of the 1884 Ordinance with reference to the searching of ships and seizure of opium on board of such ships could also be exercised by any Excise Officer. The power given to Magistrates under Section 28 of the 1884 Ordinance to issue search warrants could also be exercised by any Justice of the Peace. A Police Officer could require any person who was apparently a vagrant to accompany him to appear before a Police Magistrate. The Police Magistrate could make a summary enquiry into the circumstances of the apparent vagrant.

1887   Ordinance no. 14 of 1887 was enacted to consolidate and amend the law for the establishment and regulation of the Police Force. The Governor had the power to diminish or increase the Police Force. Terms and conditions on members of the Police Force were presented. Regulations made by the Captain Superintendent of Police under Section 19 of Ordinance no. 14, for the general government and discipline of the Police Force, focused mainly on police conduct and bribery problems.

1890   The Captain Superintendent or any other Superintendent or Inspector of the Police Force had the power, by virtue of his office, to enter at all times, with such constables as he thought necessary, into and upon every ship, boat or other vessel lying in Hong Kong waters.

1895   The strength of the Police Force had risen to 627.

1898   The Water Police exercised surveillance over boats and launches, enforced quarantine on all vessels, and arranged the removal of plague patients to hospitals and the dead to mortuaries.

1903   Police were deployed in the New Territories. In addition to the usual police duties, they collected Crown rent and acted as Bailiffs for the execution of Land Court Distress Warrants. The Water Police issued licences to boats and received fees on account of the Harbour Master.

1904   The Assistant Harbour Master was appointed Acting Assistant Superintendent of Police, and was given immediate control of the Water Police. It prevented unnecessary overlapping and duplication of work between the Force and the Harbour Master's Office.

1909   Until the Second World War and the Japanese occupation of Hong Kong, there were deliberate efforts to preserve a careful racial balance in the composition of the Force. In 1909, with a strength of 1,054, there were 511 Chinese (48%), 411 Indians (39%) and 132 Europeans (13%).

1914   The Special Police Reserve Ordinance was passed on October 23. The Special Constables replaced the Indian Police, who were temporarily withdrawn to perform land and harbour patrols.

1915   On June 23, a notice was issued calling upon persons who remained in Hong Kong for more than one week to register themselves at the Registration of Persons Office.

1917   The Police Reserve Ordinance no. 20 of 1917 was passed on September 14 altering the name from Special Police Reserve to Hong Kong Police Reserve.

1919   The Hong Kong Police Reserve was disbanded.

1922   The Criminal Investigation Department (CID) was established but commenced operations in 1923. The control and staffing of the Fire Brigade were transferred to the newly recruited professional firemen.

1927   The Hong Kong Police Reserve which disbanded in 1919 was re-established on a permanent basis. The Emergency Unit was set up on Hong Kong Island to respond to calls, fires, outrages and minor disturbances.

1928   The Pass Office (later known as the Passport Office) was set up to take offenders of various nationalities (other than Chinese, Indian and Japanese) before the courts for offences of vagrancy, stowaways and the violation of the Passport Ordinance.

1931   An Emergency Unit, modelled on the Hong Kong Emergency Unit, was set up in Kowloon.

1935   An additional CID was set up in the New Territories.

1936   The Immigration and Passport Office and the Registration Office were placed under the Special Branch.

1938   The Special Branch undertook complete control of passport work formerly performed by the Colonial Secretariat.

1939   On the eve of the outbreak of the Second World War, the regular Force was 2,234-strong; with an additional 255 Chinese Water Police and a civilian staff of 300.

1941   The Police Force was a self-contained department charged with the prevention and detection of crime. It was equipped with the usual branches: Special, Detective, Traffic, Water Police; special units were maintained in reserve for emergencies. It was assisted by a Police Reserve and was also responsible for the provision of anti-piracy guards. The pre-war Force included 277 posts for officers of the Inspector grade or above.

1945   On liberation, the Police Force was reconstituted on the lines of the pre-war days. The Commissioner of Police was responsible, in addition to his pre-war duties, for the administration of the Prisons Department; for the control of immigration to such extent as may be decided by the Government; for the control of dangerous drugs that included opium; and for civil defence measures. Liaison was established with the police in Canton, Chungking and Shanghai, and with the police administration of the Straits Settlements and the Philippines.

1946   Acting as general criminal process servers and prosecutors for all government departments, the Police Force was responsible for the prevention and detection of all activities subversive to the peace and good order of Hong Kong. The Force was organized into the Headquarters and five commands: Hong Kong Island, Kowloon and New Territories, Detective Branch, Special Branch and Police Training School. The duties of the Force were carried out by two functional teams: Uniformed Branch and CID. The Uniformed Branch covered the Hong Kong Island District, Kowloon and New Territories District, Traffic Branch and Marine Police. The CID (comprised the identification and fingerprint bureaux, handwriting and photographic sections and a forensic science laboratory) was in charge of the Special Branch and the Detective Branch. The greater part of the Police Force's strength was deployed on Hong Kong Island and in Kowloon. Watch and ward operations on the islands, in the harbour and in the waters of Hong Kong were performed by the Marine Police, which was an integral part of the Force. The New Territories Division was responsible for the control of the land frontier with mainland China.

1950   In addition to the usual administrative work, the Headquarters also supervised four sections: Auxiliary Forces (including the Police Reserve, Special Constabulary, Village Guards, Ship Watchmen, Private Watchmen and Civilian Employees); Communications Branch; Financial Office and Police Training School.

1951   The Anti-Corruption Branch was established to handle all matters relating to corruptive practices and to operate as a central records office.

1955   The Force was restructured into six separate commands: Police Headquarters (directed the Auxiliary Police Formations, Communications and Transport Branch, Police Band, Police Training School and Traffic Branch); Criminal Investigation Branch; Special Branch; Anti-Corruption Branch and Narcotics Bureau; Hong Kong Island District; Kowloon and New Territories District.

1956   The Commissioner of Police was concurrently the Immigration Officer.

1957   The Marine District was set up as a new command.

1958   The Police and the British Military made plans to integrate operations at various levels in emergency situations. The Police Force was organized into seven parts: Operational and Administrative Headquarters (supervised the Communications and Transport Branch, Immigration Office, Police Training Contingent, Police Training School, Traffic Branch); CID (controlled the Anti-Corruption and Narcotics Bureaux); Special Branch; Hong Kong Island District; Kowloon District; New Territories and Marine District; and Auxiliaries.

1959   The Hong Kong Police Reserve and the Hong Kong Special Constabulary were amalgamated to form the Auxiliary Police Force according to the Hong Kong Auxiliary Police Force Ordinance of 1959. A new driving test procedure was introduced; police driving test examiners were replaced by civilians under the supervision of the Traffic Branch.

1961   The Police Commissioner was relieved of the responsibility for immigration. The abolition of compulsory part-time service in the Auxiliary Police Force was implemented. Service in the Auxiliary Police Force became entirely voluntary. The Anti-Corruption and Narcotics Bureaux were restructured into the Anti-Corruption Branch and the Narcotics Bureau.

1962   To deal with the illegal immigration problem, the Anti-Illegal Immigration Branch was established in September; the Marine Division were transferred from the New Territories District to its command.

1965   The Anti-Illegal Immigration Branch and the Marine Division were merged to form the new Marine District.

1966   The Kowloon District was divided into two subdistricts: Kowloon East and Kowloon West.

1967   The Headquarters was reorganized in the Operations Wing and the Administration Wing. The Commissioner of Police delegated his statutory duties for the licensing of vehicles and drivers and the regulation of public transport services to the head of the Transport Office.

1968   The Police Public Information Bureau was formed in March to take up most of the duties previously performed by the Information Services Department. It dealt with the supply information to the press, radio and television; and all aspects of police public relations on behalf of the Force. The two Kowloon Subdistricts were abolished. The Traffic Branch was reorganized and the command of the Traffic Branch personnel was delegated by the Commissioner of Police to the Chief Superintendent of Police (Traffic) and the District Commanders.

1969   The Police Force was renamed Royal Hong Kong Police Force. A Planning and Research Division was established under the Headquarters. The new division comprised four sections: Building Planning and Research, Operational Planning and Research, Organizational Planning and Research, Reference and Analysis. The CID was reorganized into two wings and a bureau: Operations Wing (Commercial Crime Office, General Investigation Office and Triad Society Bureau); Narcotics Bureau; and Support Wing (Criminal Records Office, Ballistics Office, Department of Forensic Pathology, Deportation and Supervision Section, Drug Disposal Unit, Registries and Administration Office). The Anti-Corruption Branch was separated from the CID and became directly responsible to the Deputy Commissioner (Operations).

1971   The Headquarters was organized into three wings: Civil and Administration, Establishment and General, and Operations.

1972   The Operations Wing of the CID was restructured to form the three units of Criminal Intelligence Unit, Homicide Squad and Special Crimes Squad.

1973   The Police Public Information Bureau was renamed Police Public Relations Bureau. The Police Cadet School was established to prepare youths for entry into the Police Force and other disciplined services of the Government.

1976   The Force was made up of five major parts: Special Branch; CID; Personnel and Support Wing; Civil and Administration Wing; and Field Operations (supervised the four districts of Hong Kong, Kowloon, New Territories and Marine).

1979   The Police Force was led by two directorates: Operations and Administration. The Operations Directorate supervised four departments: Operations ('A' Department) (comprised the Support Wing, Anti-Illegal Immigrants, Police Districts), Special Branch ('B' Department), Criminal Investigation Directorate ('C' Department) and Public Relations Bureau. The Administration Directorate directed the Personnel and Training ('D' Department); Management and

Development ('E' Department): included Management Services, Complaints and Discipline Wing; and Civil and Administration ('F' Department).

1980   The third directorate — Management — was set up. The Personnel and Training ('D' Department) was transferred from the Administration to the Management. The Management also directed the Management and Development ('E' Department).

1981   The Police Force was led by three directorates — Operations, Management and Administration — which supervised six major departments. The Operations Directorate controlled the Operations and Support ('A' Department): divided into the three wings of Operations, Support and Police Public Relations; Special Branch ('B' Department); Criminal Investigation ('C' Department): included the Special Operations Group, Commercial Crime Group, Narcotics Bureau, Administration and Support Group. The Management Directorate supervised the Personnel and Training ('D' Department):contained the two wings of Personnel and Training; Management and Inspection Services ('E' Department): comprised the two wings of Management Services and Force Inspection. The Administration Directorate directed the Civil and Administration ('F' Department): consisted of the Civil and Administration Branch, Planning and Development Branch.

1982   The Police Force's structure was revised and its duties were carried out by five departments instead of six. They were: Operations ('A' Department), Special Branch ('B' Department), Personnel and Training ('C' Department), Management and Inspection Services ('D' Department), and Civil and Administration ('E' Department). The former Operations and Support ('A' Department) was restructured into Operations ('A' Department) which assumed additional responsibility for the former Criminal Investigation ('C' Department). The post of Director of Criminal Investigation was deleted and the Director of Operations was responsible for the criminal investigation work.

1992   The Kowloon District was divided into two: Kowloon West and Kowloon East in January.

1994   The Crime ('A1' Department) was established under the Operations Wing. The Management and Inspection Services ('D' Department) was renamed Management Services ('D' Department).

1995   The Crime ('A1' Department) and the Special Branch ('B' Department) were combined to form Crime and Security ('B' Department). The new Department was composed of two wings: Crime and Security.

1996   A new wing — Administration — was created to deal with financial and stores management. It comprised three divisions: Finance, Internal Audit and Stores Management.

1997   The Royal Hong Kong Police Force was renamed Hong Kong Police Force. The newly created Administration Wing was integrated with the Administration, Finance and Planning ('E' Department). The Police Force was organized into five major departments. Operations ('A' Department): comprised the Support Wing, Operations Wing and Police Regions; Crime and Security ('B'

Department): consisted of the two wings of Crime and Security; Personnel and Training ('C' Department): contained the two wings of Training and Personnel; Management Services ('D' Department): made up of the two wings of Service Quality and Information Systems; and Administration, Finance and Planning ('E' Department): divided into the Planning and Development Branch, Administration Wing and Finance Wing. They were led by two Deputy Commissioners - Operations (Departments 'A' and 'B') and Management (Departments 'C' and 'D'); and a civilian Director of Finance Administration and Planning ('E' Department), who was directly responsible to the Commissioner of Police.

2002   The Police Force structure remained unchanged.

Sources:

1. *Annual Report on Hong Kong Police Force 1946-1947*, Hong Kong Government Printer, 1947, pp.5, 20, 30-32.
2. Crisswell, Colin, and Watson, Mike, *The Royal Hong Kong Police (1841-1945)*, Hong Kong, Macmillan, 1982, pp.25-26.
3. Endacott, G.B., *A History of Hong Kong*, London, Oxford University, 1964, pp.150-154.
4. *Hong Kong Annual Departmental Report by the Commissioner of Police*, Hong Kong, Government Printer, 1948-1972.
5. *Hong Kong Government Gazette*, Hong Kong Government, 1847-1891.
6. "Hong Kong Police Annual Report", *Hong Kong Administration Reports 1931,* Appendix K, Hong Kong Government, 1932.
7. Earl of Kimberley to the Officer Administering the Government, *British Parliamentary Papers China 25 Hong Kong 1862-1881*, 1 April 1871, Shannon, Irish University Press, 1971, p.349.
8. "Police", *Hong Kong Directive*, Hong Kong, 1945, HKRS 211, D&S no.2/4.
9. "Report of the Captain Superintendent of Police", *Hong Kong Administrative Reports*, Hong Kong Government, 1911-1929.
10. "Reports of the Captain Superintendent of Police and of the Superintendent of Fire Brigade", *Hong Kong Administrative Reports*, Hong Kong Government, 1909-1910.
11. "Report of the Commissioner of Police", *Hong Kong Administration Reports*, Hong Kong Government, 1937-1940.
12. "Report of the Inspector General of Police", *Hong Kong Administration Reports*, Hong Kong Goverment, 1932-1936.
13. "Report of the Inspector General of Police", *Hong Kong Administrative Reports 1930*, Appendix K, Hong Kong Government, 1931.
14. *Royal Hong Kong Police Review*, Hong Kong, Government Printer, 1976-77; 1979- 1986; 1991-1997.
15. www.info.gov.hk/police/index.htm

Hong Kong Police Force — Changes in Names and Directors

Year	Name of Department	Title	Name of Director
1841-1844	Police	Chief of Police	Caine, William
1844-1862	Police Force	Captain Superintendent of Police	May, Charles
1862-1867	Police Force	Captain Superintendent of Police	Quin, William
1867-1892	Police Force	Captain Superintendent of Police	Deane, Walter Meredith
1892-1893	Police Force	Captain Superintendent of Police	Gordon, Alexander Herman Adam
1893-1901	Police Force	Captain Superintendent of Police	May, Francis Henry
1901-1913	Police Force	Captain Superintendent of Police	Badeley, Francis Joseph
1913-1918	Police Force	Captain Superintendent of Police	Messer, Charles McIlvaine
1918-1929	Police Force	Captain Superintendent of Police	Wolfe, Edward Dudley Corscaden
1929-1934	Police Force	Inspector General of Police	Wolfe, Edward Dudley Corscaden
1934-1938	Police Force	Inspector General of Police	King, Thomas Henry
1938-1940	Police Force	Commissioner of Police	King, Thomas Henry
1940-1941	Police Force	Commissioner of Police	Pennefather-Evans, John Pennefather
1946	Police Force	Commissioner of Police	Pennefather-Evans, John Pennefather
1946-1954	Police Force	Commissioner of Police	MacIntosh, Duncan William
1954-1959	Police Force	Commissioner of Police	Maxwell, Arthur Crawford
1959-1967	Police Force	Commissioner of Police	Heath, Henry Wylde Edwards
1967-1969	Police Force	Commissioner of Police	Eates, Edward Caston
1969-1974	Royal Hong Kong Police Force	Commissioner of Police	Sutcliffe, Charles Payne

Year	Name of Department	Title	Name of Director
1974-1979	Royal Hong Kong Police Force	Commissioner of Police	Slevin, Brian Francis Patrick
1979-1985	Royal Hong Kong Police Force	Commissioner of Police	Henry, Robert Thomas Mitchell
1985-1989	Royal Hong Kong Police Force	Commissioner of Police	Anning, Raymond Harry
1989-1994	Royal Hong Kong Police Force	Commissioner of Police	Li, Kwan-ha
1994-1997	Royal Hong Kong Police Force	Commissioner of Police	Hui, Ki-on
1997-2001	Hong Kong Police Force	Commissioner of Police	Hui, Ki-on
2001-2002	Hong Kong Police Force	Commissioner of Police	Tsang, Yam-pui

Sources:
1. Crisswell, Colin N., & Watson, Mike, *The Royal Hong Kong Police (1841-1945)*, Hong Kong, Macmillan, 1982.
2. *Hong Kong Blue Book*, Hong Kong, Noronha & Co., 1844-1939.
3. *The Hong Kong Civil Service List*, Hong Kong Government, 1947-1958.
4. *Staff Biographies Hong Kong Government*, Hong Kong, Government Printer, 1974, 1976, 1978, 1982, 1984, 1988, 1990, 1993.
5. *Staff Biographies the Government of the Hong Kong Special Administrative Region*, Hong Kong, Government Printer, 1998, 2001.
6. *Staff List Hong Kong Government*, Hong Kong, Government Printer, 1959-1996.
7. *Staff List the Government of the Hong Kong Special Administrative Region*, Hong Kong, Government Printer, 1997-2000.
8. www.info.gov.hk/police/index.htm

Gaol, Police (1841-1920)
Prisons Department (1920-1982)
Correctional Services Department (1982-2002)

1841 The first gaol was instituted on Hong Kong Island on August 9. In the first instance the Gaol was administered as a branch of the Police under the general control of the Chief Magistrate of Police.

1843 The Gaol was placed under a Sheriff who was responsible to the Police Magistrate.

1853 Ordinance no. 1 of 1853 for the regulation of the Gaol of Hong Kong was enacted. Certain rules prescribed for the government of the Gaol received the sanction of a legislative enactment, and that certain penalties be provided for the breach of such rules. Any three Justices of the Peace could propose any modification of the said rules. The Sheriff and Justices of the Peace should be previously notified of the modifications. It was lawful for the Sheriff to punish by imprisonment in a solitary or refractory cell for not exceeding three days.

1863 An ordinance to repeal Ordinance no. 1 of 1853 was enacted to provide gaols and debtors' wards, and for the due control of prisoners. The head of gaols was known as Superintendent of Victoria Gaol.

1876   On December 31, the number of prisoners in Victoria Gaol was: 30 European, 398 Chinese males, and 23 Chinese females. Common larceny was the most common offence, with gambling coming second. The larger portion of European prisoners were soldiers and sailors for breaches of military and naval discipline and for committing crimes against the civilian population.

1877   The Office of the Gaol was composed of the Superintendent, one Warden, one Head Turnkey, one Clerk, one Interpreter and Assistant Clerk, one Matron, one Chaplain and one Medical Officer. Other turnkeys and guards would be appointed from time to time.

1879   The Gaol was organized separately from the Police Office with the transfer of gaol guards from the Police to the control of the Superintendent of Victoria Gaol.

1885   Rules and regulations for the management of Victoria Gaol of Hong Kong, and for the guidance of its officers were made by the Governor-in-Executive-Council, under Section 17 of the Prison Ordinance 1885 on November 18. The average daily number of prisoners was 530.

1887   The gaol staff began to change the training venue from the Gaol to the Army.

1920   The Gaol was renamed Prisons Department, with the title of the department head changed to Superintendent of Prisons.

1932   A new female prison at Lai Chi Kok was opened.

1937   The Hong Kong Prison at Stanley came into operation.

1938   The Superintendent of Prisons was renamed Commissioner of Prisons. Probation services came under the administration of the Prisons Department.

1941   During the Sino-Japanese War, the Prisons Department was administered as a branch of the Police Force under the general control of the Commissioner of Police.

1945   The number of prisoners was as follows: 1,467 in Hong Kong Prison (Stanley); 166 in Victoria Remand Prison; 200 in Lai Chi Kok Female Prison. Efforts were made to provide useful employment for prisoners.

1946   Industrial training for prisoners began. The first delinquent institution was established as a temporary reformatory institution to receive boys between 8 and 16 years old.

1947   The Young Prisoners Training Centre was set up at Stanley Prison.

1948   Probation services were transferred to the Social Welfare Office of the Secretariat for Chinese Affairs.

1951   The Discharged Prisoners' Aid Subcommittee under the Hong Kong Council of Social Service was set up to arrange aftercare services.

1953   The Earnings Scheme, providing incentive to production, was implemented in the Training Centre at Stanley Prison to replace gratuities paid on discharge.

1955   Open visits were introduced at Stanley and Lai Chi Kok Prisons.

1956   The first open prison, Chi Ma Wan Prison, was put into use. The Tung Tau Wan Training Centre for boys in older age groups was inaugurated.

1958   The first Staff Training School was established at the Tung Tau Wan Training Centre.

1959   The programme for rehabilitation of drug addicts at Tai Lam Prison was implemented.

1961   The Psychiatric Observation Unit at Victoria Prison was established.

1966   Capital punishment was suspended following the last execution on November 16.

1967   The Department was organized into seven units: Headquarters Unit, Reception Centre, Prisons for Men, Prisons for Women, Treatment Centre, Training Centre and Staff Training School.

1968   New Life House, the first halfway house for the rehabilitation of ex-drug inmates, was opened. The Drug Addiction Treatment Centres Ordinance was enacted.

1969   A new female prison at Tai Lam was completed to replace the Lai Chi Kok Female Prison.

1972   A detention centre was set up at Shek Pik of Lantau Island. The Siu Lam Psychiatric Centre was set up to take care of prisoners with psychiatric problems.

1973   A Board of Enquiry was set up to investigate a disturbance at Stanley Prison.

1974   A Public Relations Unit was established to publish general activities and policies of the Department through the press and other forms of media. An Escort Unit was set up to convey persons in custody to and from courts, hospitals, clinics and institutions.

1976   A Geriatric Unit was established to provide geriatric services for geriatric prisoners. Psychological services were first introduced.

1979   A Complaints Investigation Unit was set up to investigate and deal with complaints against the Department.

1980   Tai Tam Gap Correctional Institution for young female offenders was established.

1982   The Prisons Department was retitled Correctional Services Department. It also provided a closed centre for Vietnam refugees at Chi Ma Wan and carried out detention of refugees.

1983   The Department was organized into five divisions: Administration and Industries (divided into seven sections of Accounts Section, Administration of Department, Industries, Information, Planning Section, Statistics Section and Works Section); Inspectorate and Refugees (comprised the Complaints Investigation Unit, Inspectorate Unit, Security, Internal Audit Section and Refugee Unit); Personnel and Training (consisted of sections of Personnel and Staff Training Institution); Psychological Services and Programme Development (which directed the sections of Education and Psychological Services); and Operations (composed of the sections of Adult Offenders, Aftercare Services, Treatment Centres and Young Offenders).

1985   The Psychological Services and Programme Development Division and the Operations Division were merged to form two new divisions: Young Offenders Division (comprised the three sections of Education, Psychological Services and Young Offenders) and Adult Offenders Division (included the three sections of Adult Offenders, Aftercare Services and Treatment Centres).

1986   The Young Offenders Assessment Panel was introduced.

1988   The Council of European Convention on the Transfer of Sentenced Persons was extended to Hong Kong.

1989   The Inspectorate and Refugees Division was replaced by the Inspectorate Division. The Young Offenders Division and the Adult Offenders Division were merged to form the Operations Division. The Vietnamese Unit was established.

1991   The Inspectorate Division was retitled Inspectorate and Management Services Division.

1995   The first half-way house solely for adult offenders, Pelican House, was founded. The half-way house programme was extended to young drug offenders.

1998   The last detention centre for Vietnamese migrants, High Island Detention Centre, was closed. The Vietnamese Migrants Division was abolished. A new Rehabilitation Division was set up to provide rehabilitation services for prisoners and inmates. The Criminal Procedure (Amendment) Ordinance 1998 was enacted which allowed prisoners under 18 years of age to have their cases reviewed.

1999   Pak Sha Wan Correctional Institution came into operation.

2000   The Department was structured into five divisions: Administration and Industries (Accounts Section; Business Units 1, 2, and 3; Central Supplies Office; Computer Services Unit; Departmental Transportation Office; General Administration Unit; Industries Section; Internal Audit Office; Public Relations Section; Statistics and Research Section; Translation Office; Works and Planning Section); Inspectorate and Management Services (Inspectorate Unit, Management Services Unit and Complaints Investigation Unit); Personnel and Training (Appointments Registry, Establishment Unit, Human Resource Section, Personnel Registry, Personnel Unit, Staff Relations and Welfare Unit); Operations (Penal Administration Section and Penal Operations Section); and Rehabilitation (Aftercare Unit, Education Unit, Pre-sentence Assessment Unit, Psychological Services Section, Rehabilitation Section and Vocational Training Unit).

2001   The Personnel and Training Division was reorganized and renamed Human Resource Division.

2002   The Department was organized into a Public Relations Section and five functional divisions: Civil Secretary (Accounts Section, Administration Section, Statistics and Research Section, Works and Planning Section); Human Resource (Human Resource Section); Quality Assurance (Complaints Investigation Unit, Management Services Unit, Inspectorate, Security Unit); Operations (Industries Section, Penal Administration Section, Penal Operations Section); and Rehabilitation (Psychological Services Section, Rehabilitation Section).

Sources:

1. *A Summary of the Work of the Prisons Department by the Commissioner of Prisons 1979-1980*, Hong Kong, Government Printer, 1980.
2. *Annual Report of the Commissioner of Prisons 1947-1948*, Hong Kong Government, 1948.
3. *Annual Review by the Commissioner of Correctional Services*, Hong Kong, Government Printer, 1983-1998.
4. *The Government of the Hong Kong Special Administrative Region Telephone Directory 2000*, Hong Kong, Government Printer, 2001.
5. *Hong Kong Annual Departmental Report by the Commissioner of Prisons*, Hong Kong Government, 1951-1972.
6. *Hong Kong Annual Report by the Commissioner of Prisons 1950-1951*, Hong Kong Government, 1951.
7. "Hong Kong Civil Affairs Policy Directives, Prisons", *Hong Kong Directives*, Hong Kong, 1945, HKRS211, D&S no.2/4.

8. *Hong Kong Government Gazette*, Hong Kong Government 1853-1890.
9. *Prisons Department Annual Report for 1946-1947*, Hong Kong Government, 1947.
10. "Report of the Superintendent of Prisons", *Hong Kong Administration Reports*, Hong Kong Government, 1931-1939.
11. "Report of the Superintendent of Prisons", *Hong Kong Administrative Reports*, Hong Kong Government, 1909-1931.
12. www.correctionalservices.gov.hk/

Correctional Services Department — Changes in Names and Directors

Year	Name of Department	Title	Name of Director
1841-1845	Gaol, Police	Chief of Gaol	Caine, William
1846	Gaol, Police	Sheriff of the Gaol	Hillier, C. B.
1847-1850	Gaol, Police	Sheriff of the Gaol	Holdforth, C. G.
1851-1857	Gaol, Police	Sheriff of the Gaol	Mitchell, William
1857	Gaol, Police	Governor of the Gaol	Inglis, A. L.
1858-1863	Gaol, Police	Governor of the Gaol	Scott, Joseph
1863-1874	Victoria Gaol, Police	Superintendent of Victoria Gaol	Douglas, Francis
1874-1875	Victoria Gaol, Police	Superintendent of Victoria Gaol	Lister, Alfred
1875-1885	Victoria Gaol, Police	Superintendent of Victoria Gaol	Tonnochy, Malcolm Struan
1885-1892	Victoria Gaol, Police	Superintendent of Victoria Gaol	Gordon, Alexander Herman Adam
1892-1920	Victoria Gaol, Police	Superintendent of Victoria Gaol	Lethbridge, Henry Bridgman Henderson
1920	Victoria Gaol, Police	Superintendent of Victoria Gaol	Franks, John William
1920-1938	Prisons Department	Superintendent of Prisons	Franks, John William
1938-1941	Prisons Department	Commissioner of Prisons	Willococks, James Lugard
1946-1951	Prisons Department	Commissioner of Prisons	Shillingford, William

Year	Name of Department	Title	Name of Director
1951-1953	Prisons Department	Commissioner of Prisons	Burdett, John Tunstall
1953-1968	Prisons Department	Commissioner of Prisons	Norman, Cuthbert James
1968-1972	Prisons Department	Commissioner of Prisons	Pickett, Gilbert Roy
1972-1982	Prisons Department	Commissioner of Prisons	Garner, Thomas Gerad
1982-1985	Correctional Services Department	Commissioner of Correctional Services	Garner, Thomas Gerad
1985-1990	Correctional Services Department	Commissioner of Correctional Services	Chan, Wa-shek
1990-1995	Correctional Services Department	Commissioner of Correctional Services	McCosh, Frederic Samuel
1995-1999	Correctional Services Department	Commissioner of Correctional Services	Lai, Ming-kee, Raymond
1999-2002	Correctional Services Department	Commissioner of Correctional Services	Ng, Ching-kwo, Benny

Sources:
1. *The Hong Kong Civil Service List*, Hong Kong Government, 1947-1958.
2. *Staff Biographies Hong Kong Government*, Hong Kong, Government Printer, 1974, 1976, 1978, 1982, 1984, 1986, 1988, 1990, 1993.
3. *Staff Biographies the Government of the Hong Kong Special Administrative Region*, Hong Kong, Government Printer, 1998, 2001.
4. *Staff List Hong Kong Government*, Hong Kong, Government Printer, 1959-1996.
5. *Staff List the Government of the Hong Kong Special Administrative Region*, Hong Kong, Government Printer, 1997-2000.
6. www.correctionalservices.gov.hk/

Fire Brigade, Police (1868-1941)
Fire Brigade (1941-1961)
Fire Services Department (1961-2002)

1868   The firefighting force of Hong Kong had previously consisted mainly of volunteer firemen, police and troops. An ordinance was passed putting the volunteer fire brigade on an official basis under an officer, in which both police and civilians were enrolled.

1886   The Fire Brigade consisted of 150 staff. Eleven hundred and twelve fires and alarms occurred during this year.

1887   The Brigade possessed four steam engines and 127 staff.

1895   The Fire Brigade was placed under the head of the Police Force, then known as the Captain Superintendent of Police. The Fire Brigade was made up of European Police Sergeants and permanent Chinese firemen.

1904   A. Lane held the post of Station Officer in the Fire Brigade until his retirement in 1921. He had under him 16 European Police Sergeants and 38 Chinese firemen at the Main Fire Station. The firefighting equipment consisted of two steam engines, three despatch boxes, two hose reels and two wheeled escapes. There were four substations, located at the Nam Pak Hong Association, Bonham Strand West, no. 7 Police Station and Shau Ki Wan. Each substation had two firemen and one despatch box. There were two small fire floats, one of which was fitted with a monitor. A fireman was on duty to keep watch in a watch tower situated on the roof of the Main Fire Station. At the first sight of a fire or upon receipt of a call, he gave the alarm by ringing a bell. This acted as a signal to the coolies in the vicinity, who immediately placed themselves at the disposal of the Fire Brigade to assist the firemen to manoeuvre the fire-fighting equipment to the scene of the fire. The coolies were paid on each occasion; the amount of award depended on the distance run.

1916   The Hong Kong Fire Brigade had its first motor fire appliances.

1921   The status of the officer-in-charge of the Brigade was raised to the rank of Superintendent. The first Superintendent appointed was H. T. Brooks, formerly of the London Fire Brigade. Trained fire officers were recruited from the United Kingdom to take the place of Police Sergeants on fire duty.

1923   Posts were created to recruit local Chinese as Subofficers.

1926   There was a staff shortage. The shortage of Chinese recruits was due to poor conditions of service.

1941   The Fire Brigade became an independent department; J. C. Fitz-Henry was the first professional fire officer appointed as Chief Officer of the Hong Kong Fire Brigade.

1946   W. M. Smith was appointed Chief Officer and served until 1949. The establishment consisted of 10 British, 1 Portuguese and 250 Chinese. Its duties included the inspection of all entertainment buildings, stores for dangerous goods, boarding houses etc., with a view to issuing instructions and giving advice regarding fire security matters. The Brigade installed fire hydrants in government buildings; provided fire calls, fire alarm systems and ambulance services.

1948   The Brigade acted as the licensing authority for dangerous goods and the storage of cinematograph films.

1949   A committee giving advice to the Government on the administration of the Dangerous Goods Ordinance was appointed.

1952   Ambulance services were placed under the control of the Chief Officer of the Fire Brigade. The rescue squad was transferred to the Civil Aid Services.

1953   The Fire Brigade took over the airport rescue and firefighting services.

1954   The Brigade was composed of Central Fire Station with four substations on Hong Kong Island, two in Kowloon, and seven in the New Territories. It consisted of 596 officers and clerical staff.

1961   The Fire Brigade was retitled Fire Services Department. The Department was structured into five major parts: Administration (included Accounts, General Office, Personnel, Registry, Stores, Typist Pool), Hong Kong District Command (directed Fire Prevention), Kowloon and New Kowloon District Command (directed Fire Prevention), New Territories Command (directed Fire Prevention), and Operations (consisted of Ambulance Division, Auxiliary Fire Service, Fire Prevention and Inspection, Staff, Training School, Workshop Division).

1962   A new Fire Prevention Bureau was set up to issue licences for private schools.

1963   The Hong Kong Fire Services Training School was established. The Administration was restructured into two divisions: Planning and Training, and Logistic and Technology. A new unit of Secretary was created.

1964   The Department was reorganized into five parts: Fire Prevention Bureau (Fire Prevention Bureau Training Division, Fire Investigation Squad); Hong Kong Island and Marine (Ambulance Mobilization Centre, Fire Control, General Staff and Auxiliaries, and Search and Rescue Division); Mainland (Airport Contingent, Fire Control, General Staff and Auxiliaries, Mainland Fire Control and Ambulance Mobilization Centre, Search and Rescue Division, and Sub-mainland Fire Control and Ambulance Mobilization Centre); Training Welfare Technology Education Assistance APSO (Administration of Welfare and Sports Fund, Officer Examination Board, PE); and Transport and Logistic (Auxiliaries Training, Commandant Training Establishment).

1965   The Department was restructured into four parts: Fire Service Headquarters (Principal, Secretary), Fire Prevention Bureau (General, Training), Hong Kong Island and Marine Command (Central and Western Division, Eastern Division, Fire Control, Marine Division, Search and Rescue Division), and Mainland Command (Airport Division, Kowloon City Division, New Territories Division, Search and Rescue Division, Terminus Division).

1966   An Ambulance Division was established.

1970   The Department was reorganized into six divisions: Headquarters; Ambulance Division; Fire Prevention Bureau; Hong Kong and Marine Fire Command (Central Division, Eastern Division, Western Division, Marine Division); Kowloon Fire Command (Eastern Division, Southern Division, Western Division); and New Territories Command (Eastern Division, Western Division).

1975 The Departmental Secretariat was set up.

1976 The MTR Division was established.

1992 The Ambulance Command transferred the function of handling non-emergency cases to the Hospital Authority.

2000 The Department was structured into seven parts: Fire Service Headquarters; Ambulance Command; Fire Safety Command; Licensing and Control Command; Hong Kong Island, Islands and Marine Fire Command Headquarters; Kowloon Fire Command Headquarters; and New Territories Fire Command Headquarters.

2002 The Department was organised into seven commands and a secretariat: Headquarters Command (Airport Fire Contingent; Fire Services Training School; Information Unit; Management Group; Mobilizing and Communication Group; Physical Training Establishment; Planning Group; Recruitment, Training and Examination Group; Stores and Supplies; Welfare Section; and Workshop and Transport); Departmental Secretariat (Chinese Language Section, Finance and Establishment Division, and Personnel and General Division); Ambulance Command (Administration Group; Hong Kong Region — East and West Divisions; Kowloon Region — East and West Divisions; New Territories Region — East, South and West Divisions; Training School), Fire Safety Command (Building Improvement and Support Division, Commercial Buildings and Premises Division, Community Relations Division, Fire Service Installation Task Force, Loan Scheme Supporting Team, Railway Development Strategy Division, Special Projects Division, Theme Park Projects Division); Licensing and Certification Command (Administration Group, Dangerous Goods Division, Fire Service Installations and Ventilation Division, Hong Kong Regional Office, Kowloon Regional Office, New Territories Regional Office, New Projects Division, Policy Division); Hong Kong Operational Command (Administration Group, Central Division, East Division, West Division, Marine and Offshore Islands Division); Kowloon Operational Command (Administration Group, Central Division, East Division, South Division, West Division); New Territories Operational Command (Administration Group, East Division, South Division, South West Division, West Division, North Division). The Headquarters Command formulated and reviewed departmental policies, staff planning, management, training and recruitment; dealt with legislative drafting instructions and resources allocations; handled public complaints as well as public relations; and provided fire and rescue services for the Hong Kong International Airport at Chek Lap Kok. The Departmental Secretariat was responsible for the overall management of civilian staff; establishment and personnel matters; co-ordination of the Department's resource requirements and annual estimates; and liaison with ICAC on specific issues. The Ambulance Command supervised ambulance command and liaised with other government departments and the general public. The Fire Safety Command was responsible for drawing up fire safety policies, enforcing safety regulations and public awareness on fire safety, maintaining fire service installations and equipment for fire safety improvement work. The Licensing and Certification Command enforced fire safety regulations and policies, assisted and advised the public on fire protection measures and the abatement of fire hazards. The

Hong Kong, Kowloon and New Territories operational commands were responsible for the implementation of policies, personal command of firefighting and rescue operations at no. 5 alarm fires and major calamities.

Sources:

1. *125th Anniversary of the Hong Kong Fire Service 1868-1993*, Hong Kong, Government Printer, 1993.
2. *Annual Departmental Report by the Chief Officer, Fire Brigade*, Hong Kong Government, 1950-1951.
3. *Annual Departmental Report by the Chief Officer*, Fire Brigade, Hong Kong, Government Printer, 1952-1957.
4. "Fire Brigade", *Hong Kong Directives*, Hong Kong, 1945, HKRS 211, D&S, no 2/4.
5. Gorman, W. J., Chief Officer of Fire Brigade , "The Fire Brigade" in *Hong Kong Symposium*, Hong Kong, *South China Morning Post*, 1957.
6. *The Government of the Hong Kong Special Administrative Region Telephone Directory 2000*, Hong Kong, Government Printer, 2001.
7. *Hong Kong Annual Departmental Report by the Director of Fire Services*, Hong Kong, Government Printer, 1960-1972.
8. *Hong Kong Departmental Report by the Director of Fire Service*, Hong Kong, Government Printer, 1972-1975.
9. *Hong Kong Fire Services Review*, Hong Kong Government, 1985-1986; 1991-1992; 1995-1996.
10. *Hong Kong Government Gazette*, Hong Kong Government, 1887-1889.
11. "Reports of the Captain Superintendent of Police and of the Superintendent of Fire Brigade", *Hong Kong Administrative Reports*, Hong Kong Government, 1909-1910.
12. "Reports of the Captain Superintendent of Police", *Hong Kong Administrative Reports*, Hong Kong Government, 1911-1929.
13. *Report of the Chief Officer, Hong Kong Fire Brigade*, Hong Kong Government, 1946-1950.
14. "Report of the Commissioner of Police", *Hong Kong Administration Reports*, Hong Kong Government, 1937-1940.
15. "The Report of the Committee appointed to consider suggestions for the improvement of the firefighting organization of the Colony", *Hong Kong Sessional Papers*, Hong Kong, Noronha & Co., 27 May 1926, no.6.
16. "Report of the Inspector of General of Police", *Hong Kong Administration Reports*, Hong Kong Government, 1932-1936.
17. "Report of the Inspector General of Police", *Hong Kong Administrative Reports*, 1930 Appendix K, Hong Kong Government, 1931.
18. www.info.gov.hk/hkfsd/home/

Fire Services Department — Changes in Names and Directors

Year	Name of Department	Title	Name of Director
1868-1878	Fire Brigade, Police	Superintendent, Fire Brigade	May, Charles
1878-1883	Fire Brigade, Police	Superintendent, Fire Brigade	Creach, C. V.
1883-1895	Fire Brigade, Police	Superintendent, Fire Brigade	Wodehouse, Henry Ernest
1895-1902	Fire Brigade, Police	Superintendent, Fire Brigade	May, Francis Henry

Year	Name of Department	Title	Name of Director
1902-1913	Fire Brigade, Police	Superintendent, Fire Brigade	Badeley, Francis Joseph
1913-1918	Fire Brigade, Police	Superintendent, Fire Brigade	Messer, Charles McIlvaine
1918-1922	Fire Brigade, Police	Superintendent, Fire Brigade	Wolfe, Edward Dudley Corscaden
1922-1935	Fire Brigade, Police	Chief Officer, Fire Brigade	Wolfe, Edward Dudley Corscaden
1935-1940	Fire Brigade, Police	Chief Officer, Fire Brigade	King, Thomas Henry
1940	Fire Brigade, Police	Chief Officer, Fire Brigade	Fitz-Henry, Jack Copper
1941	Fire Brigade	Chief Officer, Fire Brigade	Fitz-Henry, Jack Copper
1946-1949	Fire Brigade	Chief Officer, Fire Brigade	Smith, William McIntosh
1949-1961	Fire Brigade	Chief Officer, Fire Brigade	Gorman, William James
1961	Fire Services Department	Director of Fire Services	Gorman, William James
1961-1965	Fire Services Department	Director of Fire Services	Cox, Ronald Godfrey
1965-1970	Fire Services Department	Director of Fire Services	Milner, Joseph
1970-1975	Fire Services Department	Director of Fire Services	Wood, Alfred Evelyn Harry
1975-1984	Fire Services Department	Director of Fire Services	Watson, Frederick Morphet
1984-1987	Fire Services Department	Director of Fire Services	Holmes, Robert
1987-1992	Fire Services Department	Director of Fire Services	March, John Howard
1992-1995	Fire Services Department	Director of Fire Services	Lam, Chek-yuen, Jerry
1995-1998	Fire Services Department	Director of Fire Services	Cheung, Peter
1998-2002	Fire Services Department	Director of Fire Services	Tsang, Kwong-yu

Sources:
1. *125th Anniversary of the Hong Kong Fire Service*, Hong Kong, Government Printer, 1993, p. 66, Appendix.
2. *The Hong Kong Civil Service List*, Hong Kong Government, 1947-1958.
3. *Staff Biographies Hong Kong Government*, Hong Kong, Government Printer, 1974, 1976, 1978, 1982, 1984, 1986, 1988, 1990, 1993.
4. *Staff Biographies the Government of the Hong Kong Special Administrative Region*, Hong Kong, Government Printer, 1998, 2001.
5. *Staff List Hong Kong Government*, Hong Kong, Government Printer, 1959-1996.
6. *Staff List the Government of the Hong Kong Special Administrative Region*, Hong Kong, Government Printer, 1998, 2000.
7. www.info.gov.hk/hkfsd/home/

Registration of Persons Office (1954-1976)

1954   The Office was established under the Registration of Persons Ordinance and Rules (Cap. 177). The Office was responsible for the registration of persons and free issuance of ID cards; provision of mobile registration and photographic services to New Territories residents; maintenance of statutory requirements in respect changes of particulars such as employment and address, and lost card replacements; prosecutions.

1955   New functions were undertaken: compilation of the electoral register of the Urban Council; ascertainment of Chinese name on the jurors lists; revision of ID cards for members of the consular corps.

1960   The Office registered new arrivals; persons qualified and liable for jury service; recorded and provided maintenance of the registers of electors and common jurors.

1966   The Office registered citizens who were unable to register before the final re-registration deadlines and replaced lost or defaced ID cards and those requiring amendments.

1967   The Office provided special identification, lamination or photographic facilities for other government departments.

1968   The Office verified birth certificates.

1969   The Office issued certificates of registered particulars to applicants and selected qualified persons for service as jurors under the Jury Ordinance.

1970   The Office supplied information to the Immigration Department to aid in the processing of applications for British passports, and located new arrivals for conducting clearance investigations. It was structured into three branches: Head Office, Hong Kong, Kowloon. The Head Office comprised the Accounts and Stores Section, Central Records Division, Electoral and Jury Section, and Secretary. The Hong Kong Branch consisted of the General Office, Hong Kong Mobile Team, Identity Card Issues, Registration, Replacement Section. The Kowloon Branch consisted of the General Office, New Territories Mobile Team, Identity Card Issues, Registration, Replacement Section.

1976   The Office was amalgamated with the Immigration Department, and duties for the registration of persons were transferred to the Immigration Department.

Sources:

1. *Hong Kong Annual Departmental Report by the Commissioner of Registration*, Hong Kong, Government Printer, 1954-1977.
2. *Hong Kong Annual Departmental Report of the Director of Immigration*, Hong Kong, Government Printer, 1977-1978.

Registration of Persons Office — Changes in Directors			
Year	Name of Department	Title	Name of Director
1954	Registration of Persons Office	Commissioner of Registration of Persons	Orchard, W. D.
1955-1960	Registration of Persons Office	Commissioner of Registration of Persons	Bates, Robert Alfred
1960-1977	Registration of Persons Office	Commissioner of Registration of Persons	Mitchell, John Vanham Green

Sources:
1. *The Hong Kong Civil Service List*, Hong Kong Government, 1954-1958.
2. *Staff List Hong Kong Government*, Hong Kong, Government Printer, 1960-1976.

Immigration Department (1959-2002)

1959   The control of immigration was detached from the Police Force and became an independent Immigration Department under Immigration Ordinance no.34 of 1958.

1961   The Department was organized into three divisions: Headquarters (administered the Accounts Section, General Office, Investigation Section, Registries Section and Stores); Immigration Control Division (directed the Airport Control Section, Harbour Control Section, Kowloon Suboffice and Re-entry Permit Offices); and Travel Documents (supervised the Aliens Section, British Section and Chinese Section). The Headquarters Division controlled immigration, prevented illegal immigration, issued travel documents, traced all persons contravening the immigration laws and instituting proceedings against them. The Immigration Control Division checked on persons arriving in and departing from Hong Kong by air or by sea. The Travel Documents Division authorized entry, re-entry, and transit visas for aliens; registered aliens and prepared alien statistics. It also issued, renewed and endorsed British passports, handled British naturalization cases, and dealt with Chinese with no travel documents, passports issued by the People's Republic of China and travel documents issued by Taiwan.

1966   The Statistical Section was established under the control of the Headquarters Division to record movements of travellers and carry out statistical analysis. The Naturalization Section was set up under the supervision of the Travel Documents Division to handle British naturalization applications.

1967	The Department was reorganized into three divisions: Administrative Division (consisted of eight sections: Accounts, Confidential, General Registries, Open, Personnel, Stores, Training and Welfare); Control Division (included the five sections of Airport, Border, Harbour, Investigation and Travel Index); and Documents (comprised the five sections of Aliens, British and Commonwealth, Chinese, Macau Visitors, Naturalization; and the Re-entry Permits Offices).
1969	The British and Commonwealth Section under the Documents Division was spilt into two sections: British Section and Commonwealth Section.
1970	An Enquiries Section was set up under the Administrative Division. The Department began to provide 24-hour clearance service for shipping in the western quarantine anchorage and day-time service for eastern anchorage, and implemented a system of pre-arrival immigration clearance for cargo ships not carrying passengers.
1971	The Travel Index and Investigation Sections of the Control Division were separated from the Control Division and became an independent division — Investigation Division.
1972	The British Section of the Documents Division was renamed British Passport Section. The Commonwealth Section of the Documents Division was retitled United Kingdom and Commonwealth Section.
1973	The Overseas Visas Section under the supervision of the Documents Division was established to deal with applications for visas and entry certificates to the United Kingdom, Commonwealth countries and dependent territories. The Chinese Section was spilt into two sections: Chinese Residents and Chinese Visitors.
1975	The Aliens Section and the United Kingdom and Commonwealth Section were merged to form the Aliens and Commonwealth Section under the Documents Division. The Operational Research Section was established under the Investigation Division to collect, evaluate and disseminate immigration intelligence.
1976	The Aliens and Commonwealth Section was retitled Aliens Section. The Registration of Persons Office was integrated into the Immigration Department. The Office was responsible for supplying personal information to other government departments and the issue of certificates of registered particulars.
1979	The duties for the registration of births, deaths and marriages were transferred from the Registrar General's Department.
1997	The Department was reorganized into six branches: Administration and Planning (three divisions: Administration, General Duties, Management Audit); Control and Investigation (four divisions: Airport, Border, Harbour, Investigation); Information Systems (two divisions: Information Systems (Development), Information Systems (Production)); Liaison and Support (two sections: Liaison and Support, Vietnamese); Personal Documentation (two divisions: Registration, Documents); Visa and Policies (two divisions: Visa Control (Administration), Visa Control (Operation)).
2000	The structure remained similar to that in 1997. The Management Audit Division of the Administration and Planning Branch was abolished. The Control and Investigation Branch was renamed Control Branch; its Investigation Division was transferred to the newly established Enforcement and Liaison Branch. The former Liaison and Support Branch was abolished.

2002   The Department controlled the movement of people into and out of Hong Kong; issued HKSAR passports and other travel documents, visas and identity cards; handled nationality matters and registered births, deaths and marriages. It also detected and prosecuted immigration law offenders and removed illegal immigrants. The Department was structured into six major branches. The Administration and Planning Branch was responsible for the overall support programme including general administration, finance, planning and development, staffing, personnel matters and management audit. The Control Branch formulated and implements control policy on exit and entry; examined passengers arriving and department by sea, land and air. The Enforcement and Liaison Branch negotiated and promoted the acceptance of HKSAR travel documents; handled matters relating to Vietnamese refugees, migrants and illegal immigrants; formulated and implementd policy in respect of investigation, prosecution, deportation and removal. The Information Systems Branch planned and implemented information system systems, operated existing information systems and managed records. The Personal Documentation Branch was responsible for the issuance of HKSAR passports, other travel documents and identity cards; the processing of applications relating to claims to right of abode under the Basic Law and the Chinese nationality law; the compilation of the provisional list of jurors; and the registration of births, deaths and marriages. The Visa and Policies Branch dealt with visa control policy research and review; and the overall visa control operations including the issue of visas and the granting of extension of stay.

Sources:

1.   *Annual Departmental Report by the Director of Immigration*, Hong Kong, Government Printer, 1997-1998, 2000.
2.   *CO 129/133*, 19 Oct 1868.
3.   *Hong Kong Government Gazette*, Hong Kong Government, 21 April 1860, p.112.
4.   "Immigration control", *Hong Kong Directives*, Hong Kong, 1945, HKRS 211, D&S no. 2/4.
5.   *Hong Kong*, Hong Kong Government Printer, 1980, 1982, 1983, 1987, 1991-1992.
6.   *Hong Kong Annual Departmental Report by the Director of Immigration*, Hong Kong, Government Printer, 1961-1978.
7.   www.immd.gov.hk/index.html

Immigration Department — Changes in Directors			
Year	Name of Department	Title	Name of Director
1961-1965	Immigration Department	Director of Immigration	Moore, John
1965-1974	Immigration Department	Director of Immigration	Collard, Walter William Edgar
1974-1978	Immigration Department	Director of Immigration	Rowlands, John Martin
1978-1983	Immigration Department	Acting Director of Immigration	Bridge, Ronald George Blacker
1983-1989	Immigration Department	Director of Immigration	Carter, Alan John
1989-1996	Immigration Department	Director of Immigration	Leung, Ming-yin
1996-1998	Immigration Department	Director of Immigration	Ip Lau, Suk-yee, Regina
1998-2002	Immigration Department	Director of Immigration	Lee, Siu-kwong, Ambrose

Sources:
1. *Staff Biographies Hong Kong Government*, Hong Kong, Government Printer, 1976-1996.
2. *Staff Biographies the Government of the Hong Kong Special Administrative Region*, Hong Kong, Government Printer, 1997-2001.
3. *Staff List Hong Kong Government*, Hong Kong, Government Printer, 1961-1996.
4. *Staff List the Government of the Hong Kong Special Administrative Region*, Hong Kong, Government Printer, 1997-2001.
5. www.immd.gov.hk/index.html

Auxiliary Forces

Auxiliary Fire Service (1950-1975)

1950   The Auxiliary Fire Service (AFS), being a branch of the Essential Services Corps, was formed to attend and assist the regular Fire Brigade in firefighting operations. It was established under the terms of the Essential Services Corps (Auxiliary Fire Service) Regulations and consisted of both volunteers and conscripts.

1952   An Auxiliary Fire Service Brass Band was formed.

1956   The Auxiliary Fire Service Training Centre at North Point was opened on October 18 to undertake overnight training at weekends.

1959   The AFS carried out surveys for water relays, plotting positions and pumping points for base pumps, intermediate pumps, etc, to ensure that water could be supplied in any emergency from a permanent static supply to areas otherwise devoid of water.

1961   The Superintendent was renamed Commandant and his immediate subordinates were retitled Staff Officers. The control room staff of AFS was developed and training programmes throughout the Service. were revised.

1963   Auxiliaries were posted to fire stations nearest to their homes and places of work to enable a more active role in the day-to-day work of their professional colleagues.

1966   In training and organization spheres concentration was put on the complete integration of professional and auxiliary personnel and resources. A combined Fire Service/ Auxiliary Fire Service exercise was held on January 30 to test the degree of integration.

1968   The organizational structure of the AFS was revised as further step towards complete integration with the professionals.

1970   All fully trained auxiliaries when on duty were assigned to man fire appliances and attend emergency calls with their professional colleagues.

1972   Due to the introduction of new training, fitness and age requirements, the membership of the Service was reduced rapidly.

1975   The AFS was disbanded on March 31.

Sources:

1.   *Annual Departmental Report by the Chief Officer of Fire Brigade*, Hong Kong, Government Printer, 1952-1974.
2.   *Hong Kong Administration Reports 1939*, Hong Kong Government, 1939-1940, K(1).
3.   *Hong Kong 1976*, Hong Kong, Government Printer, 1977, p.15.

Special Police Reserve (1914-1917)
Hong Kong Police Reserve (1917-1919, 1927-1959)
Hong Kong Auxiliary Police Force (1959-1969)
Royal Hong Kong Auxiliary Police Force (1969-1997)
Hong Kong Auxiliary Police Force (1997-2002)

1886   Under the Peace and Preservation Ordinance of 1886, the Governor could appoint any citizens to serve as temporary "special constables" whenever the police seemed under-strength and when there were emergencies. The Special Constables assisted the Police in a part-time capacity and could be called up and disbanded at any time. Three hundred and fifty-two men served in this capacity on October 1.

1914   Britain declared war on Germany on August 4 and British expatriates began to volunteer their services on the Western Front. Their absence left the Police Force reduced and in need of reinforcements. The Special Police Reserve was established in October.

1915   Two hundred and fifty men joined the Special Police Reserve.

1916   The fourth company and an ambulance section were formed.

1917   On September 14, under Police Reserve Ordinance no. 20 of 1917, the corps was renamed Hong Kong Police Reserve. The duties and privileges remained unchanged. All men were called out for service.

1919   Hong Kong police officers who had left returned to Hong Kong after the War, and the Hong Kong Police Reserve was disbanded.

1927   The Hong Kong Police Reserve was re-established due to political instability on mainland China and the rapid growth in the number of Chinese refugees flooding into Hong Kong. All members of the 1914-1919 Reserve were re-enrolled.

1938   Two hundred and ninety men in the Reserve were assigned to active duty.

1939   The Civil Defence Corps Regulations came into effect, under which all British subjects of non-Chinese origin between the ages of 18 and 55 were required to sign up with one of the ten auxiliary support groups.

1940   The strength of the Reserve was increased to 1,000 men and a company of auxiliary street guards was formed.

1941   Three thousand Chinese enrolled in a new adjunct to the regular Police Force: Special Constabulary; they assisted the regular and reserve forces in the event of an emergency.

1946   The Police Reserve was formally disbanded on November 29 to absolve all reservists from liability for any contraventions of the Police Reserve regulation during the Japanese occupation. Under the Police Reserve Amendment Ordinance, a new Hong Kong Police Reserve was established. It consisted mainly of English-speaking Chinese. Its duties remained as the first line of support for the regular Police Force. The 300 members were organized into two companies.

1947   A further amendment to the Police Reserve Ordinance was passed. Under the Ordinance, the Commissioner of Reserve Police could issue a call-out order independently. It also removed the stipulation that gave reservists the same powers and privileges as Europeans of equal rank in the regular Force.

1952   Intensive training in the form of a rigorous two-week annual camp at Castle Peak was introduced. The Reserve was expanded in numbers and in fields of operation. It was divided into four sections: General Duties, Emergency Units, Marine and Communications.

1957   The reorganization of the Hong Kong Police Force following the riots of 1956 led to the complete integration of the Police Reserve and the Special Constabulary into the regular Force. To facilitate full integration, the new Hong Kong Auxiliary Police Force (HKAPF) was structured on similar lines to the uniformed branch of the regular Force. Members were distributed on a command and divisional basis with specialized Emergency Units, Communications and Marine Branches. The auxiliaries assisted the administration groups and operated the radio and telephone networks, as well as providing relief policing in all police divisions. The two Emergency Units, based on either side of the harbour, acted as anti-riot companies. Training programmes of the auxiliaries remained unchanged; there were day courses at the Police Training School, periodic mobilization exercises and a new advanced training course for Inspectors and Non-Commissioned Officers.

1959   The Police Reserve was retitled Hong Kong Auxiliary Police Force officially.

1963   The HKAPF underwent a major reorganization in January. A new division, Wong Tai Sin, was created in addition to the existing eight territorial divisions of Central, Wanchai, Western, Bay View, Yau Ma Tei, Sham Shui Po, Kowloon City and Hung Hom. Senior officers of the HKAPF directed the two commands located on Hong Kong Island and in Kowloon.

1965   Women auxiliary police constables were recruited for the Communications Unit.

1969   The HKAPF was retitled Royal Hong Kong Auxiliary Police Force (RHKAPF).

1972   Auxiliary police were called out for day-to-day crime fighting duties, and not just used as an emergency back-up force. From January 13, an average of 650 auxiliaries turned out each evening for eight-hour or four-hour shifts.

1977   The training of each auxiliary recruit involved instruction in law, drill, weapons, general police work and riot drill; requiring the completion of a total of 96 hours of basic training. Successful candidates also had to perform eight hours of training per month with the division or unit to which they were attached.

1980   The entire corps was trained in normal beat patrol, crime-fighting and report room procedures.

1984   The RHKAPF was restructured into regions, districts and special units. An auxiliary team was attached to regular police districts. Titles were kept in line with overall police policy. The head of a formation at district level was called District Superintendent, to correspond to a divisional commander of the regulars.

1994   A new Auxiliary Headquarters Branch was established. The new Headquarters Branch was under the command of an Auxiliary Chief Superintendent. The Branch was divided into two wings; one undertook all administrative and support matters and the other assisted the regulars with personnel and training.

1997   The RHKAPF was renamed Hong Kong Auxiliary Police Force (HKAPF).

2000   The HKAPF was organized in five regions: Hong Kong Island (Headquarters, Western District, Central District, Wanchai District, Eastern District); Kowloon West (Headquarters, Mongkok District, Shamshuipo District, Kowloon City District, Yau Tsim District); Kowloon East (Headquarters, Wong Tai Sin District, Sau Mau Ping District, Kwun Tong District), New Territories South (Headquarters, Lantau District, Kwai Tsing District, Tsuen Wan District, Shatin District); New Territories North (Headquarters, Tai Po District, Tuen Mun District, Yuen Long District, Border District).

2002   The organization structure remained unchanged. The Force Committee on Auxiliary Police formulated policies relating to the role, establishment, structure and command, personnel, deployment and training of the Auxiliary Police Force. The Support Wing determined and promulgated duties, deployment and operational efficiency policies. Under the command of the Support Wing, the Auxiliary Support Bureau was responsible for providing a 'one-stop-shop' service at the Force level to both regular and auxiliary officers in respect of administration, management and training of auxiliary members. The HKAPF continued to render the form and amount of support to the regular force as determined by the Commissioner of Police.

Sources:

1. *Fujing tuxing duoxiang gaige* (Reforms in the Auxiliary Police Force), *Jingxin* (Voice of Police), no. 653, 21 April - 4 May 1999, p.1.
2. Lam Branson, Clare, *Looking Back with Pride and Glory*, Hong Kong, Royal Hong Kong Auxiliary Police Force, 1997, p.136.
3. Royal Hong Kong Auxiliary Police Force, *Silver Jubilee, 1959-1984*, Hong Kong, Silver Jubilee Publication Committee, 1984.
4. *Wanzhai caiqu duoxiang caoshi congfen liyong fujing ziyuan* (New policies at Wan Chai District to fully utilize the Auxiliary Police Force), *Jingxin* (Voice of Police), 4 Nov - 17 Nov 1998.
5. www.info.gov.hk/police/career/auxpolice/eng/index.htm

Hong Kong Auxiliary Police Force — Changes in Names and Directors			
Year	Name of Department	Title	Name of Director
1959-1962	Hong Kong Auxiliary Police Force	Commandant	Turner, Michael
1962-1969	Hong Kong Auxiliary Police Force	Commandant	Clague, John Douglas
1969-1980	Royal Hong Kong Auxiliary Police Force	Commandant	Clague, John Douglas
1980-1981	Royal Hong Kong Auxiliary Police Force	Commandant	Young, Chun-sheung, Ramon
1981-1983	Royal Hong Kong Auxiliary Police Force	Commandant	Bedford, Trevor John
1983-1987	Royal Hong Kong Auxiliary Police Force	Commandant	Ts'o, Nylon Leonard

Year	Name of Department	Title	Name of Director
1987-1996	Royal Hong Kong Auxiliary Police Force	Commandant	Chan, Tai-wing, Archilbald
1996-1997	Royal Hong Kong Auxiliary Police Force	Commandant	Chau, Cham-chiu, Peter
1997-2001	Hong Kong Auxiliary Police Force	Commandant	Chau, Cham-chiu, Peter
2001-2002	Hong Kong Auxiliary Police Force	Commandant	Kwok, Chi-shun, Arthur

Sources:
1. Lam, Branson Clare, *Hong Kong Auxiliary History Book*, Hong Kong, Royal Hong Kong Auxiliary Police Force, 1997.
2. *Royal Hong Kong Auxiliary Police Force, Silver Jubilee, 1959-1984*, Hong Kong, Silver Jubilee Publication Committee, 1984.
3. www.info.gov.hk/police/career/auxpolice/eng/index.htm

Civil Aid Services (1952-1997)
Civil Aid Service (1997-2002)

1939   Under the threat of impending war, a rudimentary organization — Air Raid Precaution Corps (APRC) — was formed to assist the civil population in the event of air attacks or sabotage. It is considered to be the precursor of the Civil Aid Services.

1945   The organization was officially disbanded at the end of the Sino-Japanese War.

1952   In 1949, the Essential Services Corps (ESC) was formed to handle emergency rescue problems. The Civil Aid Services (CAS) was established as an independent unit of the (ESC) in January 1952 with an initial strength of 300 volunteers, the majority of whom were old members of the APRC.

1961   Compulsory service was abandoned. A greater emphasis was placed on civil aid and civil involvement. The CAS assisted other government departments and civil organizations during natural disasters.

1968   A Youth wing was added to the CAS and two units of cadets were formed in Wong Tai Sin and Chai Wan.

1974   The CAS was reorganized into two establishments: Permanent Establishment and Volunteer Establishment. The Commissioner was head of the Volunteer Establishment whilst the Chief Staff Officer, a full-time government officer, was head of the Permanent Establishment. He was vested with the authority to ensure that the CAS function in line with current government counter-disaster strategy and be kept abreast of situational changes. He had to make sure that volunteer service members were properly trained, equipped and were operationally efficient. The Permanent Establishment was divided into two divisions: Training (consisted of three subsections: Cadet, Hong Kong, Kowloon) and Administration (directed three subsections: Accounts, Administration, Supplies). The Volunteer Establishment was commanded by a Colony Command Unit under which there were two Regional Command Units, 21 Warden Zones, two Rescue Units, a Mountain Rescue Team and a Pay and Records Unit. Subunits were located under the Colony Command Unit, and were responsible for stores, recruit and training, etc.

1975   An independent and self-administering Civil Aid Services Cadet Corps was established on October 16. The independent Cadet Corps (for youths aged between 12 and 18) comprised a volunteer Cadet Corps headquarters and twenty units.

1976   The Volunteer Establishment was reorganized into an Adult Service and a Cadet Corps. The former had two wings: Administration and Operations. The Director of Administration commanded all Service Support Units and the Cadets Corps. The Service Support Units included Stores, Pay and Records, Recruitment, Welfare, Public Relations, Sports and Recreation, and the CAS Reserve Officers. The Operations Wing comprised the Hong Kong Region, Kowloon/New Territories Region, Mountain Rescue Unit and Liaison Unit.

1977   The Cadet Corps was reorganized into two units in Hong Kong. Two new units were formed in Yuen Long and Tuen Mun in the New Territories.

1982   The Volunteer Establishment was reorganized into two wings: Administration and Development Wing, and Operations Wing. The Administration and Development Wing, commanded by the Deputy Commissioner (Administration and Development), was divided into two divisions: Administration and Development. The Operations Wing, headed by the Deputy Commissioner (Operations), was restructured into three operational regions (Hong Kong, Kowloon and New Territories) and a Tactical Force. Three regional rescue units were combined to form the Emergency Unit. The newly created Emergency Unit was grouped with the Mountain Rescue Unit and the Liaison Unit to form the Tactical Force under the Operations Wing. The Permanent Establishment was reorganized into two main functional divisions: Administration, Operations/Training. The main objectives of the Permanent Establishment were to administer and train the volunteers to ensure a high standard of operational efficiency and to provide a support service to the volunteer organization and other resources for the effective functioning of the CAS.

1983   Three new units — Recruiting Unit, Sports Unit and Welfare Unit — were set up under the Administration and Development Wing of the Volunteer Establishment.

1988   The CAS managed the Vietnamese refugee centres at the Green Island Reception Centre, Harbour Reception Centre and Argyle Camp IV Detention Centre; and assisted in setting up the refugee centres at the San Yick Closed Centre and Erskine Camp Detention Centre.

1989   A Special Operations Unit was set up to manage the centres for Vietnamese migrants.

1996   The CAS helped to promote public awareness of mountain safety by conducting training courses on mountain/hiking safety for organized groups, school teachers and hiking group leaders. It provided basic mountain rescue training for members of the emergency services.

1997   The name was changed from Civil Aid Services to Civil Aid Service.

2002   The CAS remained organized into the two parts of Permanent Establishment and Volunteer Establishment. Under the Permanent Establishment were two divisions — Operations and Training, Administration. The Operations and Training Division was divided into Adults and Cadets. The Adults Division was composed of six sections: Headquarters, Administration and Support Force, Tactical Force, Hong Kong, Kowloon and New Territories. The Cadets Division was made up of three sections: Cadet Hong Kong, Cadet Kowloon and Cadet New Territories. The Administration Division controlled four sections: Administration/Personnel, Accounts/General, Supplies, Translation. Under the Volunteer Establishment were the three wings of Administration and Support (Administration and Support Force); Operations (Hong Kong Region, Kowloon Region, New Territories Region, Tactical Force); and Youth (Cadet Corps).

Sources:

1. *Annual Departmental Report of the Civil Aid Services, Hong Kong*, Hong Kong, Government Printer, 1973-1982.
2. *Annual Review of Civil Aid Services by the Commissioner Civil Aid Services for the Year 1983-1984*, Hong Kong, Government Printer, 1984.
3. *CAS in Action 1952-1997*, Hong Kong, Government Printer, 1997, pp.19, 36.
4. *CAS Review*, Hong Kong, Government Printer, 1962-1975.
5. *Civil Aid Services Silver Jubilee 1952-1977*, Hong Kong, Civil Aid Services, 1977.
6. *Hong Kong*, Hong Kong, Government Printer, 1989-1997.
7. www.cas.gov.hk/

	Civil Aid Service — Changes in Names and Directors		
Year	**Name of Department**	**Title**	**Name of Director**
1952-1968	Civil Aid Services	Commissioner, Civil Aid Services	Terry, Charles Edward Michael
1968-1977	Civil Aid Services	Commissioner, Civil Aid Services	Woo, Pak-chuen
1977-1992	Civil Aid Services	Commissioner, Civil Aid Services	Lobo, Roger
1993-1997	Civil Aid Services	Commissioner, Civil Aid Services	Leung, Nai-ping, Norman
1997-2002	Civil Aid Service	Commissioner, Civil Aid Service	Leung, Nai-ping, Norman

Sources:
1. *Civil Aid Services Silver Jubilee 1952-1977*, Hong Kong, Civil Aid Services, 1977.
2. *Civil and Miscellaneous List Hong Kong Government*, Hong Kong, Government Printer, 1991, 1996, 2000.
3. www.cas.gov.hk/

Essential Services Corps (1949-1961)
Essential Services Corps and Directorate of Manpower (1961-1976)

1949   Legislation to provide an organization to aid, during times of emergencies, in the operation of essential services was enacted under the title of the Essential Services Corps Ordinance 1949 (Cap. 197). The Government raised and maintained a body of persons by voluntary enrolment to assist in the maintenance of the performance of essential services. A Commissioner of the Essential Services Corps was appointed on October 24. The Essential Services Corps consisted of a number of units, each responsible for maintaining an essential service such as the supply of electricity, gas, water, communications, etc. Apart from the staff employed in the services, the Corps contained an element of others normally employed in non-essential industries or departments who would be called upon to assist in the maintenance of specific services if need arose.

1950   The Auxiliary Medical Services and the Auxiliary Fire Service were established by regulations under the Essential Services Corps Ordinance.

1952   The Essential Services (Civil Aid Services) Corps Regulations of 1952 were passed under which a separate Civil Aid Services unit was set up. In addition to the Royal Hong Kong Defence Force, the Special Constabulary and the Hong Kong Police Reserve, a number of other services were raised and organized to assist in the defence of Hong Kong in an emergency. All units attached to the Corps were composed partly of volunteers and partly of conscripts. The conditions of services of the Essential Service Corps were equivalent with those of the Defence Force and with broadly the same training obligations.

1957   The Commissioner of the Essential Services Corps also became the ex officio head of the Manpower Directorate with effect from September.

1961   The Essential Services Corps was renamed Essential Services Corps and Directorate of Manpower.

1975   The Auxiliary Fire Service was disbanded on March 31 after several decades of service. Its membership was less than 200 at the time of disbandment.

1976   The Essential Services Corps and Directorate of Manpower, as a standing body, was disbanded on April 1, with the exception of a few specialist units. However, the Corps could still mobilize at short notice all its 70 units to help maintain public utilities and other essential services in times of need.

Sources:

1. *Annual Departmental Report by the Chief Officer of Fire Brigade for the Financial Year 1951-52*, Hong Kong Government 1952, p.10.
2. Hamilton, G. C., *Government Departments in Hong Kong 1841-1969*, Hong Kong, Government Printer, 1969, p.34.
3. *Hong Kong Annual Departmental Report by the Director of Medical and Health Services, 1953-1954*, Hong Kong, Government Printer, 1954, pp.67-68.
4. *Hong Kong Annual Report, 1954-1955*, Hong Kong, Government Printer, 1955, pp.231-233.
5. *Hong Kong*, Hong Kong, Government Printer, 1964, 1976-1977.
6. *Regulations of Hong Kong 1952, Hong Kong*, Government Printer, 1953, Vol. 94, pp.1-2.

Essential Services Corps and Directorate of Manpower — Changes in Names and Directors			
Year	Name of Department	Title	Name of Director
1949-1950	Essential Services Corps	Commissioner, Essential Services Corps	Ashdowne, Kenneth
1950-1951	Essential Services Corps	Commissioner, Essential Services Corps	Walton, Arthur, St. George
1951-1953	Essential Services Corps	Commissioner, Essential Services Corps	Tingle, Geoffrey Marsh
1953-1955	Essential Services Corps	Commissioner, Essential Services Corps	Clarke, Vernon Forster
1955-1956	Essential Services Corps	Commissioner, Essential Services Corps	Rowe, George Tippett
1956-1957	Essential Services Corps	Commissioner, Essential Services Corps	Alexander, David Richard Watson
1957-1960	Essential Services Corps	Commissioner, Essential Services Corps and Director of Manpower	Coyne, John Flanders
1952-1953	Manpower Directorate	Director of Manpower	Finne, John
1954-1956	Manpower Directorate	Director of Manpower	Gumbleton, Albert Ernest
1957	Manpower Directorate	Director of Manpower	Clarke, Vernon Forster
1957-1960	Manpower Directorate	Commissioner, Essential Services Corps and Director of Manpower	Coyne, John Flanders
1960-1964	Essential Services Corps and Directorate of Manpower	Commissioner, Essential Services Corps and Director of Manpower	Bruce, Ian Denhola

Year	Name of Department	Title	Name of Director
1964-1972	Essential Services Corps and Directorate of Manpower	Commissioner, Essential Services Corps and Director of Manpower	Hillard, John Lambton
1972-1975	Essential Services Corps and Directorate of Manpower	Commissioner, Essential Services Corps and Director of Manpower	Higgins, John Anthony

Sources:
1. *The Hong Kong Civil Service List,* Hong Kong Government, 1947-1958.
2. *Staff List Hong Kong Government,* Hong Kong, Government Printer, 1959-1975.

Government Flying Service (1993-2002)

1993   The Government Flying Service (GFS) superseded the Royal Hong Kong Auxiliary Air Force on April 1 and became a full-time disciplined service. Operating in accordance with civil aviation rules, it provided 24-hour emergency air ambulance, search and rescue services, as well as flying services to various government departments. The GFS was organized into four sections: Administration, Engineering, Flying and Supplies.

1997   The GFS supported the Hong Kong Police Force in law enforcement duties, assisted the Fire Services Department by water-bombing hill fires, and carried out aerial mapping and surveys for the Lands Department.

2000   The GFS launched an Air Medical Officer Programme to enhance its emergency air medical service. This programme provided a higher level of medical care to the injured right on the spot and during transit to hospital.

2002   The GFS was sections into four sections: Administration, Quality, Engineering and Flying. The Administration Section was responsible for central administration and it also provided personnel supporting services. The Quality Section was charged with the maintenance of airworthiness standards, flight standards, flight safety and quality assurance. The Engineering Section was concerned with in-house maintenance and the servicing of all aircraft and related aircraft and ground equipment. The Flying Section undertook all flying tasks required by the Government which included specialized support to the Hong Kong Police Force, emergency medical evacuation, internal security, search and rescue operations both offshore and locally, airborne fire-fighting, aerial surveys, radio frequency interference surveys etc.

Sources:

1. *Hong Kong A New Era*, Hong Kong Government Printer, 1997, p.294.
2. *Hong Kong Government Telephone Directory 1993*, Hong Kong, Government Printer, 1994, p.198.
3. *Hong Kong*, Hong Kong, Government Printer, 1994-2000.
4. www.info.gov.hk/gfs/

Government Flying Service — Changes in Directors			
Year	Name of Department	Title	Name of Director
1993-1996	Government Flying Service	Controller, Government Flying Service	Cluter, Christopher Brian
1996-2002	Government Flying Service	Controller, Government Flying Service	Butt, Yiu-ming, Brian

Sources:
1. *Staff Biographies Hong Kong Government*, Hong Kong, Government Printer, 1993-1996.
2. *Staff Biographies the Government of the Hong Kong Special Administrative Region*, Hong Kong, Government Printer, 1997-2001.
3. *Staff List Hong Kong Government*, Hong Kong, Government Printer, 1993-1996.
4. *Staff List the Government of the Hong Kong Special Administrative Region*, Hong Kong, Government Printer, 1997-2000.
5. www.info.gov.hk/gfs/

Auxiliary Medical Services (1950-1997)
Auxiliary Medical Service (1997-2002)

1950   The Auxiliary Medical Services (AMS) was established on May 22 under the Essential Services Corps regulations as a Medical Civil Defence Unit. The Director of Medical and Health Services was the Unit Controller of the AMS. Its members included professional doctors, nurses and trained volunteers. The major duties of the AMS were broadly divided into emergency and regular duties. Emergency duties included the provision of first aid, casualty evacuation and support duties at major disaster sites such as fires, flooding, landslides and other accidents; the operation of emergency medical centres; the reinforcement of casualty-clearing hospitals and clinics with personnel and emergency supplies; and the reinforcement of regular ambulance services. Regular duties included the provision of training courses for AMS members, the conduct of annual regional field exercises to prepare for natural disasters, and the setting up of first aid posts.

1959   The AMS was divided into three parts: General Office, AMS Store Officers and Civil Defence Staff, Training.

1970   The AMS extended its scope of services and recruited more full-time training staff to provide additional services that included the organization of seminars, exhibitions, school talks and demonstrations to spread the message of home safety, accident prevention and health education. The Training Section offered a wide range of training to volunteer members as well as civil servants in various governmental departments. The Transport Division was created to control the ambulance service and the Auxiliary Band was set up.

1975   The AMS provided round-the-clock services at the clinics set up in various refugee camps. Its duties included dispensing, manning of milk kitchens, nursing, patient enrolment and other related clinical duties.

1983   The AMS became an independent government department under the Security Branch of the Government Secretariat. The Director of Medical and Health Services, serving a dual role as head of the regular health services and medical auxiliaries (in a volunteer capacity), was the ex officio Commissioner of AMS. The Chief Staff Officer of the Headquarters was responsible for its daily operations and reported to the Commissioner. The AMS consisted of two parts: Government Section and Volunteer Section.

1986   Volunteer service was carried out on a geographical basis, which had three regions and 18 districts. Each region or district was under the control of a Regional Commander or a District Commander respectively. Each district had four teams of auxiliary nurses and auxiliary dressers.

　　　　1.　The Hong Kong Training Centre was divided into five districts: Central and Eastern District, Wanchai District, Eastern District, South-Eastern District and Island District.

　　　　2.　The Kowloon Regional Headquarters included six districts: Kowloon City District, Kwun Tong District, Mong Kok District, Sham Shui Po District, Wong Tai Sin District and Yau Ma Tei District.

3.   The New Territories Headquarters contained seven districts: Sha Tin District, Northern/Tai Po District, Tsuen Wan District, Tuen Mun District, Yuen Long District, Sai Kung District and Kwai Chung/Tsing Yi District.

1988   The AMS participated in the early batches of repatriation of Vietnamese refugees.

1989   The first batch of AMS personnel attended disaster management training at the Asian Institute of Technology in Thailand.

1990   The Government Section of AMS was restructured into: Headquarters, Regional Headquarters, Refugee Section, Operation Section, Civil Servant Training Section, Departmental Administration Section and Supplies Section. The Volunteer Section was divided into three parts: Operations, Medical, Administration and Operations.

1991   The Clinic and Hospital Team of the Government Section was established.

1992   The Emergency Response Task Force under the volunteer services was established to provide on-the-spot paramedic services. This special squad was available on a 24-hour basis to respond to emergency calls.

1993   The AMS members visited the Beijing Emergency Centre. This marked the first step in establishing intellectual exchanges between Hong Kong and their Chinese counterparts in the disaster medicine field.

1995   The Volunteer Section of the AMS was restructured into: Headquarters Column, Operations Wing, Hospital Wing, Resource Column and Logistics Wing. The Operations Wing was responsible for first aid, casualty evacuations, ambulance services and operation of emergency medical centres. The Hospital Wing acted as buffers for casualty-clearing hospitals by treating the lightly injured and accepting casualties from the site of incidents. It also acted as general dispensaries or clinics for the general public living in the vicinity. The Logistics Wing supervised the 24-hour enquiry hotline through an interactive voice response system and provided necessary logistic support.

1996   The Government Section of the AMS was reorganized into: Administration Division, Operation and Training Division.

1997   The name was changed from Auxiliary Medical Services to Auxiliary Medical Service.

2000   Structure of the AMS (Government Section):

I.   Administration Division

II.   Operation and Training Division

   1. Civil Service Training and Administration Section
   2. Clinics and Hospitals Section
   3. Operation Section
   4. Special Duties Section
   5. Supplies Section
   6. Ambulance Section

Structure of the AMS (Volunteer Section):

I.   Headquarters Column

II.   Operations Wing

1. Hong Kong Island Region
2. Kowloon Region
3. New Territories Region
4. Service Training Branch
5. Emergency Response Task Force
6. Ambulance Section

III. Hospital Wing

1. Training and Development Branch
2. Medical Branch
3. Nursing Branch
4. Paramedic Branch
5. Dressing Stations
6. Casualty Clearing Hospital
7. Convalescent Units

IV. Resource Column

V. Logistics Wing

1. Welfare and Liaison Branch
2. General Support Branch
3. Non-Emergency Ambulance Transfer Service
4. Transport
5. General Store
6. General Administration

2002   The AMS Volunteer Section was structured into four major parts: Headquarters (Headquarters Column), Operations (Operations Wings 1 and 2), Human Resource (Training and Development Column, Medical and Paramedic Column), Logistics and Support (Logistics and Support Column). The Director of Health was the ex officio Commissioner of the AMS.

Sources:

1. *Auxiliary Medical Services for 40th Anniversary*, Hong Kong, Government Printer, 1991, pp.12-23.
2. Auxiliary *Medical Services for 45th Anniversary*, Hong Kong, Government Printer, 1995, pp. 17-49.
3. *The Government of the Hong Kong Special Administrative Region Telephone Directory*, Hong Kong, Government Printer, 1997-2000.
4. *Hong Kong Annual Departmental Report by the Director of Medical and Health Services*, Hong Kong, Government Printer, 1954, pp.1-8, 89.
5. *Hong Kong Government Telephone Directory*, Hong Kong, Government Printer, 1959-1996.
6. www.info.gov.hk/ams/

Auxiliary Medical Service — Changes in Names and Directors

Year ·	Name of Department	Title	Name of Director
1950-1952	Auxiliary Medical Services	Unit Controller	Newton, Isaac
1952-1958	Auxiliary Medical Services	Unit Controller	Yeo, Kok-cheang
1958-1963	Auxiliary Medical Services	Unit Controller	MacKenzie, David James Masterton
1963-1970	Auxiliary Medical Services	Unit Controller	Teng, Pin-hui
1970-1976	Auxiliary Medical Services	Unit Controller	Choa, Gerald Hugh
1976-1982	Auxiliary Medical Services	Unit Controller	Thong, Kah-leong
1982-1988	Auxiliary Medical Services	Commissioner of Auxiliary Medical Services	Thong, Kah-leong
1988-1994	Auxiliary Medical Services	Commissioner of Auxiliary Medical Services	Lee, Shiu-hung
1994-1997	Auxiliary Medical Services	Commissioner of Auxiliary Medical Services	Chan Fung, Fu-chun, Margaret
1997-2002	Auxiliary Medical Service	Commossioner of Auxiliary Medical Service	Chan Fung, Fu-chun, Margaret

Sources:

1. *Auxiliary Medical Services for 40th Anniversary*, Hong Kong, Government Printer, 1990.
2. *Auxiliary Medical Services for 45th Anniversary*, Hong Kong, Government Printer, 1995.
3. *Civil and Miscellaneous Lists Hong Kong Government*, Hong Kong, Government Printer, 1982; 1989; 1996.
4. *The Hong Kong Civil Service List*, Hong Kong Government, 1950-1957.
5. *Staff List Hong Kong Government*, Hong Kong, Government Printer, 1959-1963.
6. www.info.gov.hk/ams/

Chapter 4
Infrastructure and Construction

Headquarters Drawing Staff, Royal Engineers, HK, 1909

Opening of the British Section of Kowloon-Canton Railway, 1910

Evolvement of Infrastructure and Construction

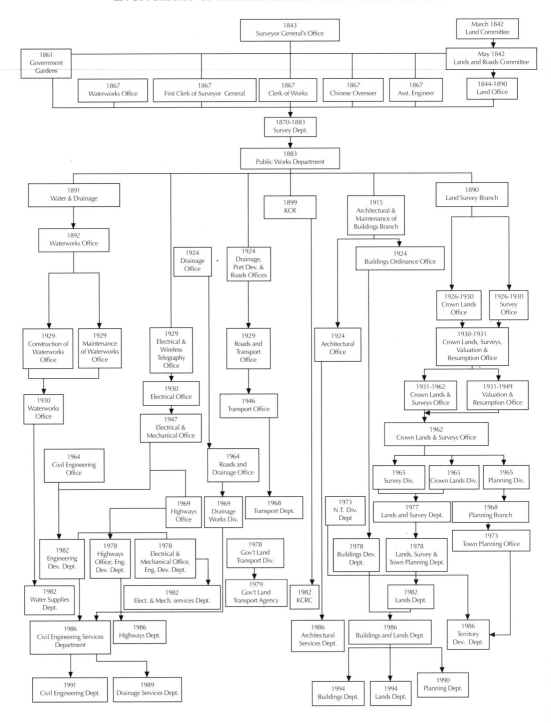

The development of the City of Victoria since the second half of the nineteenth century relied mainly on the pace of construction and infrastructure work of the Government, for the Colony was lacking in natural resources and faced continuously increasing population pressures. As builders of the urban Hong Kong, the establishment history of construction-related government departments reflected the urbanization process of Hong Kong. Their organizational evolution can be divided into four stages.

The first stage, 1843-1883, starting with the nomination of the Surveyor General and ending in the foundation of the Public Works Department, was related to the establishment of the City of Victoria. The second stage, 1883-1941, covered the period up to the Japanese invasion of Hong Kong; it was the period of systemization of construction works. The third stage, 1946-1982, involved post-war restoration works and culminated in the restructuring of the Public Works Department; this was the era of urban expansion from Hong Kong Island and New Kowloon to the New Territories. The fourth stage, 1982-2002, spanned the period from the independence of individual construction departments to the present day, signified the glamour of the metropolitan city through its immense construction and new architectural works.

The Surveyor General, appointed in 1843, was not only responsible for basic infrastructure construction works of the City of Victoria; he also managed the major sources of revenue of the Colony through land registrations and land auctions. During the second half of the nineteenth century, financial capability defined the pace of construction work and quality. The major construction works concentrated on areas where the primitive City of Victoria was in urgent need: roads and streets, public buildings, markets, piers and wharfs. Expenditure on public works and building represented over 46% of total

expenditure of the Colonial Government in 1845 and exceeded 30% from 1844 to 1883. The Surveyor General's Office functioned with a few engineers and under ten permanent supporting staff. Engineers had to undertake various construction-related duties that did not necessarily correspond to their professional fields. The early urban development pace moved in a rather limited and slow rhythm.

Construction workload increased tremendously due to rapid growth in population and commercial activities. To deal with worsening public hygiene, the Public Works Department was established in 1883. Emphases were placed on drainage, water provision and fundamental construction works. From 1883 to 1940, the number of works offices grew steadily to between ten and fourteen offices. The principal offices included the Accounts and Stores Office; Architectural Office; Buildings Ordinance Office; Crown Lands, Surveys and Valuation and Resumption Office; Drainage Office; Electrical Office; General Works Office; Port Development Office; Roads Office; and Waterworks Office. Most of the offices remained functional until 1939. Through the continued existence of these construction works offices, one can deduce that the organization was oriented towards the installation of modern infrastructural facilities in Hong Kong. More professional engineers were hired from England and other countries. Expenditure on public works still represented a high proportion of the total expenditure; it varied between 20% and 40% each year. The basic structure of the works departments in the early twentieth century had laid the foundation for further development of Hong Kong.

The emergency post-war restoration works and the unexpected population growth due to massive inflows from Mainland China were the driving force behind the expansion of the Public Works Department. Numerous new offices were established during late 1940s. The major responsibilities of the Public Works Department were on buildings and lands, communications, engineering and water. New ideas such as town planning, mass communications and more than construction of transport networks were strongly stressed. By 1969, the Public Works Department had more than 10,500 staff. Each construction works office possessed comprehensive facilities that were well equipped for vast and immediate development works. The redundancy of subordinate sections appeared to be the reason behind frequent combinations and abolitions of various works offices. Important construction works done during this period had focused on new town areas, and the construction of new transport and communications facilities, such as the expansion of Kai Tak airport and the building of highways.

In 1982, the Public Works Department was transformed into the Lands and Works Branch, the policy maker responsible for nine independent works departments. Each of these departments was fully equipped with comprehensive facilities. The rapid growth pace of the city reflected their work. Construction works no longer had to face financial constraints. Although the government spent generously on construction works, it only represented around 10% of the total expenditure from 1982 to 2000. The Government was much more financially endowed compared to the nineteenth century. In 1989 The Lands and Works Branch was reorganized and spilt into two branches: Planning, Environment and Lands; and Works. The former continued to be under the control of the Government Secretariat while the latter was transferred to the Department of Finance. In 2002, prior to July1, there were 13 works departments under the direction of three different bureaux: Planning and Lands (four departments), Transport (two departments) and Works (seven departments).

Planning and Development

Surveyor General's Office (1843-1870)
Survey Department (1870-1883)
Public Works Department (1883-1982)

1843   The post of Surveyor General was created with a salary of £1,000 per annum.

1844   The Surveyor General was nominated officially on May 9.

1852   The Surveyor General was responsible for the development planning and inspection of construction of the City of Victoria.

1854   The Market Ordinance of 1854 ordained the Surveyor General to approve the construction and reconstruction of markets. The Surveyor General was also responsible for the letting and sale of land.

1856   The major duties of the Surveyor General's Office included the supervision of building construction, public lighting erection and nuisance prevention of the City of Victoria according to the Buildings and Nuisances Ordinance of 1856.

1860   Construction work planning comprised Bowring Praya, Ice House Road Pier, Pedder's Wharf, Pokfulam Reservoir, and the reclamation of praya in front of Pedder's Wharf.

1861   A Superintendent of Government Gardens under the supervision of Surveyor General was nominated.

1862   The Surveyor General's Office was responsible for the construction of roads, streets, drains, markets, nullahs, praya, bridges, piers, public buildings, planning and preparation of land sale.

1867   Duties of the Surveyor General's Office were mainly distributed through six subdepartments: First Clerk of Surveyor General, Clerk of Works, Public Gardens Branch, Waterworks Branch, Chinese Overseer and Assistant Engineer. The Surveyor General ensured that the provisions of the building ordinances were strictly carried out; executed surveys or drawings that required quantity specifications; superintended public works; and examined the daily reports of subordinate departments. The First Clerk of Surveyor General was in charge of the Land Office that registered all transfers of landed properties; collected burial and monumental and deed registry fees; and superintended the official correspondence of the Office. The Clerk of Works was responsible for the construction and repairs of public buildings, drains and streets in the City of Victoria; and the provision of daily reports on all works and quarterly reports on the state of repairs. The Public Gardens Branch managed public gardens and superintended the planting of trees. It prepared monthly reports on the state of the public gardens; kept daily labour books; and provided monthly requisitions for flowers and tools. The Waterworks Branch superintended waterworks; took charge of water services in the event of fire; provided daily reports of duties performed; weekly reports on supplies to public hydrants; and monthly reports on general waterworks. The Chinese Overseer superintended the repairs of all roads and drains on Hong Kong Island; repaired police stations and schools in villages; marked out grounds under the direction of the Surveyor General for Chinese Crown tenants; assisted in surveying; and prepared daily reports of duties performed. The Assistant Engineer was in charge of the sea walls and reclamation, and prepared returns of squatter licences for houses and land in Kowloon.

1870   The Surveyor General's Office became known as Survey Department.

1879   The Public Gardens Branch's duties were transferred out of the Department and the Government Gardens and Plantations Department was formed.

1883   The Survey Department was renamed Public Works Department.

1891   The Surveyor General changed his title to Director of Public Works. The Department consisted of: Inspection of Buildings, Praya Reclamation, Public Works, Public Recurrent, Land Survey Branch, Squatters, Staff — a total of seven administrative units.

1903   The passing of the Public Health and Building Amendment and Consolidation

Ordinance of 1903 affected the duties and responsibilities of the Public Works Department. The Director of Public Works, as a member of the Sanitary Board, supervised the improvement of permanent sanitary conditions in Hong Kong.

1915   The Department comprised: Accounts, Correspondence and Stores, Architectual and Maintenance of Buildings Ordinance, Crown Lands and Surveys, Public Health and Waterworks, and General Staff — a total of seven subdepartments.

1924   A new subdepartment by the name of Port Development was established on August 14. The Department was divided into eight administrative units: Administration of the Buildings Ordinance, Architecture, Drainage, Electrical, General Works, Port Development, Roads and Waterworks.

1929   The Public Works Department consisted of 14 offices: Accounts and Stores; Administrative Staff and Correspondence; Architectural and Maintenance of Buildings; Buildings Ordinance; Construction of Waterworks; Crown Lands; Drainage; Electrical and Wireless Telegraphy; General Works; Maintenance of Waterworks; Port Works; Roads and Transport; Surveys; and Valuation and Resumption. There were 156 European officers and 535 non-European staff in the Department.

1930   The Department was restructured into: Head Office; Accounts and Stores Office; Architectural Office; Buildings Ordinance Office; Crown Lands, Surveys and Valuation and Resumption Office; Drainage Office; Electrical Office; General Works Office; Port Development Office; Roads Office; and Waterworks Office. The basic structure of the Department remained unchanged until 1939.

1946   The Department resumed its pre-war duties.

1947   The Department was organized into a headquarters and eight offices. The Headquarters comprised the Accounts Office, Administration Office, Town Planning Office and Valuation and Resumption Office. The eight Offices were: Architectural, Buildings Ordinance, Crown Lands and Surveys, Drainage, Electrical and Mechanical, Port Works, Roads, Waterworks. The Electrical and Mechanical Office was a combination of the Electrical Office and the Transport Office. It supervised all electrical, transport and mechanical equipment and plants within the Department.

1949   The Headquarters was under the direction of the Director, who was assisted by a Deputy Director, an Assistant Director (Engineering), an Assistant Director (Buildings), a Secretary and a Senior Accountant. The Assistant Director (Engineering) directed the Architectural Office while the Assistant Director (Buildings) supervised the Buildings Ordinance Office. The Deputy Director controlled the Waterworks Office, the Crown Lands and Surveys Office and the Town Planning Office. The Valuation and Resumption Office was absorbed into the Crown Lands and Surveys Office.

1951   The Town Planning Office was dissolved.

1953   The Crown Lands and Surveys Office took over all town planning matters and a new post of Assistant Superintendent of Crown Lands was created.

1958   The Development Office was established in March to respond to rapid and large-scale development of Crown land and reclaimed land.

1961   The work of the Department was divided into three spheres of responsibilities-buildings and land, communications, and water.

1962   The three major spheres of responsibilities were buildings and land,
        engineering and water. The Crown Lands and Surveys Office changed its
        name to Crown Lands and Survey Office.

1964   The Offices of Roads, Drainage, Port Works and Development were merged to form
        the new Civil Engineering Office. The Civil Engineering Office was responsible for
        roads, drainage, port works, major reclamation and traffic engineering works. The
        Department comprised six offices: Architectural, Buildings Ordinance, Civil
        Engineering, Crown Lands and Survey, Electrical and Mechanical, and Waterworks.

1965   The Department was headed by the Director of Public Works and comprised four
        main sections which were further subdivided into six technical offices. The Director
        of Engineering Services headed the section which included the Civil Engineering
        Office and the Electrical and Mechanical Office. He was in charge of port works,
        roads, drainage, sewage disposal, land development, traffic engineering, and
        electrical and mechanical engineering. The Director of Building Services headed the
        section that included the Architectural Office and the Buildings Ordinance Office.
        He was responsible for the design and construction of government buildings and
        control of private developments. The Director of Water Supplies headed the section
        that comprised the Waterworks Office. He supervised the design and construction of
        water impounding and purification works and distribution. The Superintendent of
        Crown Lands and Survey headed the Crown Lands and Survey Office and was in
        charge of the disposal of Crown land, survey and town planning.

1969   Staff numbered more than 10,500, of which 628 were professional or assistant
        professional officers. The Highways Office was established on September 1 to
        plan, construct, and maintain public roads, bridges, associated sewerage and
        drainage systems. It also collected and analyzed all data relating to passenger
        transport. With the newly created Highways Office, the Department consisted
        of seven offices: Architectural, Buildings Ordinance, Civil Engineering, Crown
        Lands and Survey, Electrical and Mechanical, Highways and Waterworks.

1973   The Public Works Department was made up of four main sections (buildings,
        engineering, land and water) which were further subdivided into six technical
        subdepartments: Buildings Development, Engineering Development, Lands and
        Survey, New Territories Development, Water Supplies and Mass Transit Studies.
        The Town Planning Office was re-established to formulate town planning policies
        and to co-ordinate all activities related to town and country planning. The New
        Territories Development Department was established on August 1 and took over
        responsibility for the planning and co-ordination of development for the three
        new towns at Sha Tin, Tuen Mun and Tsuen Wan and the New Territories rural
        centres. The Mass Transit Unit under the Highways Office became an
        independent office: Mass Transit Studies Office. It was responsible for the
        administration and co-ordination of all matters related to mass transit services.

1977   A new Geotechnical Control Office was formed to investigate the safety of
        natural and man-made slopes. The Crown Lands and Survey Office was
        renamed Lands and Survey Department.

1978   The Department was reorganized into five subdepartments: Buildings

Development; Engineering Development; Lands, Survey and Town Planning; New Territories Development; Water Supplies. The Buildings Development Department controlled the Architectural Office and Buildings Ordinance Office. The Engineering Development Department supervised the Civil Engineering Office, Highways Office, Electrical and Mechanical Office, and Geotechnical Control Office. The Lands, Survey and Town Planning Department administered the Crown Lands and Survey Office and the Town Planning Office. The New Territories Development Department co-ordinated the New Town Development Offices at Sha Tin, Tsuen Wan, Tuen Mun and the New Territories Development Branch. The Director of the Water Supplies Department controlled the Waterworks Office.

1982   The Public Works Department was abolished. Its subordinate departments — Buildings Development; Electrical and Mechanical Services; Engineering Development; Lands, Survey and Town Planning and Water Supplies — became independent departments. The above departments were under the Lands and Works Branch. In addition to its policy setting responsibility. The Lands and Works Branch also oversaw the planning and development of public works programmes, and co-ordinated and monitored their progress.

Sources:

1. *150 Years of Public Works Foundation for the Future*, Hong Kong, Government Printer, 1994.
2. *Annual Departmental Report by the Director of Public Works*, Hong Kong, Government Printer, 1952-1977.
3. Braga, J.M., *Hong Kong Business Symposium: A Compilation of Authorative View on Administration and Resources of Britain Far Eastern Outpost*, Hong Kong, South China Morning Post, 1957.
4. *CO129/126* no 190 of Nov 1867; *CO129/150* no 7598-7, 1 May 1871; *CO129/244*, 15 Feb 1890; *CO129/422* no.206, 29 May 1915; *CO129/484*, 12 July 1924.
5. Organisation and Methods Branch, Colonial Secretariat, *Report on Public Works Department, Organisation, Methods and Staff Survey*, Government of Hong Kong, 1949.
6. *Hong Kong*, Hong Kong, Government Printer, 1978-1982.
7. *Hong Kong Annual Report by the Director of Public Works*, Hong Kong, Government Printer, 1950.
8. *Hong Kong Government Gazette*, Hong Kong Government, 17 Jan. 1852, p.18; 15 July 1854, pp.163-164; 29 Mar.1856, no.39, vol. 1; 14 June 1856, p.5; 4 Feb.1860, p.20; 8 Dec 1860, p. 264; 22 Feb.1862, p.54; 23 Oct 1863, p.282; 12 Dec 1863, p.363; 2 May 1891, pp.351-353; 19 Mar 1892.
9. *Report of the Director of Public Works*, Hong Kong Government, 1946-1949.
10. Public Works Department, *Public Works Department - Organization and Functions*, Hong Kong, Government Printer, 1978.
11. Town Planning Office, Planning Department, *50th Anniversary of the Planning Department (1947-1997)*, Hong Kong, Government Printer, 1998.

Public Works Department — Changes in Names and Directors

Year	Name of Department	Title	Name of Director
1842	Land and Road Committee	Inspector of Road	Raynolds, Glascot Eward
1842	Land Office	Land Officer	Mylius, George F.
1843-1844	Land Office	Land Officer	Gordon, Alexander Thomas
1844-1845	Surveyor General's Office	Surveyor General	Gordon, Alexander Thomas
1845-1865	Surveyor General's Office	Surveyor General	Cleverly, Charles St. George
1865-1868	Surveyor General's Office	Surveyor General	Wiberforce, Wilson
1868-1870	Surveyor General's Office	Surveyor General	Moorsom, Lewis Henry
1870-1873	Survey Department	Surveyor General	Moorsom, Lewis Henry
1873-1883	Survey Department	Surveyor General	Price, John MacNeile
1883-1889	Public Works Department	Surveyor General	Price, John MacNeile
1889-1891	Public Works Department	Surveyor General	Brown, Samuel
1891-1897	Public Works Department	Director of Public Works	Cooper, Francis Alfred
1897-1901	Public Works Department	Director of Public Works	Ormsby, Robert Daly
1901-1921	Public Works Department	Director of Public Works	Chatham, William
1921-1923	Public Works Department	Director of Public Works	Perkins, Thomas Luff
1923-1932	Public Works Departmen	Director of Public Works	Creasy, Harold Thomas
1932-1939	Public Works Department	Director of Public Works	Henderson, Richard McNeil
1939-1941	Public Works Department	Director of Public Works	Purves, Alexander Bruce
1946-1949	Public Works Department	Director of Public Works	Kenniff, Victor
1949-1950	Public Works Department	Director of Public Works	Boyce, Edward Audley

Year	Name of Department	Title	Name of Director
1950-1957	Public Works Department	Director of Public Works	Bowring, Theodore Louis
1957-1963	Public Works Department	Director of Public Works	Inglis, Allan
1963-1969	Public Works Department	Director of Public Works	Wright, Alec Michael John
1969-1974	Public Works Department	Director of Public Works	Robson, James Jeavons
1974-1982	Public Works Department	Director of Public Works	McDonald, David Wylie

Sources:
1. *Hong Kong Blue Book,* Hong Kong, Noronha & Co, 1844-1939.
2. Hamilton, G. C., *Government Departments in Hong Kong 1841-1969*, Hong Kong, Government Printer, 1969, p.52
3. *The Hong Kong Civil Service List 1948*, Hong Kong Government, 1948.
4. *The Hong Kong Civil Service List*, Hong Kong Government, 1950; 1952; 1957.
5. *Staff List Hong Kong Government*, Hong Kong, Government Printer, 1963; 1969; 1974.

Town Planning Office, Public Works Department (1947-1951)
Town Planning Division, Crown Lands and Surveys/Survey Office, Public Works Department (1953-1968)
Planning Branch, Crown Lands and Survey Office, Public Works Department (1968-1973)
Town Planning Office, Public Works Department (1973-1982)
Town Planning Office, Lands Department (1982-1986)
Town Planning Office, Buildings and Lands Department (1986-1989)
Planning Department (1990-2002)

1947   The Town Planning Office under the Headquarters of the Public Works Department was first established on April 1 to prepare land utilization plans, detailed zoning plans, layouts for land reclamation, and the industrial layouts for Tsuen Wan and Kwun Tong. It also gave advice to district officers with layouts for new markets in the New Territories.

1951   The Town Planning Office was dissolved.

1953   In January 1953, a new post of Assistant Superintendent of Crown Lands (Planning) was created within the Crown Lands and Surveys Office of the Public Works Department to supervise all town planning matters.

1965   The Planning Division of the Crown Lands and Survey Office (name changed from Crown Lands and Surveys Office in 1962) prepared outline plans, outline zonings, development plans and population distribution forecasts; it was responsible for the scrutiny of public and private development projects.

1968   The Planning Division was expanded into Planning Branch; it comprised two divisions: District Planning Division and Colony Outline Planning Division. The District Planning Division prepared draft plans, departmental layout plans and reserved sites for government and community use. The Colony Outline Planning Division revised land use plans, conducted structural and sample surveys, and prepared Hong Kong's outline plan.

1973   The Planning Branch was expanded into The Town Planning Office. It was responsible for the formulation of town planning policies, the establishment of planning standards and co-ordination of all activities related to town and country planning. It consisted of the District Planning Branch and the Colony Planning Division.

1978   The Public Works Department was restructured into five main subdepartments. The Town Planning Office was subordinated to the Lands, Survey and Town Planning Department.

1982   The Public Works Department was abolished. The Town Planning Office was subordinated to the newly established Lands Department, whcih was transformed from Lands, Survey and Town Planning Department.

1986   The Lands Department was transformed into Buildings and Lands Department.

1990   The Planning Department was established on January 1, through the amalgamation of the Town Planning Office of the Buildings and Lands Department and the various district planning sections of the Territory Development Department. The organization of the Department was as follows:

I.   Territorial and Subregional Planning Branch

    1. Territorial and Subregional Planning Division
    2. Transport Studies
    3. Central Data Section
    4. Planning and Development Strategy Section

II.   District Planning Branch

    1. Town Planning Board and Design Division
    2. Metro District Planning Division
    3. New Territories District Planning Division
    4. Town Planning Ordinance Review Division

III.   Departmental Administration Division

1995   The Housing and Land Supply Division was established in February to co-ordinate the planning and provision of housing land to meet forecast demand and ensure timely delivery of identified housing sites.

1996   The Territorial and Subregional Planning Branch was reorganized with effect from January 29, 1996. It consisted of two divisions: Territorial and Subregional Planning Division, Housing and Land Supply Division. The Town

Planning Ordinance Review Division of the District Planning Branch was renamed Ordinance Review and Technical Administration Division.

1997   Restructuring of the District Planning Branch: the Town Planning Board and Design Division was renamed Board Division; the Ordinance Review and Technical Administration Division became Technical Services Division.

2002   The structure of the Department remained basically the same. Under the District Planning Branch, there was an additional division: Urban Renewal Division. The Urban Renewal Division assumed overall responsibilities on urban renewal matters, in particular on the implementation of the urban renewal policy which was published in 1996.

Sources:

1.   *Planning Department Annual Report*, Hong Kong, Government Printer, 1995, pp.7-8; 1996, pp. 8-10; 1997, p.58; 1998, pp.12-13.
2.   www.info.gov.hk/planning/index_e.htm

	Planning Department — Changes in Directors		
Year	Name of Department	Title	Name of Director
1990-1991	Planning Department	Director of Planning	Upton, Robert Ian William
1991-1999	Planning Department	Director of Planning	Pun, Kwok-shing
1999-2002	Planning Department	Director of Planning	Fung, Chee-keung, Bosco

Sources:
1.   *Staff Biographies Hong Kong Government*, Hong Kong, Government Printer, 1986, 1988, 1990, 1993.
2.   *Staff Biographies the Government of the Hong Kong Special Administrative Region*, Hong Kong, Government Printer, 2001.
3.   *Staff List Hong Kong Government*, Hong Kong, Government Printer, 1989-1996.
4.   www.info.gov.hk/planing/index_e.htm

New Territories Development Department, Public Works Department (1973-1982)
New Territories Development, Lands and Works Branch (1982-1986)
Territory Development Department (1986-2002)

1973   The New Territories Development Department was established on August 1 to take over the responsibilities for the planning and co-ordination of development for the three new towns at Sha Tin, Tuen Mun and Tsuen Wan; and the New Territories rural centres; with Project Managers appointed at each of the new towns.

1986 The New Territories Development Department and the Urban Area Development Organization of the Lands and Works Branch under the Government Secretariat were merged to form the Territory Development Department. The Department consisted of the Headquarters and six regional development offices: Sha Tin Development Office (covering Sha Tin and Ma On Shan); North East New Territories Development Office (covering Tai Po, Fanling, Sha Tau Kok and Pak Shek Kok); Tsuen Wan Development Office (covering Tsuen Wan, Kwai Chung, Sham Tseng and Tsing Yi); North West New Territories Development Office (covering Tuen Mun, Yuen Long and Tin Shui Wai); South New Territories Development Office (covering Junk Bay, Sai Kung and Island); and Urban Area Development Office (covering Hong Kong Island, Kowloon and New Kowloon). The Headquarters oversaw the work of the six Development Offices. The Development Offices were responsible for all engineering, district town planning, building and landscaping related to development in their areas; and co-ordination with other government departments on public housing, transport and community facilities.

1988 The North West New Territories Development Office was spilt into two offices: Tuen Mun Development Office, Tin Shui Wai and Yuen Long Development Office. The Tuen Mun Development Office focused on works associated with the Light Rail Transit System while the Tin Shui Wai and Yuen Long Development Office oversaw the development works in Yuen Long Town, and the rural areas of Sha Tin, Kam Tin, Ping Shan, Lau Fau Shan and Hung Shui Kiu.

1990 The Sha Tin Development Office was integrated with the North East New Territories Development Office. The Tin Shui Wai and Yuen Long Development Office was retitled North West New Territories Development Office. The South New Territories Development Office was spilt into two offices: South East New Territories Development Office (covering Tsueng Kwan O and Sai Kung) and South West Development Office (covering North Lantau and the rural areas in the Island Districts such as Tung Chung, Cheung Chau, Peng Chau, Mui Wo and Tai O).

1994 The regional development offices were restructured into five : Hong Kong Island and Islands; Kowloon; New Territories North (covering Yuen Long, Tai Po, Fanling, Sheung Shui and Sha Tau Kok); New Territories East (covering Sha Tin, Ma On Shan, Tseung Kwan O and Sai Kung); and New Territories West (covering Tsuen Wan, Kwai Chung, Tsing Yi, Stonecutters Island and Tuen Mun).

2002 The structure of the Department remained unchanged, with a Headquarters and five Development Offices.

Sources:

1. Public Records Office, Administrative History Folder, No.73.
2. www.info.gov.hk/tdd/

Territory Development Department — Changes in Directors			
Year	Name of Department	Title	Name of Director
1986-1989	Territory Development Department	Director of Territory Development	Kwok, Wai-kai, Kenneth
1989-1993	Territory Development Department	Director of Territory Development	Nip, Kam-fan
1993-1994	Territory Development Department	Director of Territory Development	Chow, Che-king
1994-2000	Territory Development Department	Director of Territory Development	Lee, Shing-see
2000-2002	Territory Development Department	Director of Territory Development	Wong, Hung-kin, James

Sources:
1. *Staff Biographies Hong Kong Government,* Hong Kong, Government Printer, 1986, 1988, 1990, 1993.
2. *Staff Biographies the Government of the Hong Kong Special Administrative Region,* Hong Kong, Government Printer,1998, 2001.
3. *Staff List Hong Kong Government,* Hong Kong, Government Printer, 1986-96.
4. www.info.gov.hk/tdd/

Land and Architectural Development

Architectural and Maintenance of Buildings Branch, Public Works Department (1915-1924)
Architectural Office, Public Works Department (1924-1982)
Architectural Office, Buildings Development Department (1982-1986)
Architectural Services Department (1986-2002)

1915   The Public Works Department was restructured. The Architectural and Maintenance of Buildings Branch was first established.

1924   The Architectural and Maintenance of Buildings Branch was retitled Architectural Office. It undertook the design, preparation of work drawings, specifications and quantities and construction of all new government buildings and quarters; and was responsible for the improvements and maintenance of all existing government buildings.

1946   The Architectural Office resumed its pre-war duties. It prepared designs and estimates for building projects; approved schemes to proceed with detailed planning and preparation of contracts; supervised the construction and maintenance of buildings.

1965   The Public Works Department was reorganized. The Director of Building Services headed the Architectural Office and the Buildings Ordinance Office. The Architectural Office comprised five divisions. The Architectural Division (Hong Kong, Kowloon and New Territories) was in charge of the overall supervision and control of building works under construction. The Structural Engineering Division provided general advice on the structural of buildings. The Quantity Surveying Division prepared estimates, specifications and bills of quantities for building works, contracts, and payments of accounts for building works. The Building Services Division was responsible for the design and installation of electrical and air-conditioning services in buildings. The Maintenance Division was in charge of the maintenance of existing buildings.

1966   The Office was also responsible for the construction and maintenance of the majority of buildings used by the British Armed Forces.

1970   All divisions, except the Architectural Division (Hong Kong, Kowloon and New Territories), had their titles changed from divisions to branches. Their major duties remained unchanged.

1971   A new Architectural Branch in charge of the Resettlement and Government Low Cost Housing Programme was established.

1978   The Architectural Office was merged with the Buildings Ordinance Office to form the Buildings Development Department. The new Architectural Office under the Buildings Development Department had five branches: Architectural, Structural Engineering, Building Services, Quantity Surveying and Maintenance. It provided architectural services to all governmental departments, prepared all building estimates, controlled expenditure of all government building projects and maintained government buildings.

1982   The Buildings Development Department became independent. The Architectural Office remained its subordinate department.

1986   The Architectural Office of the Buildings Development Department was transformed into an independent department: Architectural Services Department. It consisted of six branches: Architectural Services Department Headquarters, Architectural Branch, Maintenance Branch, Quantity Surveying Branch, Structural Engineering Branch and Building Service Branch.

1989   The Antiquities Section under the Maintenance Branch was set up to advise on and restore historical buildings in Hong Kong.

1991   The Maintenance Branch was renamed Property Services Branch to provide professional maintenance services to government properties.

1996   The Project Management Branch was set up to monitor the implementation of all government and client projects such as costs, disbursements and completion time.

2001   The Architectural Services Department comprised the Headquarters and six branches: Architectural, Building Services, Project Management, Property Services, Quantity Surveying and Structural Engineering.

2002   The structure of the Department has remained unchanged.

Sources:

1. *Hong Kong*, Hong Kong, Government Printer, 1990, pp.203-204; 1991, pp.206-208; 1993, pp. 211-214, 1998, pp.216; 2000, pp.230-232.
2. www.archsd.gov.hk/english/index1024.asp

	Architectural Services Department — Changes in Directors		
Year	Name of Department	Title	Name of Director
1986-1991	Architectural Services Department	Director of Architectural Services	Lei, Meng-can, Joseph
1991-1993	Architectural Services Department	Director of Architectural Services	Corser, Paul Jeremy
1993-1997	Architectural Services Department	Director of Architectural Services	Chan, Yat-sun, Kenneth
1997-2002	Architectural Services Department	Director of Architectural Services	Pau, Shiu-hung

Sources:
1. *Staff Biographies Hong Kong Government*, Hong Kong, Government Printer, 1990-1996.
2. *Staff List the Government of Hong Kong Special Administrative Region*, Hong Kong, Government Printer, 1998.
3. www.archsd.gov.hk/english/index1024.asp

Architectural and Maintenance of Buildings Branch, Public Works Department (1915-1924)
Buildings Ordinance Office, Public Works Department (1924-1978)
Buildings Development Department, Public Works Department (1978-1982)
Buildings Development Department (1982-1986)
Buildings and Lands Department (1986-1994)
Buildings Department (1994-2002)

1854   The Market Ordinance of 1854 enabled the Surveyor General to approve all construction works of buildings in the markets.

1856   The Buildings and Nuisances Ordinance of 1856 was enacted for better regulation of buildings and prevention of nuisances.

1867	The Surveyor General was responsible for the construction and repairs of all buildings in the Colony whether public or private, and the execution of the buildings ordinances. The Clerk of Works of the Surveyor General's Office was in charge of all construction and repairs of public buildings, drains and streets; he also provided quarterly reports on the state of repairs of public buildings.
1883	The Survey Department was restructured to form the Public Works Department. The Inspection of Buildings Branch was established.
1915	The Public Works Department was reorganized. The Construction of New Buildings Branch was integrated with the Architectural and Maintenance of Buildings Branch and placed under an Executive Engineer.
1924	The duties of the Public Works Department were divided mainly into six categories, of which the Administration of the Buildings Ordinance Office was an independent office that handled all public buildings construction works.
1929	The Administration of the Buildings Ordinance Office was retitled Buildings Ordinance Office. It was responsible for the examination and approval of all private building work plans in connection with the Public Health and Buildings Ordinance; approval for all verandahs, scavenging lanes and wells; prosecutions and notices for defective drainage and non-compliance with the Public Health and Buildings Ordinance.
1946	The Office was restored after the Sino-Japanese War. Inspection, reconstruction of and repairs to old buildings, issuance of dangerous building notices and occupation certificates were the major duties of the Office.
1965	The Buildings Ordinance Office was responsible for the administration of the Buildings Ordinance, which was related to the design and construction of all private building works. Records were maintained which made it possible to gauge the stage and rate of redevelopment in any particular area. The Buildings Ordinance Office comprised two divisions: General Division and Dangerous Buildings Division. The General Division was responsible for the scrutiny and approval of all site formations, building structures and access roads submitted by authorized architects; inspection of materials used by private buildings; and giving structural advice to other governmental departments. The Dangerous Buildings Division conducted surveys of buildings considered to be in dangerous structural conditions.
1973	A Works Division was established to prepare estimates for the subdepartments of the Public Works Department, to demolish buildings included in the pilot scheme for urban renewal, and to carry out, for defaulting owners, works ordered under the Buildings Ordinance to eliminate dangers.
1978	The Public Works Department was reorganized and a subdepartment, Buildings Development Department, was established. It consisted of two main offices: Architectural Office and Buildings Ordinance Office. The Buildings Ordinance Office ensured compliance with building legislation and dealt with private buildings in dangerous conditions and comprised four branches: General, Specialist, Structural Engineering and Geotechnical Control.
1982	The Buildings Development Department became an independent department.
1986	The Buildings Development Department was abolished. The Buildings Ordinance Office

of the Department was merged with the Lands Department to form the Buildings and Lands Department. The Architectural Office became an independent Architectural Department. The Buildings and Lands Department comprised five offices: Lands Administration Office, Buildings Ordinance Office, Town Planning Office, Survey and Mapping Office, and Departmental Administration Office.

1990   The Town Planning Office was transferred to the newly established Planning Department on January 1.

1992   The Legal Advisory and Conveyance Section of the Lands Division of the Registrar General's Department was transferred to the Building and Lands Department to form the Legal Advisory and Conveyance Office. The Office provided legal advice on all government land matters and conducted all government property conveyances.

1994   The Buildings and Lands Department was spilt into two independent departments: Buildings Department and Lands Department. The Buildings Department consisted of six divisions. The Development Division was responsible for all matters relating to new building developments, alteration and additions to existing buildings, and the quality of completed work. The Litigation and Legislation Division was responsible for the prosecutions and disciplinary cases under the Buildings Ordinance; responding to appeals and providing expert opinion in litigation involving the Building Authority; and conducted research on changes in legislation. The Specialist Division dealt with the dilapidated and dangerous buildings; served as the Licensing Authority under the Buildings Regulations; advised other government agencies on the suitability of premises for licensing or registration purposes. The Control and Enforcement Division handled unauthorized building works as well as defective and polluting drainage systems; and assisted the Building Management Co-ordination Committee of the City and New Territories Administration to improve standards of building management. The Structural Engineering Division dealt with structural submissions and construction control in the Development Division; and assessed structural engineering systems and materials for use under the Buildings Ordinance and Building (Construction) Regulations. The Headquarters directed the overall performance of the Department.

1995   The Legal and Management Division was set up to assume the duties of the former Litigation and Legislation Division.

2001   The Buildings Department was reorganized into the following major units: New Buildings Divisions 1 and 2, Existing Building Divisions 1 and 2, Support Division, Special Duties and Headquarters.

2002   The Departmental structure was as follows: New Buildings Divisions 1 and 2, Existing Buildings Divisions 1 and 2, Support Division, Departmental Administration Section, Accounts and Supplies Section, Information Section, Building Innovation Unit and Internal Audit Unit.

Sources:

1. *Annual Departmental Report by the Director of Public Works*, Hong Kong, Government Printer, 1952-1978.
2. *Buildings Department*, Hong Kong, Government Printer, 1997.
3. *Hong Kong*, Hong Kong, Government Printer, 1978-1995.
4. *Hong Kong Annual Report by the Director of Pulbic Works*, Hong Kong, Government Printer, 1950.
5. "Report of Director of Public Works", Hong Kong Government, 1946-1949.
6. www.info.gov.hk/bd/english/index.html

Buildings Department — Changes in Names and Directors

Year	Name of Department	Title	Name of Director
1982-1983	Buildings Development Department	Director of Buildings Development	Aitken, John Blyth
1983-1984	Buildings Development Department	Director of Buildings Development	Lei, Meng-can, Joseph
1984-1986	Buildings Development Department	Director of Buildings Development	Chau, Cham-son
1986-1989	Buildings and Lands Department	Director of Buildings and Lands	Chau, Cham-son
1989-1992	Buildings and Lands Department	Director of Buildings and Lands	Eason, Anthony Gordon
1992-1994	Buildings and Lands Department	Director of Buildings and Lands	Chen, Darwin
1994-1996	Buildings Department	Director of Buildings	Yu Lai, Ching-ping, Helen
1996-1999	Buildings Department	Director of Buildings	Choi, Yu-leuk
1999-2002	Buildings Department	Director of Buildings	Leung, Chin-man

Sources:
1. *Staff List Hong Kong Government*, Hong Kong, Government Printer, 1980-1998.
2. www.info.gov.hk/bd/english/index.html

Land Committee (March-May 1842)
Lands and Roads Committee (May 1842-1844)
Land Office, Surveyor General's Office / Survey Department /
Public Works Department (1844-1890)
Land Survey Branch, Public Works Department (1890-1909)
Land Survey Office, Public Works Department (1909-1926)
Crown Lands Office, Public Works Department (1926-1930);
Surveys Office, Public Works Department (1926-1930)
Crown Lands, Surveys and Valuation and Resumption Office,
Public Works Department (1930-1931)
Valuation and Resumption Office, Public Works Department
(1931-1949)
Crown Lands and Surveys Office, Public Works Department
(1931-1962)
Crown Lands and Survey Office, Public Works Department
(1962-1977)
Lands and Survey Department, Public Works Department
(1977-1978)
Lands, Survey and Town Planning Department, Public Works
Department (1978-1982)
Lands Department (1982-1986)
Buildings and Lands Department (1986-1994)
Lands Department (1994-2002)

1842   The Land Committee was appointed on March 29. Captain George F. Mylius was nominated as Land Officer. The Committee was responsible for the estimation of value of land possessed by native Chinese, and the selection of eligible land for public and government use. The post of Land Officer was subsequently temporarily abolished and a Lands and Roads Inspector was appointed on May 27, 1842. The Committee was renamed Lands and Roads Committee.

1843   Five principles governing the control and availability of land were laid down and remained in effect. Firstly, all land was Crown land and was leased out by the Crown. Secondly, public auction was to be the normal method of sale. Thirdly, a minimum expenditure on building was to be specified. Fourthly, the Government reserved the right to re-enter if lease conditions were not complied. Fifthly, in order to prevent the Government from over-exploiting land as a source of revenue, the central allocation of land and its use were to be made in response to public demand and with regard to public interests.

1844   To prevent secret and fraudulent conveyances in Hong Kong and to provide the means whereby the titles to real and immovable property might be easily traced and ascertained, Ordinance no. 3 of 1844 which was responsible for the registration of deeds, was enacted. The Lands and Roads Committee was replaced by the Land Office, a unit under the Surveyor General's Office. The Land Office was responsible for the registration of deed conveyances and the keeping of the indexes of places and names in the registry book. The Land Officer controlled the allocation of land.

1854   The Surveyor General approved the letting and sale of land.

1862   The sale of land by public auction was held on the ground that was to be sold. The Surveyor General's Office was responsible for the publication of the schedule of lots for sale and made it known to the general public.

1867   The First Clerk of Surveyor General administered the Land Office which registered all transfers of landed properties, leases, rent-roll and collected burial and monumental and deed registry fees.

1883   The Land Registry was set up under the Survey Department. It was under the control of the Land Officer and Official Receiver.

1886   The Land Commission was established on April 30. Land Commissioners were appointed for the purpose of inquiring into and reporting upon the system of leasing or disposing of Crown land; to suggest alterations or improvements to facilitate the transfer of land; and to check overcrowding in the populated parts of the City of Victoria.

1890   The Land Survey Branch was formed to carry out land surveys; its land agent was in charge of the valuation and sale of properties.

1906   The Land Survey Branch's major duties were connected with the surveying of Tax Claims in the New Territories and sale of numerous small lots there.

1909   The Land Survey Branch was expanded into an office of the Public Works Department. The Principal Land Surveyor was the executive officer for all matters relating to Crown land. He submitted reports on all applications for land, conducted all sales of areas to be let on long leases; prepared permits for temporary occupation of land and licences for temporary piers; and attended to the preparation of lease plans for land lots, quarries, and permanent piers. The Land Survey Office issued its own annual reports under the Public Works Department. The eight Land Surveyors were responsible for preventing illegal squatting and encroachments upon Crown land.

1912   The Land Officer and Official Receiver changed its title to Land Officer.

1926   The Crown Lands and Surveys Office was split into two separate units of Crown Lands Office and Surveys Office in the Public Works Department.

1930   The Crown Lands Office and the Surveys Office were recombined to form the Crown Lands, Surveys and Valuation and Resumption Office.

1931   The Crown Lands, Surveys and Valuation and Resumption Office was spilt into two: Crown Lands and Surveys Office, and Valuation and Resumption Office. The Crown Lands and Surveys Office dealt with Crown land sales; agreements and issue of conditions for leases for all properties; development schemes, conversions and exchanges; pier rents and permits for land and quarries; preparation of plans for the issue of title deeds; ordinance enforcement and trigonometrical surveys for the City of Victoria, Hong Kong,

Kowloon and New Territories; and demarcation of boundaries of roads and properties and preparation of lease plans.

1946   The Crown Lands and Surveys Office resumed its previous duties after the Sino-Japanese War.

1949   The Crown Lands and Surveys Office was responsible to the Director of Public Works; it performed land agency functions for the Government, prepared and maintained triangulation and traverse records, and made surveys and prepared plans for leases and land development. The Valuation and Resumption Office once again merged with the Crown Lands and Surveys Office and ceased to exist as an independent entity. Its works, which included valuation for town planning, rehabilitation of damaged properties, purchase of properties and grant of new Crown leases, were performed by the Crown Lands and Surveys Office. After the merger, the Office was divided into five main groups: Valuation and Resumption, Drawing Office, Land Agency Functions, Land Surveys and Clerical.

1951   The Crown Lands and Surveys Office became responsible for keeping all the work progress photographs of the Public Works Department.

1953   The Crown Lands and Surveys Office took over all town planning matters.

1962   The Crown Lands and Surveys Office changed its name to Crown Lands and Survey Office.

1965   The Public Works Department was reorganized. The Crown Lands and Survey Office was restructured into three divisions: Planning, Crown Lands, Survey. The Planning Division prepared outline plans, outline zonings, development plans and population distribution forecasts; it was also responsible for the scrutiny of public and private development projects. The Crown Lands Division was in charge of the disposal of Crown land for private development, public auction or tender, control of private land by enforcement of lease conditions, the acquisition of land for public purposes, valuation for government transaction, and the leasing and management of government buildings. The Survey Division was responsible for all basic survey plans and maps of Hong Kong required for land administration, ground control and field checking for air surveys, site planning for government building and development projects, training of land survey workers, and co-ordination with related service departments.

1972   The Lease Renewal Branch was established to manage all lease renewals, assessment of Crown rent and calculation of installments. The Valuation Branch was set up.

1977   The Crown Lands and Survey Office was retitled Lands and Survey Department.

1978   The Department was renamed Lands, Survey and Town Planning Department with effect from March 15 due to the reorganization of the Public Works Department. The Lands, Survey and Town Planning Department comprised two offices: Crown Lands and Survey Office (in charge of the Land Branch, Valuation Branch and Survey Branch) and Town Planning Office (in charge of the District Planning Branch and Hong Kong Outline Planning Division).

1982   The Lands, Survey and Town Planning Department became an independent Lands Department due to the abolition of the Public Works Department. The new Department took over all land administration duties carried out by the former New Territories Administration. The Department was organized into a headquarters and 12 district offices (4 in the urban areas and 9 in the New Territories). The Headquarters comprised an administration division and three main functional divisions: Lands, Survey and Town Planning.

1983   The Special Committee on Land Supply and the Land Disposal Subcommittee was formed.

1984   According to the Sino-British Joint Declaration, the policy with regard to land grants and leases was governed by the provisions of Annex III to the Joint Declaration.

1985   Normal land grants throughout the whole of the territory were made for terms expiring not later than June 30, 2047.

1986   The Lands Department was merged with the Buildings Ordinance Office of the Buildings Development Department to form the new Buildings and Lands Department. The Buildings and Lands Department comprised five offices: Lands Administration, Buildings Ordinance Office, Town Planning Office, Survey and Mapping Office, and Departmental Administration.

1990   The Town Planning Office was transferred to the newly established Planning Department on January 1.

1992   The Legal Advisory and Conveyance Section of the Lands Division of the Registrar General's Department was transferred to the Building and Lands Department to form the Legal Advisory and Conveyance Office. The Office provided legal advice on all government land matters and conducted all government property conveyances.

1994   The Buildings and Lands Department was abolished. The Lands Department was re-established on August 1. The Department acquired land and made land available for government's development programmes, managed all unallocated government land, and ensured that the use of private land complied with its lease conditions. The Department consisted of the Administration Office and three other offices: Land Administration Office, Survey and Mapping Office, Legal Advisory and Conveyancing Office.

1996   The Land Survey Ordinance came into force in January. The Ordinance stated that land subdivisions for registration in the land registry had to be surveyed by authorized land surveyors.

2000   A new procedure for land sales by application was introduced with the aim of improving flexibility by making sufficient land available to meet market demands.

2002   The structure remained up changed. The Department was made up of four offices: Land Administration, Survey and Mapping, Legal Advisory and Conveyancing, and Departmental Administration.

Sources:

1. Bristow, Roger, *Land-use Planning in Hong Kong, History , Policies and Procedures*, Hong Kong, Oxford University Press, 1984, p.23.
2. *Friend of China and Hong Kong Government Gazette*, Hong Kong Government, 31 Mar 1842, no.2, vol.1; 13 April 1842, no.55, vol. 2; 5 May 1842, vol.1, no.7; 9 Mar 1844, supplement to no.113, p.277; 4 Feb, 1860, vol. VI, no.5.
3. *Hong Kong Almanac and Directory for 1846*, Hong Kong, *China Mail*, 1846.
4. *Hong Kong*, Hong Kong, Government Printer, 1978-1983.
5. *Hong Kong Annual Report*, Hong Kong, Government Printer, 1947-1976.
6. Organisation and Methods Branch, Colonial Secretariat, *Report on Public Works Department, Organisation, Methods and Staff Survey*, Government of Hong Kong, September 1949.
7. "Report from the Land Commission of 1886-87", *Hong Kong Sessional Papers*, Hong Kong, Noronha & Co., 1887, p.xiii.
8. www.info.gov.hk/landsd/index.htm

Lands Department — Changes in Names and Directors			
Year	Name of Department	Title	Name of Director
1982-1986	Lands Department	Director of Lands	Todd, John Rawling
1986-1989	Buildings and Lands Department	Director of Buildings and Lands	Chau, Cham-son
1989-1992	Buildings and Lands Department	Director of Buildings and Lands	Eason, Anthony Gordon
1992-1994	Buildings and Lands Department	Director of Buildings and Lands	Chen, Darwin
1994-2002	Lands Department	Director of Lands	Pope, Robert Douglas
2002	Lands Department	Director of Lands	Lau, Lai-chiu, Patrick

Sources:
1. *Staff Biographies Hong Kong Government*, Hong Kong, Government Printer, 1986, 1988, 1990, 1993.
2. *Staff Biographies the Government of the Hong Kong Special Administative Region*, 1998, 2001.
3. *Staff List Hong Kong Government*, Hong Kong, Government Printer, 1983-1996.
4. www.info.gov.hk/landsd/index.htm

Engineering Development

Civil Engineering Office, Public Works Department (1964-1982)
Engineering Development Department (1982-1986)
Civil Engineering Services Department (1986-1991)
Civil Engineering Department (1991-2002)

1843   The construction works of piers, roads and reclamation of land were carried out irregularly by subdepartments such as Lands, Buildings Ordinance and General Works of the Surveyor General's Office since 1843.

1924   The Office of Drainage, Port Development and Roads were first established to deal with urban construction works. The Drainage Office was responsible for the construction, maintenance and consultation of public sewers, drains, nullahs and septic tanks. The Port Development Office designed, constructed and maintained piers, sea walls and reclamation projects; examined marine structure projects and private operators' proposals. The Roads Office dealt with the construction and maintenance of roads, pavements and tunnels. These offices were the precursors of the Engineering Development Department.

1958   In order to accelerate the urban development, the Development Office was established in March in the Public Works Department to handle new engineering works at development areas and reclamation works.

1964   The Offices of Roads, Drainage, Port Works and Development were merged to form the Civil Engineering Office. It was responsible for drainage, major reclamation, port works, roads and traffic engineering. The Department comprised six offices: Architectural, Buildings Ordinance, Civil Engineering, Crown Lands and Survey, Electrical and Mechanical, and Waterworks.

1965   The Civil Engineering Office was the largest Public Works Department office. The two Assistant Government Civil Engineers were each responsible for three suboffices. The Hong Kong Assistant Government Civil Engineer controlled the Hong Kong Roads and Drainage Office, Traffic Engineering Office, and Port Works and Development Office. The Mainland Assistant Government Civil Engineer controlled: the Kowloon Roads and Drainage Office, New Territories Roads and Drainage Office, and Development Office.

1969   The Civil Engineering Office was reorganized into three divisions. The Development and Airport Division designed, constructed and maintained civil engineering works in connection with airport development. It also prepared feasibility reports on major development schemes for Kowloon and the New Territories, and supervised reclamation works. The Drainage Works Division planned, built and investigated sewerage and storm-water drainage. The Port Works Division was responsible for the design, construction and maintenance of all public piers and sea walls.

1978   The Public Works Department was restructured. The Engineering Development Branch of the Headquarters office comprised four offices: Civil Engineering Office,

Electrical and Mechanical Office, Highways Office and Geotechnical Control Office. The Civil Engineering Office administered the Consultants Management Division, Development and Airport Division, Drainage Works Division, Port Works Division and Railway Division. It was responsible for site formations, marine works, storm-water drainage and sewage disposal systems. The Electrical and Mechanical Office undertook electro-mechanical equipment installation and maintenance works. The Highways Office consisted of three branches: Works, Traffic and Transport, and Management and Planning. The Highways Office was in charge of the planning, construction and maintenance of public road system, surveillance of traffic management system, and carrying out traffic and transport surveys. The Geotechnical Control Office co-ordinated the Engineering Branch and Land Survey Section. It controlled all geotechnical engineering aspects of slopes relating to building development and was responsible for the management of quarries, laboratory testing and site investigation.

1982   The Engineering Development Branch of the Headquarters office of the Public Works Department was restructured on April 1 and became an independent department . It was mainly divided into seven units: Headquarters, Civil Engineering Office, Electrical and Mechanical Office, Geotechnical Control Office, Highways Office, Mass Transit Office and Railway Development Office. The Mass Transit Office monitored and co-ordinated the operations of the MTR and planned surface transport and traffic facilities. The Railway Development Office designed and executed all major works connected with the modernization of the Kowloon-Canton Railway (British Section). On August 1, the Electrical and Mechanical Office was separated from the Engineering Development Department to become the Electrical and Mechanical Services Department.

1986   The Highways Office was separated from the Department and became the Highways Department. It was responsible for the highways development programmes. The Engineering Development Department was restructured to form the Civil Engineering Services Department with effect from June 1. The structure of the Department was as follows:

I.   Headquarters

II.   Civil Engineering Office

    1. Drainage Branch
       i. Urban Drainage Division
       ii. New Territories Drainage Division
       iii. Drainage (Construction) Division
       iv. Drainage (Design) Division
    2. General Engineering Branch
       i. Port Works Division
       ii. Development and Airport Division

III.   Geotechnical Control Office

    1. Island Branch
       i. Island East Division
       ii. Island West Division

    2. Mainland Branch
      i. Mainland East Division
      ii. Mainland West Division
      iii. Design Division
    3. Development Branch
      i. Special Projects Division
      ii. Planning Division
      iii. Materials Division

IV.   Railway Development Office

     Railway Division

1989 The Drainage Branch was separated from the Department and became Drainage Services Department. Sewage treatment and storm-water drainage of the Civil Engineering Services Department were transferred to the Drainage Services Department.

1991 The Civil Engineering Services Department was renamed Civil Engineering Department. The Director of Civil Engineering Services was appointed Commissioner of Mines. The Mines Division of the Labour Department was transferred to the Island Branch of the Geotechnical Engineering Office (formerly Geotechnical Control Office). The Mine Division controlled the possession, conveyance, storage, manufacture and use of explosives; it also enforced legislation and safety regulations relating to mining, quarrying and explosives.

1996 The Civil Engineering Office of the Department was reorganized. It comprised three branches: General Engineering, Project Management, and Port and Airport Development Strategy. The General Engineering Branch co-ordinated the Development and Airport Division, Port Works Division and Technical Services Division. The Port and Airport Development Strategy Branch administered the West Kowloon Reclamation Division and Port Development Division.

2001 The structure of the Civil Engineering Department was as follows:

I.   Administrative and Technical Services Branch

    1. Administrative Division
    2. Accounts and Supplies Division
    3. Survey Division
    4. Technical Support Group

II.   Civil Engineering Office

    1. Land Development
      i. Development Division
      ii Housing Sites Division
    2. Project Management Branch
    3. Port Branch
      i. Port Works Division
      ii. Technical Services Division

III. Geotechnical Engineering Office

     1. Hong Kong Island Branch

        i. Advisory Division
        ii. Island Division
        iii.Slope Safety Division
     2. Mainland Branch
        i. Mines and Quarries Division
        ii. Mainland East Division
        iii.Mainland West Division
     3. Development Branch
        i. Fill Management Division
        ii. Planning Division
        iii.Materials Division
     4. Landslip Preventive Measures Branch
        i. Design Division
        ii. Works Division
        iii.Landslip Investigation Division

IV.   Special Duties Office

     1. Special Duties (Co-ordination) Division
     2. Special Duties (Works) Division

2002   The structure of the Department remained largely the same, apart from two changes. In the Development Branch of the Geotechnical Engineering office, a Special Projects Division had been added.

Sources:

1.   *Civil Engineering Department, Performance Pledge*, Hong Kong, Government Printer, 1996.
2.   *Civil Engineering Department, Serving the Community in Slope Safety, Port Development and Land Formation*, Hong Kong, Government Printer, 1997.
3.   *Hong Kong Annual Department Report by the Director of Public Works*, Hong Kong, Government Printer, 1952-1978.
4.   *Hong Kong*, Hong Kong, Government Printer 1989-1998.
5.   Public Works Department, *Public Works Department — Organization and Functions*, Hong Kong, Government Printer, 1978, pp.3-11.
6.   "Report of the Director of Public Works Report", *Hong Kong Administrative Reports*, 1924, Appendix Q.
7.   www.ced.gov.hk/eng/index.htm.

Civil Engineering Department — Changes in Names and Directors

Year	Name of Department	Title	Name of Director
1982-1984	Engineering Development Department	Director of Engineering Development	Short, Frank Edmond
1984-1986	Engineering Development Department	Director of Engineering Development	Nip, Kam-fan
1986-1990	Civil Engineering Services Department	Director of Civil Engineering Services	Nip, Kam-fan
1990	Civil Engineering Services Department	Director of Civil Engineering Services	Brand, Edward William
1991-1996	Civil Engineering Department	Director of Civil Engineering and Commissioner of Mines	Brand, Edward William
1996-1999	Civil Engineering Department	Director of Civil Engineering and Commissioner of Mines	Lam, Moon-tim, Bernard
1999-2000	Civil Engineering Department	Director of Civil Engineering and Commissioner of Mines	Lo, Yiu-ching
2000-2002	Civil Engineering Department	Director of Civil Engineering and Commissioner of Mines	Lau, Ching-kwong

Sources:
1. *Staff Biographies Hong Kong Government*, Hong Kong, Government Printer, 1982, 1984, 1986, 1988, 1990, 1993.
2. *Staff Biographies the Government of the Hong Kong Special Administrative Region*, Hong Kong, Government Printer, 1998, 2001
3. *Staff List Hong Kong Government*, Hong Kong, Government Printer, 1982-1996.
4. *Staff List the Government of the Hong Kong Special Administrative Region*, Hong Kong, Government Printer, 1997-2000.
5. www.ced.gov.hk/eng/index.htm

Electrical and Wireless Telegraphy Office, Public Works Department (1929-1930)
Electrical Office, Public Works Department (1930-1947)
Electrical and Mechanical Office, Public Works Department (1947-1982)
Electrical and Mechanical Services Department (1982-2002)

1913   A new post of Electrician to give advice to the Director of Public Works on electrical matters was created.

1929   The Electrical and Wireless Telegraphy Office of the Public Works Department was responsible for the maintenance of the wireless telegraphy and radio broadcasting stations, installation and maintenance of fans, lights and lifts in government buildings. It also gave advice on the rules and regulations for public electric and telephone companies.

1930   The Electrical and Wireless Telegraphy office was retitled Electrical Office.

1946   The Electrical Office under the Public Works Department was restored after the war. The Office was in charge of the installation and maintenance of electrical equipment and mechanical plants in government buildings, and the supervision of rules and regulations on electrical and mechanical matters.

1947   The Electrical Office of the Public Works Department was transformed into the Electrical and Mechanical Office. The Office comprised two sections. The Electrical Section installed and maintained electrical equipment and lifts in government buildings, and managed the electrical workshops. The Mechanical Section assumed the duties of the former Transport Office of the Public Works Department. It repaired and serviced the government land transport and operated a motor car pool for official business use.

1965   The Government Electrical and Mechanical Engineer was responsible for the installation and maintenance of all government mechanical and electrical plants other than those controlled by the Director of Water Supplies.

1967   The Military Division was created to plan, install and maintain military installations of an electrical and mechanical nature.

1968   The Electrical and Mechanical Office was reorganized into two divisions. The Design and Projects Division was responsible for all new projects — both electrical and mechanical — and the administration of lifts and escalators. The Operation and Maintenance Division installed and maintained government plants and equipment, including vehicles and electrical facilities.

1978   The Public Works Department was restructured into five subdepartments. The Electrical and Mechanical Office became a branch of the Engineering Development Department. Its duties remained unchanged.

1982   The Electrical and Mechanical Office was spilt from the Engineering Development Department on August 1 and restructured into an independent department: Electrical and Mechanical Services Department. The Department consisted of four branches: Headquarters, Works and Services Branch, Projects and Development Branch, and Gas Adviser's Office. The Headquarters dealt with the overall administrative planning, financial and supplies control; and the management of technical and contract services of the Department and other government departments. The Works and Services Branch operated and maintained the electrical and mechanical services for all government departments. The Projects and Development Branch designed, installed and commissioned the engineering services and various telecommunication services for all government departments; enforced legislation, regulations and codes of practices related to electrical and mechanical installations and equipment. The Gas Adviser's Office monitored hazard surveys of gas depots; supervised the work and performance of the gas industry; and provided advice on gas matters to all government departments.

1984   The Building Services Branch of the Architectural Office under the Buildings Development Department was transferred to the Electrical and Mechanical Services Department with effect from April 1. The Building Services Branch was responsible for the supervision on matters related to building services in government buildings: design and consultancy of lifts, air-conditioning and refrigeration, electrical, mechanical and liquefied petroleum gas services in public works projects and new military works.

1989   The proposal for the Electrical and Mechanical Services Trading Fund was initiated.

1990   The Electricity Ordinance was enacted to protect the public over the safe supply, delivery and use of electricity.

1991   The Gas Safety Ordinance was introduced on April 1 and the Director of Electrical and Mechanical Services was appointed Gas Authority under the Ordinance.

1996   The Department was reorganized into 10 administrative units: Business Development Branch, Contract Adviser's Unit, Dedicated Services Branch, Department Safety Unit, Departmental Administration Division, Electricity Legislation Division, Energy Efficiency Office, Gas and General Legislation Branch, General Services Branch and Staff Relations Unit.

1997   The Contract Adviser's Unit, Dedicated Services Branch and General Services Branch were restructured into two engineering services branches: Engineering Services Branches 1 and 2.

2001   The Department comprised six major units: Business Development Branch (made up of the Management Services Division, Marketing Unit, Business Support Unit and Service Development Unit); Electricity Legislation Division; Energy Efficiency Office (consisted of the Energy Efficiency Division and Utility Monitoring Subdivision); Engineering Services Branch 1 (administered the Supplies Subdivision; Vehicle Engineering Division; Transport, Security and Central Services Division; and Project Division); Engineering Services Branch 2 (with four subordinate divisions — General Engineering Services, Municipal Sector, Health Sector and Airport Sector); Gas and General Legislation Branch which directed the Gas Standards Office (made up of the Gas Production and Supply Division and Gas Utilization Division) and Gas Legislation Division.

2002   In the Energy Efficiency Office, the Energy Efficiency Division had been split into two divisions: Energy Efficiency Divisions A and B; the Utility Monitoring Subdivision had also been split into Utility Monitoring Subdivisions A and B. There was also an Electricity Team. The remaining organization structure was the same.

Sources:

1.   Electrical and Mechanical Services Department, *50 Years of Electrical and Mechanical Services*, Hong Kong: Printing Department, 1998.
2.   www.emsd.gov.hk/emsd/

Electrical and Mechanical Services Department — Changes in Directors

Year	Name of Department	Title	Name of Director
1982-1990	Electrical and Mechanical Services Department	Director of Electrical and Mechanical Services	Osborne, Graham John
1990-1993	Electrical and Mechanical Services Department	Director of Electrical and Mechanical Services	Miao, Chi
1993-1994	Electrical and Mechanical Services Department	Director of Electrical and Mechanical Services	Kwok, Ping-ki
1994-1999	Electrical and Mechanical Services Department	Director of Electrical and Mechanical Services	Phillipson, Hugh Brian
1999-2001	Electrical and Mechanical Services Department	Director of Electrical and Mechanical Services	Leung, Cham-tim
2001-2002	Electrical and Mechanical Services Department	Director of Electrical and Mechanical Services	Lai, Sze-hoi, Roger

Sources:
1.   *Staff Biographies Hong Kong Government*, Hong Kong, Government Printer, 1990, 1993.
2.   *Staff Biographies the Government of the Hong Kong Special Administrative Region*, Hong Kong, Government Printer, 1998, 2001.
3.   *Staff List Hong Kong Government*, Hong Kong, Government Printer, 1982-1996.
4.   www.emsd.gov.hk/emsd/

Transportation

Government Land Transport Division, Finance Branch (1978-1979)
Government Land Transport Agency, Administration Branch (1979-2002)

1978 The Government Land Transport Division within the Finance Branch was set up. It was responsible for the management of government vehicles in the transport pool; ensured the most efficient use of vehicles; the recruitment and training of government motor drivers; and the review of all government regulations on the use of vehicles and hired-transport supplied to the Government. Headed by the Controller of Government Land Transport, the Department consisted of the Administration Section and the Transport Operations Section.

1979 The Government Land Transport Division was transformed into the Government Land Transport Agency under the Administration Branch of the Government Secretariat. Its main duties included the provision of centralized management for the operation of the government vehicle fleet; giving advice to all departments and secretariat branches on modern methods of transport management; and the maintenance of a Transport Management Information System to provide evaluation of vehicle utilization statistics.

1980 The Agency took over the control of the transport pool from the Electrical and Mechanical Office in April. It was also responsible for the testing of government driver applicants and keeping records of government drivers.

1984 Computerization of the transport management information systems.

1988 The Agency was divided into: Administration Division, Management and Review Division, and Headquarters.

1992 The Controller of Government Land Transport was retitled Government Land Transport Administrator with effect from October 13.

1993 The Management and Review Division was transformed into the Planning and Development Division.

1999 The Agency consisted of three divisions: Administration, Planning and Operations. The Planning Division formulated policy on the management of government vehicles, conducted departmental transport reviews, procured general purpose vehicles for use by the Government, conducted trials and evaluation of vehicles, and scrutinized requests for additional or replacement of departmental vehicles. The Operations Division formulated training policies for drivers, administered tenders for contract hiring and provided transport services to government departments, monitored the maintenance and repair services of the pooled vehicles, and controlled the operation of the transport pool.

2000 The Management Division was established to maintain all government management data related to vehicles and drivers, to monitor traffic accident cases involving government vehicles, and to promote customer services and marketing services of the Agency.

2002   The Agency was made up of four divisions: Administration, Procurement, Operations and Management. The Procurement Division had taken over all the functions of the former Planning Division, as well the contract-hiring tender work from the Operations Division.

Sources:

1. *Hong Kong Government Telephone Directory*, Hong Kong, Government Printer, 1999.
2. www.info.gov.hk/glta/

	Government Land Transport Agency — Changes in Directors		
Year	**Name of Department**	**Title**	**Name of Director**
1978-1987	Government Land Transport Agency	Controller	Gray, John Walter
1987-1992	Government Land Transport Agency	Controller	Walker, Peter Brian
1992-2002	Government Land Transport Agency	Government Land Transport Administrator	Walker, Peter Brian

Sources:
1. *Staff List Hong Kong Government,* Hong Kong, Government Printer, 1984, 1988, 2001.
2. www.info.gov.hk/glta/

Highways Office, Public Works Department (1969-1978)
Highways Office, Engineering Development Department (1978-1986)
Highways Department (1986-2002)

1969   The Highways Office under the control of the Public Works Department was first established. The Office comprised four divisions. The Traffic and Transport Survey Unit collected and analyzed data relating to passenger transport. The Highways Division (Hong Kong, Kowloon and New Territories Branches) planned, designed, constructed and maintained public roads, bridges, sewerage and drainage systems. The Traffic Engineering Division (Hong Kong and Mainland Branches) planned and designed road systems, and provided technical advice and information on traffic management control and regulating measures. The Mass Transit Unit investigated, planned and co-ordinated all activities pertaining to Mass Transit Railway.

1978   The Highways Office was put under the control of the Engineering Development Department, a sudepartment of the Public Works Department. It was restructured into three branches: Works Branch, Traffic and Transport Branch, and Management and Planning Branch. The Works Branch was responsible for the design and construction of new roads and maintenance of existing roads, drainage and sewerage systems. The Traffic and Transport Branch was in charge of the planning and improvement of road systems and investigation of day-to-day traffic management. The Management and Planning Branch was concerned with the administrative procedures of Highways Office such as the implementation of computerized planning, programming and budgeting systems, resource scheduling and financial control.

1982   The Engineering Development Department became independent of the Public Works Department. The Highways Office became a subordinate unit of the Department. Its duties remained the same.

1984   The Highways Office was reorganized in December on a regional basis and was divided into three regions: Hong Kong, Kowloon and New Territories.

1986   The Highways Office became independent and became known as Highways Department. It was responsible for the implementation of transport policies and the construction and maintenance of roads. The Department was mainly divided into three parts: Headquarters (comprised the Structure Division, Lighting Division, Research and Development Unit, Land Surveying Unit, Maintenance Accounting and Information Unit, Contract Advisory Unit, Surveying Unit and Landscape Unit); Highways Regions (Hong Kong, Kowloon and New Territories); and Eastern Harbour Crossing Unit.

1990   The Eastern Harbour Crossing Unit was abolished; the Western Harbour Link Office and the North Lantau Link Office were set up.

1991   The Western Harbour Link Office and the North Lantau Link Office were abolished. Two new units were set up: Airport and Port Access Office and Lantau Fixed Crossing Project Management Office. The Airport and Port Access Office was responsible for the planning and co-ordination of administrative and technical arrangements regarding the Western Harbour Crossing, West Kowloon Expressway and Route 3. The Lantau Fixed Crossing Project Management Office was in charge of the administration and implementation of the Airport Railway Lantau Fixed Crossing and the North Lantau Expressway projects.

1992   The Airport and Port Access Office was retitled Airport and Port Access Project Management Office on October 16.

1995   A Major Works Project Management Office was established to manage non-airport core programme projects. The Railway Development Office was set up to oversee and co-ordinate all necessary administrative arrangements related to railway development.

2001   The Highways Department comprised four main parts: Headquarters, Regional Highways Offices (Hong Kong, Kowloon and New Territories), Railway Development Office and Major Works Project Management Office. Major works supervised by the Railway Development Office included KCR West Rail; MTR Tseung Kwan O extension; Ma On Shan-Tai Wai rail link; KCR East Rail Hung

Hom-Tsim Sha Tsui extension; Sheung Shui-Lok Ma Chau spur line; and Penny's Bay rail link. Capital works under the supervision of the Major Works Project Management Office involved: Routes 7, 9 and 10; Tsing Yi North Coastal Road; Tuen Mun Road improvement; the widening of Tolo and Fanling Highways; the improvement of Island Eastern Corridor's link with the Central-Wan Chai Bypass; the widening of Yuen Long Highway and Central Kowloon Route.

2002   The structure of the Department remained unchanged.

Sources:

1. Government Information Services, *Hong Kong: The Fact Highways*, Hong Kong, Government Printer, June 1986, May 1988, August 1990, October 1991, 1996, p.19.
2. *Staff List Hong Kong Government,* Hong Kong, Government Printer,1986, p.296; 1991, p.340; 1995, p.411.
3. *Staff List the Government of Hong Kong Special Administrative Region*, Hong Kong, Government Printer, 1997, p.438; 2000, p.490.
4. www.hyd.gov.hk/

	Highways Department — Changes in Director		
Year	**Name of Department**	**Title**	**Name of Director**
1986-1989	Highways Department	Director of Highways	Beaton, Harold Campbell
1989-1993	Highways Department	Director of Highways	Kwei, See-kan
1993-1996	Highways Department	Director of Highways	Kwong, Hon-sang
1996-2000	Highways Department	Director of Highways	Leung, Kwok-sun
2000-2002	Highways Department	Director of Highways	Lo, Yiu-ching

Sources:
1. *Staff List Hong Kong Government,* Hong Kong, Government Printer, 1986-96.
2. *Staff Biographies Hong Kong Government,* Hong Kong, Government Printer, 1986, 1988, 1990, 1993.
3. *Staff Biographies the Government of the Hong Kong Special Administrative Region,* Hong Kong, Government Printer, 1998, 2001.
4. www.hyd.gov.hk/

Kowloon-Canton Railway (1899-1982)
Kowloon-Canton Railway Corporation (1982-2002)

1899   A preliminary agreement on the construction of Kowloon-Canton Railway (KCR) was signed between British and Chinese Corporation and the Director of the Imperial Chinese Railway Administration on March 28. P. T. Somerville Large, Director of British and Chinese Corporation, was in charge of the preliminary survey for the railway.

1905   J. C. Bruce, Chief Surveying Engineer of the Public Works Department, carried out surveys on the cost of the eastern and western routes of the railway.

1906   The construction project was divided into three sections: Section one from Kowloon to Beacon Hill Tunnel; Section two the Beacon Hill Tunnel; and Section three from Beacon Hill to the frontier. The Colonial Office approved the project in February. The whole project was under the auspices of the Crown Agents, with the firm of John Wolfe Barry and Leslie acting as consultant engineers.

1909   Yau Ma Tei Station, Fanling Station and Tai Po Tunnel were completed.

1910   The British Section was opened for traffic on October 1. The management of the Railway was carried out through five administrative units: Administration (comprised the Accounts Office and Store Office), Locomotive Superintendent's Office, Traffic Department, Carriages and Wagons Department, and Engineering Department.

1911   The constant rise in construction costs faced many criticisms. Traffic with Canton commenced on October 5.

1912   The supervision of work and maintenance on telephone poles and lines were transferred to the Public Works Department.

1921   The Railway Night School was established in 1921 and was closed in 1925.

1924   The Railway First Aid Division was set up.

1936   Various employees of the railway formed a unit known as the Railway Operating Department Cadre as part of the Hong Kong Volunteer Defence Force. The unit consisted two parts: an operating detachment to carry out ordinary combat duties and run the Railway under conditions of war; and a construction detachment to carry out demolition.

1941   The General Manager of the Railway was appointed a member of the War Supplies Board that had direct responsibilities for the Colony's war efforts.

1946   British military authorities were involved in the reconstruction of the railway. The re-establishment of civilian control of the Railway was difficult due to the loss of accounting and other records during the Japanese occupation. Reconstruction of information was made from the memories of clerical staff. The Railway was handed over to civilian management in the same year. Traffic between the British and Chinese Sections continued on the basis of the pre-war agreement. Insufficient seat capacity had resulted in a black market trade in railway tickets, and unlicensed lorries operated along the Tai Po Road routinely to compete with KCR. The organization of KCR was divided into five main sections: Traffic Section, Way and Works Section, Operation Section, Mechanical Workshops, Store Section.

1947   To combat competition from unlicensed lorries, a local company was permitted to serve along the Tai Po Road with fares set at the same level as the Railway's. The workshop staff went on strike for a month which caused a loss of revenue of $420,000.

1949   From October onwards, all British Section trains terminated at Lo Wu.

1951   More than five million passengers were carried during the year. The British tried to balance arrivals and departures by introducing a quota system whereby the number of people allowed out was limited to the number coming in the previous day; the move aroused protests from the Chinese Government. A new timetable was introduced with reduced services to curb operating costs.

1952   KCR hired 88 permanent and pensionable staff, 304 monthly-paid employees and 390 daily-paid workers.

1954   A through-mail service between Kowloon and Canton was reintroduced.

1955   A new fare tariff for local services was introduced. A new station was built at Ma Liu Shui between Sha Tin and Tai Po Kau.

1956   KCR employed 117 permanent and pensionable staff, 446 non-pensionable staff and 108 daily-paid staff.

1960   The posts of General Manager and Engineer of Way and Works were combined.

1961   A temporary isolation centre was set up at Kowloon Station, Tsim Sha Tsui, as a precautionary measure against the outbreak of cholera on August 16. From August 18, the Chinese Section required all passengers from Hong Kong to have a valid certificate showing that they had been inoculated against cholera at least six days before. The requirement was implemented again in 1964 and 1965.

1962   Extensive damage was done to railway embankment and sea walls between Sha Tin Station and Tai Po Market Station by Typhoon Wanda. KCR suffered damage amounting to HK$469,069.

1963   A new power signalling system was installed at Kowloon Station on November 28.

1967   A new passenger timetable was introduced. The last train leaving Kowloon Station was extended to 2230 hours on weekdays and 2300 hours on Saturdays, Sundays and public holidays; but the two last outbound trains terminated their journeys at Sheung Shui instead of Lo Wu due to the lack of passengers. Railway services were disturbed by bomb disturbances.

1968   The removal plan of the railway terminus from Tsim Sha Tsui to Hung Hom was approved. Yau Ma Tei Station was renamed Mong Kok Station on December 31.

1972   Construction works done included the double-tracking of the railway line between the new terminus in Hung Hom and Sha Tin; rebuilding of Mong Kok and Sha Tin Stations; provision of signalling equipment for the tunnel section; and construction of a spur line from the railway workshops in Ho Tung Lau to the racecourse site in Sha Tin.

1973   Torrential rainstorms caused by Typhoon Dot caused extensive damage to railway properties.

1975	Several new posts such as Project Manager, Marketing Manager and Training Manager were created. The Project Manager was responsible for liaison with other government departments, and improvement of project implementation. The Marketing Manager exploited more value from the Railway's assets. The Training Manager planned and carried out professional training. The most significant construction project this year was the opening of the new Kowloon Station at Hung Hom on November 24.
1976	The revision of the railway standing orders was completed. The Railway suffered a major disruption between Tai Wai and Sha Tin when a rainstorm destroyed the bridge over Shing Mun River in August.
1977	KCR was reorganized into four major units. The Planning and Administration Division was responsible for the general administration of KCR. The Traffic Division was responsible for the trains, terminal and station operations, marketing and public relations. The Way and Works Division dealt with the development of civil engineering projects. The Workshops Section was in charge of the maintenance of mechanical workshops and signalling system.
1978	The Workshops Section and the Ways and Works Division were replaced by the Technical Division, which comprised the Electrical and Mechanical Section and the Civil Engineering Section. The Electrical and Mechanical Section supervised the maintenance works such as telecommunications and electronic equipment at Hung Hom Terminus, new colour light signaling system between Hung Hom and Sha Tin Stations, and the operation of locomotives. The Civil Engineering Section liaised with the Public Works Department, ensured the safety of railway operations, and supervised the construction of capital projects undertaken by contractors.
1979	The agreement between KCR and Guangzhou Railway Administration to reinstate a through-passenger train between Kowloon and Canton after a break of 30 years was concluded.
1982	The first stage of electrification programme of the Railway was completed. Kowloon-Canton Railway Corporation (KCRC) was established on December 24 under the Kowloon-Canton Railway Corporation Ordinance (Cap. 372). The Corporation was entirely owned by the Hong Kong Government. One thousand four hundred and sixty employees were transferred from KCR to KCRC.
1983	KCRC was divided into four divisions: Engineering, Operations, Personnel and Administration, and Finance. Apart from the operation of the railway system between Kowloon and Lo Wu, KCRC developed associated commercial activities including advertising sales, marketing of concessions and property leasing.
1984	The Commercial Division was set up to supervise all revenue-earning activities. KCRC was also responsible for the construction and subsequent operation of the western New Territories Light Rail Transit system (LRT).
1985	The Planning and Development Department was established to centralize all project planning, survey work, industrial engineering and administration. The Fo Tan Station and the Racecourse Station were put into operation.
1986	Legislation empowering KCRC to construct and operate LRT was enacted.

1987	KCRC was restructured into the following divisions: Bus, Freight, Heavy Rail, Light Rail, Property.
1988	LRT came into operation in September 1988.
1989	The Planning and Projects Division was established.
1990	The construction of an extension of LRT to Tin Shui Wai was scheduled to operate in 1992.
1993	The Tin Shui Wai extension of light rail was put into operation in January.
1998	KCRC conducted detailed studies and proposals to build new railway lines. The largest one — Phase 1 of West Rail — would run from north-west New Territories to Kowloon. Others new projects included a line connecting Ma On Shan to East Rail at Tai Wai; an extension of East Rail from Hung Hom Terminus to Tsim Sha Tsui; and a spur line running from Sheung Shui to Lok Ma Chau.
2002	The organization structure of KCRC was as follows: East Rail Division (Domestic and Lo Wu Services, Intercity Passenger Services and Freight Department); Light Rail Division (Light Rail Services and Bus Services); Property Division (Property Services Department and Property Development Department); Planning and Works Group (West Rail Division, East Rail Extensions Division and Capital Projects Planning Department); Finance and Management Services Division (Financial Services and Control Department, Corporate Treasury, Procurement Department, Information Technology Services Department, Revenue Department and Quality Department); Company Secretariat and Legal Department; Corporate Affairs Department; Human Resource Department; Internal Audit Department.

Sources:

1. *Annual Report of the General Manager, Kowloon Canton Railway*, 1946-1948, 1949-1961 Hong Kong, Government Printer.
2. *Hong Kong Annual Departmental Report by the General Manager, Kowloon Canton Railway, 1951-1979*, Hong Kong, Government Printer.
3. *The Hong Kong Civil Service List 1948*, Hong Kong, Local Printing Press, 1949, pp.65-66.
4. "Kowloon Canton Railway (British Section)", *Hong Kong Administration Reports*, Hong Kong Government, Appendix S, 1934, S21; 1935, S24.
5. "Kowloon Canton Railway (British Section)", *Hong Kong Administrative Reports*, Hong Kong Government, Appendix Q, 1909, Q2, Q3.
6. "Kowloon Canton Railway (British Section)", *Hong Kong Administrative Reports* Hong Kong Government, Appendix R, 1913, R20.
7. "Kowloon Canton Railway (British Section)", *Hong Kong Administrative Reports*, Hong Kong Government, Appendix S, 1920, S2; 1923, S7; 1924, S6, S14; 1925, S24; 1926, S8, S25, S31.
8. *Kowloon-Canton Railway Corporation Annual Report,* Hong Kong, Government Printer, 1983, 1985-1991, 1993.
9. Phillips, Robert, *Kowloon-Canton Railway (British Section)*, Hong Kong: Urban Council, 1990.
10. Trevor, I.B., General Manager of Kowloon-Canton Railway, British Section, "The Kowloon-Canton Railway" in Braga, J.M. ed., *Hong Kong Business Symposium*, Hong Kong, *South China Morning Post*, 1957.
11. www.kcrc.com/

Kowloon Canton Railway Corporation — Changes in Names and Directors

Year	Name of Department	Title	Name of Director
1906-1909	Kowloon-Canton Railway	Chief Resident Engineer	Eves, Graves William
1909-1911	Kowloon-Canton Railway	Chief Resident Engineer	Lindsey, Edward Sergint
1911-1927	Kowloon-Canton Railway	Manager, Kowloon Canton Railway	Winslow, Herbert Pinckney
1927-1934	Kowloon-Canton Railway	Manager and Chief Engineer, Kowloon-Canton Railway	Baker, Robert
1934-1941	Kowloon-Canton Railway	Manager and Chief Engineer, Kowloon-Canton Railway	Walker, Reginald David
1946-1958	Kowloon-Canton Railway	General Manager, Kowloon-Canton Railway	Trevor, Ivan Bernard
1958-1960	Kowloon-Canton Railway	General Manager, Kowloon-Canton Railway	Lam, Po-hon
1960-1965	Kowloon-Canton Railway	Manager and Chief Engineer	Lam, Po-hon
1965-1974	Kowloon-Canton Railway	General Manager, Kowloon-Canton Railway	Lam, Po-hon
1974-1978	Kowloon-Canton Railway	General Manager, Railway and Chief Resident Engineer	Gregory, Reginald Edward
1978-1981	Kowloon-Canton Railway	General Manager, Kowloon-Canton Railway	Howes, Douglas Martin
1981-1983	Kowloon-Canton Railway	General Manager, Kowloon-Canton Railway	Wong, U-lam
1983-1990	Kowloon-Canton Railway Corporation	Chairman	Forsgate, Hugh Moss Gerald
1990-1996	Kowloon-Canton Railway Corporation	Chairman	Hyde, Kelvin O
1996-2001	Kowloon-Canton Railway Corporation	Chairman	Yeung, Kai-yin
2001-2002	Kowloon-Canton Railway Corporation	Chairman	Tien, Puk-Sun, Michael

Sources:
1. Hamilton, G.C., *Government Departments in Hong Kong 1841-1969*, Hong Kong, Government Printer, 1969.
2. *Hong Kong Annual Departmental Report by the General Manager, Railway and Chief Resident Engineer*, Hong Kong Government Printer, 1974-1975.
3. *Hong Kong Annual Departmental Report by the General Manager, Railway*, Hong Kong, Government Printer, 1977-1978.
4. *The Hong Kong Civil Service List*, Hong Kong Government, 1948-1960.
5. *Staff List Hong Kong Government*, Hong Kong, Government Printer, 1959-1982.
6. *Staff Biographies Hong Kong Government*, Hong Kong, Government Printer, 1974, 1976, 1978, 1982.
7. www.kcrc.com/

Roads and Transport Office, Public Works Department (1929-1940)
Transport Office, Public Works Department (1946-1968)
Transport Department, Public Works Department (1968-1982)
Transport Department (1982-2002)

1929	The Roads and Transport Office dealt with the design and construction of bridges, roads, streets and paths, small markets, small bathhouses, latrines, culverts, reclamation and retaining walls; works in connection with the airport and erection of hangars; supervision of bathing sheds and beaches; maintenance of all public roads and street lighting by electricity and gas; control of the work and output of government quarries; and upkeep of vehicles, road and quarry plants.
1946	The Transport Office was formed in October to advise the Director of Public Works on land transport matters, to repair and serve government land transport, and to operate a motor car pool for use on official business.
1965	Before 1965, transport services were distributed among the Public Works Department, the Police Force and the Financial Secretary. The Civil Engineering Office of the Public Works Department had a Traffic Engineering Division that planned and designed road system; provided the Police Force with technical advice and information of traffic management control and regulation measures on street parking; rendered technical advice and information to the newly established Transport Advisory Committee. The Police Force was responsible for the issuance of vehicle and driving licences. On October 26, a new Transport Office was established.
1967	The Transport Office took over all the vehicle and driving licensing powers from the Police Force and the statutory powers under road traffic and public transport legislation.
1968	On December 1, the Transport Office was upgraded to became Transport Department. The Department comprised six sections: Administration, Transport Advisory Committee Secretariat, Transport Survey, Public Transport, Licensing and Lion Rock Tunnel. It gave advice on future transportation; co-ordinated transportation activities of the public transport companies as well as the related government departments; carried out statutory duties vested under the various road traffic ordinances; and took charge of the operation of Lion Rock Tunnel.

1969	The Department co-ordinanted interdepartmental policies on road use and water transport services. The Commissioner for Transport was Chairman of the Standing Committee on Waterborne Transport the membership of which included representatives from the Marine Department, Port Works Office and Highways Office of the Public Works Department; and chairman of a standing committee on road use.
1972	The Cross Harbour Tunnel was open to traffic and the green minibus was introduced. In the Public Works Department, a new Traffic Branch under the control of the Highways Office was created. It comprised the Traffic Engineering Division, Traffic and Transport Survey Division, and Area Traffic Control Unit. The Transport Department was reorganized into three divisions: Licensing and Administration Division, General Division and Public Transport Division.
1973	The Environment Branch within the Government Secretariat was established to co-ordinate transport policy development following the McKinsey's review. The execution of policy rested with the Transport Department.
1974	A green paper on "Transport in Hong Kong" which aimed at improvements of the public transport system was tabled in the Legislative Council on June 19.
1975	The General and Traffic Division was set up to collect revenue and maintain parkingmeters. The Licensing and Administration Division was retitled Licensing Division.
1976	The Transport Department was represented on committees dealing with development in the New Territories, especially on transport facilities in new towns such as Sha Tin, Tsuen Wan and Tuen Mun. Regulations were made relating to the design of diesel-engine vehicles to meet European emission control standards on gaseous pollutants and the requirement of safety belts on the front seats of private cars.
1977	The Tunnel Management Division was set up in November to manage road tunnels such as Lion Rock Tunnel, Aberdeen Tunnel and Airport Tunnel.
1978	The Tunnel Management Division was renamed Road Tunnels Management Division. The Traffic Management Division was established to take over the functions of the former General and Traffic Division for general traffic matters, control and management of government-owned car parks.
1979	The Transport Department comprised five divisions: Licensing, Planning, Public Transport, Traffic Management and Road Tunnels Management.
1980	The Department was reorganized into three branches. The Administration Branch consisted of Licensing Division, Traffic Management Division and Road Tunnels Management Division. The Public Transport Branch administered Operations Division and Public Transport Planning Division. The Commissioner's Office dealt with overall policy and administration.
1981	The Transport Branch of the Government Secretariat controlled transport and highways construction policies. The Railway Development Division under the Public Transport Branch was set up to manage the construction of the Mass Transit Railway's Island Line, Tsuen Wan extension, and the modernization and electrification project. The North-West Development Division was set up to deal with the construction of the Light Rail Transit system in Tuen Mun.
1982	The Public Works Department was dissolved and the Transport Department became

an independent department. The Traffic and Transport Branch of the Highways Office of the Public Works Department was transferred to the Transport Department. In October, the Department was restructured on a regional basis. The Department comprised two administrative units — Administration and Licensing Branch, and Planning and Research Branch — and three regional branches. The Administration and Licensing Branch comprised five main divisions: Information and Public Relations, Licensing, Motor Vehicle Examination, Tunnels and Administration, and Vehicle Examination. The Planning and Research Branch consisted of four divisions: Public Transport Planning, Traffic and Transport Surveys, Traffic Control and Surveillance, and Road Safety. The regional branches were Hong Kong Island, Kowloon and the New Territories.

1985   The Bus Engineering Division under the Planning and Research Branch was established to monitor the maintenance of all public buses.

1986   The Traffic and Transport Surveys Division was abolished. The Comprehensive Transport Division was set up to carry out comprehensive transport studies.

1989   The Transport Department was reorganized into two regions: Urban Regional Offices and New Territories Regional Offices; and three branches — Management and Licensing Branch, Technical Services and Planning Branch, and Public Transport Development Branch.

1993   The Urban Regional Offices and the New Territories Regional Offices were combined and became Urban and New Territories Regional Offices. A new branch, Port and Airport Development Branch, was established.

1994   The Public Transport Development Branch was spilt into two branches: Bus Development Branch, and Ferry and Paratransit Branch. The Bus Development Branch was responsible for the development and planning of public bus and tram services; the Ferry and Paratransit Branch dealt with ferry, taxi and public light bus services.

1998   The Strategic Infrastructure Branch was established. It was responsible for the planning and implementation of strategic road projects and port development.

2000   The Technical Services and Planning Branch and Strategic Infrastructure Branch were merged and became two new branches: Planning Branch and Technical Services Branch. The Bus Development Branch was transformed into Bus and Railway Branch. A new branch, VALID Project Branch, was established.

2002   The Department was organized into: five branches (Administration and Licensing; Bus and Railway; Management and Paratransit; Planning; and Technical Services), and two groups of Regional Offices (Urban and New Territories).

Sources:

1.   *Hong Kong Annual Departmental Report by the Commissioner for Transport,* Hong Kong, Government Printer, 1971, pp.1-28; 1973, pp.1-24; 1973-1974, pp.1-37; 1974-1975, pp.4-8, 29; 1975, pp.4-9; 1976, pp.1-8; 1977, pp.1-8; 1978, pp.4-8; 1979, pp.3-9; 1980, pp.4-8; 1981, pp.4-9; 1982, pp.5-20; 1983, pp.5-13; 1984, pp.1-14; 1985, pp.1-14; 1986, pp.1-12.

Transport Department — Changes in Directors

Year	Name of Department	Title	Name of Director
1982-1987	Transport Department	Commissioner for Transport	Leeds, Peter Frederick
1987-1989	Transport Department	Commissioner for Transport	So, Yiu-cho, James
1989-1992	Transport Department	Commissioner for Transport	Siu, Kwing-chue, Gordon
1992-1995	Transport Department	Commissioner for Transport	Hui, Si-yan, Rafael
1995-1997	Transport Department	Commissioner for Transport	Yam Kwan, Pui-ying, Lily
1997-1998	. Transport Department	Commissioner for Transport	Law Fan, Chiu-fun, Fanny
1998-2002	Transport Department	Commissioner for Transport	Footman, Robert Charles Law

Sources:
1. *Staff Biographies Hong Kong Government,* Hong Kong Government Printer, 1968-1996.
2. *Staff Biographies the Government of the Hong Kong Special Administrative Region,* Hong Kong Government Printer, 1998, 2001.
3. Transport Department, *30th Anniversary (1968-1998),* Hong Kong, Government Printer, 1998.
4. www.info.gov.hk/td/

Water and Drainage Works

Water and Drainage Subdepartment, Public Works Department (1891-1892)
Waterworks Office, Public Works Department (1892-1924)
Drainage Office, Public Works Department (1924-1964)
Roads and Drainage Offices, Civil Engineering Office of the Public Works Department (1964-1969)
Drainage Works Division, Civil Engineering Office of the Public Works Department (1969-1982)
Drainage Works Division, Engineering Development Department (1982-1986)
Drainage Branch, Civil Engineering Services Department (1986-1989)
Drainage Services Department (1989-2002)

1862	Construction of drains was one of the major duties of the Surveyor General's Office.
1891	The Water and Drainage Subdepartment was established to handle water and drainage construction works and systems maintenance.
1892	The Water and Drainage Subdepartment was renamed Waterworks Office.
1924	The Drainage Office was set up under the charge of an Executive Engineer, with the title of Drainage Engineer.
1925	The Drainage Office undertook the design and construction of all extensions to sewers and storm-water drains; nullah drainage in connection with anti-malarial work; water supplies from wells and nullahs; and the maintenance and cleansing of the existing sewers and public septic tanks.
1946	The Drainage Office was reinstated after the Sino-Japanese War. It constructed and maintained public sewers, drains, nullahs and septic tanks, advised the Buildings Ordinance Office on drainage matters of privately-owned buildings, and for all drainage and sewer works required on behalf of the Government.
1964	The Offices of Drainage, Development, Port Works and Roads were merged to form the Civil Engineering Office. There were three Roads and Drainage Offices (Hong Kong, Kowloon and New Territories), each under the control of an Assistant Government Civil Engineer. These Offices constructed and maintained all sewerage and drainage systems, investigated and designed works to improve the overloading situations of the existing sewerage systems in the urban areas.
1965	The Civil Engineering Office was the largest Office of the Public Works Department. The two Assistant Government Civil Engineers were each responsible for three suboffices. The Hong Kong Assistant Government Civil Engineer controlled the Hong Kong Roads and Drainage Office, Traffic Engineering Office,

and Port Works and Development Office. The Mainland Assistant Government Civil Engineer controlled the Kowloon Roads and Drainage Office, New Territories Roads and Drainage Office, and Development Office.

1969 The Public Works Department was reorganized. The Roads and Drainage Offices were transformed into the Drainage Works Division under the supervision of the Civil Engineering Office. The Drainage Works Division was responsible for the planning, construction and investigation of sewerage and storm-water drainage.

1986 The Drainage Work Branch was restructured and became the Drainage Branch in the Civil Engineering Services Department. It was made up of four divisions: Drainage (Construction) Division, Drainage (Design) Division, Urban Drainage Dvision and New Territories Drainage Division.

1989 The Drainage Branch was restructured to form an independent department, Drainage Services Department. Its major duties included the operation and maintenance of drainage systems, treatment and disposal of foul water, and storm-water drainage.

1991 Groundwork for the creation of a new Land Drainage Ordinance was completed to deal with the maintenance of natural streams in the New Territories. An Emergency and Storm Damage Organization was set up to deal with emergency flooding cases.

1992 A Land Drainage Bill empowering the Government to gain access and maintain the running of the important watercourses was prepared.

1993 The Department comprised three branches. The Operations and Maintenance Branch assumed the overall strategic planning on drainage. The Projects and Development Branch was responsible for the implementation of major projects. The Electrical Mechanical Branch dealt with the research, design, installation, operation and maintenance of the electrical facilities of sewage treatment plants, sewage pumping stations and flood pumping stations.

1994 The Sewage Services Trading Fund Branch was set up. The Director of Drainage Services was nominated as General Manager of the Sewage Services Trading Fund. A sum of $6.8 billion was invested to improve the water quality of Victoria Harbour.

1995 By virtue of the Sewerage Services Ordinance enacted in December 1994, a sewage-charging scheme was introduced in April 1995. The scheme was established on the "polluter pays" principle.

1997 Waste water disposal projects implemented by the Department were divided into two categories: Sewerage Master Plans and Strategic Sewage Disposal Scheme, to collect and treat sewage discharges.

1998 The drainage services focused on the enhancement of sewerage systems in three flood-prone areas: North-West New Territories, North New Territories and West Kowloon.

2001 The Department comprised one administrative unit: Headquarters (controlled the Hong Kong and Islands Division, Mainland South Division, Mainland North Division and Land Drainage Division), and three technical branches: Projects and Development Branch, Electrical and Mechanical Branch, and Sewage Services

Branch. The Projects and Development Branch consisted of four divisions: Drainage Projects, Sewerage Projects, Project Management and Consultants Management. The Electrical and Mechanical Branch was composed of three divisions: Electrical and Mechanical Projects Division, and Sewage Treatment Divisions I and II. The Sewage Services Branch was made up of two divisions: Strategic Sewage Disposal Scheme Division and Sewage Charge Division.

2002   The four divisions formerly under the Headquarters were placed under the Operations and Maintenance Branch. For the Sewage Services Branch, the Strategic Sewage Disposal Scheme Division was renamed Harbour Area Treatment Scheme Division. All the four branches were under the direction of the Headquarters. Apart from these changes, the structure has remained the same.

Sources:

1. *Hong Kong*, Hong Kong, Government Printer, 1997, pp.214-217; 1998, pp.222-223; 1999, pp. 238-240; 2000, pp.231-233; 1998, pp.213-215.
2. *Staff List Hong Kong Government*, Hong Kong, Government Printer, 1990, p.219; 1991, p.227; 1994, p.224.
3. *Staff List the Government of Hong Kong Special Administrative Region*, Hong Kong, Government Printer, 1997, p.274; 2000, p.290.
4. www.dsd.gov.hk/index.htm

Drainage Services Department — Changes in Directors

Year	Name of Department	Title	Name of Director
1989-1990	Drainage Services Department	Director of Drainage Services	Saunders, Charles Robert
1990-1991	Drainage Services Department	Director of Drainage Services	Kuo, Ketsing Taty
1991-1994	Drainage Services Department	Director of Drainage Services	Siu, Chuen
1994-1996	Drainage Services Department	Director of Drainage Services	Ng, Yee-yum
1996-2002	Drainage Services Department	Director of Drainage Services	Collier, John
2002	Drainage Services Department	Director of Drainage Services	Cheung, Tat-kwing

Sources:
1. *Staff Biographies Hong Kong Government*, Hong Kong, Government Printer, 1990, 1993.
2. *Staff Biographies the Government of the Hong Kong Special Administrative Region*, Hong Kong, Government Printer, 1998, 2001.
3. *Staff List Hong Kong Government*, Hong Kong, Government Printer, 1989-1996.
4. *Staff List the Government of the Hong Kong Special Administrative Region*, Hong Kong, Government Printer, 1998, 2001.
5. www.dsd.gov.hk/index.htm

Waterworks Office, Surveyor General's Office / Survey Department / Public Works Department (1867-1891)
Water and Drainage Subdepartment, Public Works Department (1891-1892)
Waterworks Office, Public Works Department (1892-1982)
Water Supplies Department (1982-2002)

1842	A Land and Roads Inspector was appointed in May, he was responsible for safeguarding public watering places from damage.
1860	The Colonial Government started to provide and maintain constant supply of pure water to the City of Victoria. A rate estimated at 2% per annum on the gross value of property was charged for the maintenance of waterworks.
1863	Completion of the first reservoir, Pokfulam Reservoir, to collect fresh water.
1891	The Water and Drainage Subdepartment, was established under the direction of the Public Works Department.
1892	The Water and Drainage Subdepartment was renamed Waterworks Office.
1889	Completion of Tai Tam Reservoir with a storage capacity of 312 million gallons (mg).
1899	Completion of the 30-mg-capacity Wong Nai Chung Reservoir.
1902	Water meterage system was set up for households on Hong Kong Island and levies were charged according to consumption.
1903	A rider main system was installed to provide free water supply to Western and Central Districts of the Island.
1910	Completion of the 353-mg-capacity Kowloon Reservoir.
1917	Completion of the 1,420-mg-capacity Tai Tam Tuk Reservoir.
1923	Completion of the 116-mg-capacity Shek Lei Pui Reservor.
1930	Completion of the first cross-harbour submarine pipeline to convey fresh water to Hong Kong Island.
1931	Completion of the 360-mg-capacity Aberdeen Upper and Lower Reservoirs.
1932	Abolition of the rider main system.
1935	Completion of the second cross-harbour pipeline.
1936	Completion of the 3,000-mg-capacity Shing Mun (Jubilee) Reservoir.
1939	Completion of the third cross-harbour pipeline.
1958	Seawater flushing supply system was installed at Shek Kip Mei and Li Cheng Uk.
1959	Completion of the 4,500-mg-capacity Tai Lam Chung Reservoir.
1960	The first agreement was concluded between the Guangdong Provincial Government and the Hong Kong Government for the purchase of Dongjiang water to satisfy the rapid increase in water demand.
1963	Completion of the 5,515-mg-capacity Shek Pik Reservoir.

1965   The Waterworks Office became one of the four main subdepartments under the supervision of the Public Works Department. The two main professional subdivisions — New Works Division, Maintenance and Operation Division — supervised the following sections: Distribution, Construction, Mechanical and Electrical, and Planning.

1967   The Water Quality Control Section was established to regularly test all samples of water from raw, treated and tap sources to safeguard the quality of water supply, and to ensure the most economic use of water.

1968   Completion of the 37.4-billion-gallon-capacity Plover Cove Reservoir.

1970   The Distribution Division was set up to control maintain and extend the water distribution system. The Supply Division was set up to operate and maintain reservoirs, treatment works, trunk mains, and to provide processed hydrological data.

1971   The Desalting Division was established to operate and maintain the experimental desalter, and to supervise the manufacturing work of the desalting plant.

1973   The extension of Plover Cove Reservoir to reach a capacity of 51.8 billion gallons was completed.

1974   The Projects Division was created to plan and design the desalting plant and equipment. The Operations Division was formed to operate and maintain the desalting plant at Lok On Pai.

1975   A desalination plant was commissioned to produce fresh water from seawater.

1978   The Waterworks Office was reorganized into: Supply and Distribution Branch, Mechanical and Electrical Branch, and Desalting Branch. High Island Reservoir was completed with a capacity of 60.2 billion gallons.

1982   The Water Supplies Department became a fully autonomous department to supply, distribute fresh filtered water and to maintain and improve the waterworks system in Hong Kong. The Department consisted of the following administrative units: Headquarters, Accounts, Consultants Management, Consumer Services, Distribution, Supply, Mechanical and Electrical Operations and Maintenance, Mechanical and Electrical Projects, Design, Construction, Research Development, Water Science, Desalination.

1987   The Department was reorganized into:

       I.   Administration and Planning Branch

           1. Planning Division
           2. General Administration

       II.   Supply and Distribution Branch

           1. Mainland South East Region
           2. Mainland South West Region
           3. Mainland North West Region
           4. Mainland North East Region
           5. Hong Kong and Islands Region

 6. Regional Administration Division
 7. Water Science Division

III. New Works Branch

 1. Construction Division
 2. Consultants Management Division
 3. Design Division

IV. Mechanical and Electrical Branch

 1. Projects Division
 2. Maintenance Division
 3. Lok On Pai Desalter

1989   The China Water Supply Branch was established in February to undertake the planning, design and construction of reception and the distribution of the water supply from China.

1995   The Sewage Services Ordinance came into effect on April 1. Sewage charges and water charges were combined into one single bill and the Water Supplies Department acted as an agent to collect general sewage charges on behalf of the Drainage Services Department. The Efficiency and Management Branch was set up to review and propose measures to improve efficiency of the Department.

1998   The Efficiency and Management Branch was dissolved. The Financial Management Branch and Departmental Administration Division were established to improve the implementation of general policies of the Department.

2001   The Department comprised the Department Administration Division and five main branches: Administration and Planning Branch, New Works Branch, Mechanical and Electrical Branch, Supply and Distribution Branch, and Financial Management Branch.

2002   The structure of the Department remained unchanged.

Sources:

1. *Hong Kong Government Gazette*, Hong Kong, Noronha & Co., 2 June 1842, no. 11, vol.2; vol. 1; 14 July 1860, p.179m; 9 Oct 1903, p.145.
2. *Hong Kong,* Hong Kong, Government Printer,1984, pp.162, 166-168; 1985, pp.140-141; 1986, pp.190-191; 1991, pp.209-210; 1994, pp.206-208; 1997, pp.220-222.
3. *Hong Kong's Water*, Hong Kong, The Information and Public Relations Unit, Lands and Works Branch, March 1987, pp.18-20.
4. Ho Pui-yin, *Water for a Barren Rock: 150 Years of Water Supply in Hong Kong*, Hong Kong, The Commercial Press, 2001, p.244.
5. Jackson, Leonard, *The Hong Kong Waterworks*, Hong Kong, The Local Printing Press Ltd., 1949.
6. Waterworks Office, *Hong Kong Waterworks Data Book*, Hong Kong, Issue 1965-1966.
7. Water Supplies Department, *Annual Report,* Hong Kong, Government Printer, 1996-1998.
8. Water Supplies Department, *Water Service*, Hong Kong, Government Printer, 1996-99.
9. Woodward, W., *Report on the Water Supply of Hong Kong*, Hong Kong, Government Printer, 1937.
10. www.info.gov.hk/wsd/index.htm

Water Supplies Department — Changes in Directors

Year	Name of Department	Title	Name of Director
1982-1987	Water Supplies Department	Director of Water Supplies	Tomlinson, Thomas Herbert
1988-1992	Water Supplies Department	Director of Water Supplies	Wong, Kwok-lai
1992-1999	Water Supplies Department	Director of Water Supplies	Hu, Man-shiu
1999-2001	Water Supplies Department	Director of Water Supplies	Phillipson, Hugh Brian
2001-2002	Water Supplies Department	Director of Water Supplies	Ko, Chan-gock, William

Sources:

1. *Annual Departmental Report by the Director of Public Works,* Hong Kong, Government Printer, 1965-1973
2. Ho, Pui-yin, *Water for a Barren Rock: 150 Years of Water Supply in Hong Kong,* Hong Kong, The Commercial Press, 2001, p.150.
3. *Staff Biographies Hong Kong Government,* Hong Kong, Government Printer, 1974, 1976, 1978, 1982, 1984, 1986, 1988, 1990, 1993.
4. *Staff Biographies the Government of the Hong Kong Special Administrative Region,* Hong Kong, Government Printer, 1998, 2001.
5. *Staff List Hong Kong Government,* Hong Kong, Government Printer, 1977-1996.
6. www.info.gov.hk/wsd/index.htm

Chapter 5
Social Services

A resettlement estate in Wong Tai Sin
Kowloon, 1964

A child receiving vaccine
against poliomyelitis, 1963

Evolvement of Social Services

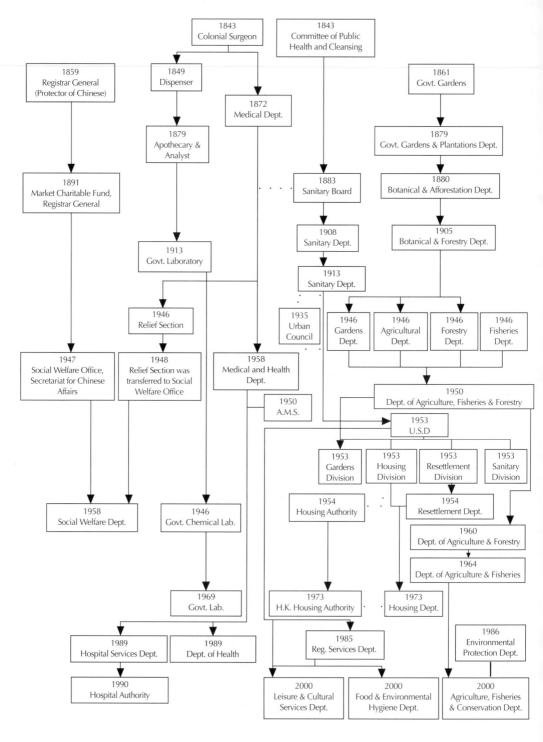

It took more than a century for Hong Kong to transform into a modern city equipped with comprehensive social welfare facilities. The social services provided by the Hong Kong Government, according to their functions and their establishment dates, can be mainly grouped into five important parts: medical; sanitary, leisure and culture; housing; environmental conservation; and social welfare. In this chapter, the presentation of the concerned departments in the social sector will follow this grouping in order to trace the origins of different kinds of social services and give some general information on the evolving characteristics of social services in Hong Kong.

The earliest social services administered by the Hong Kong Government can be traced back to 1843 when the Colonial Surgeon was first nominated. At that time the medical services served mainly European citizens and government officials. From 1850 onwards, preventive measures such as control of hygiene conditions had been adopted due to the rapid growth of the Chinese population after the Taiping Rebellion. To imitate the British medical service pattern, professional qualifications and skills were required within the medical department. Professional branches such as the Dispenser and Government Analyst were found in the middle to late nineteenth century. The early structure laid the foundation for today's medical services. The Medical Department expanded its functions and changed its name to Medical and Health Department in 1958. In 1989, it was spilt into two departments — Department of Health and Hospital Services Department. In 1990, an autonomous organization, the Hospital Authority, was set up to improve the management of hospital services.

Another early-established department that provided public health services was the Sanitary Department. Although a Committee of Public Health and Cleansing had been set up in 1844, it was not until 1883, when the Sanitary Board was established, that Chinese citizens' health conditions attracted the Government's attention. The inspection of Chinese hospitals and the control of hygiene conditions of Chinese households had been reinforced from the late nineteenth century onwards. At that time, Hong Kong had experienced the invasion of bubonic plague, the maintenance of proper hygiene conditions was considered an essential element to protect human lives and the economic development of the city.

The dimension of sanitary services changed its nature after the Sino-Japanese War, due to the rapid population growth since the 1950s. In 1951, the Urban Services Department was established and the Sanitary Department was downgraded and became a division under the Urban Services Department. The Urban Services Department contributed its work mainly on sanitary control, housing services, public leisure and cultural development. New divisions such as Housing, Resettlement and Gardens were created to satisfy the continued demands of the growing population. Construction and management of public housing estates became one of the most urgent tasks of the Government after the disastrous fire that broke out in the Shek Kip Mei squatter area in December 1953. The Resettlement Department was created in 1954, and was absorbed into the Housing Department in 1973. In January 2000, the Urban Services Department was dissolved to make way for the Food and Environmental Hygiene Department and the Leisure and Cultural Services Department.

The idea of environmental conservation had concentrated mainly on local afforestation in the early days. In 1861, a Superintendent of Government Gardens attached to the Surveyor General's Office was appointed to take care of tree plantation and public gardens. In 1879, an independent department, the Government

Gardens and Plantations Department, was set up to centralize the management of plantation and forestry. Although the Department had gone through name changes — first to Botanical and Afforestation Department and then to Botanical and Forestry Department — its functions remained unchanged until 1939. In 1940 the exploration of agriculture development and management of agricultural affairs became the new tasks of the Botanical and Forestry Department. After the Sino-Japanese War, more emphasis was put on promoting the economic performance of agriculture and fisheries. The Botanical and Forestry Department was split into four departments in 1946. They were: Gardens, Forestry, Agriculture and Fisheries. These four departments were later merged to form the Department of Agriculture, Fisheries and Forestry to reinforce local economic production. This Department was in charge of afforestation conservation and the management of the wholesale market of the vegetables and fisheries since the 1960s. In the mid 1970s its the Director became the Country Park Authority. Its focus on environmental conservation was reiterated again in the late 1990s.

Private charitable associations had borne the major responsibilities for providing assistance to the poor and emergency relief, working with the Secretariat for Chinese Affairs. The 1909 Charitable Fund run by the Secretariat for Chinese Affairs was considered the earliest government social welfare foundation in Hong Kong. The Social Welfare Office was set up in 1947 (much later than the provision of medicalservices), as a subdepartment of the Secretariat for Chinese Affairs, to act as the general liaison between the Government and the kaifong welfare associations, women's welfare clubs and other bodies with district or clan allegiance. The independent Social Welfare Department was established in 1958. Since then social services were extended to Chinese citizens down to the lower classes. It protected women and girls, carried out arbitration inneighbourhood and family disputes and provided large-scale emergency relief assistance subsequent to sudden disasters. The wide scope of services rendered signified improvements in living conditions of society.

The evolution of social services in Hong Kong began by attending to the basic survival needs, namely, the medical and health services. Their remit was gradually expanded to take in the provision and management of public housing, conservation of the countryside and the environment, and the organization of cultural and leisure activities to satisfy the growing demands of the much larger population. The dimensions of social services are no longer restricted to the provision of emergency assistance to the poor; they also create a better living environment for everyone in Hong Kong.

Medical Services

Colonial Surgeon (1843-1897)
Medical Department (1872-1958)
Medical and Health Department (1958-1989)
Department of Health (1989-2002)
Hospital Services Department (1989-1999)
Hospital Authority (1990-2002)

Colonial Surgeon / Medical Department

1843   A Colonial Surgeon was nominated. The Medical Board was established and its members included: Colonial Surgeon, Senior Naval and Military Medical Officer, two registered medical practitioners and three other appointed members. The Colonial Surgeon's Office catered for the needs of government officers and overseers of roads; the police, and their wives and children, prisoners; and verified the qualifications of persons applying to be medical and surgical practitioners.

1850   A government hospital was constructed.

1864   The post of Medical Superintendent was created.

1866   A qualified medical practitioner was appointed Medical Inspector. He inspected houses and controlled the sanitary conditions in Hong Kong.

1867   An Inspector of Hospital and Visiting Surgeon were appointed.

1868   A Medical Officer were appointed to examine immigrants.

1872   The Medical Department was established. Its areas of responsibilities included hospital and apothecary services, port health, lunatic asylum and quarantine hospital.

1890   The Medical Department was divided into three branches: Government Civil Hospital, Medical Office and Government Analyst.

1895   The Medical Department was restructured. It consisted of six branches: Colonial Surgeon and Medical Officer, Medical Officer of Victoria Gaol, Hospital, Public Mortuary, Medical Officer of Port and Government Analyst. The Colonial Surgeon and Medical Officer was in charge of the executive and administrative work and provided consolation services to government officers and reports or certificates to the Police Magistrate for serious criminal cases. The Medical Officer of Victoria Gaol provided medical services for the prisoners and police staff. The Hospital was in charge of the management of government hospitals. The Public Mortuary was responsible for the reception and burial of dead. The Medical Officer of Port inspected all ships and vessels entering the harbour, performed health control on board, signed certificates of health and examined all out-going emigrants. The Government Analyst analyzed food, drug, liquors, mineral, pharmaceutical products, opium, building materials and public water quality.

1897   The Colonial Surgeon was renamed Principal Civil Medical Officer.

1900   The New Territories Section was created to provide routine services to Tai Po, Sheung Shui, Sha Tau Kok, Au Tau, San Tin and Ping Shan districts in the New Territories. The provision of medical care was under the supervision of Chinese Medical Officers.

1902   The Government Public Dispensaries were set up to give medical treatment to patients. The Bacteriological Institute was established to carry out routine bacteriological examinations.

1908   The Sanitary Department was set up as an attachment to the Medical Department.

1913   The Government Laboratory was set up to take over the work of the Government Analyst Division. The Sanitary Department became independent.

1923   The Radiological Section, responsible for radiographic examinations including visualization of deeper organs, was established.

1929   The Principal Civil Medical Officer was renamed Director of Medical and Sanitary Services. European Medical Officers were appointed with part-time duties in the New Territories. To provide opportunities of acquiring first hand information of sanitary work, the Director of Medical and Sanitary Services was nominated as a member of the Sanitary Board. The Medical Department was restructured as follows:

I.   Health Division

    1. Port Health Branch
    2. Venereal Diseases Branch
    3. Maternity and Child Welfare Branch
    4. Chinese Hospital and Dispensaries Branch
    5. School Inspection Branch

II.   Medical Division

    1. Clinical Branch
    2. Pharmacy Branch
    3. Radiology Branch
    4. New Territories Branch

III.   Investigative Division

    1. Bacteriological Institute

IV.   Division of Chemical Analysts

    1. Government Laboratory

Assuming the duties of the Medical Officer of Port, the Health Division was responsible for vaccinations for emigrants, supervision of Chinese hospitals and dispensaries, implementation of preventive measures against infectious diseases, provision of maternity and child welfare, medical inspections of school and promotion work for public health and hygiene for students. The Medical Division was in charge of the management of hospitals and the provision of Western medical care for residents in the New Territories. The Investigative Division controlled the public mortuaries and examined disinfectants and pathological materials. The Division of Chemical Analysts inspected and analyzed food, drug, liquors, mineral, pharmaceutical products, opium, building materials and public water quality.

1930   The Malariological Branch, also known as the Malaria Bureau, was established under the Investigative Division to carry out scientific investigations of malaria and render assistance to government departments with respect to mosquito nuisances.

1932   The head of the Department — Director of Medical and Sanitary Services — became the Registrar of Births and Deaths. It was planned to transfer the function of registering births and deaths to the Medical Department. Statistics were collected from 11 registration offices in Hong Kong Island, seven offices in Kowloon and 11 offices in the New Territories.

1934   The registration function of births and deaths was formally transferred to the Medical Department.

1936   The Director of Medical and Sanitary Services was renamed Director of Medical Services.

1939   The Nutrition Research Committee and the Technical Committee were established. The Director of Medical Services was Chairman of both Committees. The Nutrition Research Committee was responsible for devising and promoting an economic but satisfactory diet for the poor. The Technical Committee was concerned with the reorganization and improvement of existing government hospitals and clinical facilities. Special war measures including the recruitment and training of medical personnel; the establishment of casualty clearing and relief hospitals; the collection of ambulances, stretchers, instruments and dressing and planning for first aid posts were adopted.

1946   The Medical Department comprised the following units: Health Services, Medical Services, Births and Deaths Registry, Government Chemical Laboratory (formerly Government Laboratory), Pathological Institute, Relief Section, Nursing Staff and Almoners. Health Services was responsible for the general management of public health work such as the promotion of health education, the prevention of infectious diseases, and the provision of maternity and child welfare. The Medical Services was in charge of the registration of pharmacists, the issue of wholesale licences and the control of the use of all medicines, the management of government and government-assisted hospitals, out-patient clinics, dispensaries, health centres and dental clinics.

1948   The Relief Section of the Medical Department was transferred over to the Social Welfare Office. After the transfer of the Relief Section, Almoners became responsible for the medical social welfare activities.

1950   The title of the Director of Medical Services was changed to Director of Medical and Health Services. The administration of dangerous drugs was transferred from the Commerce and Industry Department to the Medical Department. The Auxiliary Medical Services was established to supplement the emergency work of the Medical Department such as ambulances and first aid services and to provide trained men for the treatment of casualties.

1951   The units of Government Chemical Laboratory, Pathological Institute, Almoners and Nursing Staff were placed under the Medical Services.

1952   The administration of ambulance services was transferred to the Fire Brigade.

1954   The Department was reorganized into two divisions: Health Division and Medical Division. Special services such as physiotherapy and ophthalmiatrics were provided.

1956   The Nursing Services unit was established. The Occupational Therapy Services unit was set up to provide long term services to psychiatric cases at the Mental Hospital.

1957   The function of registering births and deaths was transferred to the Registrar General's Department with effect from April 1.

Medical and Health Department

1958   The Medical Department changed its name to Medical and Health Department. The Radiation Board was set up to issue licences, to control import, export, possession and the use of radioactive substances according to Ordinance no. 35 of 1957.

1959   The Planning Unit was established to prepare an outline for the development of medical and health facilities, to liaise with government departments and give assistance to voluntary organizations and philanthropic bodies.

1965   A committee was formed in February to ensure maximum co-operation and co-ordination of the anti-tuberculosis services. The Registration of Medical Clinics was set up to control service standards of private clinics.

1973   The Medical Development Advisory Committee (MDAC) was set up in March to review and advise on the development of medical and health services in Hong Kong.

1974   The Narcotics and Drug Administration Division was formed to undertake treatment and rehabilitation of drug addicts.

1977   Regionalization of medical and health services based on geographical distribution was implemented in April. The Department had three divisions: Health, Medical and Administration.

1980   The School Dental Services unit was established to provide regular dental examination and simple dental treatment for primary school children.

1981   Further regionalization of medical and health services through the reorganization of headquarters. The Department was restructured into four divisions: Health Services and Planning, Medical Services, Administration and Non-regional Services.

1987   Integration of government and subvented hospitals to form an independent statutory hospital authority.

1988   The Provisional Hospital Authority was set up in October.

1989   The Medical and Health Department was reorganized into the Department of Health and the Hospital Services Department.

Department of Health

1989   The Medical and Health Department was reorganized. A new Department of Health was established on April 1. The Department was the principal health authority in Hong Kong on health-related matters. Its duties were to develop health services for the promotion of positive health and to prevent diseases; it also trained health personnel and liaised with the Hospital Services Department. The Department consisted of five divisions: Personal Health Services, Special Health Services, Non-regional Health Services, Health Administration and Planning, General Administration and Public Health Nursing.

1990   A new division of the Hygiene Division was established to control food safety and to maintain advisory services to public on food. It also carried out pest control and promotion of hygienic practices and behaviours.

1992   The Dental Service Section was transformed into the Dental Division in April.

1995   A Student Health Service unit was set up to promote and maintain the physical and psychological health of primary and secondary school students.

1996   Two Deputy Directors supervised the services of the Department. The first Deputy Director oversaw the Personal Health Services, Elderly Health Services, Non-regionalized Health Services, Hygiene, Nursing and Accounts Services. The second Deputy Director was put in charge of the Special Health Services, Health Administration and Planning, and another group of Non-regionalized Services.

1997   The Traditional Chinese Medicine Division was established to develop a statutory framework for the future regulation of the practice, use and trading of Chinese medicine.

1999   The Hospital Services Department was merged with the Department of Health. The Hospital Staff Division was set up to advise the Hospital Authority head office and individual hospitals on administrative, manpower and other personnel matters.

2000   The Hygiene Division was transferred to the Food and Environmental Hygiene Department. The Disease Prevention and Control Division was established to strengthen the control of diseases.

2002   The Department was organized into three major areas, led by two Deputy Directors of Health and a Consultant-in-charge. One Deputy Director had control over the Non-regionalized Health Services, Elderly Health Services, Personal Health Services, Public Health Nursing Division, Finance and Supplies Division. Another Deputy Director directed another group of Non-regionalized Health Services, Special Health Services, Traditional Chinese Medicine, Health Administration and Planning, Administration, Boards and Councils, Hospital Staff Division. The Consultant-in-charge oversaw the Dental Care Services.

Hospital Services Department

1989   The Hospital Services Department was established on April 1. It was responsible for the operation of regional, district and convalescent hospitals, specialist outpatient clinics, day care centres and rehabilitative services. A regional approach was adopted in planning and administration of medical and health services. The services were provided based on geographical distribution: Hong Kong, Kowloon, New Territories East and New Territories West. The Department was divided into three sub-departments: Hospital and Clinic Services, Rehabilitative Services and Special Services.

1991   The formal transfer of the public hospital system to the Hospital Authority took place on December 1, 1991. The Director and Deputy Director of the Hospital Services Department were renamed Administrator and Deputy Administrator respectively.

1999   The Hospital Services Department merged with the Department of Health and became the Hospital Staff Division of the Department of Health.

Related Organization: Hospital Authority (1990-2002)

1987   The Government took the initiative to establish a Hospital Authority to administer hospital services in Hong Kong.

1988   The Provisional Hospital Authority was formed on October 1 to prepare for the formal statutory body.

1990   The Hospital Authority was set up on December 1 by the Hospital Authority Ordinance.

1991   The formal transfer of management responsibilities for the public hospital system to the Hospital Authority took place on December 1. The management of 36 hospitals, and 56 specialist centres and institutions from 16 organizations, was transferred to the Hospital Authority. It comprised three main branches: Operations, Development and Secretary General.

2002   Under the Chief Executive's Office, the Hospital Authority was organized into the following functional areas: Professional Services and Planning, Professional Services and Public Affairs, Professional Services and Human Resources, Professional Services and Medical Development, Finance, Cluster Chief Executives (Hong Kong East, New Territories East and Kowloon East).

Sources:

1. *Annual Departmental Report by the Director of Medical and Health Services for the Financial Year 1950-1951*, Hong Kong, Government Printer, pp.1-7, 66-67.
2. Choa, G.H., *The Life and Times of Sir Kai Ho*, Hong Kong, The Chinese University of Hong Kong Press, 1981, p.29.
3. *CO129/480*, Governor R.E. Stubbs to Duke of Devonshire, 27 Feb, 26 July, 1923.
4. *Hong Kong Annual Departmental Report by the Director of Health*, Hong Kong, Government Printer, 1989-1999.
5. *Hong Kong Annual Departmental Report by Director of Hospital Services*, Hong Kong, Government Printer, 1989-1991.
6. *Hong Kong Annual Departmental Report by the Director of Medical Health Services*, Hong Kong, Government Printer, 1951-1989.
7. *Hong Kong Annual Report by the Director of Medical Services*, Hong Kong Government, 1948-1950.
8. "Hong Kong Civil Affairs Policy Directives Medical and Health Policy", *Hong Kong Directives*, Hong Kong, 1945, HKRS 211 D&S no 2/4.
9. *Hong Kong Government Annual Report of the Medical Department for 1946*, Local Printing Press, 1947, pp.1-3, 24-25.
10. *Hong Kong Government Gazette*, Hong Kong Governemnt, July 27, 1867; Nov. 16, 1872, p.484; March 21, 1891, p.196; July 18, 1891, pp.581-586.
11. *Hospital Authority Annual Report*, Hong Kong, Hospital Authority (Public Affairs Division), 1990-2000.
12. "Joint Report of the Principal Civil Medical Officer and the Medical Officer of Health", in *Hong Kong Administrative Reports*, Hong Kong Government, 1910.

13. *Report of the Director of Medical Services for 1947*, Hong Kong Government, 1948, pp1-28.
14. www.info.gov.hk/dh/

Medical Department — Changes in Names and Directors

Year	Name of Department	Title	Name of Director
1843-1844	Colonial Surgeon	Colonial Surgeon	Anderson, Alexander
1844-1846	Colonial Surgeon	Colonial Surgeon	Dill, Francis
1846-1847	Colonial Surgeon	Colonial Surgeon	Young, Peter
1847-1854	Colonial Surgeon	Colonial Surgeon	Morrison, William
1854-1858	Colonial Surgeon	Colonial Surgeon	Dempster, James Carroll
1858-1859	Colonial Surgeon	Colonial Surgeon	Harland, William Aurelius
1859-1872	Colonial Surgeon	Colonial Surgeon	Murray, John Ivoy
1872-1873	Medical Department	Colonial Surgeon	McCoy, Robert
1873-1897	Medical Department	Colonial Surgeon	Ayres, Philip Bernard Chenery
1897-1912	Medical Department	Principal Civil Medical Officer	Atkinson, John Mitford
1912-1923	Medical Department	Principal Civil Medical Officer	Johnson, John Taylor Connell
1923-1929	Medical Department	Principal Civil Medical Officer	Addison, Joseph Bartlett
1929-1936	Medical Department	Director of Medical and Sanitary Services	Wellington, Arthur Robartes
1936-1938	Medical Department	Director of Medical Services	Wellington, Arthur Robartes
1938-1941	Medical Department	Director of Medical Services	Selwyn-Clarke, Percy Selwyn
1946-1950	Medical Department	Director of Medical Services	Newton, Isaac
1950-1952	Medical Department	Director of Medical & Health Services	Newton, Isaac
1952-1958	Medical Department	Director of Medical & Health Services	Yeo, Kok-cheang

Sources:
1. *The Hong Kong Civil Service List*, Hong Kong Government, 1948; 1950-53.

Department of Health — Changes in Names and Directors			
Year	Name of Department	Title	Name of Director
1938-1941	Medical Department	Director of Medical Services	Selwyn-Clarke, Percy Selwyn
1947-1950	Medical Department	Director of Medical Services	Newton, Isaac
1950-1952	Medical Department	Director of Medical & Health Services	Newton, Isaac
1952-1958	Medical Department	Director of Medical & Health Services	Yeo, Kok-cheang
1958-1963	Medical and Health Department	Director of Medical & Health Services	MacKenzie, David James Masterton
1963-1970	Medical and Health Department	Director of Medical & Health Services	Teng, Pin-hui
1970-1976	Medical and Health Department	Director of Medical & Health Services	Choa, Gerald Hugh
1977-1988	Medical and Health Department	Director of Medical & Health Services	Thong, Kah-leong
1988-1989	Medical and Health Department	Director of Medical & Health Services	Lee, Shiu-hung
1989-1994	Department of Health	Director of Health	Lee, Shiu-hung
1994-2002	Department of Health	Director of Health	Chan Fung, Fu-chun, Margaret

Sources:
1. *The Hong Kong Civil Service List,* Hong Kong Government, 1948-1958.
2. *Staff List, Hong Kong Government,* Hong Kong, Government Printer, 1963-1996.
3. *Staff Biographies Hong Kong Government,* Hong Kong, Government Printer, 1970; 1978; 1990.
4. *Staff Biographies the Government of the Hong Kong Special Administrative Region,* Hong Kong, Government Printer, 1997-2002.
5. www.info.gov.hk/dh/

Government Laboratory (1969-2002)

1849   The Dispenser of the Government Civil Hospital was first appointed to carry out chemical analyses.

1864   The Dispenser was renamed Apothecary.

1879   The title of Apothecary was changed to Apothecary and Analyst.

1890   The Government Analyst Branch of the Medical Department was in charge of the analysis of food, drug, liquors, mineral, pharmaceutical products, opium, building materials and public water quality.

1913   The Government Analyst Division was replaced by the Government Laboratory.

1946   The name was changed to Government Chemical Laboratory.

1969   The Government Chemical Laboratory was spilt from the Medical and Health Services Department and became an independent department with the title of Government Laboratory. Acting as the main centre for analytical chemistry, it provided analytical, investigation and advisory services to government departments as well as selected private entities. It was divided into: Forensic, Toxicology, Commerce and Industry, Urban Services, Drug and General.

1978   The Department was restructured into the General Division and the Forensic Division. The General Division provided analytical support services to food, dutiable products, pharmaceuticals, dangerous goods and a wide range of commodities. The Forensic Division provided scientific services in the areas such as narcotics, toxicology, scheduled poisons and general forensic science to the Hong Kong Police Force, Customs and Excise Department, ICAC, Immigration Department and other law enforcement organizations.

1979   The General Division also examined products submitted for registration under the Pharmacy and Poisons Regulations, pharmaceutical products purchased for use in governmental hospitals and clinics, and physical and chemical testings of food under the Public Health and Urban Services Ordinance.

1980   The Department commenced environmental science study and the installation of computerized data systems.

1981   The General Division of the Department undertook subsequent analysis of heavy metal contained in flying ashes emitted from incinerators. The Environment Science Section was established under the General Division to provide supporting services to the Environmental Protection Agency, and to perform scientific work for the Consumer Council.

1985   The General Division was replaced by the Analytical and Advisory Services Division. It monitored environmental pollution and conducted commodities testing for health and safety evaluation. The Forensic Division was renamed Forensic Science Division. It provided comprehensive forensic scientific services to the criminal justice system on crimes such as arsons, burglaries, counterfeiting, deceptions, document forgeries, frauds, hit-and-run traffic accidents, homicides, illegal manufacture and possession of drugs, drug abuse, rapes and robberies.

1989   The Forensic Science Division detected possible adulteration of Chinese herbal medicines with Western synthetic drugs. The Analytical and Advisory Services Division monitored nitrosamines and radioactive contaminants in food.

1994   The Physical and Biochemical Evidence Group was established under the Forensic Science Division and it was responsible for DNA compiling work to solve sex crimes, among other functions.

1996   An Administration Division was set up to deal with financial budgeting, centralization of stocks and supplies services and human resources and quality management.

2002   The structure of the Department was as follows:

    I.   Forensic Science Division

        1. Physical and Biochemical Evidence Group

        2. Drugs and Toxicology Group

    II. Analytical and Advisory Services Division

        1. Environmental Chemistry and Other Scientific Services Group

        2. Health Science and Commodities Testing Services Group

    III. Administration Division

        1. Physical Resource Management Section

        2. Human Resource and Quality Management Section

Sources:

1. *Goverment Laboratory Annual Report*, Hong Kong, Government Printer, 1978, pp.1-3.
2. *Hong Kong*, Hong Kong, Government Printer, 1980-1996.
3. www.info.gov.hk/govlab/

Government Laboratory — Changes in Directors

Year	Name of Department	Title	Name of Director
1969-1984	Government Laboratory	Government Chemist	Nutten, Albert John
1984-1996	Government Laboratory	Government Chemist	Lee, Nam-sang
1996-1998	Government Laboratory	Government Chemist	Daily, Bryce Nelson
1998-1999	Government Laboratory	Government Chemist	Chan, Chi-kin
1999-2002	Government Laboratory	Government Chemist	Clarke, David George

Sources:
1. *Staff List the Government of the Hong Kong Special Administrative Region*, Hong Kong, Government Printer, 2000.
2. *Staff Biographies Hong Kong Government*, Hong Kong Government Printer, 1993.
3. *Staff Biographies the Government of the Hong Kong Special Administrative Region*, Hong Kong, Government Printer, 1998; 2001.
4. www.info.gov.hk/govlab/

Health, Leisure and Cultural Services

Sanitary Board (1883-1935)
Sanitary Department (1908-1953)
Urban Services Department (1953-1999)
Food and Environmental Hygiene Department (2000-2002)
Leisure and Cultural Services Department (2000-2002)

Sanitary Board

1843   A Committee of Public Health and Cleansing was established.

1844   The first ordinances relating to sanitation were enacted.

1883   The Sanitary Board was set up under the provisions of Ordinance no. 7 of 1883 to supervise and control all matters relating to sanitation. Members of the Board included the Surveyor General, Registrar General, Captain Superintendent of Police and Colonial Surgeon. A Sanitary Inspector and staff were appointed under the direction of the Board.

Sanitary Department

1908   The Sanitary Department was established and was attached to the Medical Department. The Department was divided into two major divisions:

I.   Sanitary Division

1. Drainage Works
2. Disinfecting Section
3. Bath Houses
4. Cemeteries

II.   Veterinary Division

1. Animal Depots and Slaughterhouses
2. Cattle Crematorium
3. Markets
4. Plague Section

Major duties of the Sanitary Division of the Department included: maintenance of environmental hygiene, scavenging of night soil and keeping the city clean, inspection of wells and drains; control of ambulances; removal of sick persons to hospital and removal of the dead to mortuary; supervision of public bath houses; control and management of cemeteries.

Major duties of the Veterinary Division were: control of sanitary conditions of government depots, slaughterhouses and cattle diseases; issue of licences for the keeping of animals; inspection and examination of animals, carcasses and food;

investigation of all unnatural animal deaths; special visits to districts where plague rats were found; control and inspection of sanitary conditions of factories and workshops.

1909   To facilitate the inspection work of public health, the City of Victoria was divided into 10 Health Districts and Kowloon was divided into 3 Health Districts under the supervision of the Sanitary Department. In the same year, the Plague Section under the Veterinary Division was abolished. New functions of the Department such as the registration of births and deaths, the control of vaccination and letting of market stalls were transferred from the Registrar General to the Sanitary Department.

1913   The Sanitary Department was separated from the Medical Department. The Department had as its head an Officer of the Cadet Services and consisted of 2 Medical Officers of Health, 2 Veterinary Surgeons and 53 Inspectors.

1932   On January 1, the Director of Medical and Sanitary Services became the Registrar of Births and Deaths.

1934   After the enactment of the Births and Deaths Ordinance no.21 of 1934, the registration function of births and deaths was transferred to the Medical Department.

1935   The Sanitary Board was abolished and replaced by the Urban Council. The Chairman of the Urban Council was responsible for the administration of the Sanitary Department.

1939   Health Districts were reduced in size. Eight new Health Districts were formed, four on Hong Kong Island and four in Kowloon. A Price Board was set up to maintain the prices of main foodstuffs at reasonable levels.

1945   The Sanitary Department was re-established after the Sino-Japanese War; its duties remained unchanged.

1952   A new section of Pest Control Section under the Veterinary Division was created. This section was responsible for pest control; the provision of pest identification services; disinfestation treatment of government premises and land, and private premises and the supply of biological materials.

1953   The Sanitary Department was abolished with the establishment of the Urban Services Department. The duties of the former Sanitary Department were transferred to the Sanitary Division under the direction of the Urban Services Department.

Urban Services Department

1953   Established in 1953, the Urban Services Department (USD) was divided into four divisions: Sanitary Division, Housing Division, Gardens Division and Resettlement Division. The duties of the Sanitary Division included the functions previously carried out by the Sanitary Department such as the maintenance of environmental hygiene, inspection of foodstuffs, slaughter-houses, markets, dairies, etc. in each Health District; disinfection work, pest control, scavenging and conservancy services; disposal of the dead;

management of hawkers, bathing beaches, bathhouses and public latrines. The Housing Division functions included preliminary work and the selection of possible housing sites, the planning of general policy and execution of the decisions of the Housing Authority. The Gardens Division was responsible for the maintenance of horticultural and botanical work and recreation. The Resettlement Division was responsible for the management of building structures and materials, and squatter control.

1954 The Resettlement Division was transferred out to form an independent Resettlement Department. The Senior Veterinary Office and its staff from the USD were transferred to the Department of Agriculture, Fisheries and Forestry.

1960 The Department was reorganized and divided into five divisions: Cleansing Division, Amenities and General Division, Hygiene Division, New Territories Division and Housing Division.

1962 The City Hall Division was set up to manage the City Hall.

1966 The Amenities and General Division was spilt into two new divisions: Parks, Recreation and Amenities Division, and General Division.

1973 Services provided by Urban Services Department were administered through three regions instead of six central divisions: Hong Kong, Kowloon and the New Territories. The Housing Division was abolished. Functions related to housing were transferred to the Housing Department. Major divisions of the Urban Services Department included: Hygiene Division, Cultural Services Division, Administration Division, Department Secretary Division, Treasury Division and Public Relation Division. The major duties of USD were to maintain public health and environmental hygiene and to provide and manage recreation facilities and cultural services.

1974 The Planning Division was established.

1979 The City Services Department was set up to manage all urban services on a regional or district basis.

1982 The Department was reorganized into five divisions:

I.   Central Administration
     1. Public Information Unit
     2. Cultural Services Department
        i. Cultural and Entertainment
        ii. Museum and Libraries
     3. City Services Department
     4. New Territories Services Department

II. Accounting and Supplies Division

III. Hygiene Division

IV. Legal Advisor's Office

V.   Planning and Development

Among the above divisions, the Legal Advisor's Office that provided legal advice to the Urban Council was a new addition.

1985 Together with other parts of the Urban Services Department, the New

Territories Services Department was transferred out to form the Regional Services Department.

1997   On July 1, the Urban Council was renamed Provisional Urban Council and the Chinese title of USD was changed. The organization structure and functions remained unchanged.

1999   On December 31, both the Provisional Urban Council and the USD were dissolved.

2000   Two independent departments — Food and Environmental Hygiene Department and Leisure and Cultural Services Department — assumed the duties previously carried out by the USD and the Urban Council with effect from January 1, 2000.

Leisure and Cultural Services Department

2000   The Department was mainly grouped into three parts:

I.   Administration Branch

1. Administration and Planning Division
2. Finance and Supplies Division
3. Information Technology Division
4. Quality Assurance Section

II.   Cultural Services Branch

1. Performing Arts Division
2. Heritage and Museums Division
3. Libraries and Development Division
4. Grade Management and Support Section

III.   Leisure Services Branch

1. Division 1
2. Division 2
3. Division 3
4. Grade Management and Support Section

Duties of this Department could be divided into two main categories: leisure services and cultural services. Leisure services included the organization of leisure activities, provision of leisure facilities, beautification of the environment and the promotion of synergy among sports, cultural and community organizations. Cultural services involved the preservation of cultural heritage, management of museums, libraries and organization of cultural activities.

2002   The structure remained the same, except that the Information Technology Division was placed under the Cultural Services Branch instead of the Administration Branch.

Food and Environmental Hygiene Department

2000   The Department comprised three branches:

I.   Food and Public Health Branch

      1. Food Surveillance and Control Division
      2. Risk Assessment and Communication Division
      3. Policy and Legislation Division
      4. Food and Public Health Administration Division

II.   Environmental Hygiene Branch

      1. Headquarters Division
      2. Support Services Division

III.   Administration and Development Branch

      1. Administration Division
      2. Grade Management and Development Division
      3 Finance and Supplies Division
      4. Public Information and Education Division
      5. Information Technology Division
      6. Internal Audit Division

Major duties of the Department included cleansing services, hawker control, food safety surveillance and public health promotion, issue of licences, public education, and the provision of cemeteries and crematoria.

2002   There was only one change in the organization structure. The Headquarters Division of the Environmental Hygiene Branch was replaced by Operations Divisions 1 to 3.

Sources:

1. *Annual Departmental Report by the Chairman of the Urban Council and Head of the Sanitary Department*, Hong Kong, Government Printer, 1950-1953.
2. *Annual Report of the Chairman, Urban Council, and Head of the Sanitary Department, for the Year Ending 31st March, 1947*, Hong Kong Government, 1948.
3. *Hong Kong Annual Departmental Report by the Chairman, Urban Council and Director of Urban Services*, Hong Kong, Government Printer, 1954-1978.
4. *Hong Kong Government Gazette*, Hong Kong Government, 21 April 1844, p.363; 26 May 1883, pp.426-427; 7 May 1887, pp.458-459.
5. *Hong Kong Report of the Urban Council and Sanitary Department for the Financial Year, 1st April, 1948 - 31st March, 1949*, Hong Kong, Government Printer.
6. *Provisional Urban Council Annual Report*, Hong Kong, Government Printer, 1997-1999.
7. "Report of the Head of the Sanitary Department", *Hong Kong Administration Reports*, Hong Kong Government, 1931-1939.
8. "Report of the Head of the Sanitary Department", *Hong Kong Administrative Reports* Hong Kong Government, 1909-1930.
9. "Report on the Health and Sanitary Condition of the Colony of Hong Kong", *Hong Kong Sessional Papers*, Hong Kong, Noronha & Co., 1899-1908.
10. Richards, H.G., Director of Urban Services, "The Urban Council, the Housing Authority, and the Urban Services Dept" in Braga, J.M. ed., *Hong Kong Business Symposium*, Hong Kong, South China Morning Post, 1957.
11. *Urban Council Annual Report*, Hong Kong, Government Printer, 1978-1997.
12. www.fehd.gov.hk/
13. www.lcsd.gov.hk/indexe.html/

Regional Services Department (1985-1999)

1985   The Provisional Regional Council was formed to prepare for the establishment of a municipal authority in the Regional Council area. The municipal authority was financially autonomous and administratively independent. The Regional Services Department, was formed in April by combining the New Territories Department of the USD with component units from the Recreation and Culture Department and the Cultural Services Department of the USD operating in the areas covered by the Regional Council. It was the executive arm of the Regional Council. The head of the Department, Director of Regional Services, was responsible for the implementation of the Council's policies, decisions, and the overall administration. The Director was assisted by two Deputy Directors who each headed one branch. The Department was organized into: Administration Branch (comprised the Administration Division, Finance and Supplies Division, Information Division, Management Services Division and Planning Division); and Operations Branch (consisted of the Culture and Entertainment Division, Environmental Hygiene Division, Leisure Services Division and Transport Division).

1986   The Regional Council was established in April to oversee the provision of municipal, recreational and cultural services for residents living in areas covered by the Regional Council.

1988   The Department launched the financial management reforms. Under the new scheme, budget control officers were required to present their estimates through aims and objectives which would then be measured against performance. The Department prepared the Regional Council's five-year revenue and expenditure forecast. A Legal Advice Unit under the Administration Branch was established to provide independent legal advice to the Council and the Department.

1990   Street cleansing services for six selected townships were being contracted out into two phases.

1991   The Festival Office was created under the Operations Branch. The Office was responsible for the District Festival Subsidy Scheme under which district bodies received subsidies from the Council to organize large-scale festive events.

1993   An additional Assistant Director of Regional Services was appointed, making a total of two in charge of the environmental hygiene workforce. One Assistant Director was to deal with the efficient delivery and management of environmental hygiene services. The other Assistant Director was responsible for all policy matters as well as legislative amendment and training of health inspectors and supervisory grade staff. The functions of the Environmental Hygiene Division were transferred to two new divisions — Environmental Health Services Division and Environmental Health Policy Division — under the direction of the Operations Branch. The Environmental Health Services Division oversaw the efficient provision of public health services, including street cleansing, refuse collection and district environmental hygiene operation; it also managed the Department's fleet of vehicles. The Environmental Health Policy Division was responsible for policy and management matters concerning hawkers, markets, licensing, abattoirs, food hygiene, cemeteries and crematoria as well as the development of the health inspectorate. The Transport Division became a section of the Environmental Health Services Division.

1995   The Music Office of the Government Secretariat's Recreation and Culture Branch was transferred to the Regional Council and the Urban Council in August.

1997   On July 1, the Regional Council was replaced by the Provisional Regional Council.

1999   The Provisional Urban Council and the Provisional Regional Council were abolished on December 31, along with the Ubran Services Department and the Regional Services Department. On January 1, 2000, the Leisure and Cultural Services Department and the Food and Environmental Hygiene Department assumed the duties of the two Councils and the two Departments.

Sources:

1. *Leisure and Cultural Services Department Annual Report 2000*, Hong Kong, Government Printer, 2001, p.2.
2. *Regional Council Annual Report*, Hong Kong, Regional Council, 1986-1987; 1988-1989, pp.33-36; 1989-1990, p.17; 1990-1991, pp.33-47; 1991-1992, pp.44-45; 1993-1994, pp.42-44; 1994-1995, p.44; 1997-1998, p.4.

Sanitary Department — Changes in Names and Directors

Year	Name of Department	Title	Name of Director
1883-1888	Sanitary Board	President of the Sanitary Board	Price, John MacNeile
1888-1889	Sanitary Board	President of the Sanitary Board	Ayres, Philip Bernard Chenery
1889-1891	Sanitary Board	President of the Sanitary Board	Brown, Samuel
1891-1895	Sanitary Board	President of the Sanitary Board	Lockhart, James Haldane Stewart
1895-1897	Sanitary Board	President of the Sanitary Board	Cooper, Francis Alfred
1897-1908	Sanitary Board	President of the Sanitary Board	Atkinson, John Mitford
1908	Sanitary Department	Head of Sanitary Department	Messer, Charles McIlvaine; Kemp, Joseph Horsford
1909-1913	Sanitary Department	Head of Sanitary Department	Wolfe, Edward Dudley Corscaden
1913-1917	Sanitary Department	Head of Sanitary Department	Orme, Geoffrey Norman
1917-1918	Sanitary Department	Head of Sanitary Department	Tratman, David William
1918-1919	Sanitary Department	Head of Sanitary Department	Carpmael, Ernest Vincent

Year	Name of Department	Title	Name of Director
1919-1920	Sanitary Department	Head of Sanitary Department	Gibson, Adam
1920-1924	Sanitary Department	Head of Sanitary Department	Sayer, Geoffrey Robley
1924-1928	Sanitary Department	Head of Sanitary Department	Smith, Norman Lockhart
1928-1929	Sanitary Department	Head of Sanitary Department	Sayer, Geoffrey Robley; Carrie, William James
1929-1930	Sanitary Department	Head of Sanitary Department	Carrie, William James
1930-1933	Sanitary Department	Head of Sanitary Department	Sayer, Geoffrey Robley
1933-1934	Sanitary Department	Head of Sanitary Department	Megarry, Thomas; Sayer, Geoffrey Robley
1934-1936	Sanitary Department	Head of Sanitary Department	Carrie, William James; Forrest, Robert Andrew Dermod
1936	Sanitary Department	Head of Sanitary Department, Chairman of the Urban Council	Burgess, Claude Bramall
1936-1939	Sanitary Department	Head of Sanitary Department, Chairman of the Urban Council	Todd, Ronald Ruskin
1939-1940	Sanitary Department	Head of Sanitary Department, Chairman of the Urban Council	Carrie, William James
1940	Sanitary Department	Head of Sanitary Department, Chairman of the Urban Council	Kennedy-Skipton, George Stacy
1940-1941	Sanitary Department	Head of Sanitary Department, Chairman of the Urban Council	Carrie, William James
1946	Sanitary Department	Head of Sanitary Department, Chairman of the Urban Council	Megarry, Thomas
1946-1951	Sanitary Department	Head of Sanitary Department, Chairman of the Urban Council	Frehily, Joseph Patrick
1951-1953	Sanitary Department	Head of Sanitary Department, Chairman of the Urban Council	Barnett, Kenneth Myer Arthur

Sources:
1.   *The Hong Kong Civil Service List,* Hong Kong Government, 1948; 1952.

Food and Enviounmental Hygience Department/Leisure and Cultural Services Department — Changes in Names and Directors

Year	Name of Department	Title	Name of Director
1953	Urban Services Department	Chairman, U.C. ; Director of Urban Services	Barnett, Kenneth Myer Arthur
1954-1955	Urban Services Department	Chairman, U.C. ; Director of Urban Services	Richards, Harold Giles
1955-1957	Urban Services Department	Chairman, U.C. ; Director of Urban Services; Chairman, Housing Authority	Holmes, David Ronald
1957-1959	Urban Services Department	Chairman, U.C. ; Director of Urban Services; Chairman, Housing Authority	Morrison, Colin George Mervyn
1959-1963	Urban Services Department	Chairman, U.C. ; Director of Urban Services; Chairman, Housing Authority	Kinghorn, Kenneth Strathmore
1963-1968	Urban Services Department	Chairman, U.C. ; Director of Urban Services; Chairman, Housing Authority	Tingle, Geoffrey Marsh
1968-1973	Urban Services Department	Chairman, U.C. ; Director of Urban Services; Chairman, Housing Authority	Alexander, David Richard Watson
1973	Urban Services Department	Director of Urban Services	Alexander, David Richard Watson
1973-1983	Urban Services Department	Director of Urban Services	Wilson, Brian Denis
1983-1985	Urban Services Department	Director of Urban Services	Barnes, Graham
1985-1986	Urban Services Department	Director of Urban Services	Chui, Augustine Kam
1986-1989	Urban Services Department	Director of Urban Services	Purves, Alexander Lamont
1989-1991	Urban Services Department	Director of Urban Services	So, Yiu-cho, James
1991-1992	Urban Services Department	Director of Urban Services	Barma, Haider Hatim Tyebjee

Year	Name of Department	Title	Name of Director
1993-1997	Urban Services Department	Director of Urban Services	Lam, Chi-chiu, Albert
1997-1999	Urban Services Department	Director of Urban Services	Chung, Lai-kwok, Elaine
1999-2000	Urban Services Department	Director of Urban Services	Lau Ng, Wai-lan, Rita
1985-1986	Regional Services Department	Acting Director of Regional Services	Hammond, Joseph Charles Anthony
1986-1988	Regional Services Department	Acting Director of Regional Services	Suen, Ming-yeung, Michael
1988-1989	Regional Services Department	Acting Director of Regional Services	Barma, Haider Hatim Tyebjee
1989-1991	Regional Services Department	Director of Regional Services	Barma, Haider Hatim Tyebjee
1991-1998	Regional Services Department	Director of Regional Services	Hsu, Hsuang, Adolf
1998-1999	Regional Services Department	Director of Regional Services	Yu Lai, Ching-ping, Helen
2000-2002	Food and Environmental Hygiene Department	Director of Food and Environmental Hygiene	Lau Ng, Wai-lan, Rita
2000-2002	Leisure and Cultural Services Department	Director of Leisure and Cultural Services	Leung, Sai-wah, Paul

Sources:

1. *The Hong Kong Civil Service List,* Hong Kong Government, 1954-1958.
2. *Staff List Hong Kong Government,* Hong Kong, Government Printer, 1959- 1996.
3. *Staff List the Government of the Hong Kong Special Administrative Region,* Hong Kong, Government Printer, 1997- 2001.
4. *Staff Biographies Hong Kong Government,* Hong Kong Government Printer, 1976; 1978; 1982; 1984; 1986; 1988; 1990; 1993.
5. *Staff Biographies the Government of the Hong Kong Special Administrative Region,* Hong Kong, Government Printer, 1998; 2001.
6. www.fehd.gov.hk/
7. www.lcsd.gov.hk/indexe.html

Housing Services

Hong Kong Housing Society (1948-2002)
Resettlement Department (1953-1973)
Hong Kong Housing Authority (1954-2002)
Housing Department (1973-2002)

Hong Kong Housing Society

1947	A donation from the Lord Mayor of London's Air Raid Distress Fund to the Hong Kong Social Welfare Council initiated the establishment of a subcommittee for housing development. The subcommittee was the predecessor of the Housing Society.
1948	The Hong Kong Housing Society was formally set up in 1948. Its first official meeting, held on 17 April, 1948, included members of the Social Welfare Council.
1951	The Hong Kong Housing Society was incorporated by the Hong Kong Housing Society Incorporation Ordinance with its own constitution.
1952	The Hong Kong Housing Society was granted a site at Sham Shui Po at one-third of the market value. The site was developed into the Society's first rental estate: Sheung Li Uk.
1958	The Hong Kong Housing Society focused on rental estates development, providing more than 11,000 units in Hung Hom Chuen, Tanner Hill, Kwun Lung Lau, Healthy Village, Yue Kwong Chuen, Chun Seen Mei Chuen, Garden Estate and Moon Lok Dai Ha.
1976	At the Government's request, the Hong Kong Housing Society participated in urban development. The first project under the Urban Improvement Scheme — Block A of Mei Sun Lau — was completed in 1976 and sold at market price. Construction works on other rental estates — Ming Wah Dai Ha, Lai Tak Tsuen and Lok Man Sun Chuen — were also completed.
1993	Through the Sandwich Class Housing/Loan Scheme, the Hong Kong Housing Society took over the main functions of the former Resettlement. Administration Office and the Mobile Resettlement Unit. A Works Section was transferred over from the Public Works Department.helped middle-income families to purchase their own homes. Phase I of the loan scheme was launched in August 1993. It also raised funds from the financial market for the first time to meet its expansion needs.
1996	The first project under the Sandwich Class Housing Loan Scheme was completed.
2002	The Hong Kong Housing Society was organized into five divisions: Projects, Planning and Development, Finance, Corporate Services, Estate Management; and three other units: Quality Assurance Unit, Internal Audit Unit, Corporate Communications Section.

Resettlement Department

1951   A subdepartment under the Urban Council was set up in July to prepare a resettlement scheme to meet the rapid growth of the Chinese population.

1953   The Hong Kong Government decided to build 6- to 7-storey resettlement estates to rehouse five the victims of the Shek Kip Mei squatter area. The Resettlement Division under the Urban Services Department was established to administer the resettlement areas in Hong Kong.

1954   The Resettlement Division was transferred out to form the nucleus of the Resettlement Department. D. R. Holmes was appointed Commissioner for Resettlement. The Department consisted of five sections:

    I.   Screening, Surveys and Documentation

    II.   Squatter Patrols

    III.   Clearance and Resettlement Operations

    IV.   Resettlement Administration Office

    V.   Mobile Resettlement Unit

The Department operated under the Urban Council for clearance and under the Commissioner for Resettlement's authority for squatter control. The Screening, Surveys and Documentation Section carried out surveys of squatter areas and prepared the preliminary documentation before each clearance. The Squatter Patrols Section prevented the construction of illegal huts and buildings. The Clearance and Resettlement Operations Section undertook clearance operations. The Mobile Resettlement Unit was responsible for the routine and emergency resettlements of people displaced due to squatter clearances or squatter fire accidents. The Resettlement Administration Office administered and maintained the multi-storey resettlement estates and cottages.

1956   The organization of the Department was restructured into: Squatter Control Section, Screening Section, Mobile Resettlement Unit and Resettlement Administrative Office.

1957   The Rooftop Squatter Prevention Section was set up to prevent the erection of new structures or extensions of existing structures on rooftops.

1958   The emergency regulations operated by the Department were replaced by the Resettlement Ordinance no. 16 of 1958. The Department was restructured into two divisions — Squatter Prevention and Control Division; and Administration and Operations Division, Kowloon. The Squatter Prevention and Control Division had two sections: Squatter Control Section and Rooftop Squatter Prevention Section. The Administration and Operations Division took over the main function of the former Resettlement Administration Office and the Mobile Resettlement Unit. A works Section was transferred over from the Public Works Department. The Works Section was responsible for the maintenance of the settlement, the construction and maintenance work in the cottage areas, and the preparation of plans for cultivation clearances.

1962   The Administration and Operations Division was spilt into Estate and Cottage

Areas Division and Operations Division. The Estate and Cottage Areas Division administered the estates, cottages areas and factory blocks. The Operations Division was responsible for clearance planning and maintaining constant liaison with the Architectural Office of the Public Works Department.

1965   The Government appointed a Housing Board in June. It reviewed the progress made in the construction of permanent domestic housing by major types of premises, kept under review the need of housing over the succeeding 10 years and evaluated the suitability of the balance between various types of housing being constructed and projected. The organization of the Department had evolved into: Headquarters, Estates and Areas Division, Operations Division and Works Division.

1973   On April 1, the new Housing Department was established. It assumed all duties previously exercised by the Resettlement Department and the Housing Division of the Urban Services Department.

Hong Kong Housing Authority

1954   The Housing Authority was established on April 29, under Housing Ordinance no. 18 of 1954 to provide accommodation for the poor. It was composed of all members of the Urban Council, ex officio government officials, and not more than three persons nominated by the Governor. It consisted of eight committees: General Administration Select Committee, Site Select Committee, Architectural and Planning Select Committee, Tenancy Select Committee, Estates Organization Select Committee, Finance and Accountancy Select Committee, By-laws and Rules Select Committee, and Publicity Select Committee. Its major duties were to draft basic housing development plans, to co-ordinate the recommendations of Select Committees and to administer staff matters of the Housing Division.

1957   On May 22, the Commissioner for Housing of the Housing Division became an ex officio member of the Housing Authority.

1961   The Select Committees were restructured on April 1. Four committees were set up: Executive Committee, Building Committee, Management Committee and Finance Committee.

1964   The Temporary Housing Scheme was launched for residents who were not immediately eligible for permanent public housing but who could not afford private housing.

1972   Governor Murray MacLehose announced the 10-year Housing Programme to provide self-contained housing for 1.5 million people.

1973   The reconstituted Hong Kong Housing Authority was formally established on April 1 under the Housing Ordinance of 1973. The new Authority was vested with the powers and functions that were previously fragmented — those of the Urban Council and the Resettlement Department for the management of resettlement estates and control of squatters, and those of the Housing Board on giving advice on housing policy. Five committees under the supervision of the Housing Authority were formed: Appeals Committee, Building Committee, Finance Committee, Management Committee and Operations Committee.

1976	Home Ownership Scheme was introduced to provide flats for sale at below-market price, to enable lower-middle income families to own their own homes.
1979	The Home Ownership Scheme was supplemented by a Private Sector Participation Scheme. Private developers were involved in the public housing projects.
1985	The clearance of substandard blocks in 11 middle-aged estates was carried out.
1987	HK$2.76 billion was allocated for the clearance of the Kowloon Walled City. A Special Committee on Clearance of Kowloon Walled City was set up to prepare rehousing for and make compensation to the 32,500 residents in the area.
1988	The Housing Authority was reorganized on April 1 and was given a separate financial identity and autonomy. The Housing Authority's general powers and duties remained as those defined by Section 4 of the Housing Ordinance (Cap. 283). As a government agency, it was responsible for liaising with other bodies concerned with housing in both public and private sectors; the planning, building and redeveloping of public housing estates, Home Ownership Scheme courts and temporary housing areas; the management of flatted factories and commercial facilities in public housing estates and Home Ownership Scheme courts; and the management of Home Purchase Loan Scheme. It comprised nine committees: Building Committee, Commercial Properties Committee, Complaints Committee, Development Committee, Establishment and Finance Committee, Home Ownership Committee, Management Committee, Operations Committee and Tenancy Appeals Committee. There was also an ad hoc Committee — Special Committee on Clearance of Kowloon Walled City.
2001	The Housing Authority consisted of 25 non-official and four official members, who were appointed by the Chief Executive of the HKSAR for a two-year term. It advised the Chief Executive on all public housing matters such as the management of its rental housing estates and home ownership estates including interim housing, cottage areas, transit centres, flatted factories and extensive commercial facilities. It also dealt with land clearance, prevention and control of squatters and the implementation of improvements to squatter areas. The Housing Authority comprised eight standing committees: Strategic Planning, Building, Commercial Properties, Human Resources, Finance, Home Ownership, Rental Housing and Complaints.
2002	The Housing Authority still had the same eight standing committees. It had 28 non-official and four official members who were appointed by the Chief Executive of the HKSAR for a two-year term. Ad hoc committees were appointed when need arose.

Housing Department

1935   Established in 1935, the Housing Commission is considered the precursor of the Housing Department.

1938   A permanent Town Planning and Housing Committee was established to advise the Government on housing development policy.

1973   The Resettlement Department and the Housing Division of the Urban Services Department were amalgamated to form the Housing Department on April 1. The Housing Department was the executive arm of the Housing Authority. It comprised five operational units: Housing Authority Secretariat, Administration Division, Construction Branch, Estate Management Branch and Operations Branch. The Housing Authority Secretariat maintained the administrative link between the Housing Authority and the Housing Department. It reviewed housing policies, provided basic secretarial services and processed tender documents. The Administration Division was responsible for all general and personnel matters, normal financial and accounting duties and publication of Housing Authority's policies and activities. The Construction Branch planned and built domestic and commercial accommodation and ancillary facilities. The Estate Management Branch was responsible for the letting, management and maintenance of all public housing estates, cottage areas and factory estates. The Operations Branch controlled illegal building structures, cleared squatter structures, arranged housing for victims of fires and natural disasters, and redeveloped squatter areas.

1977   A new branch, Administration and Planning Branch, was established to co-ordinate the work of the Housing Authority Secretariat and the Administration Division. Its responsibilities covered personnel, finance, planning, committees and public relations.

1981   The squatter control function in the New Territories was transferred from the New Territories Administration to the Operations Branch of the Department.

1985   The Administration and Planning Branch was renamed Administration Branch.

1986   The Department took over the functions of environmental improvement and clearance from the City and New Territories Administration.

1987   The Administration Branch was changed back to Administration and Planning Branch.

1988   The Administraiton and Planning Branch was renamed Administration and Policy Branch.

1990   The Estate Management Branch and the Operations Branch were combined to form the Housing Management Branch.

1994   The Housing Management Branch was spilt into Estate Management Branch and Housing Administration Branch. The Construction Branch was split into Maintenance and Construction Services Branch and New Development Branch.

1997   In April the Housing Department was restructured along business lines into four core business branches (Allocation and Marketing, Commercial and Services, Development and Construction, Management) and two supporting branches (Financial and Accounting, Corporate Services), the Director Office and a Corporate Strategy Unit. At the strategic level, an executive board was set up to map out strategies, formulate policies, set performance targets and monitor progress.

1999   The Commercial Services Branch was changed to Commerical and Business Development Branch.

2001   The Department provided public housing assistance, management, maintenance and other housing related services to the public. The structure of the Department in 2001 was as follows:

I.   Director's Office
    1. Technical Audit
    2. Internal Audit
    3. Independent Checking

II.   Finance and Information Branch
    1. Financial Management and System
    2. Investment and Risk Management
    3. Information Technology
    4. Supplies and Counterparty List Management

III. Corporate Services Branch
    1. Administration and Personnel
    2. Information and Community Relations
    3. Legal Advice
    4. Management Services

IV.   Management Branch
    1. Building Services
    2. Central Investigation
    3. Estate and Interim Housing Management
    4. Maintenance and Repair
    5. Management Policies (Estate and Interim Housing)
    6. Management Support Services
    7. Property Services Contractors Administration
    8. Structural Engineering, Quantity Surveying, Civil Engineering and Geotechnical Engineering Services related to Maintenance

V.   Allocation and Marketing Branch
    1. Agency Management
    2. Applications and Allocations
    3. Home Ownership Scheme
    4. Redevelopment
    5. Rental Estate Land Management
    6. Tenants Purchase Scheme

VI.   Commercial and Business Development Branch
    1. Commercial Properties
    2. Driving Private Sector Involvement

VII. Development and Construction Branch
    1.   Architecture
    2.   Building Services
    3.   Civil Engineering
    4.   Consultant Management
    5.   Geotechnical Engineering
    6.   Landscape
    7.   Planning
    8.   Project Management
    9.   Quantity Surveying
    10. Structural Engineering

VIII. Corporate Strategy
    1.   Policy
    2.   Research and Statistics

2002   The structure of the Department remained largely unchanged.

Sources:

1. *Annual Report of Housing Authority,* Hong Kong, Government Printer, 1973-1999.
2. *Hong Kong Annual Departmental Report by the Commissioner for Resettlement*, Hong Kong Government Printer, 1954-1972.
3. *Annual Report of the Hong Kong Housing Authority*, Hong Kong Government, 1954-1957.
4. *Hong Kong Housing Authority Annual Report*, Hong Kong, Government Printer, 1959-1976.
5. *Hong Kong Housing Authority Annual Report*, Hong Kong Graphic Printing & Design Co. Ltd, 1976-1979.
6. *Hong Kong Housing Authority Annual Report*, Hong Kong, Fok Hing Co., 1979-1994.
7. *Report of the Hong Kong Housing Authority*, Hong Kong, Government Printer, 1958-1959.
8. Richards, H.G., "The Urban Housing Authority and the Urban Service Department" in Braga, J.M., *Hong Kong Business Symposium: A Compilation of Authoritative View on Administration and Resources*, Hong Kong, *South China Morning Post*, 1957.
9. www.housingauthority.gov.hk/en

Resettlement Department — Changes in Directors

Year	Name of Department	Title	Name of Director
1954-1955	Resettlement Department	Commissioner for Resettlement	Holmes, David Ronald
1955-1958	Resettlement Department	Commissioner for Resettlement	Walton, Arthur, St. George
1958-1961	Resettlement Department	Commissioner for Resettlement	Aserappa, John Philip
1960-1963	Resettlement Department	Commissioner for Resettlement	Morrison, Colin George Mervyn
1963-1965	Resettlement Department	Commissioner for Resettlement	Barty, Dermont Campbell
1965	Resettlement Department	Commissioner for Resettlement	Wakefield, James Tinker
1965-1968	Resettlement Department	Commissioner for Resettlement	Barty, Dermont Campbell
1968-1970	Resettlement Department	Commissioner for Resettlement	Aserappa, John Philip
1970-1971	Resettlement Department	Commissioner for Resettlement	Tsui, Ka-cheung, Paul
1971-1972	Resettlement Department	Commissioner for Resettlement	Lightbody, Ian MacDonald

Sources:
1. *The Hong Kong Civil Service List*, Hong Kong Government, 1955-1958.
2. *Staff List Hong Kong Government*, Hong Kong, Government Printer, 1960-72.

The Hong Kong Housing Authority — Changes in Directors

Year	Name of Department	Title	Name of Director
1973-1977	The Hong Kong Housing Authority	Chairman, Housing Authority	Lightbody, Ian MacDonald
1977-1980	The Hong Kong Housing Authority	Chairman, Housing Authority	Scott, Alan J.
1980-1985	The Hong Kong Housing Authority	Chairman, Housing Authority	Liao, Poon-huai, Donald

Year	Name of Department	Title	Name of Director
1985	The Hong Kong Housing Authority	Chairman, Housing Authority	Ford, David Robert
1985-1986	The Hong Kong Housing Authority	Chairman, Housing Authority	Pang, Yuk-ling
1986-1988	The Hong Kong Housing Authority	Chairman, Housing Authority	Todd, John Rawling
1988-1993	The Hong Kong Housing Authority	Chairman, Housing Authority	Akers-Jones, David
1993-2000	The Hong Kong Housing Authority	Chairman, Housing Authority	Wong, Yik-ming, Rosanna
2000-2002	The Hong Kong Housing Authority	Chairman, Housing Authority	Cheng, Hon-kwan

Sources:
1. *Civil and Miscellaneous Lists Hong Kong Government*, Hong Kong, Government Printer, 1999.
2. Leung, Mei-yee, *From Shelter to Home, 45 Years of Public Housing Development in Hong Kong*, Hong Kong Housing Authority, 1999.
3. www.housingauthority.gov.hk/en

Housing Department — Charges in Directors

Year	Name of Department	Title	Name of Director
1973-1980	Housing Department	Director of Housing	Liao, Poon-huai, Donald
1980-1983	Housing Department	Director of Housing	Williams, Bernard Vaughan
1983-1985	Housing Department	Director of Housing	Ford, David Robert
1985-1990	Housing Department	Director of Housing	Pang, Yuk-ling
1990-1996	Housing Department	Director of Housing	Fung, Tung
1996-2002	Housing Department	Director of Housing	Millier, John Anthony

Sources:
1. *Staff Biographies Hong Kong Government*, Hong Kong, Government Printer, 1974, 1982, 1986, 1990, 1993.
2. *Staff Biographies the Government of the Hong Kong Special Administrative Region*, Hong Kong, Government Printer, 2001.
3. www.housingauthority.gov.hk

Environmental Conservation

Government Gardens (1861-1879)
Government Gardens and Plantations Department (1879)
Botanical and Afforestation Department (1880-1905)
Botanical and Forestry Department (1905-1941)
Gardens Department (1946-1950)
Forestry Department (1946-1950)
Agricultural Department (1946-1950)
Fisheries Department (1946-1950)
Department of Agriculture, Fisheries and Forestry (1950-1960)
Department of Agriculture and Forestry (1960-1964)
Department of Agriculture and Fisheries (1964-1999)

Co-operative and Marketing Department (1950-1958)
Co-operative Development Department (1959)
Co-operative Development and Fisheries Department (1960-1964)

Agriculture, Fisheries and Conservation Department (2000-2002)
Environmental Protection Department (1986-2002)

Government Gardens

1861   A Superintendent of Government Gardens attached to the Surveyor General's Office was appointed.

1872   The Government Gardens under the supervision of the Surveyor General was established. The Government Gardens consisted of two divisions: Government Gardens Division and Forestry Division.

Government Gardens and Plantations Department

1879   The Government Gardens changed its name to Government Gardens and Plantations Department and became independent.

Botanical and Afforestation Department

1880   The Department became known as the Botanical and Afforestation Department. It comprised two divisions: Botanic Garden Division and Afforestation Division. The Botanic Garden Division was responsible for the planning and management of trees and shrubs in the Botanic Garden, the Government House, government gardens and forestry. The Afforestation Division was in charge of operational planning, preservation of water and ground for plants, distributing and exchanging plants and seeds with other countries and sales of plants.

1898   The Afforestation Division was changed to Forestry Division and a new division, New Territories Division, was set up. The Division was responsible for tree planting in the New Territories, the management of two Chatannooga Sugar Mills in the New Territories, the setting up of experimental gardens to introduce and distribute plants of economic value to cultivators and organization of exhibitions.

Botanical and Forestry Department

1905   The Botanical and Afforestation Department was renamed Botanical and Forestry Department. The Department began to manage agricultural and other industries and to invite English experts to examine tea plantations in Hong Kong.

1938   A new division, New Museum Committee, was set up to make preparations for the new biological, geological, archaeological museums of Hong Kong.

1941   The Agricultural Section was set up to assess the possibilities of developing New Territories agricultural areas, to give practical demonstrations of agricultural possibilities and assistance such as water supply, financial support, etc., to cultivators. This Section was for the first time included in the Estimates of 1941-42.

1946   The Botanical and Forestry Department was split into four departments: Gardens Department, Agriculture Department, Forestry Department and Fisheries Department.

Gardens Department (1946-1950)

The Gardens Department consisted of four sections: Botanic Garden, Herbarium, Library and Sookunpoon Vegetable Garden. Its major duties included the rehabilitation of gardens, restoration of the plant nurseries and recreation grounds, production of crops and usual supplies such as vegetables and fruits for the Government House.

Forestry Department (1946-1950)

The Forestry Department comprised four sections: Afforestation Section, Forest Protection Section and Routine Section. The Department was responsible for the conservation work of local afforestation, sales of seedlings to the public, and to establish and distribute forest plants of economic importance.

Agricultural Department (1946-1950)

The Agricultural Department was divided into six administrative parts:

Experimental Station, Wholesale Vegetable Market, Night Soil Maturation and Distribution Scheme, Pig Breeding Stations, Distribution of Animal Food, and Distribution of Seeds. In 1948, the Department was reorganized into two divisions: Agricultural Division and Animal Husbandry Division. The Agricultural Division investigated and advised on conditions and methods of agriculture. The Animal Husbandry Division improved local breeds and investigated disease control in connection with animal husbandry.

Fisheries Department (1946-1950)

The Fisheries Department was established to administer the fishing industry and fleet. The Department had two divisions: Wholesale Marketing Scheme and Fisheries Vernacular School. Its major duties were to run the Wholesale Marketing Scheme under the Co-operative Movement and the Fisheries Vernacular School.

Department of Agriculture, Fisheries and Forestry (1950-1960)

1950   Four departments — Agriculture, Fisheries, Forestry and Gardens — were merged to form the Department of Agriculture, Fisheries and Forestry in October 1950. The Department comprised four divisions: Agriculture and Animal Husbandry Division, Fisheries Division, Forestry Division and Gardens Divisions. The Agriculture and Animal Husbandry Division was responsible for the importation, selection, production and distribution of improved livestock, fertilizers and seeds with a view to increase local production of food crops and improve the living standards of farmers. It also conducted surveys on land utilization, introduced practical methods of pest and disease control and co-operated with the New Territories district administration, Public Works Department, Education Department and other interested governmental departments to improve farming conditions. The Fisheries Division investigated pond fish culture, oyster farming and fish export to other countries and worked closely with the Co-operative and Marketing Department. The Forestry Division protected vegetation growing, encouraged forestry operations by villagers and carried out scenic and roadside tree planting. The Gardens Division was responsible for the maintenance of public gardens and recreation grounds. It also constructed and rehabilitated planting areas to provide favourable conditions for planting.

1951   The Gardens Division was detached from the Department and placed under the Sanitary Department.

1954   The Senior Veterinary Office and its associated staff were transferred over from the Urban Services Department to form a new division: Division of Animal Industries.

Department of Agriculture and Forestry

1960   The Department of Agriculture, Fisheries and Forestry was renamed

Department of Agriculture and Forestry in July. It comprised three divisions: Agriculture, Animal Husbandry and Forestry.

Co-operative and Marketing Department

1946   The Wholesale Marketing Scheme proved to be beneficial to the producers. A similar scheme was introduced in September to help vegetable farmers by co-operating with self-supporting fish and vegetable marketing organizations.

1950   The Co-operative and Marketing Department was formed to manage marketing organizations. The Department comprised two divisions: Co-operative and Marketing. The Co-operative Division was responsible for the registration, accounting service and audit of co-operative societies. The Marketing Division provided transport facilities, supervised all sales and financial transactions of wholesale marketing of vegetables and fisheries, and granted loans to fishermen for production purposes at a low interest rate, and provided loans for the mechanization of Hong Kong's fishing fleets.

1952   The Audit Section was set up to maintain control over all inventories and building records.

1955   The Department was reorganized into four administrative divisions: Executive Office, Marketing Division, Co-operative Division and Fish Marketing Organization Schools.

Co-operative Development Department

1959   The Co-operative and Marketing Department was retitled Co-operative Development Department.

Co-operative Development and Fisheries Department

1960   The Co-operative Development Department merged with the Fisheries Division of the Department of Agriculture and Forestry and was renamed Co-operative Development and Fisheries Department.

1964   The Department was amalgamated with the Department of Agriculture and Forestry.

Department of Agriculture and Fisheries

1964   Upon amalgamation with the Co-operative Development and Fisheries Department, the Department of Agriculture and Forestry was renamed Department of Agriculture and Fisheries and consisted of four parts: Group of Agriculture and Forestry Services, Field Services, Veterinary Services and Group of Fisheries Services. The major duties of the Group of Agriculture and Forestry Services included the protection and provision of advisory services to natural vegetation and afforestation, supervision of vegetable marketing and ensuring the smooth functioning of the 26 Vegetable Marketing Co-operative Societies in the New Territories. The Field Services was responsible for the improvement of farm production and provision of direct financial assistance to farmers through loan funds, agricultural credits, etc. The Veterinary Services inspected all animals imported for slaughter and dealt with matters such as rabies control, issue of licenses and certificates for livestock and livestock products, and wild life preservation. The Group of Fisheries Services was in charge of the administration of marine fisheries, fish marketing, provision of credit facilities to fishermen, propagation of the co-operative movement, examination of relief claims, inspection of boats engines, training of fishermen and management of Fish Marketing Schools. The administrative structure of the Department was as follows:

I.   Group of Agriculture and Forestry Services

    1. Agriculture Services
      i. Crop Division
      ii. Land Utilization and Farm Management Division
      iii.Chemistry Division
      iv. Farms Division
    2. Vegetable Marketing Services
      - Vegetable Marketing Organization
    3. Forestry Services
    4. Group of Field and Veterinary Services

II.   Field Services

    1. Division of Extension
    2. Division of Rural Co-operatives

III. Veterinary Services

    1. Division of Livestock Regulatory
    2. Division of Livestock Husbandry and Health

IV.   Group of Fisheries Services

    1. Marketing, Co-operation and Credit
    2. Fisheries Extension and Development Division
    3. Schools
    4. Research

1966   The Department was reorganized into four parts:

I.   Agriculture Branch

    1. Extension Division
    2. Crop Husbandry and Health Division
    3. Livestock Husbandry and Health Division

II.   Fisheries Branch

    1. Fisheries Extension and Development Division
    2. Fisheries Research Division

III. Headquarters

1. Administration Division
2. Accounts and Stores Division
3. Economic and Marketing Division

IV. Forestry Branch

1971   The Forestry Branch was renamed Conservation and Forestry Division in April. It emphasized on the research and development of local afforestation work and provided conservation services on flora and fauna.

1976   The Conservation and Forestry Division was separated into two divisions: Conservation Division and Country Parks Division. The Country Parks Division was responsible for the planning, development and management of country parks and protection of wild animals.

1981   The Conservation Division and the Country Parks Division were merged into one branch: Conservation and Country Parks Branch. The Agricultural Waste Control Division under the supervision of the Agriculture Branch was set up. It controlled all aspects of pollution caused by agricultural waste and co-ordinated with other government departments such as the Environmental Protection Agency, Public Works Department, and the New Territories Administration.

1995   The Agriculture Branch was renamed Agricultural and Regulation Branch. The Conservation and Country Parks Branch was separated into two branches: Country and Marine Parks Branch, and Conservation Branch.

Agriculture, Fisheries and Conservation Department

2000   On January 1, 2000, the Department of Agriculture and Fisheries was renamed Agriculture, Fisheries and Conservation Department. It became the main agency for nature and wildlife conservation under the Environment and Food Bureau. Its structure was as follows:

I.   Agriculture and Administration Branch

1. Agricultural Development Division
2. Crop Division
3. Wholesale Markets Development Division
4. Wholesale Markets Management Division
5. Administration Division

II.   Inspection and Quarantine Branch

1. Plant and Pesticides Regulatory Division
2. Veterinary Laboratory Division
3. Animal Management Division
4. Livestock Division

III.   Fisheries Branch

1. Aquaculture Development Division
2. Aquaculture Environment Division
3. Fisheries Enforcement and Special Projects Division
4. Fisheries Management Division

        5. Fisheries Supporting Services Division

IV. Country and Marine Parks Branch

        1. Country Parks (South-East) Division
        2. Country Parks (North-West) Division
        3. Country Parks Ranger Services Division
        4. Engineering Division
        5. Marine Parks Division
        6. Marine Conservation Division (East)
        7. Marine Conservation Division (West)

V. Conservation Branch

        1. Endangered Species Protection Division
        2. Biodiversity Division
        3. Wetland and Fauna Conservation Division
        4. Wetland Park Division
        5. Nature Conservation Division (Central)
        6. Nature Conservation Division (South)
        7. Nature Conservation Division (North)

VI. Accounts and Supplies Division

VII. Information Unit

2002   There were only two changes in the structure. In the Agriculture and Administration Branch, a Co-operative and Credit Union Section had been added. In the Fisheries Branch, the Aquaculture Environment Division had been abolished.

Environmental Protection Department

1959   The Government inaugurated the policy for environmental protection. However, no specific relevant organization was established.

1974   The Advisory Committee on Environmental Pollution was set up.

1977   The Environment Protection Unit (EPU) under the Government Secretariat was established to design and develop policy and legislation on environmental protection.

1981   The EPU was detached from the Government Secretariat to form the Environmental Protection Agency (EPA). It was in charge of the programmes of environmental protection activities.

1986   The Environmental Protection Department was established on April 1.

1987   The Department was responsible for planning environmental protection strategy and enforcing environmental quality under the legislative framework. The Department also provided services on the collection and disposal of waste generated from households, livestock, street, marine, commercial, industrial, construction and dredging; carried out monitoring and research programmes; gave advice on environmental implications of town plans and major developments; and centralized complaints and enquiries. It consisted of three divisions:

I.   Administration Division

II.   Air and Noise Division

    1. Air Policy Group
    2. Noise Policy Group
    3. Air Control Group
    4. Noise Control Group

III.   Water and Waste Division

    1. Liquid and Solid Waste Control Group
    2. Waste Management Policy Group
    3. Water Policy Group
    4. Liquid and Solid Waste Control Group

1993   The Department comprised seven divisions: Administration, Air and Noise, Water and Waste, Accounting Services, Environmental Assessment, Waste Facilities and Local Control.

1995   The Air and Noise Division was separated into two divisions: Air Division, Motor Vehicles Emission and Noise Division. The Department started to provide a guide on air pollution level.

1997   The Corporate Services Division was set up to issue environmental licences or permits.

1998   The Department introduced the roadside air pollution index.

2000   The Department laid stress on legislative control and the safeguard of health and welfare of the community. The Environment and Food Bureau was set up during the year. Work accomplished included a comprehensive package of air quality improvements that was launched in May, and the first stage of tunnel excavations of the Harbour Area Sewage Treatment System.

2001   The organizational structure of the Department was as follows:

I.   Air Division

    1. Air Management Group
    2. Air Policy Group
    3. Air Services Group
    4. Motor Vehicle Emissions Group

II.   Waste and Water Division

    1. Sewage Infrastructure Planning Group
    2. Waste and Water Management Group
    3. Water Policy and Planning Group
    4. Waste Policy and Services Group

III.   Local Control Division

    1. Territory East Group
    2. Territory North Group
    3. Territory South Group
    4. Territory West Group
    5. Urban East Group

   6. Urban West and Island Group

IV. Environmental Assessment and Noise Division

   1. Assessment and Audit Group
   2. Noise Management and Policy Group
   3. Territory Assessment Group
   4. Urban Assessment Group

V. Waste Facilities Division

   1. Business Services Group
   2. Facilities Development Group
   3. Facilities Management Group
   4. Facilities Planning Group
   5. Special Waste Facilities Group

VI. Corporate Services Division

   1. Accounting Services Group
   2. Administration Group
   3. Departmental Computer Unit
   4. Human Resources and Safety Unit
   5. Technical Support Unit

VII. Community Relations Unit

VIII. Media Relations Unit

2002   The structure of the Department remained unchanged.

Sources:

1. *Annual Departmental Report by the Director of Agriculture and Fisheries*, Hong Kong, Government Printer, 1964-1999.
2. *Annual Departmental Report by the Director of Agriculture and Forestry, Hong Kong*, Government Printer, 1960-1964.
3. *Annual Departmental Report by the Director of Agriculture, Fisheries and Forestry, Hong Kong* Government, 1950-1959.
4. *Annual Report of the Forestry Department of Hong Kong*, Hong Kong Government, 1946-1950.
5. Blackie, W.J., "Agriculture and Forestry in Hong Kong" in Braga, J.M.ed., *Hong Kong Business Symposium — A Compilation of Authorative View on Administration and Resources of Britain's Far Eastern Outpost*, Hong Kong, *South China Morning Post* 1957.
6. *CO129/568*, 14 June, 1938, Bontanical and Forestry Department.
7. *Environment Hong Kong*, Hong Kong, Government Printer, 1986-1998.
8. *Fisheries Depratment Report*, Hong Kong Government, 1946-1950.
9. Flippence, F., *Superintendent of Botanical and Forestry Department's Report*, June 14, 1938; Feb 6, 1939.
10. *Hong Kong Blue Book*, Hong Kong, Noronha & Co., 1898-1939.
11. *Hong Kong Government Gazette*, Hong Kong Government, 14 Oct. 1874, p.578.
12. *Hong Kong Report of the Agricultural Department for the Period 1st April, 1948 to 31st March, 1949*, Hong Kong Government, 1949.
13. *Report of the Agricultural Department*, Hong Kong Government, 1946-1950.
14. "Report of the Superintendent of the Bontanical and Afforestation Department", *Hong Kong Administration Reports*, Hong Kong Government, 1931-1939.
15. "Report on the Bontanical and Foresty Department", *Hong Kong Sessional Papers* Hong Kong, Noronha & Co., 1905-1908.
16. "Report of the Superintendent of the Botanical and Afforestation Department", *Hong Kong Sessional Papers*, Hong Kong, Noronha & Co., 1899-1904.
17. www.afcd.gov.hk/index_e.htm
18. www.epd.gov.hk/epd/

Environmental Protection Department — Changes in Directors

Year	Name of Department	Title	Name of Director
1986-1996	Environmental Protection Department	Director of Emvironmental Protection	Reed, Stuart Bennett
1996-2002	Environmental Protection Department	Director of Emvironmental Protection	Law, Robert John Steen

Sources:
1. *Staff List Hong Kong Government,* Hong Kong, Government Printer, 1986-1996.
2. *Staff List the Government of the Hong Kong Special Administrative Region,* Hong Kong, Government Printer, 1997-2000.
3. www.info.gov.hk/epd

Agriculture, Fisheries and Conservation Department — Changes in Names and Directors

Year	Name of Department	Title	Name of Director
1946-1948	Agricultural Department	Senior Agricultural Officer	Ryan, Thomas Francis
1948-1950	Agricultural Department	Senior Agricultural Officer	Strangeways, Thomas German
1946-1948	Fisheries Department	Officer of Fisheries	Cater, Jack
1948-1950	Fisheries Department	Director of Fisheries	Strangeways, Thomas German
1946-1950	Forestry Department	Forestry Officer	Tamworth, Ian Philip
1946-1947	Gardens Department	Superintendent of Gardens	Ryan, Thomas Francis
1947-1950	Gardens Department	Superintendent of Gardens	Dean, Ralph Evan
1950-1953	Department of Agriculture, Fisheries and Forestry	Director of Agriculture, Fisheries and Forestry	Strangeways, Thomas German
1953-1960	Department of Agriculture, Fisheries and Forestry	Director of Agriculture, Fisheries and Forestry	Blackie, William John
1960-1963	Department of Agriculture and Forestry	Director of Agriculture and Forestry	Chambers, Philip Cecil
1963-1964	Department of Agriculture and Forestry	Director of Agriculture and Forestry	Cater, Jack

Year	Name of Department	Title	Name of Director
1964-1965	Department of Agriculture and Fisheries	Director of Agriculture and Fisheries	Cater, Jack
1966-1980	Department of Agriculture and Fisheries	Director of Agriculture and Fisheries	Nichols, Edward Hewitt
1997-1999	Department of Agriculture and Fisheries	Director of Agriculture and Fisheries	Wei Chui, Kit-yee,
2000-2001	Agriculture, Fisheries and Conservation Department	Director of Agriculture, Fisheries and Conservation	Wei Chui, Kit-yee, Lessie
2001-2002	Agriculture, Fisheries and Conservation Department	Director of Agriculture, Fisheries and Conservation	Chan, Chun-yuen, Thomas

Sources:
1. *The Hong Kong Civil Service List,* Hong Kong Government, 1947-1958.
2. *Staff Biographies Hong Kong Government,* Hong Kong Government Printer, 1963; 1965; 1978; 1986.
3. *Staff Biographies the Government of the Hong Kong Special Administrative Region,* Hong Kong, Government Printer, 2001.
4. *Staff List, Hong Kong Government,* Hong Kong, Government Printer, 1959-1996.
5. *Staff List the Government of the Hong Kong Special Administrative Region,* Hong Kong, Government Printer, 1997-2001.
6. www.afcd.gov.hk/web/index_e.htm

Botanical and Forestry Department — Changes in Names and Directors

Year	Name of Department	Title	Name of Director
1861-1871	Government Gardens, Surveyor General's Office, Survey Department	Superintendent of Government Gardens	Donaldson, Thomas
1871-1879	Government Gardens, Survey Department	Superintendent of Government Gardens	Ford, Charles
1879-1880	Government Gardens and Plantations Department	Superintendent, Government Gardens and Plantations Department	Ford, Charles

Year	Name of Department	Title	Name of Director
1880-1904	Botanical and Afforestation Department	Superintendent, Botanical and Afforestation Department	Ford, Charles
1904-1905	Botanical and Afforestation Department	Superintendent Botanical and Afforestation Department	Dunn, Stephen Troyte
1905-1910	Botanical and Forestry Department	Superintendent, Botanical and Forestry Department	Dunn, Stephen Troyte
1910-1920	Botanical and Forestry Department	Superintendent, Botanical and Forestry Department	Tutcher, William James
1920-1937	Botanical and Forestry Department	Superintendent, Botanical and Forestry Department	Green, Harold
1937-1941	Botanical and Forestry Department	Superintendent, Botanical and Forestry Department	Flippance, Frederick

Sources:
1. *Hong Kong Blue Book*, Hong Kong, Noronha & Co., 1861-1939.
2. *The Hong Kong Civil Service List*, Hong Kong Government, 1921-1922.

Social Welfare

Social Welfare Office, Secretariat for Chinese Affairs (1947-1958)
Social Welfare Department (1958-2002)

1946   A Relief Section to provide assistance to needy residents and refugees with food and accommodation was established. The Relief Section was a unit of the Medical Department.

1947   The Social Welfare Office was first established on August 27, as a special subdepartment of the Secretariat for Chinese Affairs. Its major duties were to protect women and girls, rehabilitate the distressed, offer emergency relief after sudden disasters and play the role of arbitration in neighbourhood and family disputes.

1948   The International Red Cross at Ma Tau Chung no. 1 Camp transferred its duties to the Social Welfare Office. Two sections were established in the Social Welfare Office to help achieve its main objectives:

    I.   Relief Section (transferred from the Medical Department)

    II.   Women's and Children's Section

1949   The Camp was relocated to North Point.

1952   The Women's and Children's Section was split into: Moral Welfare Section and Child Welfare Section.

1954   The Office was restructured into: Headquarters, General Office, Relief Section, Probation Section, Youth Welfare Section, Moral Welfare Section and Children's Section.

1956   The Office comprised seven sections: Relief, Child Welfare, Youth Welfare, Women's and Girls', Probation, Community Development and Special Welfare Services.

1958   On January 1, the Office became an independent department as the Social Welfare Department. The statutory powers of the Secretary for Chinese Affairs were transferred to the Director of Social Welfare. The Community Development Section was retained by the Secretariat for Chinese Affairs. The Department comprised six sections and their functions were as follows:

I.   Relief Section

To provide assistance to persons in need and victims of natural disasters, rehabilitate the destitute, investigate applications for assistance and receive advice from members of the public.

II.   Child Welfare Section

To assume legal guardianship of young children in need of care and protect girls lacking parental guidance, to administer adoption of children under the Adoption Ordinance of 1956 and placement in temporary foster care, and to be responsible for the welfare of all infants under the age of six and in primary schools.

III. Probation Section

To operate the probation services such as the supervision of offenders, investigation of the social background of offenders at the request of courts, liaison with voluntary agencies working with delinquent boys and ex-prisoners, and the management of three institutions — the Approved School for Boys at Castle Peak, the Remand Home and the Shanghai Street Children's Centre.

IV.   Youth Welfare Section

To operate children groups to provide informal education and recreation activities, to assist voluntary agencies working with groups of children and young people and promote group work for children and young persons aged between 8 and 21, especially for youngsters not in school.

V.   Special Welfare Services Section

To be responsible for the registration of the blind, the deaf, the physically or mentally handicapped and the aged, and liaison with voluntary agencies working in the fields.

VI.   Women's and Girls' Welfare Section

To be responsible for the welfare of girls in need of care and protection, young prostitutes and unmarried mothers.

1967   Reorganization of the Department was undertaken in July, and its structure was as follows:

I.   Family Services Division

To take over the functions of the former Relief Section, Child Welfare Section, Special Welfare Services, and Women's and Girls' Welfare Section.

II.   Group and Community Work Division (formerly Youth Welfare Section)

To strengthen social cohesion through the organization of community activities.

III.   Probation and Corrections Division

To administer and develop probation services and be responsible for the various correctional institutions.

IV.   Headquarters

1970   The Department was made up of three main branches, and each branch consisted of a number of divisions.

I.   Social Work Branch

1. Families Services Division
2. Probation and Corrections Division
3. Group and Community Work Division

II.   Administration Branch

1. Administration Division
2. Operations Division

III.   General Branch

1. Public Assistance Division

1981   The Department was reorganized into five branches: Administration, Subventions, Development, Social Security and Operations. The Administration Branch was responsible for general administration, public relations, accounts and internal audit. The Subvention Branch was in charge of the administration of social welfare subventions and the evaluation of services. The Development Branch was responsible for planning and development of social work policies and services. The Social Security Branch dealt with social security policies and the administration of the Criminal and Law Enforcement Injuries Compensation Scheme and the Traffic Accident Victims Assistance Scheme. The Operation Branch administered day-to-day social welfare services such as social security, family services, group and community work, probation and correctional services, and services to the elderly and handicapped through four regional offices and 11 district offices.

1987   Two new branches were established: Family Welfare Services Branch and Youth and Rehabilitation Branch. The Family Welfare Services Branch was in charge of family, child care, elderly and medical social work services; while the Rehabilitation Branch dealt with youth and community services, probation and rehabilitation.

1992   The Elderly and Medical Social Services Branch was set up to develop and operate services for old people and perform medical social work services. The Family Welfare Services Branch was transformed into the Family and Child Welfare Branch to operate and develop family and child welfare.

1996   Four new branches were set up. The Youth and Training Branch was responsible for the development of steering services for offenders and social welfare training policies. The Rehabilitation Branch provided steering services for the disabled. The Finance Branch controlled all financial matters and finance management information systems. The Information Systems and Technology Branch assisted the appointed consultants to conduct information system strategy study, and developed office automation system.

2001   The Department comprised 11 headquarters branches and two offices:

I.   Administration Branch

II.   Social Security Branch

III.   Family and Child Welfare Branch

IV.   Youth and Corrections Branch

V.   Elderly Branch

VI.   Rehabilitation and Medical Social Services Branch

VII.   Clinical Psychological Service Branch

VIII.   Subventions and Performance Monitoring Branch

IX.   Human Resource Management Branch

X.   Finance Branch

XI.   Information Systems and Technology Branch

XII.   Corporate Affairs Office

XIII.   Licensing Office

Of these, the Clinical Psychological Service and the Human Resource Management were new branches. The major duties of the Clinical Psychological Service Branch were to provide psychological assessment and psychotherapy to psychologically distressed individuals and help them overcome their crises. The Human Resource Management Branch administered personnel matters such as promotion, staff development and training. The 11 headquarters branches were supported by 13 district offices.

2002   The organization structure remained unchanged.

Sources:

1. *Director of Social Welfare Departmental Report*, Hong Kong, Government Printer, 1993-1997
2. *Hong Kong Annual Departmental Report by the Director of Social Welfare*, Hong Kong, Government Printer, 1954-2000.
3. *Hong Kong Departmental Report by the Social Welfare Officer for the Period 1948-1954*, Hong Kong Government, 1954.
4. *Social Welfare Departmental Report*, Hong Kong, Government Printer, 1996-1998.
5. www.info.gov.hk/swd/html_eng/index.html

Social Welfare Department — Changes in Names and Directors

Year	Name of Department	Title	Name of Director
1947-1952	Social Welfare Office	Social Welfare Officer	McDouall, John Crichton
1952-1958	Social Welfare Office	Social Welfare Officer	Keen, Kenneth
1958-1966	Social Welfare Department	Director of Social Welfare	Baron, David Whinfield Barclay
1966-1968	Social Welfare Department	Director of Social Welfare	Todd, Alastair
1968-1972	Social Welfare Department	Director of Social Welfare	Rowe, George Tippett
1972-1973	Social Welfare Department	Director of Social Welfare	Li, Fook-kow
1973-1974	Social Welfare Department	Director of Social Welfare	Topley, Kenneth Wallis Joseph
1974-1980	Social Welfare Department	Director of Social Welfare	Lee, Chun-yon, Thomas
1980-1983	Social Welfare Department	Director of Social Welfare	Alleyne, Selwyn Eugene
1983-1984	Social Welfare Department	Director of Social Welfare	Chambers, John Walter
1984-1987	Social Welfare Department	Director of Social Welfare	Chan Fang, Anson
1987-1990	Social Welfare Department	Director of Social Welfare	Wong Chien, Chi-lien, Elizabeth
1990-1992	Social Welfare Department	Director of Social Welfare	Cartland, Michael David
1992-1996	Social Welfare Department	Director of Social Welfare	Strachan, Ian Robert
1996-2000	Social Welfare Department	Director of Social Welfare	Leung, Kin-pong, Andrew
2000-2002	Social Welfare Department	Director of Social Welfare	Lam Cheng, Yuet-ngor, Carrie

Sources:

1. *The Hong Kong Civil Service List*, Hong Kong Government, 1950-51; 1953; 1958.
2. *Staff List Hong Kong Government*, Hong Kong, Government Printer, 1964; 1966; 1972.
3. *Staff Biographies Hong Kong Government*, Hong Kong, Government Printer, 1974; 1978; 1982; 1984; 1986; 1988; 1990; 1993.
4. *Staff Biographies the Government of the Hong Kong Special Administrative Region*, Hong Kong, Government Printer, 1998; 2001.
5. www.info.gv.hk/swd/html_eng/index.htm/

Chapter 6
Financial Management and Economic Development

Stock Market, c 1960s.

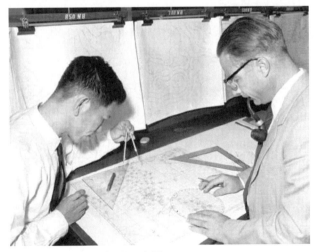

Two forecasters in the Royal Observatory
preparing the daily weather chart, 1965.

Evolvement of Financial Management and Economic Development

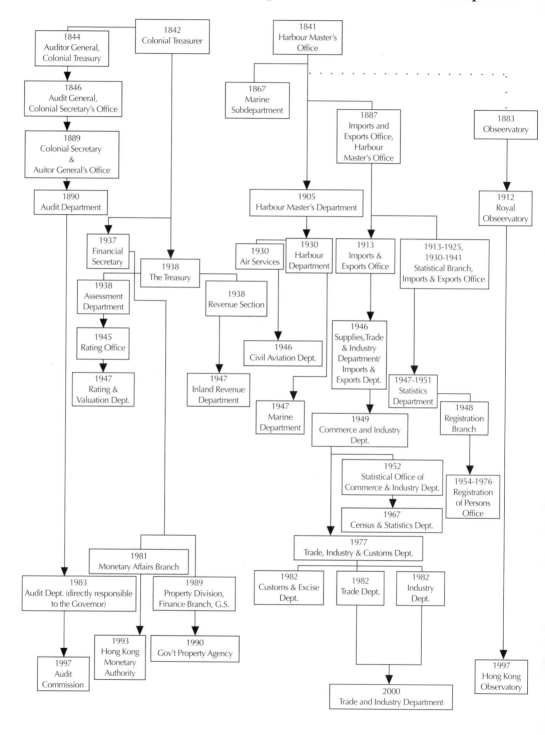

Located south of China and with access to the Pacific Ocean, the remote Hong Kong Island benefited from its geographical advantage, and became a famous entrepôt of the region under the free port policy in the nineteenth century. The control of goods and passenger transportation in the harbour was crucial to commercial development. The Harbour Master's Office was established in 1841 to oversee arrivals and departures of all vessels and preserve public order there. Harbour control was always at the core of the Government's economic strategies.

The organization structure and functions of the Harbour Master's Office from the mid-nineteenth to the mid-twentieth century support this assertion. Five subdepartments were established before the war period: Emigration and Customs Office (1854), Marine Surveyor's Office (1879), Imports and Exports Office (1887), Mercantile Marine Office (1898), and Air Services (1930). They were basically involved in controlling passengers entering and leaving the harbour; vessel registrations; keeping records on imported and exported products; checking hygiene conditions of vessels; preventing the trafficking of weapons and munitions in the harbour; managing air transport and carrying out marine surveys.

The economic strategy of the Government altered significantly after the Sino-Japanese War. The flow of financial and human resources from mainland China after 1949, and the rapidly growing demands of export-led industry, were the major causes of the change. The period marked a watershed in the development of the economic sector's administrative structure.

Changes in the economic sector were

manifold. Firstly, the control of the harbour and economic development was separated into two different parts and handled by two independent departments. In 1947, port control, ship survey and other maritime survey duties were passed to a newly established department: Marine Department. The post-war rehabilitation work and economic recovery work relied mainly on another new department: the Supplies, Trade and Industry Department (1946).

Secondly, the economic sector underwent continuous expansion. In 1949, the Supplies, Trade and Industry Department evolved into the Commerce and Industry Department, a department which specialized in fostering economic development. It enlarged its functions and became the Trade, Industry and Customs Department in 1977. In 1982, it was split into three independent departments: Trade Department, Industry Department, and Customs and Excise Department. The Trade Department and the Industry Department were merged in 2000 to form the Trade and Industry Department.

Thirdly, the economic development strategy after the war stressed the promotion of local enterprises and co-ordination between government departments and private economic organizations. The Government's economic development policy was the driving force behind rapid economic development. This policy was very different from the pre-war period. In the 1920s and the 30s, when local industrial activities were already making an important contribution to government revenue, most of the governmental bodies linked to the economic sector were still geared towards the collection of taxes, registration fees, and other sources of revenue. The development and promotion of local private enterprises had been neglected.

Finally, since the 1980s more emphasis has been placed on financial controls or development by restructuring various subdepartments offices into more sophisticated independent departments. The Government Property Agency became independent in 1990, and the Hong Kong Monetary Authority in 1993. Since the independence of the Financial Secretary gained its independency from the Government Secretariat in 1981, more policy branches on economics and finance have been set up to manage the various departments. In 2002, a total of six policy bureaux — Economic Services; Finance; Financial Services; Information,

Technology and Broadcasting; Commerce and Industry; and Works — were engaged in economic sectoral work.

In the twenty-first century, the provision of efficient economic information, the development and maintenance of good commercial relations with trading partners, and the assurance of general supporting services for industry and commerce, are the essential duties for the government departments involved in economic development work. These departments represent the largest and most important sector within the government structure. The success of its administration directly influences the future development of Hong Kong.

Financial Administration

Audit Office (1844-1889)
Colonial Secretary and Auditor General's Office (1889-1890)
Audit Department (1890-1997)
Audit Commission (1997-2002)

1844   The Audit Office was established and attached to the Colonial Treasurer.

1846   The Audit Office was annexed to the Colonial Secretary on November 19.

1857   It was the Auditor General's duties to audit the colonial and consular accounts.

1889   The Colonial Secretary also acted as the Auditor General and was in charge of audit work.

1890   An independent auditor under the Colonial Secretary was appointed on January 22. The Audit Department ceased to be connected with the Colonial Secretary's Office, and became accountable to the Comptroller and Auditor General. The Audit Department employed four clerks: one for general supervision and registration audits; one for examination of vouchers and keeping the ledger; the Audit Examiner visited every department once a month and compared counterfoils of licences, fees, receipts etc. with the registers and collectors' accounts; the fourth clerk was responsible for the copying work of the Department, supervision of the numbering of the receipts and counterfoils of all departments, and took charge of stationery and printing.

1909   The responsibilities of the Auditor included the audit and inspection of all government accounts of general revenue and expenditure, accounts of special funds and departmental accounts; examination of the bank pass books; verification of investment quarterly; and provision of guidance to store accountants. He ensured all matters of finance and accounts strictly complied fully with the laws of Hong Kong. Each year, he prepared a report on the revenue and expenditure of the year, in which he dealt with the collection of revenue, the state of arrears, how accounts were kept, the sufficiency of existing checks against fraud, nature and extent of audit tests, and any problems that arose from the accounts.

1946   The Audit Department resumed its pre-War duties: It conducted audit inspection of government departments; ensured efficiency and promptness of collection revenue and moneys due to the Government; examined losses of government moneys and stores due to theft, fraud or irregularity.

1961   The Department was organized into three main branches: Registry and Enquiries; Revenue and Stores (consisted of Hong Kong Group A, Hong Kong Group B and Kowloon Group); and Expenditure.

1962   The Department was reorganized into five main branches: Registry and Enquiries, Hong Kong A, Hong Kong B, Kowloon and Expenditure.

1967   The Registry and Enquiries Branch was abolished. The Hong Kong Group A and Hong Kong Group B were merged into the Hong Kong Branch.

1978   The Department was restructured into five divisions: Administration and Personnel, Central Accounts, Computer Audit, Works and Lands, and Kowloon.

1980   The Department comprised Headquarters, Central Accounts Division, General Division, Works and Lands Division, and Subventions Branch.

1983   The Audit Department became directly accountable to the Governor.

1986   The Department was responsible for carrying out regularity audit by examining statements of assets and liabilities and statement of receipts and payment of the General Revenue Account and the Capital Works Reserve Fund. It also carried out 'value for money' audit which examined into the economy, efficiency and effectiveness of all branches of the Government Secretariat, departments, agencies, and other public offices/ bodies.

1987   The Subventions Branch was abolished and the Social Services Branch was set up.

1997   The Department was renamed Audit Commission on July 1.

2001   There was no structural change in the Commission, which comprised the Headquarters Administration Division, Central Accounts Division, General Division, Works and Lands Division, and Social Services Division. The Headquarters Administration Division was responsible for the general administration, technical and special duties, computer audit and training. It contained the Technical and Special Duties Branch (made up of the Executive Support Section and the Research and Development Section), and the Computer Audit Branch. The Executive Support Section provided administrative and professional support and conducted quality assurance reviews on the audit work done by the line divisions. The Research and Development Section conducted research on modern auditing practices; identified subjects for broad-based 'value for money' studies; and provided technical support service, advice and training to audit staff. The Computer Audit Branch provided central technical support to all other divisions in the audit of computerized systems, in addition to its own audit responsibility for certain government bodies. The Central Accounts Division, General Division, Works and Lands Division and Social Services Division were responsible for the audit of all bureaux, government departments, statutory bodies and fund accounts, other than those covered by the Computer Audit Branch.

2002   The organization structure remained unchanged.

Sources:

1.   *CO129/ 241*, 30th March, 1899.
2.   *Hong Kong Government Gazette*, Hong Kong, Government Printer, 20th Jan, 1890.
3.   *Hong Kong Government Telephone Directory*, Hong Kong, Government Printer, 1961, 1978, 1980, 1991.
4.   *Regulations for His Majesty's Colonial Service*, Hong Kong, Government Printer, 1st June, 1909, Chapter V. Finance, pp.1-13.
5.   *Report & Certificate of Director of Auditor the Accounts of Hong Kong Government*, Hong Kong, Government Printer, 1974, 1979,
6.   *Report of the Director of Audit on the Audit of the Accounts of Hong Kong*, Hong Kong, Hong Kong, Government Printer, 1947-1967.
7.   *Report of the Director of Audit on the Accounts of the Hong Kong Government & the Results of Value for Money Audit*, Hong Kong, Government Printer, 1988-1997.
8.   *Report of the Director of Audit on the Accounts of the Hong Kong Special Administrative Region*, Hong Kong, Government Printer, 1998-2000.
9.   www.info.gov.hk/aud/

Audit Commission — Changes in Names and Directors

Year	Name of Department	Title	Name of Director
1844-1846	Audit Office	Auditor General	Shelley, Adolphus Edward
1846-1854	Audit Office	Auditor General	Caine, William
1854-1858	Audit Office	Auditor General	Mercer, William Thomas
1858-1870	Audit Office	Auditor General	Rennie, William Hephburn
1870-1878	Audit Office	Auditor General	Austin, John Gardiner
1878-1887	Audit Office	Auditor General	Marsh, William Henry
1887-1889	Audit Office	Auditor General	Stewart, Frederick
1889-1890	Colonial Secretary and Auditor General's Office	Colonial Secretary and Auditor General	Stewart, Frederick
1890-1898	Audit Department	Auditor General	Stewart, Frederick
1898-1904	Audit Department	Auditor	Nicolle, Hilgrove Clement
1904-1930	Audit Department	Auditor	Phelips, Hugh Richard
1930-1938	Audit Department	Auditor	Collisson, Percival Lorimer
1938-1941	Audit Department	Auditor	Pollard, Arnold
1946-1948	Audit Department	Director of Audit	Pollard, Arnold
1948-1955	Audit Department	Director of Audit	Jennings, Percival Henry
1955-1959	Audit Department	Director of Audit	Carter, Frank Ernest Lovell
1959-1965	Audit Department	Director of Audit	Cooper, William John Dupre
1965-1970	Audit Department	Director of Audit	Britton, Denis George
1970-1973	Audit Department	Director of Audit	Warr, Percy Thomas
1973-1982	Audit Department	Director of Audit	Lyth, Gordon Evershed
1982-1988	Audit Department	Director of Audit	Stalker, Norman Bertram
1988-1992	Audit Department	Director of Audit	Hutt, Robert Jeffrey
1992-1997	Audit Department	Director of Audit	Jenney, Brian George
1997-2002	Audit Commission	Director of Audit	Chan, Yin-tat, Dominic

Sources:
1. *Hong Kong Blue Book,* Hong Kong, Noronha & Co., 1844-1939.
2. *The Hong Kong Civil Service List,* Hong Kong, Government, 1947-1958.
3. *Staff Biographies Hong Kong Government,* Hong Kong, Government Printer, 1974, 1976, 1978, 1982, 1984, 1986, 1988, 1990, 1993.
4. *Staff Biographies the Government of the Hong Kong Special Administrative Region,* Hong Kong, Government Printer, 1998, 2000
5. *Staff List Hong Kong Government,* Hong Kong, Government Printer, 1959-1996.
6. *Staff List the Government of the Hong Kong Special Administrative Region,* Hong Kong, Government Printer, 1997-2000.
7. www.info.gov.hk/aud/

Colonial Treasurer (1842-1937)
The Treasury (1938-2002)

1842   The Colonial Treasurer was under the direct control of the British Government. He was the chief accounting officer in charge of the financial and accounting operations of the Colonial Government. His duties included the supervision of account systems in government departments, control of expenditure and other disbursements of the Government, and the provision of necessary information to the Colonial Secretary for preparing the annual estimates of the revenue and expenditure of Hong Kong.

1847   The Colonial Treasurer was responsible for the collection of licence fees from pawnbrokers and auctioneers, and the issuance of licences of sale of salt, opium, bhang, ganja, betel and betel leaf.

1868   The Treasury Vault was abolished and all receipts and payments on account of the public had to be conducted through the Oriental Bank from September 1 onwards. A receipt for each payment was required from the Oriental Bank. All sums paid into the Treasury for police, lighting and other charges were to be lodged each day not later than 1445 hours at the Oriental Bank.

1871   The Treasury was divided into three divisions. The Cashier's Office received all money paid into the Treasury. The second division was the Accountant's Office; it was responsible for the collection of police, lighting, water and fire brigade taxes. All receipts were made out and issued after being signed by the Treasurer. The third division was the Treasurer's Office. Money was paid into the Treasury from 1030 to 1500 hours. The books were written up every day between 1500 and 1600 hours. When receipts for the payment of money into the Treasury were required, they were signed first by the Accountant and then sent to the Treasurer for signature. The Treasurer had a Pass Book, which was forwarded to the Audit Office for verification of returns transmitted.

1884   The Colonial Treasurer was also responsible for making payments to schools under the grant-in-aid schemes.

1886   The Colonial Treasurer paid to executors or administrators small sums due to the deceased on account of pay or allowances.

1924	The administration of the Estate Duty Ordinance was transferred from the Registrar of the Supreme Court to the Treasury.
1935	The Assessment Office of the Treasury introduced a special rating system to parts of the New Territories.
1938	The Financial Secretary (formerly Colonial Treasurer) assumed control of the financial administration. He ceased to hold office as Assessor, Estate Duty Commissioner and Collector of Stamp Revenue. The duties for the collection of stamp revenue, estate duty and assessment of rates were transferred to the Inland Revenue section in the same year. The department of Colonial Treasurer was abolished and replaced by the Treasury, headed by the Accountant General.
1946	The Treasury was organized into five branches: Accounts, Establishment, Inspections, Payments and Revenue. The Accounts Branch was responsible for the book-keeping of Hong Kong's investments, handling of the public debt, operation of various government funds, classification of the financial transactions, and production of the final accounts. The Establishment Branch was responsible for salaries, allotments and various allowances, and the provision of pensions. The Inspections Branch liaised with other departments on any matter concerning accounts or stores accounts, ensured proper accounting systems and adequate provisions for the safeguarding of public money, and dealt with stock verification. The Payments Branch examined all payment vouchers other than salary paysheets. The Revenue Branch was in charge of revenue including rates, property tax, and rent under leases. The Stamp Office under the Revenue Branch collected stamp duty and estate duty, and fees for the Medical Department.
1947	The Assessment Department under the Treasury was transformed into Rating and Valuation Department under the direction of the Commissioner of Rating and Valuation on July 31.
1953	The Establishment Branch commenced in December the centralization of salary records and the mechanized preparation of the paysheets of monthly-paid staff of certain departments.
1954	The Revenue Branch was responsible for the collection of rents in the resettlement estates.
1955	The Stamp Office of the Revenue Branch was transferred to the Inland Revenue Department on February 1. The Inland Revenue Department also undertook the inspection work connected with the collection of entertainments tax, dance halls tax, and bets and sweeps tax.
1967	The organization of the Treasury was reduced to four branches: Establishment, Inspections, Main Accounts and Revenue. The Accounts Branch and Payments Branch were merged to form the Main Accounts Branch. Its major duties included the examination of all payments vouchers, which was performed by the former Payments Branch. A new function — control of parking meter revenue — was added to the Revenue Branch.
1968	The Computer Branch was established in November to design and organize the computerization for major accounting systems.

1972   The stock verification work was transferred from the Inspections Branch to the Government Supplies Department in November.

1973   The Inspections Branch and the Computer Branch were amalgamated to form a new Accounting Services Branch. It was in charge of the general management and supervision of the accounting operations of the Government.

1977   The Treasury was reorganized into three branches: Accounting Services, Establishment and Treasury Accounts. The Treasury Accounts Branch was a new branch that exercised accounting control over all official banking accounts; maintained the accounting records and funds; issued cheques and arranged banks transfers in payment of goods, services and salaries, subventions; and prepared the Government's annual revenue estimates.

1979   The Financial Monitoring Unit of the Economic Services Branch under the Government Secretariat was transferred to the Accounting Services Branch.

1980   The Accounting Services Branch comprised five divisions: Computer, Financial Monitoring, Internal Audit, Inspection, System and Surveys.

1983   The Accounting Services Branch was restructured into five divisions: Accounting Support, Computer, Financial Information Systems, Internal Audit and Security. The new division — Financial Information Systems Division — was responsible for the implementation of the Ledger Accounting and Financial Information System in the Medical and Health Department, Printing Department, and Electrical and Mechanical Services Department. The Security Division ensured the adequacy of security in relation to cash-handling offices and the safe-keeping of cash and valuables.

1986   The structure of the Treasury was as follows:

    I.   Accounting Services Branch
        1. Accounting Support Division
        2. Computer Division
        3. Financial Information Systems Division
        4. Financial Management Development Division
        5. Internal Audit Division
        6. Security Division

    II. Establishment Branch
        1. Passages Division
        2. Pensions Division
        3. Personnel System Support Division
        4. Salaries and Allowances Division

    III. Treasury Accounts Branch
        1. Grant and Subsidized Schools Provident Funds Division
        2. Revenue Accounts Division
        3. Treasury Accounts Division

1988   The Grant and Subsidized Schools Provident Funds Division was separated from the Treasury Accounts Branch to form the Provident Funds Branch in March.

1989   The Accounting Support Division, Financial Information Systems Division and

Financial Management Development Division were merged to form the Financial Management Services Branch in February.

1990   The Establishment Branch added two new divisions. The Allowances Division was responsible for the administration of advances and loans and the payment of allowances to all government officers. The Salaries Division was in charge of the payment of salaries to all government officers. The Personnel System Support Division was abolished; its duties were transferred to the two newly set up divisions.

1991   The Planning and Development Division was established under the Accounting Services Branch to recruit, train and manage treasury staff, as well as conducting reviews and internal audits within the Department.

1992   The Computer Division of the Accounting Services Branch was expanded into an independent Branch.

1993   The Passages Division of the Establishment Branch was renamed Passages and Education Allowances Division. The Salaries Division and the Allowances Division of the Establishment Branch were combined into one division — Salaries and Allowances Division. The Housing Benefits Division was set up under the Establishment Branch to administer and pay housing benefits to government officers.

2001   The Treasury comprised: Accounting Services Branch, Administration Branch, Computer Branch, Establishment Branch, Provident Funds Branch and Treasury Accounts Branch; and Planning and Development Division.

2002   The structure of the Treasury remained unchanged.

Sources:

1. *Accounts of the Colony and Annual Report of the Accountant General*, Hong Kong, Government Printer, 1967-1968, pp.1-13; 1968-1969, p.14; 1972-1973; pp.19-21; 1973-1974, pp.20-23; 1974-1975, pp.21-23;1977-1978, pp.22-24; 1979-1980, pp.11-12; 1980-1981, pp.11-12; 1983-1984, pp. 12-13, 1986-1987, pp.8-12; 1987-1988, p.13; 1988-1989, pp.11-12, 1990-1991, pp.10-13, 1991-1992, pp.10-12; 1992-1993, pp.10-12; 1993-1994, pp.11-14; 1994-1995, pp.11-13; 1995-1996, pp. 11-14.
2. Caine, S., "Financial Report for the year 1935", *Hong Kong Administration Reports*, Hong Kong Government, 1935, A 5.
3. *CO129/139*, 1 Sept 1869; *CO129/139*, 29 Oct 1869; *CO129/156*, 26 Oct 1871.
4. Crisswell, Colin, N., *The Taipans: Hong Kong's Merchant Princes*, Hong Kong, Oxford University Press, 1981, p.95.
5. *Friend of China*, 31 March, 1842; 15 May, 1844; 20 August, 1845; 1 January, 1845; 3 Feb, 1847; 1 Feb, 1850.
6. *Hong Kong*, Hong Kong Government, 1952, p.210.
7. *Hong Kong Annual Departmental Report by the Accountant General*, Hong Kong, Government Printer, 1955-1956, pp.7-9.
8. *Hong Kong Government Gazette*, Hong Kong Government, 24 Nov, 1853; 22 April, 1854; 15 Sept, 1855; 8 Aug. 1857; 14 Jan, 1860; 5 March, 1864; 23 April 1879; 1 March 1886; 11 Dec. 1886, p.1169; 21 March 1891, p.197; 1 Aug. 1891.
9. *Rating and Valuation Department Chronology and Events*, Hong Kong Government Printer, 1997, pp.11-12, 18-29, 45-49, 59.
10. *Regulations for His Majesty's Colonial Service*, Hong Kong Government, 1st June, 1909, Chapter V. Finance.
11. Woodroffe, B. J. C., *The History of Rates in Hong Kong: A Brief Historical Review Covering Rates over 150 years in Hong Kong*, Hong Kong, Government Printer,1999, p.27.
12. www.info.gov.hk/tsy/intrnet/index.html

The Treasury — Changes in Names and Directors

Year	Name of Department	Title	Name of Director
1842-1843	Colonial Treasurer	Colonial Treasurer	Elmslie, Edward
1843-1844	Colonial Treasurer	Colonial Treasurer	Stewart, Charles Edward
1844-1847	Colonial Treasurer	Colonial Treasurer	Martin, Robert Montgomery
1847-1854	Colonial Treasurer	Colonial Treasurer	Mercer, William Thomas
1854-1857	Colonial Treasurer	Colonial Treasurer	Rienaecker, Robert
1857-1871	Colonial Treasurer	Colonial Treasurer	Forth, Frederick Henry Alexander
1871-1879	Colonial Treasurer	Colonial Treasurer	Smith, Cecil Clementi
1879-1883	Colonial Treasurer	Colonial Treasurer	Russell, James
1883-1890	Colonial Treasurer	Colonial Treasurer	Lister, Alfred
1891-1896	Colonial Treasurer	Colonial Treasurer	Mitchell-Innes, Norman Gilbert
1896-1898	Colonial Treasurer	Colonial Treasurer	Smith, Thomas Sercombe
1898-1918	Colonial Treasurer	Colonial Treasurer	Thomson, Alexander MacDonald
1918-1931	Colonial Treasurer	Colonial Treasurer	Messer, Charles McIlvaine
1931-1937	Colonial Treasurer	Colonial Treasurer	Taylor, Edwin
1938-1941	The Treasury	Accountant General	Black, Thomas
1946-1950	The Treasury	Accountant General	Hirst, Harold Rupert
1950-1956	The Treasury	Accountant General	Lemmon, Ronald Charles
1956-1959	The Treasury	Accountant General	Thompson, Eric James
1959-1965	The Treasury	Accountant General	Heys, Harold
1965-1970	The Treasury	Accountant General	Wardle, Harold
1970-1975	The Treasury	Accountant General	Blye, Douglas William Alfred
1975-1978	The Treasury	Director of Accounting Services	Crabb, Francis
1978-1983	The Treasury	Director of Accounting Services	Eden, Geoffrey Douglas
1983-1993	The Treasury	Director of Accounting Services	O' Kelly, Conal Francis Mary

Year	Name of Department	Title	Name of Director
1993-1994	The Treasury	Director of Accounting Services	Chiu, Sze-hung
1994-1997	The Treasury	Director of Accounting Services	Richardson, Alan
1997-1999	The Treasury	Director of Accounting Services	Dagnall, Brian
1999-2002	The Treasury	Director of Accounting Services	Shum, Man-to

Sources:
1. *Civil and Miscellaneous List Hong Kong Government,* Hong Kong, Government Printer, 1996.
2. *Hong Kong Blue Book,* Hong Kong, Noronha & Co., 1844-1939.
3. *The Hong Kong Civil Service List,* Hong Kong Government, 1947-1958.
4. *Staff Biographies Hong Kong Government,* Hong Kong, Government Printer, 1974, 1976, 1982, 1987, 1990, 1993.
5. *Staff Biographies the Government of the Hong Kong Special Administrative Region,* Hong Kong, Government Printer, 1998, 2001.
6. *Staff List Hong Kong Government,* Hong Kong, Government Printer, 1959-1996.
7. *Staff List the Government of the Hong Kong Special Administrative Region,* Hong Kong, Government Printer, 1997-2000.
8. www.info.gov.hk/tsy/intrnet/index/html

Accounts and Stores Office, Public Works Department (1929-1938)
Stores Department (1938-1969)
Government Supplies Department (1969-2002)

1929 The Accounts and Stores Office of the Public Works Department was responsible for the accounts and the stores and stationery required by government departments either purchased locally or through Crown Agents. The Office also dealt with the provision and repair of all furniture items required for government offices, schools and quarters.

1938 The Stores Section of the Accounts and Stores Office was detached from the Public Works Department and became an independent Stores Department on June 1. Its major duties focused on the control of sand monopoly.

1940 The North Point central store was completed.

1946 The Stores Department resumed its pre-war duties. The Department comprised five sections: Medical Stores, Procurement, Shipping and Inspection, Storage and Distribution, and Sand Monopoly. The Medical Stores Section was in charge of the procurement, storage and issue of medical instruments and appliances. The

Procurement Section purchased goods from the local suppliers or through the Crown Agents in London and concluded contracts for the supply of stores and services. The Shipping and Inspection Section collected and delivered government cargoes and parcels; inspected unallocated stores; and initiated claims of stores lost or damaged. The Storage and Distribution Section dealt with storage of all unallocated stores. The Sand Monopoly Section operated under the Sand Ordinance no. 50 of 1935 and the Sand Amendment Ordinance no. 12 of 1938 to control the importation of sand, regulate the removal of sand by junk, lighter, truck or lorry and the sale of sand.

1947   The Department undertook the disposal of unmanifested goods seized by the Imports and Exports Department; took over the collection, storage and disposal of machinery forwarded by Japan as war reparations; implemented written store-keeping procedures; and investigated surplus and unwanted military and relief stores.

1949   The Accounts Section was set up to keep records of all financial transactions of the Department and to undertake various negotiations with banks, shipping firms and merchant houses for stores purchases from overseas. The Metal Workshop was established to repair items including office clocks, typewriters and calculating machines.

1950   The Furniture and Equipment Section was set up to provide and estimate the demand of furniture and equipment for other government departments.

1951   Stores Regulations were published.

1956   The newly established Stores Section was responsible for the operation of the Electrical and Mechanical Stores, Marine Stores and Waterworks Stores.

1958   The Dangerous Goods Store was completed.

1962   The Department was restructured into the following divisions: Accounts, Furniture and Equipment, Medical, Procurement, Sand Monopoly, Storage and Distribution, Transport and Inspection.

1969   The Department was renamed Government Supplies Department on April 4. The Controller of Stores was retitled Director of Government Supplies. The structure of the Department remained unchanged.

1970   Duties of the Sand Monopoly such as collection, storage and sale of sand were transferred to the Public Works Department.

1973   The Supplies Surveys and Stock Verification Section was set up to verify internal stocks in all sections of the Department and other government departments.

1974   The Coding and Data Processing Section was established to classify and code all new unallocated stores purchased for stocks but returned from other departments, and to investigate all documentation queries referred from the Accounts Division.

1975   The Coding and Data Processing Section was renamed Data Processing Division.

1977   The Metal Workshop was transferred to the Electrical and Mechanical Office of Public Works Department.

1988   The Department was reorganized into five administrative units: Administration Division, Data Processing Section, General Division, Procurement Division, Supplies Surveys and Stock Verification Section.

1999   The Data Processing Section was transformed into Systems Administration Section. It assumed the duties of the Data Processing Section such as the provision of systems support to the Department, electronic data interchange, and the application of information technology. The Training Section was set up to train staff and professionals in the Department.

2001   The Department comprised the following divisions and sections: Accounts Section, Administration Section, General Division, Procurement Division, Supplies Surveys and Stock Verification Section, Systems Administration Section, Training Section.

2002   The Departmental structure remained unchanged.

Sources:

1. *Annual Departmental Report by the Controller of Stores on the Government Stores and the Sand Monopoly for the Financial Year 1950-1*, Hong Kong, Noronha & Co. Ltd., 1952, p.5.
2. *Annual Report of the Government Supplies Department 1998-1999*, Hong Kong, Government Printer, 2000, p.42.
3. Government Supplies Department, *The 50th Anniversary Government Supplies Department Hong Kong*, Hong Kong, Southern Printing Co, 1988.
4. *Government Supplies Department Annual Report*, Hong Kong, Government Printer, 1995-2000.
5. *Government Supplies Department Report*, Hong Kong, Government Printer, 1991-1995.
6. *Hong Kong Annual Departmental Report by the Controller of Stores and Sand Monopoly*, Hong Kong, Noronha & Co. Ltd., 1952-1970.
7. *Hong Kong Annual Departmental Report by the Director of Government Supplies*, Hong Kong, Government Printer, 1970-1975.
8. *Hong Kong Annual Report by the Controller Stores for the Year Ended the 31st March 1950*, Hong Kong, Noronha & Co. Ltd., 1951, pp.1-5.
9. *Hong Kong Annual Report by the Director of Supplies and Distriution for the Year Ended the 31st March 1950*, Hong Kong Government, 1950.
10. *Report of the Controller of Stores for the Period 1st May 1946 to 31st March 1947*, Hong Kong, Noronha & Co. Ltd., 1948, pp.1-6.
11. www.info.gov.hk/gsd/

Government Supplies Department — Changes in Names and Directors

Year	Name of Department	Title	Name of Director
1938-1941	Stores Department	Controller of Stores	Anderson, William John
1947-1948	Stores Department	Controller of Stores	Anderson, William John
1948-1954	Stores Department	Controller of Stores	Watson, John
1954-1960	Stores Department	Controller of Stores	Perry, Arthur Edward
1960-1965	Stores Department	Controller of Stores	Peaker, Arthur James
1965-1969	Stores Department	Controller of Stores	Lemay, George Andrew
1969-1970	Government Supplies Department	Director of Government Supplies	Lemay, George Andrew
1970-1979	Government Supplies Department	Director of Government Supplies	Young, Frederick James
1979-1991	Government Supplies Department	Director of Government Supplies	Kilvert, Roy
1991-1993	Government Supplies Department	Director of Government Supplies	Lam, Chung-lun, Billy
1993-2001	Government Supplies Department	Acting Director of Government Supplies	Shipman, Nigel Christopher Leslie
2001-2002	Government Supplies Department	Director of Government Supplies	Leung, Wing-lup, Gregory

Sources:
1. *The Hong Kong Civil Service List*, Hong Kong Government, 1947-1958.
2. *Staff List Hong Kong Government*, Hong Kong, Government Printer, 1959-1996.
3. *Staff Biographies Hong Kong Government*, Hong Kong, Government Printer, 1990, 1993.
4. *Staff Biographies the Government of the Hong Kong Special Administrative Region*, Hong Kong, Government Printer, 1998, 2001.
5. www.info.gov.hk/gsd/

Hong Kong Monetary Authority (1993-2002)

1993   The Office of the Exchange Fund and the Office of the Commissioner of Banking were merged to form the Hong Kong Monetary Authority on April 1. The Authority was governed by the Exchange Fund Ordinance and the Banking Ordinance. It comprised six executive departments and two committees (Banking Advisory Committee and Deposit-Taking Companies Advisory Committee), in addition to the Administration Division. The six executive departments were:

I.   Monetary Management Department

It maintained exchange rate stability within the framework of the Linked Exchange Rate System through the management of the Exchange Fund, monetary operations and other means; monitored closely the level of inter-bank liquidity and the level of inter-bank interest rates; managed the Exchange Fund and Hong Kong's official reserves; and kept the Hong Kong dollar stable.

II. Reserves Management Department

It formulated and implemented the asset allocation decisions in the bond, currency and equity cash markets; supervised and trained portfolio managers in cash market and derivative market activities; and engaged in quantitative modelling of market dynamics to assist in asset allocation decisions.

III. External Department

It promoted international understanding of monetary and banking policies in Hong Kong; shared information with other central banks about financial trends so as to facilitate more effective policy formulation.

IV. Legal Office

It prevented abuses and activities that jeopardize Hong Kong's reputation as an international financial centre.

V.   Banking Supervision Department

It was responsible for the day-to-day supervision of authorized institutions, co-operated with internal and external auditors and monitored the growth in mortgage lending.

VI. Banking Policy Department

It developed banking supervisory policies and processed amendments to the Banking Ordinance and related legislation, and carried out interest rate risk and market risk surveys.

1994   The Monetary Management Department was renamed Monetary Policy Markets Department. Monetary management was strengthened with the adoption of revised mode of money market operations and the broadening of the scope of eligible report securities for discounting under the Liquidity

Adjustment Facility operated by the Authority. The Exchange Fund Advisory Committee was set up to advise the Financial Secretary on general policies relating to its deployment.

1997   A Land Fund Office was set up in July to take over the management of the Land Fund from the Land Fund Secretariat.

1998   The Economic Division of the External Department was separated from the Department and became an independent department: Research Department. It comprised two divisions: Economic Research and Market Research.

2000   The Corporate Development Division of the External Department was expanded into an independent department: Corporate Services Department. It was in charge of the matters relating to corporate development, human resources, administration, finance and information technology. The Legal Office was renamed Office of the General Counsel. It assumed the duties of the Legal Office and worked closely with client departments, from the initial planning and policy-making to implementation, to ensure that the Hong Kong Monetary Authority's initiatives and operations were conducted in a cost-effective manner with regard to applicable laws.

2001   The Authority consisted of nine major departments and two independent divisions:

    I.   Banking Development Department

        1. Banking Development Division A
        2. Banking Development Division B
        3. Banking Development Division C

    II.   Banking Policy Department

        1. Banking Policy Division A
        2. Banking Policy Division B

    III.   Banking Supervision Department

        1. Banking Supervision I
        2. Banking Supervision II
        3. Banking Supervision III
        4. Banking Supervision IV

    IV.   Office of the General Counsel

    V.   External Department

        1. External Relations Division
        2. Economics Division

    VI.   Reserves Management Department

        1. Direct Investment Division
        2. External Managers Division
        3. Risk Management and Compliance Division

    VII.   Monetary Policy and Markets Department

        1. Monetary Operations Division
        2. Market Systems Division

3. New York Office

4. London Office

VIII. Research Department

1. Economic Research Division

2. Market Research Division

IX. Corporate Services Department

1. Administration Division

2. Finance Division

3. Information Technology Division

4. Corporate Development Division

5. Training Division

Two independent divisions: Internal Audit Division

Support Services Division

2002   The structure remained largely the same, with some minor changes. In the Banking Development Department, an additional unit of Banking Development (Special Duties) was set up. In the External Department, it was made up of External Divisions 1 and 2, the Economics Division had been abolished. In the Reserves Management Department, the External Managers Division ceased to exist.

Sources:

1.   *Hong Kong Monetary Authority Annual Report*, Hong Kong, Government Printer, 1993-2000.
2.   www.info.gov.hk/hkma/index.htm

Hong Kong Monetary Authority			
Year	Name of Department	Title	Name of Director
1993-2002	Hong Kong Monetary Authority	Chief Executive	Yam, Chi-kwong, Joseph

Sources:
1. *Staff Biographies the Government of the Hong Kong Special Administrative Region*, Hong Kong, Government Printer, 1998, 2001.
2. *Staff List Hong Kong Government*, Hong Kong, Government Printer, 1993-1996.
3. *Staff List the Government of the Hong Kong Special Administrative Region*, Hong Kong, Government Printer, 1997-2000.
4. www.info.gov.hk/hkma/index.htm

Commerce, Industry and Trade

Harbour Master's Office (1841-1905)
Harbour Master's Department (1905-1930)
Harbour Department (1930-1947)
Marine Department (1947-2002)

1841	The Harbour Master's Office was established on July 31, 1841. It was the duties of the Habour Master to control anchoring places, departures and arrivals of all vessels in the harbour; to preserve order in the harbour and to giving notice of the intended time for closing mail. The Office consisted of the Marine Magistrate Court of which the Harbour Master was also the Marine Magistrate. The court exercised magisterial and police authority over any persons who breached the regulations issued by the Government in any harbour of the Island.
1854	The Emigration and Customs Office under the Harbour Master's Office was set up. The Harbour Master was the Emigration Officer.
1860	The Harbour Master was empowered to enter at any time on board any licensed boat and to survey, examine and seize such boat in the event of discovering fraudulent concealment of goods.
1861	The Harbour Master was in charge of the registration of seamen on board, checking hygiene condition of vessels arriving in the harbour, and preventing the traffic of weapons by sea.
1864	The Harbour Master was responsible for recording foreign trade conditions, import and export figures; registration of junks, vessels, and the number of seamen discharged; and the cases tried in the Marine Magistrate Court.
1865	Shau Ki Wan, Stanley and Aberdeen were three main stations of Harbour Master's Office.
1866	Two supplementary stations were established at Yau Ma Tei and Hung Hom.
1867	The Marine Subdepartment was under the supervision of the Harbour Master.
1874	Before the establishment of the Observatory, the Harbour Master was in charge of the typhoon reports.
1875	The first lighthouse was set up at Cape d' Aguilar.
1879	The Marine Surveyor's Office was set up to conduct surveys, control the qualification of engineers, examine the carriage of dangerous goods, and regulate medicine and medical stores.
1887	The Imports and Exports Office was formed to register steamers, vessels and the details of goods imported or exported by steamers or vessels. It also regulated the opium trade.
1889	Two new harbour stations were established on Cheung Chau and in Tai O .
1895	The Gunpowder Depot was set up to store explosive materials. Three

lighthouses, at Cape d' Aguilar, Green Island and Gap Rock, started to collect light dues and transmit daily weather reports for the Observatory.

1898	The Mercantile Marine Office was set up to supervise seamen's registration.
1900	A new harbour station was set up in Mirs Bay of Tai Po in January.
1901	The fourth lighthouse was set up on Waglan.
1902	A new harbour station was set up in Sai Kung in April.
1904	The fifth lighthouse was set up in Kap Shui Mun.
1905	A new harbour station was set up in Long Ket.
1909	The Imports and Exports Office was in charge of intoxicating liquors.
1911	A new harbour station was established in Deep Bay.
1912	A new harbour station was established on Lantau.
1921	A Government Coaling Depot and a Shipping Office were set up at Yau Ma Tei. The Government Slipway was established in the same year.
1930	The Air Services was established to manage Kai Tak Airport, issue Certificates of Airworthiness and inspect all civil aircraft in service. The Office was renamed Harbour Department.
1936	A Far East Flying Training School under the Air Services was set up to provide training courses for the Air Arm of the Hong Kong Volunteer Defence Corps.
1945	Rehabilitation was made towards the restoration and improvement of facilities and vessels after the Sino-Japanese War. Co-operation with the Ministry of Transport was stressed.
1946	The Air Services was transformed into the Civil Aviation Department. The Marine Magistrate Court resumed its duties in May. It co-operated with the Marine Police and other disciplined services to investigate marine accidents. The Gunpowder Depot was renamed Government Explosive Department. The Registry Office was established to register incoming and outgoing vessels.
1947	The Port Committee was set up to consider and advise the Government on all matters relating to the welfare, control, administration and development of the Port on February 17. The Harbour Department was transformed into the Marine Department. The Marine Department consisted of two divisions: Port Control Division (administered the Port Control Office, Mercantile Marine Office, Marine Licensing Office, Government Slipway, Lighthouse Section, Gunpowder Depot (Green Island), Harbour Pilotage Examination Board, and Registration of British Ships), and Ship Survey Division. The Port Control Office was responsible for the administration of port regulations and the operation of a buoy or anchorage allocation system. The Mercantile Marine Office worked under the provisions of the Merchant Shipping Acts and the Hong Kong Shipping Ordinance no.10 of 1899 in regard to shipping and seamen and collected the National Insurance and Income Tax (United Kingdom) contributions. It was also responsible for the recruitment, engagement and discharge of seamen. The Marine Licensing Office issued licences to vessels and boats; collected licence fees, permits fees and light dues; enforced

Dangerous Goods Regulations and Load Line Convention of lighters and the registration of all vessels; ensured the operation of the Marine Licensing Stations in accordance with Standing Orders; handled the clearance of boat squatters; and provided typhoon shelter accommodation. The Government Slipway maintained and repaired the Government's fleet and other government-owned boats. The Lighthouse Section maintained and operated all lighthouses automation light stations, navigational aids and signal stations. The Gunpowder Depot (Green Island) operated the depot, took custody of all keys, stocks, stores and equipment of the depot, and arranged for the storage of explosive according to their shipment, class and category. The Harbour Pilotage Examination Board was responsible for the licensing of working pilots and apprentices. The Ship Survey Division conducted surveys in connection with: the licensing of vessels including the emigration licences, registration, grant of certificates, and permits to carry dangerous goods; conducted examinations for certificates of competency; and took measurement of ships for registry under the Merchant Shipping Acts and the Merchant Shipping Ordinance.

1950	The Marine Licensing Office took over from the Urban Council the licensing duties of marine hawkers since October 1.
1962	The Headquarters Division was established to direct the Senior Administration Section, Mercantile Marine Office, Registry of Shipping, Accounts and Stores Section, Marine Magistrate's Court and Marine Department Secretariat. Three new sections — Small Craft Section, Convention Ships Section and New Construction Section — were set up under the Ship Survey Division.
1963	The Senior Administration Section was replaced by the Planning Office.
1966	The Department was reorganized into four divisions: Port Administration Division, Ship Safety Division, Headquarters Division and Seamen's Recruiting Office. The Port Administration Division (formerly Port Control Division) controlled the Port Control Office, Navigation Aids Section, Government Dockyard and Small Craft Licensing Section. The Ship Safety Division administered the International Convention Ships Section, Research and Development Section, Design and New Construction Section and Local Craft Section. The Seamen's Recruiting Office was responsible for the recruitment of new seamen, the supply and registration of seamen, examination of application of licences to employ local seamen, licensing of crew departments, and disciplinary actions against seamen.
1969	The Mercantile Marine Office, which was in charge of disciplinary actions against seamen, was transferred from the Headquarters Division to the Seamen's Recruiting Office.
1970	The Examinations and Shipping Casualties Section commenced its operation on September 1 to investigate all marine casualties involving Hong Kong-registered vessels, as well as conducting examinations for certificates of competency.
1973	The Crew Division was established in June. The Seamen's Recruiting Office and the Mercantile Marine Office became sections under the Crew Division.
1974	The Cargo Handling Section under the Port Administration Division was established.
1991	The Department was restructured into five divisions: Port Services Division (administered the Port Services Branch and Terminus Branch); Planning and

Local Services Division (comprised the Planning Branch and Local Services Branch); Government Fleet Division (directed the Government New Construction Section, Maintenance Section, Fleet Operations Section and Planning Section); Shipping Division (controlled the Crews Branch, Convention Ships Branch and Local Craft Safety Branch); and Technical Policy Division. The major duties of the Department included the maintenance of efficiency of the Hong Kong port, ensuring the safety of all vessels operating in Hong Kong waters, recruitment and engagement of Hong Kong seamen for service in ocean-going ships.

2001   The Marine Department comprised five divisions and an Administrative Branch. The Multilateral Policy Division supervised the Technical Policy Branch, Maritime Policy Branch and Marine Accident Investigation Branch. The Planning and Services Division controlled the Planning and Development Branch, Services Branch and Hydrographic Office. The Shipping Division administered the Ship Safety Branch, Local Vessels Safety Branch, and Shipping Registry and Seafarers' Branch. The Port Control Division comprised the Vessel Traffic Services Branch and Operations Branch. The Government Fleet Division consisted of the Fleet Operations Section, Maintenance Section, Government New Construction Section, Support Services Section, Administration and Security Section, Accounting Services Section, Industrial Safety Section and Supplies Services Unit. The Administration Branch was made up of the Administrative Secretariat, Finance Section, Information and Public Relations Unit. The Multilateral Policy Division liaised with the International Maritime Organization (IMO) and other international agencies, developed environmental protection policy, assisted the Secretary for Economic Services in concluding shipping agreements with other governments, developed policy on nautical matters and legislation, and provided assistance to the Third World countries. The Planning and Services Division was responsible for the strategic planning of port development, harbour mooring, navigation aids, management of all public cargo handling areas matters and hydrographic surveys of Hong Kong waters. The Shipping Division carried out Port State Control inspections of foreign merchant ships, provided consultancy service to the shipping industry on international safety management, reviewed and made amendments to legislation for local vessels and inspection standards, promoted maritime industrial safety, administered the Hong Kong Shipping Registry and provided executive support in ship registration policy formulation, regulated and provided services for registration and employment of Hong Kong-registered seamen. The Port Control Division planned all documentary management of vessel traffic, provided daily shipping information service to non-government agencies and organizations, unified harbour patrol, co-ordinated search-and-rescue missions for ships within Hong Kong waters, enforced the Dangerous Goods Ordinance, formulated training policy and development of training programmes, assessed impact of all marine works, processed entry and clearance formalities of all vessels, issued licences to local vessels, and be responsible for prosecution matters. The Government Fleet Division was responsible for the design, procurement, maintenance, operation and crewing of government vessels. The Administration Branch was responsible for providing administrative and accounting support, and public relations matters.

2002   The structure of the Department remained unchanged.

Sources:

1. *Annual Report of the Director of Air Services*, Hong Kong Government, 1946-1947.
2. *CO129/448*, 9 April; *CO129/602/6*, 19 Aug 1947; *CO129/602/6*, G. N. N. Nunn to P. E. Millbourn, 8 Jan 1948.
3. "Harbour Master's Report", *Hong Kong Sessional Papers*, Hong Kong, Noronha, & Co., 1895-1898.
4. *Hong Kong Almanac and Directory*, Hong Kong Government, 1846.
5. *Hong Kong Annual Report by the Director of Marine*, Hong Kong Government Printer, 1950-1951; 1963-1954, pp.12, 21; 1961-1962, p.1; 1962-1963, pp.14-26; 1963-1964, pp.7-12; 1964-1965, p.9; 1966-1967, pp.1-64; 1969-1970, pp.34-43; 1970-1971, pp.45-47; 1971-1972, p.9; 1974-1975, p.19.
6. *Hong Kong Government Gazette,* Hong Kong Government, 24 March 1842, vol.1, no.1; 21 April 1842; 5 May 1842; 12 March 1844; 15 Jan. 1845; 10 March 1855; 24 Nov. 1860, p.253; 22 Jan. 1862, pp.16-19; 11 Feb. 1865, p.38; 9 March 1867, pp.72-74; 27 March 1867, pp.275-277; 7 March 1868, pp.87-90; 20 March 1869, pp.130-133; 28 March 1874, pp.136-151; 18 July 1874, p.297; 17 Oct 1874, p.579; 18 March 1876, pp.124-127; 17 March 1877, pp.150-151; 31 March 1883, pp.274-275; 29 March 1884, pp.249-251; 25 April 1885, pp.365-367; 13 Feb. 1886, p.70; 2 July 1887, pp.731-733; 14 Jan. 1888, p.32; 21 July 1888, p.775; 8 Dec. 1888, p.1109; 27 July 1889, p.638; 31 May 1890, pp.491-494; 1 Aug 1891; 2 May 1891, pp.321-325; 7 May 1892; 14 May 1892.
7. *Port of Hong Kong the Annual Report of the Harbour Master*, Hong Kong, Government Printer, 1946-1947, pp.1-15.
8. *Port of Hong Kong - The Annual Report of the Director of Marine*, Hong Kong Government, 1948-1949.
9. "Preliminary Report on the Purchase and Sale of Rice by Government of Hong Kong During the Year 1919", *Hong Kong Sessional Papers*, Hong Kong, Noronha and Co., 1920.
10. "Report of the Harbour Master", *Hong Kong Administrative Reports*, Hong Kong, Government, 1909-1930.
11. "Report of the Harbour Master", *Hong Kong Sessional Papers*, Hong Kong, Noronha & Co., 1899-1907.
12. "Report of the Harbour Master and Director of Air Services", *Hong Kong Administration Reports*, Hong Kong, Government, 1931-1939.
13. Taylor, D. A., *The Port of Hong Kong Government*, Hong Kong, Book Marketing Ltd., 1991, pp. 12-24.
14. Welsby, George Ernest, *A History of the Preventive Service, 1909-1939*, Hong Kong, 1957.
15. www.mardep.gov.hk/

Marine Department — Changes in Names and Directors

Year	Name of Department	Title	Name of Director
1841-1853	Harbour Master's Office	Harbour Master and Marine Magistrate	Pedder, William
1854-1857	Habour Master's Office	Harbour Master, Emigration Officer & Marine Magistrate	Watkins, Thomas Vernon
1858-1860	Harbour Master's Office	Harbour Master, Emigration Officer & Marine Magistrate	Inglis, Andrew Lysaght

Year	Name of Department	Title	Name of Director
1861-1863	Harbour Master's Office	Harbour Master, Emigration Officer & Marine Magistrate	Thomsett, Henry George
1864-1887	Harbour Master's Office	Harbour Master, Marine Magistrate, Emigration and Customs Officer	Thomsett, Henry George
1888-1903	Harbour Master's Office	Harbour Master, Marine Magistrate, Emigration and Customs Officer	Rumsey, Robert Murray
1904-1905	Harbour Master's Office	Harbour Master, Marine Magistrate, Emigration, Customs Officer & Intelligence for Board of Trade	Barnes-Lawrence, Lionel Aubrey Walter
1905-1907	Harbour Master's Department	Harbour Master, Marine Magistrate, Emigration, Customs Officer & Intelligence for Board of Trade	Barnes-Lawrence, Lionel Aubrey Walter
1907-1917	Harbour Master's Department	Harbour Master, Marine Magistrate, Emigration, Customs Officer & Intelligence for Board of Trade	Taylour, Basil Reginald Hamilton
1917-1920	Harbour Master's Department	Harbour Master, Marine Magistrate and Emigration Officer	Taylour, Basil Reginald Hamilton
1920-1924	Harbour Master's Department	Harbour Master, Marine Magistrate and Emigration Officer	Beckwith, Charles William Malbeyse
1924-1930	Harbour Master's Department	Harbour Master, Marine Magistrate and Emigration Officer	Hole, George Francis
1930-1933	Harbour Department and Directorate of Air Services	Harbour Master, Marine Magistrate, Emigration Officer and Director of Air Services	Hole, George Francis
1934-1941	Harbour Department and Directorate of Air Services	Harbour Master	Hole, George Francis
1941	Harbour Department	Harbour Master	Jolly, James

Year	Name of Department	Title	Name of Director
1946-1947	Harbour Department	Harbour Master	Jolly, James
1947-1957	Marine Department	Director of Marine	Jolly, James
1957-1961	Marine Department	Director of Marine	Parker, Arthur George
1961-1967	Marine Department	Director of Marine	Hewitt, Joseph Paul
1967-1972	Marine Department	Director of Marine	Milburn, Kenneth
1972-1977	Marine Department	Director of Marine	Fletcher, Allan
1977-1980	Marine Department	Director of Marine	Alexander, Malcolm James
1980-1984	Marine Department	Director of Marine	Davy, Perry Edward John
1984-1987	Marine Department	Director of Marine	Chan, Yue-yan, Peter
1987-1988	Marine Department	Director of Marine	Higginson, Gerald Aidian
1988-1991	Marine Department	Director of Marine	Hall, Derick Arnold
1991-1992	Marine Department	Director of Marine	Sze, Cho-cheung, Michael
1992-1993	Marine Department	Director of Marine	Miller, John Anthony
1993-1996	Marine Department	Director of Marine	Pyrke, Allan Charles
1996-1998	Marine Department	Director of Marine	Dale, Ian Barry
1998-2002	Marine Department	Director of Marine	Tsui, Shung-yiu

Sources:

1. *Hong Kong Blue Book*, Hong Kong, Noronha & Co, 1844-1939.
2. *The Hong Kong Civil Service List*, Hong Kong Government, 1947-1958.
3. *Civil and Miscellaneous Lists Hong Kong Government*, Hong Kong, Government Printer, 1972, 1975, 1982, 1987, 1989, 1990, 1996.
4. *Civil and Miscellaneous Lists the Government of the Hong Kong Special Administrative Region*, Hong Kong, Government Printer, 2000.
5. *Staff Biographies Hong Kong Government*, Hong Kong, Government Printer, 1974, 1976, 1978, 1982, 1984, 1986, 1988, 1990, 1993.
6. *Staff Biographies the Government of the Hong Kong Special Administrative Region*, Hong Kong, Government Printer, 1998, 2001.
7. *Staff List Hong Kong Government*, Hong Kong, Government Printer, 1959-1996.
8. *Staff List the Government of the Hong Kong Special Administrative Region*, Hong Kong, Government Printer, 1997-2000.
9. www.mardep.gov.hk/

Civil Aviation Department (1946-2002)

1946	The Air Services was transformed into the Civil Aviation Department and separated from the Harbour Department on May 1, 1946.
1947	The responsibility for booking civilian passengers by the Royal Air Force Transport Command was taken over by the Civil Aviation Department.
1948	The Director of Air Services was retitled Director of Civil Aviation. The services provided by the Department included airport management, air traffic control services, telecommunications services, and issuance of licences and certificates for flying and engineering.
1949	An Air Advisory Board was appointed to advise the Governor on civil aviation matters on March 12.
1950	The Air Transport Licensing Authority was set up under the Air Transport (Licensing of Air Services) Regulations. The Authority was responsible for approval of licences for air services.
1953	The duties of senior staff were restructured due to the promulgation of new standing orders. The Director of Civil Aviation acted as an adviser to the Government on all civil aviation matters. He was responsible for the implementation of approved policies of civil aviation services and draft legislation; liaison with Ministry of Civil Aviation, Colonial Office, Airlines, Royal Air Force; planning and development of regional aviation with neighboring states; and overall staff and personnel matters of the Department. Senior members of the Department included the Deputy Director of Civil Aviation, Airport Manager, Senior Air Traffic Control Officer, Senior Signals Officer, and Air Registration Board Surveyor.
1954	The Government intended to introduce legislation to restrict the heights of buildings in the areas in the vicinity of the airport.
1955	The Airport Progress Committee was established to make recommendations on the layout and design of the airport terminal building, maintenance area and other requirements ancillary and the operation of the airport.
1957	The Director of Royal Observatory transferred his main forecasting office from the airport to the Royal Observatory building.
1962	The Aviation Advisory Board was formed to advise the Government on matters of importance in relation to the development of civil aviation. The new air terminal building was inaugurated.
1968	The Department comprised the following divisions: Technical Administration, Operations, Technical and Planning, Establishment and Organization, and Accident Investigation.
1971	The Finance Division was established.
1976	The Airport Administration Division was established to manage terminal buildings and property, control customs, immigration and quarantine matters.
1977	The International Affairs Division, consisting of Air Services Section and Administration Section, was set up.

1980   The Department was reorganized. The Operation Division was spilt into two divisions: Air Traffic Management Division and Aviation Safety Division. The Establishment and Organization Division was renamed Administration Division. The International Affairs Division was retitled Air Services Division.

1986   The Civil Aviation (Aircraft Noise) Ordinance was approved in June and empowered the Government to prohibit the operation of aircraft not meeting the noise standard. Legislation relating to the control of obstructions came into force in December to safeguard the take-off surface of the runway.

1987   The Airport Development Studies Division was set up in October to study the ultimate capacity of Kai Tak airport and to produce a long-term forecast of air traffic growth.

1988   The Alternative Replacement Airport Sites Consultancy Study, in co-ordination with related strategic planning studies, was conducted.

1989   The Government proceeded with the construction of a replacement airport at Chek Lap Kok as an integral part of the port and airport development strategy.

1990   The Provisional Airport Authority Ordinance of 1990 approved the establishment of the Provisional Airport Authority.

1991   The Aviation Safety Division was renamed Safety Regulation Division.

1995   An additional Deputy Director was appointed to deal with the closure of Kai Tak airport and the transfer of operations to the Hong Kong International Airport at Chek Lap Kok. The new Deputy Director was also responsible for the flight operations, air traffic control, and the procurement of the airspace management systems of the new airport. The Airport Standards Division was established in August to monitor and ensure high standards of safety and security. The Department implemented an "absolute-closure period" with effect from November 1 to prohibit aircraft movements between 0100 to 0600 hours, except in emergency.

1996   The Flight Standards and Airworthiness Division was established to monitor compliance by holders of air operator certificates. The Division was composed of the Airworthiness Office, Flight Operations Inspectorate, and Personnel Licensing Office.

1998   Chek Lap Kok airport was opened on July 6. The Airport Management Division, which was responsible for the routine management of Kai Tak airport, was abolished.

1999   The dual runway at Chek Lap Kok airport came into operation on May 26.

2000   A regulated agent regime was launched on March 6 to enhance air cargo security.

2001   The Director of the Civil Aviation was retitled Director-General of Civil Aviation. The Department was made up of seven divisions: Administration; Air Traffic Management; Air Services; Airport Standards; Engineering and Systems (a newly established division, to plan, co-ordinate, enhance air traffic control systems, radar, navigational aids and communications equipment for Chek Lap Kok airport); Flight Standards and Airworthiness; and Finance.

2002   The organization of the Department remained unchanged.

Sources:

1. *Annual Report of the Director of Air Services,* Hong Kong Government, 1946-1950.
2. *Annual Review of Civil Aviation in Hong Kong by the Director of Civil Aviation,* Hong Kong, Government Printer, 1976-1995.
3. *Hong Kong Annual Departmental Report by the Director of Civil Aviation,* Hong Kong, Government Printer, 1952-1974.
4. *Report of the Director of Civil Aviation for the Period 1st April, 1947 to 31st March, 1948,* Hong Kong, Government Printer, 1949.
5. *Review of Civil Aviation in Hong Kong by the Director of Civil Aviation,* Hong Kong, Government Printer, 1995-2001.
6. www.info.gov.hk/cad/index.htm

	Civil Aviation Department — Changes in Directors		
Year	**Name of Department**	**Title**	**Name of Director**
1946-1952	Civil Aviation Department	Director of Civil Aviation	Moss, Albert James Robert
1952-1966	Civil Aviation Department	Director of Civil Aviation	Muspratt-Williams, Mervyn Jackson
1966-1973	Civil Aviation Department	Director of Civil Aviation	Thomson, Thomas Russell
1973-1978	Civil Aviation Department	Director of Civil Aviation	Dowing, Roy Evans
1979-1984	Civil Aviation Department	Director of Civil Aviation	Keep, Brian Dennis
1984-1989	Civil Aviation Department	Director of Civil Aviation	Thorpe, John Trevor
1990-1996	Civil Aviation Department	Director of Civil Aviation	Lok, Kung-nam
1996-1998	Civil Aviation Department	Director of Civil Aviation	Siegel, Richard Alan Frank
1998-2000	Civil Aviation Department	Director of Civil Aviation	Lam, Kwong-yu
2001-2002	Civil Aviation Department	Director-General of Civil Aviation	Lam, Kwong-yu

Sources:
1. *Annual Review of Civil Aviation in Hong Kong by the Director of Civil Aviation,* Hong Kong, Government Printer, 1979-1980, 1983-1984.
2. *Civil Aviation Department Annual Report,* Hong Kong, Government Printer, 1998-1999.

3. Hamilton, G.C., *Government Departments in Hong Kong 1841-1969*, Hong Kong, Government Printer, 1969.
4. *Hong Kong Annual Departmental Report by the Director of Civil Aviation1972-1973*, Hong Kong, Government Printer, 1973.
5. *The Hong Kong Civil Service List*, Hong Kong Government, 1947-1958.
6. *Report on Civil Aviation in Hong Kong*, Hong Kong, Government Printer, 1988-1989, 1994-1995.
7. *Staff Biographies Hong Kong Government*, Hong Kong, Government Printer, 1974, 1976, 1978, 1982, 1984, 1986, 1988, 1990, 1993.
8. *Staff Biographies the Government of the Hong Kong Special Administrative Region*, Hong Kong, Government Printer, 1998, 2001.
9. *Staff List Hong Kong Government*, Hong Kong, Government Printer, 1959-1996.
10. *Staff List the Government of the Hong Kong Special Administrative Region*, Hong Kong, Government Printer, 1997-2001.
11. www.info.gov.hk/cad/index/htm

Imports and Exports Office (1887-1941, 1946)
Imports and Exports Department (1946-1949)

1887   Under the administration of the Harbour Master's Office, an Imports and Exports Office was set up on November 1. It was responsible for the inspection of all imported goods by sea. The Imports and Exports Office comprised one working office, Opium Office, which controlled directly the opium trade in Hong Kong.

1903   The Sugar Office was created to issue certificates of origin for sugar. According to the Imperial Sugar Convention Act of 1903, the Superintendent of Imports and Exports was the representative of the Fiscal Authority.

1909   The Imports and Exports Office was expanded. More authority was given to the control of intoxicating liquors and imported goods at the end of 1909. The Office supervised four subdepartments: Opium Office, Sugar Office, Revenue Office and Preventive Launch. Its major services included the collection of revenue on intoxicating liquors in nine distilleries in urban areas; issuance of warehouse licences; control of traffic of liquors, opium and sugar; and the provision of preventive services by searching incoming river steamers.

1910   The collection of the liquor revenue was extended to 14 distilleries in the New Territories.

1913   The Office provided assistance in the exclusion of Chinese currency and the protection of Post Office revenue. The Revenue Office started to collect tobacco duties in the New Territories with effect from July 1. The Imports and Exports Office was separated from the Harbour Master's Office.

1914   The Government monopolized the opium business with effect from February 28; the administration of the monopoly of opium was placed under the control of the Import and Export Office. The "Opium Farm" system had been abolished. The Opium Factory (Boiling Department), Packing Department and Sale Department were set up within the Office.

1915	The Military Store Exportation Ordinance was replaced by the Importation and Exportation Ordinance, under which, with a few exceptions, no goods could be exported from Hong Kong or imported into Hong Kong without permit.
1916	The Revenue Office was responsible for the collection of tobacco duties in urban areas from July 7.
1917	The Statistical Branch was set up to publish trade statistics of Hong Kong. The Revenue Office started to collect tobacco duties in the New Territories with effect from July 1.
1918	The Statistical Branch collected and published imports and exports statistics.
1919	The Rice Office was established to deal with the management of the transactions of rice trade. The Superintendent of Imports and Exports was appointed Rice Controller on October 24.
1925	The Statistical Branch was dissolved.
1930	The Statistical Branch was re-established to resume its previous duties — collection and publication of trade statistics.
1931	Perfume, medicated spirits and toilet preparation containing more 10% of alcohol were considered dutiable liquors.
1932	The Revenue Office took over the licensing of street squatters from the Police Force. All tobacco retailers were under the direct control of the Superintendent of Imports and Exports.
1933	The Opium Factory was closed.
1935	The Imports and Exports was authorized by the Governor-in-Council to exercise in Hong Kong the powers of the Commissioners of the UK Customs and Excise under the Treaty of Peace (Covenant of the League of Nations).
1941	The Office was disbanded due to the Sino-Japanese War.
1945	The opium monopoly was abolished. Responsibility for the suppression of opium and illicit possession of opium was transferred to the Police Force. Some Chinese Revenue Officers were allocated detective work under the War Crimes Commission of the British Military Administration and others were assigned duties in connection with the control of rice, firewood and peanut oil under the Supplies, Transport and Industry Section of the British Military Administration.
1946	The Supplies, Trade and Industry Department was formed to continue the functions performed by a similar branch of the British Military Administration. Its functions included: the procurement of raw materials for industry; identification from shipping all government cargoes; collation and indention the second six-month food programme and programmes for other essentials; control of commodities prices; procurement and distribution of commodities in short supply; and assisting the rehabilitation of industry. The Imports & Exports Office recommenced its operations and became Imports & Exports Department.
1949	The Supplies, Trade and Industry Department was combined with the Imports and Exports Department to form the Commerce and Industry Department.

Some temporary functions were to be carried on by the Department of Supplies and Distribution.

Sources:

1. Braga, J.M., "Trade Development in Hong Kong and the Department of Commerce and Industry in Hong Kong", *Hong Kong Symposium*, Hong Kong, *South China Morning Post*, 1957.
2. *CO129/448*, 9 April 1918; *CO129/44*, 29 Dec 1917; *CO129/622*, 7 Nov 1949.
3. *Customs and Excise Department 75th Anniversary* , Hong Kong, Government Printer, 1984.
4. *Customs and Excise Department 90th Anniversary(1909-1999)*, Hong Kong, Government Printer, 1999.
5. *Hong Kong Administration Reports*, Hong Kong, Government Printer, 1931-1939.
6. *Hong Kong Administrative Reports*, Hong Kong, Government Printer, 1909-1939.
7. *Hong Kong Government Gazette*, Hong Kong Government, 29 April 1886; 1 May 1886; 14 Jan, 27 July 1888; 25 July 1891, p.629; 25 Nov, 1904.
8. "Preliminary Report on the Purchase and Sale of Rice by Government of Hong Kong During the Year 1919", *Hong Kong Sessional Papers*, Hong Kong, Noronha & Co., 1920.

Supplies, Trade and Industry Department (1946-1949)
Commerce and Industry Department (1949-1977)
Trade, Industry and Customs Department (1977-1982)
Trade Department (1982-2000)
Industry Department (1982-2000)
Trade and Industry Department (2000-2002)

Supplies, Trade and Industry Department

1946   The Supplies, Trade and Industry Department was formed to continue the functions performed by the British Military Administration. Its major duties included price control and the procurement and distribution of goods in short supply in Hong Kong. The Department comprised nine sections: Directorate, Procurement, Price Control, Marketing, Rice, Trade and Industry, Fuel Oil, Coal and Firewood, and Accounting. The Department was responsible for the procurement of raw materials for industry; identification from shipping all government cargoes; collation and indention of the second six-month food programme and other essentials programmes; control of commodities prices; procurement and distribution of commodities in short supply; and assisting the rehabilitation of industry.

1949   The Department was abolished. Its major functions were taken over by the newly established Commerce and Industry Department. The Department of Supplies and Distribution also assumed some temporary functions.

Commerce and Industry Department

1949   In order to exercise control over imports and exports, giving advice on new industries, and keeping in touch with the commercial community and with trade developments abroad, all relevant departments were fused to form the Commerce and Industry Department.

1950   The Department of Supplies and Distribution ceased to operate and was integrated into the Commerce and Industry Department on September 1.

1951   The Department was organized into three divisions: Economic, Revenue and Supplies. The Economic Division comprised seven offices: Import Control, Export Control, Essential Supplies, Price Control, Economic Intelligence, Statistical and Trade Promotion. It was responsible for the issuance of import licences, export licences and essential supplies certificates for strategic commodities; control of the importation and exportation of strategic articles; and analyses of statistical data. The Revenue Division was in charge of collection of revenue; prevention of smuggling; and capture of illegal commodities. The Supplies Division maintained records of stocks of essential foodstuffs and fuels for emergency purposes.

1952   The Statistics Department was closed at the end of December 1951 and its duties were transferred to the Statistical Office of the Economic Division of the Commerce and Industry Department from January. A Business Registration Office under the Revenue Division was set up to issue business registration certificates.

1953   The Economic Division was renamed Trade Control Division. The Price Control Office was abolished in April. The Trade Development Division was established. It was divided into three sections: Trade Promotion, Comprehensive and Tourist Certificates of Origin, and Imperial Preference Certificates of Origin. Also added were the Headquarters Division (handled administration and prosecution work), "B" Division (in charge of preventive work and industry supervision), and "C" Division (responsible for revenue collection).

1955   Upon reorganization Administration Division and Controls Division were set up. The Administration Division comprised Staff and Office Section, Accounts and Stores Section, Statistical Branch and Industry Section. The Controls Division consisted of two main branches — Trade Licensing Branch and Preventive Branch. The Supplies and Revenue Divisions were merged into one : Supplies and Revenue Division. It was made up of: Revenue Branch, Supplies Branch and Business Registration Office. An Trade Development Division was also established.

1957   The various branches of the Department were grouped into three main divisions: Administration Division (comprised the Administrative Branch and Statistical Branch); Controls Division (consisted of the Trade Licensing Branch, Dutiable Commodities Branch, Supplies Branch and Preventive Service); and Development Division (included the Industrial Development and Certification Branch, and Trade Promotion Branch). Of these the Dutiable Commodities Branch was a new unit set up to assess and collect import and excise duties.

1958   The Administration Branch under the Administration Division was renamed

Accounts and Administration Branch. The Overseas Trade Relations Branch under the Development Division was set up to keep a watch on changes in tariffs and quotas in overseas countries; to pass on information to chambers of commerce and trade associations concerned; to deal with trade complaints; and to study the activities and development of international institutions concerned with trade.

1959   An Industry Branch under the Development Division was established in August to deal with the registration of factories for certificates of origin of all kinds, and to act as a means of liaison with other government departments.

1960   The Overseas Trade Relations Branch was renamed Trade Agreements and Market Research Branch; the Industrial Development Branch (previously Industry Branch) was temporaryly merged with the Export Promotion Branch to from the Industrial and Trade Development Branch.

1961   The Industrial and Trade Development Branch was demerged. The Export Promotion Branch was renamed Trade Development Branch. It was responsible for the organization of trade missions, promotion of trade, and the handling of written and personal trade inquires from overseas businessmen.

1962   The Textiles and Certification Division was established to deal with quota allocation and export licensing of cotton textiles destined for restricted markets and origin certification of Hong Kong products. It comprised two branches: Certification and Textiles.

1964   The Industry Inspection Branch was set up under the Textiles and Certification Division and was responsible for physical policies of administrative controls, issuance of certificates of various types relating to specific exports to factories, and routine factory inspections. The Export Promotion Division was established. The Trade Development Branch under the Development Division was transferred to the Export Promotion Division; and a new Trade Licensing Branch was also created.

1967   The Department was reorganized into five divisions: Industry Division (comprised the Administration and Accounts Branch, Statistical Branch, Certification Branch, Industrial Development Branch and Industry Inspection Branch); Controls Division (consisted of the Dutiable Commodities Branch, Trade Licensing Branch and Preventive Service); Textiles Division (divided into the Overseas Trade Relations Branch and Overseas Offices); Commercial Relations 'E' Division (Europe); and Commercial Relations 'R' Division (Outside Europe). The Statistical Branch was latter transferred out and became the Economic Statistics Division of the newly created Census and Statistics Department.

1969   The Controls Division was replaced by the Preventive Service and Dutiable Commodities Division and the General Duties Branch.

1971   The Industry Division had the following reorganization: the Administration and Accounts Branch was renamed Administration Branch and Finance and Supplies Branch; and the Industry Inspection Branch was renamed Trade Investigation Branch.

1974   Two new divisions were established. The Administration Division was set up to manage the Department and to liaise with overseas offices. The Trade Division was set up for certification and documentation procedures, operation of trade investigation service, handling trade complaints, and control of reserved commodities (of which rice was the most important). The Textiles Division was retitled Textile Controls Division. The Preventive Service and Dutiable Commodes Division was renamed Preventive Service.

Trade, Industry and Customs Department

1977   The Commerce and Industry Department was reorganized and became Trade, Industry and Customs Department in July. The new department consisted of two subdepartments: Trade (supervised the two Commercial Relation Divisions, Textile Controls Division and Overseas Offices), and Industry and Customs (administered the Industry Division, Trade Division, and Customs and Excise Service). The Commercial Relation Divisions conducted trade negotiations with other governments; and collected and disseminated information on trade policy measures of other countries. The Textile Controls Division was responsible for the general licensing of textile exports, and the implementation of restraint agreements reached with importing countries. The Overseas Offices were in charge of commercial relations work and provided information on international developments that may affect Hong Kong. The Industry Division provided liaison between industry and other government departments, promoted overseas investment in local industry, and dealt with specific industrial issues. The Trade Division was responsible for certification and trade documentation procedures; management of the Trade Investigation Branch that undertook regular inspection of factories and goods; and handling trade complaints. The Customs and Excise Service's duties included the collection of revenue derived from four dutiable commodities (alcoholic liquors, tobacco, methyl alcohol and hydrocarbon oils used as fuel for motor vehicles and aircraft); administration of the Dutiable Commodities Ordinance which imposed controls over the import, export, manufacture, sale and storage of commodities; prevention and suppression of illicit trafficking in narcotics, other dangerous drugs and acetylating substances under the Dangerous Drug Ordinance, Pharmacy and Poisons Ordinance and the Acetylating Substance (Control) Ordinance; and the enforcement of the Copyright Ordinance.

1978   The Industry Division was restructured into Industrial Support Division and Industrial Development Division. The Industrial Support Division liaised with other government departments and dealt with specific issues affecting industry, such as infrastructure and the health and safety standards set in Hong Kong's overseas markets. The Industrial Development Division promoted overseas investment in local industry, encouraged industrial co-operation between Hong Kong and overseas manufacturers, and liaised with the Hong Kong Trade Development Council and the Hong Kong General Chamber of Commerce. The Trade Division was retitled Trade Controls Division. Another Commerical Relations Division was added.

1979   The Department was reorganized into three subdepartments: Trade (administered the External Affairs Group, Internal Affairs Group and Overseas Offices); Industry (supervised the Industry Support and Liaison Division and

Industrial Development Division); and Customs and Controls (directed the Trade Control Division, and Customs and Excise Service).

1980   The Trade Subdepartment was restructured into two main groups: EEC and Multilateral Group, and Rest of the World and Textile Systems Group.

1981   The Industry Subdepartment had the following changes: The Industry Support and Liaison Division was renamed Environment and Resources Division; and two new divisions was created: Promotion Consultancy Division and Science and Technology Division.

1982   The Trade, Industry and Customs Department was split into three independent departments: Trade Department, Industry Department, and Customs and Excise Department.

Trade Department

1982   The Trade Department was responsible for overseas commercial relations liaison work; issuance of certificates of origin, export and import licensing; administration of quotas in respect of United States, Canada, EEC, Portugal, Spain and Turkey markets; planning and implementation of the computerization programme of the textile controls system. It consisted of two groups: Multilateral and North America Group (supervised the Multilateral Division and North America Division), Rest of the World and Systems Group (directed the EEC Division, Other Regions Division, and Systems Division).

1990   The EEC Division was renamed Europe Division.

1995   The Department was restructured. The Multilateral and Regional Co-operation Group supervised two divisions: Multilateral Division and Regional Co-operation Division. The Commercial Relations and Control Group directed three divisions: Europe, Africa and Middle East Division; Americas Division; and Systems Division. The major duties of the Multilateral Division involved preparatory work for joining the World Trade Organization (WTO). The Regional Co-operation Division dealt with activities related to the Asia-Pacific Economic Co-operation forum (APEC), the Pacific Economic Co-operation Council (PECC), and commercial relations with Asia, Australia and New Zealand. The Systems Division was responsible for the textiles export control system; the Textiles Trader Registration Scheme; non-restrained textile licensing; the computerization of the Department's licensing systems; the import and export licensing of commodities other than textiles; the rice control scheme; and common services.

1997   The Europe, Africa and Middle East Division and the Americas Division were reorganized into two new divisions: Europe Division, Asia and Americas Division.

2000   The Trade Department and the Industry Department were combined to form the Trade and Industry Department.

Industry Department

1982   The Trade, Industry and Customs Department was spilt into three independent departments. The Industry Department comprised four divisions: Environment and Resources, Industrial Development, Promotion Consultancy, and Science and Technology. The Environmental and Resources Division was responsible for liaison with local trade organizations and relevant government departments; control of raw material supplies such as fuel and essential products; provision of adequate infrastructure facilities; and administration of environmental legislation on industry. The Industrial Development Division was in charge of the industrial promotion policy; and co-ordination between industrial promotion programmes and industry and trade organizations. The Promotion Consultancy Division provided comprehensive information on Hong Kong to potential investors. The Science and Technology Division advised on the provision of industrial support facilities and technical back-up services, transfer of technology, research and development; provided calibration services to the public as well as private sectors; administered quality certification, product standard services and accreditation of testing laboratories; and provided overseas consultancy for the planning of international exhibitions in Hong Kong.

1985   The Department was reorganized into five divisions. The Data and Services Division was responsible for liaison with local and international trade and industry organizations; promotion of industrial investment; collection and collation of industrial data; and conduct of research and surveys on industry. The Industrial Infrastructure Division monitored raw material supplies; ensured the provision of adequate infrastructure facilities; and advised the government on industrial land matters. The Industrial Promotion Division carried out promotion work through overseas offices and gave comprehensive advice and assistance to potential investors. The Industrial Support Division dealt with industrial support facilities and technical back-up services. The Product Standards Branch under the Industrial Support Division was responsible for providing information on overseas standards requirements and issues relating to industrial product design, packaging and quality assurance. The fifth division was Laboratory Services Division.

1988   The Data and Services Division was reorganized into two sections: Data and Services Section, and Industrial Extension Service Section. The Industrial Infrastructure Division was renamed Infrastructure Support Division; it consisted of two sections: Land Section, and Environment and Resources Section. The Industrial Promotion Division was retitled Inward Investment Division; it comprised three administrative units: Industrial Promotion Branch, One Stop Unit, and Research and Targeting Unit. The Industrial Support Division was renamed Development Support Division. The Laboratory Services Division was renamed Quality Services Division; it consisted of Laboratory Accreditation Scheme, Hong Kong Government Standards and Calibration Laboratory, and Product Standards Information Bureau.

1992   The Inward Investment Division was renamed Investment Promotion Division. The Technology Development Division was established.

1994   The Technical Section was added to the Data and Services Division. The

Research and Targeting Section under the Investment Promotion Division was abolished, and a new Support Section was created.

1996   The Data and Services Division was abolished. The Development Support Division was restructured into three sections: Productivity and Technology Support Section, Industrial Data and Liaison Section, and Technical Support Section. New sections — Secretariat for Industry and Technology Applied Research Development Council, Industrial Support Fund Section, and Technical Support Section — were set up under the direction of the Technology Development Division.

1997   The Environment and Resources Section of the Infrastructure Support Division was enlarged and became the Environment, Resources and Hong Kong Industry and Technology Co-operation Centre (HKITCC) Section. The Science Park Section was set up under the supervision of the Infrastructure Support Division. The Services Support Fund Section and the Asia Pacific Economic Co-operation/Small and Medium Enterprises (SME) Section were added to the Development Support Division. A new section, Biotechnology Section, was created under the Technology Development Division.

1999   The Infrastructure Support Division was reorganized: the Environment, Resources and HKITCC Section, and the Science Park Section were restructured to form the HKITCC, Hong Kong Productivity Council (HKPC), and Manpower, Environment and Resources Section; the Land Section was retitled Industrial Land Section; and the Applied Sciences and Technology Research Institute Section was established. A SME Policy Development Section was added to the Development Support Division. The Industrial Support Fund Section of the Technology Development Division was abolished and replaced by the Innovation and Technology Fund Section.

2000   The Industry Department ceased its operations on July 1. The Industry Department and the Trade Department were restructured to form the Trade and Industry Department.

Trade and Industry Department

2000   The Trade Department and the Industry Department were merged into the Trade and Industry Department. It handled commercial relations with trading partners, implemented trade policies and agreements, and provided general supporting services for the industrial sector and small and medium enterprises. The Department was organized into two major groups: Multilateral, Regional Co-operation and Europe Group (comprised the three divisions of Europe, Multilateral, Regional Co-operation); and the Commercial Relations, Controls and Support Group (directed the four divisions of Americas, Asia, Industrial Support, Systems). The Commercial Relations, Controls and Support Group dealt with bilateral commercial relations with Hong Kong's trading partners in Americas and Asia; administered the textiles export control system and the origin certification system, and co-ordinated the related policies; provided general industrial support services as well as services specific to small and medium enterprises. The Multilateral, Regional Co-operation and Europe Group dealt with the multilateral aspects of Hong Kong external commercial relations and bilateral commercial relations with Hong Kong's trading partners in Europe. The Department also has 10 Overseas Offices: Brussels, Geneva, London, Washington DC, New York, San Francisco, Toronto, Tokyo, Sydney and Singapore; an Administration Branch and a Public Relations and Information Unit.

2002　The structure of the Department remained unchanged.

Sources:

1. *Annual Report by the Director of Commerce and Industry*, Hong Kong, Government Printer, 1951-1952, p.4-16; 1952-1953, pp.15-16; 1952-1953, pp.8-13; 1953-1954, pp.7-38; 1955-1956, pp. 5-46; 1956-1957, pp.12-13; 1959-1960, pp.11-12; 1956-1957, pp.28-49; 1958-1959, pp.17, 24, 46, 89; 1959-1960, pp.9-10, 96; 1960-1961, pp.7-10, 89, 1962-1963, pp.7-8, 10; 1963-1964, p.100; 1964-1965, pp.20-21, 34-35, 67, 79, 89; 1965-1966, p.88; 1966-1967, pp.31, 75, 91; 1967-1968, pp.12-13, 16; 1968-1969, pp.10, 60; 1969-1970, p.66; 1970-1971, p.82; 1971-1972, pp.46-47, 66-80.
2. *Annual Statistical Review of Trade Department*, Hong Kong, Government Printer, 1982, p.3, 1983, p.3.
3. *CO 129/619/4*, pp.37-43, 46-64; *CO129/619/4*, 15 July 1848, 19 March 1949, 27 Sept 1949.
4. *Hong Kong*, Hong Kong, Government Printer, 1978, pp.19-20, 123-124; 1979, p.19, 1980, pp. 27-28; 1981, pp.25-26; 1982; 1983, pp.21-22; pp.28-29; 1997, pp.103-104; 2000, p.116.
5. *Hong Kong A New Era*, Hong Kong, Government Printer, 1997, p.100.
6. *Hong Kong Annual Report of the Director of Supplies, Trade and Industry*, Hong Kong Government, 1948-1949, p.12; 1951, p.4.
7. *Hong Kong Government Telephone Directory*, Hong Kong, Government Printer, Issue No. 2, 1982, pp.137-139.
8. *Hong Kong Annual Report*, Hong Kong Government, 1947, pp.148.
9. *Trade and Industry Department Handbook*, Hong Kong, Government Printer, 2001.
10. *Trade Department Handbook*, Hong Kong, Government Printer, 1990, Appendix A.
11. www.tid.gov.hk/

Trade and Industry Department — Changes in Names and Directors

Year	Name of Department	Title	Name of Director
1887	Imports and Exports Office	Superintendent of Imports and Exports	Seth, Arathan
1887-1903	Imports and Exports Office	Superintendent of Imports and Exports	Rumsey, Robert Murray
1904-1906	Imports and Exports Office	Superintendent of Imports and Exports	Barnes-Lawrence, Lionel Aubrey Walter
1907-1908	Imports and Exports Office	Superintendent of Imports and Exports	Taylor, Basil Reginald Hamilton
1909-1910	Imports and Exports Office	Superintendent of Imports and Exports	Beckwith, Charles William Malbeyse
1909-1910	Imports and Exports Office	Superintendent of Imports and Exports	Beckwith, Charles William Malbeyse
1910-1911	Imports and Exports Office	Superintendent of Imports and Exports	Tratman, David William

Year	Name of Department	Title	Name of Director
1911-1921	Imports and Exports Office	Superintendent of Imports and Exports	Hutchison, Robert Oliphant
1921-1923	Imports and Exports Office	Superintendent of Imports and Exports	Smith, Norman Lockhart
1923-1927	Imports and Exports Office	Superintendent of Imports and Exports	Lloyd, John Daniel
1927-1932	Imports and Exports Office	Superintendent of Imports and Exports	Sayer, Geoffrey Robley
1932-1933	Imports and Exports Office	Superintendent of Imports and Exports	Hamilton, Eric William
1933-1935	Imports and Exports Office	Superintendent of Imports and Exports	Lloyd, John Daniel
1935-1937	Imports and Exports Office	Superintendent of Imports and Exports	Hamilton, Eric William
1937-1941	Imports and Exports Office	Superintendent of Imports and Exports	Hamilton, Eric William; Megarry, Thomas
1946	Imports and Exports Office	Superintendent of Imports and Exports	Thomson, Walter Morris
1946-1949	Imports and Exports Department	Superintendent of Imports and Exports	Himsworth, Eric
1946-1947	Supplies, Trade & Industry Department	Acting Director, Supplies, Trade & Industry Deparrtment	Thomson, Walter Morris
1947-1948	Supplies, Trade & Industry Department	Acting Director, Supplies, Trade & Industry Deparrtment	Cowperthwaite, John James
1949-1950	Commerce and Industry Department	Director of Commerce and Industry	Keen, Kenneth
1949	Suppies and Distribution Department	Director of Supplies and Distribution	Barnett, Kenneth Myer Arthur
1950	Suppies and Distribution Department	Director of Supplies and Distribution	Clarke, Arthur Grenfell
1950-1951	Commerce and Industry Department	Director of Commerce and Industry	Clarke, Arthur Grenfell
1951-1953	Commerce and Industry Department	Director of Commerce and Industry	Sedgwick, Patrick Cardinall Mason
1953-1962	Commerce and Industry Department	Director of Commerce and Industry and Commissioner of Preventive Service	Angus, Herbert Alexander

Year	Name of Department	Title	Name of Director
1962-1966	Commerce and Industry Department	Director of Commerce and Industry and Commissioner of Preventive Service	Holmes, David Ronald
1966-1970	Commerce and Industry Department	Director of Commerce and Industry and Commissioner of Preventive Service	Sorby, Terence Dare
1970-1972	Commerce and Industry Department	Director of Commerce and Industry and Commissioner of Preventive Service	Cater, Jack
1972-1977	Commerce and Industry Department	Director of Commerce and Industry and Commissioner of Preventive Service	Jordan, David Harold
1977-1979	Trade, Industry and Customs Department	Director of Trade, Industry & Customs and Commissioner of Customs & Excise	Jordan, David Harold
1979-1982	Trade, Industry and Customs Department	Director of Trade, Industry & Customs and Commissioner of Customs & Excise	Dorward, William
1982-1987	Trade Department	Director of Trade	Macleod, Nathaniel William Hamish
1987-1990	Trade Department	Director of Trade	Sze, Cho-cheung, Michael
1990-1991	Trade Department	Director-General of Trade	Chau, Tak-hay
1991-1992	Trade Department	Director-General of Trade	Tsang, Yam-kuen, Donald
1993-1996	Trade Department	Director-General of Trade	Miller, John Anthony
1996-2000	Trade Department	Director-General of Trade	Law, Chi-kong, Joshua
1982-1986	Industry Department	Director of Industry	Yaxley, John Francis
1986-1988	Industry Department	Director of Industry	Yeung, Kai-yin, Andrew
1988-1989	Industry Department	Director of Industry	Leung, Kin-pong
1989-1992	Industry Department	Director of Industry	Barma, Tyebjee Hatam
1993-1995	Industry Department	Director- General of Industry	Yue, Cheung-yee, Denise

Year	Name of Department	Title	Name of Director
1996	Industry Department	Director- General of Industry	Ip Lau, Suk-yee, Regina
1997-2000	Industry Department	Director- General of Industry	Ho, Suen-wai
2000-2002	Trade and Industry Department	Director-General of Trade and Industry	Law, Chi-kong, Joshua

Sources:
1. *Customs and Excise Department 90th Anniversary (1909-1999)*, Hong Kong, Government Printer, 1999.
2. *Hong Kong Blue Book*, Hong Kong, Noronha & Co., 1909-1939.
3. *The Hong Kong Civil Service List*, Hong Kong Government, 1947-1958.
4. *Staff Biographies Hong Kong Government*, Hong Kong, Government Printer, 1974, 1976, 1978, 1982, 1984, 1986, 1988, 1990, 1993.
5. *Staff Biographies the Government of the Hong Kong Special Administrative Region*, Hong Kong, Government Printer, 1998, 2000
6. *Staff List Hong Kong Government*, Hong Kong, Government Printer, 1959-1996.
7. *Staff List the Government of the Hong Kong Special Administrative Region*, Hong Kong, Government Printer, 1997-2000.
8. www.tid.gov.hk/

Customs and Excise Department (1982-2002)

1982   The Customs and Excise Department became independent in August upon the split-up of the former Trade, Industry and Customs Department.

1983   The Department was divided into two major divisions: the Administration and Trade Controls Division, and the Customs and Excise Service. The former division comprised five branches: Administrative Branch, Accounts and Supplies Branch, Trade Controls Operations Branch, Trade Controls Investigation Branch and Trade Administration Section. It was responsible for factory and consignment inspections in support of the origin and preference certification system; the enforcement of import and export legislation, including the textile quota control system; prosecution of all cases handled by the Investigation and Trade Controls Operations and Investigation Branches; liaison with the Legal Department; and assisting settlement of commercial disputes between Hong Kong businesses and overseas complainants. The latter division consisted of six administrative units — Command Headquarters, Customs Technical Bureau, Customs Investigation Bureau, Hong Kong Island Region, Kowloon Region and New Territories Region. This Division was responsible for revenue collection and licensing control on dutiable commodities such as tobacco, hydrocarbon oil and alcohol. The major inspection work stressed on the manufacturing and selling of narcotic drugs, copyright offences and smuggling of illegal cargoes.

1984   The Department was divided into three main branches: Headquarters, Operation and Investigation. The structure of the Department was as follows:

I.   Headquarters Branch
   1. Departmental Administration (formerly Administrative Branch)
   2. Service Headquarters
   3. Departmental Accounts and Supplies (formerly Accounts and Supplies Branch)
   4. Dutiable Commodities Administration
      i.   Excise System
      ii. Excise Verification and Intelligence
      iii. Valuation and Dutiable
      iv. Commodities Office

   5. Departmental Training
   6. Trade Controls Administration (formerly Trade Administration Section)

II. Operation Branch
   1. Hong Kong Island Region
      i.   Marine Strike and Search (formerly Strike and Search Division)
      ii. Anti-Smuggling Division
      iii. Sea-Cargo Examination Division
      iv. Island Administration and Controls Division

   2. Kowloon Region
      i.   Air-Cargo Examination Division
      ii. Air Passenger Examination Division
      iii. Kowloon Administration and Controls Division

   3. New Territories Region
      i.   Anti-Smuggling Division
      ii. Container-Cargo Examination Division
      iii. New Territories Administration and Controls Division
      iv. Border Controls

   4. Trade Inspection Group
      i.   Hong Kong Island
      ii. Kowloon
      iii. New Territories

III. Investigation Branch
   1. Customs Investigation Bureau
      i.   Narcotics Division
      ii. Intelligence and General Investigation Division
      iii. Copyright Division
      iv. Prosecution Division
      v.   Regional Intelligence Liaison Office

   2. Trade Investigation Bureau
      i.   Origin Fraud Investigation
      ii. Licensing Fraud Investigation (formerly General (Licensing) Investigation Section)

3. Trading Standards Investigation Bureau
  i. Industrial Property Investigation Section
  ii. Trade Complaints and Prosecution Division (formerly Trade Complaints Unit)

1989   Two new branches were established: Trade Controls Branch and Civil Secretariat. The Trade Controls Branch enforced programmes against origin fraud, controlled quota systems; managed trade matters under the Schedule of the Trade and Industry Bureau; detected smuggling of endangered species and medicines; inspected factories and consignments. The Civil Secretariat was in charge of internal audit, departmental and financial administration of the Department.

1996   The Department underwent a reorganization and was regrouped into five branches: Administration and Excise (directed the Office of Dutiable Commodities Administration, Office of Management Service, Office of Service Administration and Training, Prosecution Intelligence and Investigation Bureau); Trade Controls (supervised the Trade Investigation Bureau, Trade Licensing Investigation Bureau, Trade Controls Headquarters, Trading Standards Investigation Bureau, Trade Inspection and Verification Bureau); Border and Drugs (administered the Airport Command, Control Points Command and Customs Drug Investigation Bureau); Control and Intellectual Property (comprised the Intellectual Property Investigation Bureau, Marine and Land Enforcement Command, Ship Search and Cargo Command); and Civil Secretariat (consisted of the Office of Information Technology, Office of Departmental Administration, Office of Financial Administration, Statistics Office and Information Unit).

2001   With effect from April 17, the Trade Controls Branch was reconstructed into five new bureaux: Trade Inspection and Verification, Textiles Fraud Investigation, Textiles Tactical and Intelligence, General Investigation and Systems, Consumer Protection and Prosecution.

2002   The Department was organized into six branches: Administration and Excise (consisted of the Office of Dutiable Commodities Administration, Office of Management Services, Office of Service Administration, Office of Training and Development); Boundary and Drugs (comprised the Airport Command, Control Points Command, Customs Drug Investigation Bureau); Control and Intellectual Property (supervised the Intellectual Property Investigation Bureau, Marine and Land Enforcement Command, Ship Search and Cargo Command, Special Task Force); Customs Co-operation and Intelligence (composed of the Customs Intelligence and Liaison Bureau, World Customs Organization Group); Trade Controls (made up of the General Investigation and Systems Bureau, Trade Inspection and Verification Bureau, Fraud Investigation Bureau, Textiles Tactical and Intelligence Bureau, Consumer Protection and Prosecution Bureau); Civil Secretariat (directed the Office of Departmental Administration, Office of Financial Administration, Office of Information Technology, Internal Audit Division, Information Unit, Statistics Office). The Department was also supported by the Complaints Investigation Group, the Formation Inspection Team and the Management Support Team (contained the Statistics Unit).

Sources:

1. *Customs and Excise Department 75th Anniversary*, Hong Kong, Government Printer, 1984.
2. *Customs and Excise Department 90th Anniversary (1909-1999)*, Hong Kong, Government Printer, 1999.
3. *Customs and Excise Department 1986-1993*, Hong Kong, Government Printer, 1994.
4. *Customs and Excise Department Review*, Hong Kong, Government Printer, 1983.
5. *Hong Kong Customs and Excise Annual Review*, Hong Kong, Government Printer, 1996-2000.
6. www.info.gov.hk/customs/ieflash.shtml

Customs and Excise Department — Changes in Directors

Year	Name of Department	Title	Name of Director
1982-1984	Customs & Excise Department	Commissioner of Customs & Excise	Jordan, Douglas Arthur
1984-1986	Customs & Excise Department	Commissioner of Customs & Excise	Grewal, Harnam Singh
1986-1990	Customs & Excise Department	Commissioner of Customs & Excise	Williamson, Patrick John
1990-1993	Customs & Excise Department	Commissioner of Customs & Excise	Oxley, Clive William Baker
1993-1996	Customs & Excise Department	Commissioner of Customs & Excise	Watson, Donald McFarlane
1996-1999	Customs & Excise Department	Commissioner of Customs & Excise	Li, Shu-fai, Lawrence
1999-2001	Customs & Excise Department	Commissioner of Customs & Excise	Tsang, Chun-wah, John
2001-2002	Customs & Excise Department	Commissioner of Customs & Excise	Wong, Hung-chui, Raymond

Sources:
1. *Customs and Excise Department 90th Anniversary (1909-1999)*, Hong Kong, Government Printer, 1999.
2. *Staff Biographies Hong Kong Government*, Hong Kong, Government Printer, 1984, 1986, 1988, 1990, 1993.
3. *Staff Biographies the Government of the Hong Kong Special Administrative Region*, Hong Kong, Government Printer, 1998, 2001.
4. *Staff List Hong Kong Government*, Hong Kong, Government Printer, 1968-1996.
5. *Staff List the Government of the Hong Kong Special Administrative Region*, Hong Kong, Government Printer, 1997-2000.
6. www.info.gov.hk/customs/ieflash.shtml.

Statistical Branch, Imports and Exports Office (1913-1925, 1930-1941)
Statistics Department (1947-1951)
Statistical Branch, Commerce and Industry Department (1952-1967)
Census and Statistics Department (1967-2002)

1913	The Statistical Branch within the Imports and Exports Office was set up to publish trade statistics of Hong Kong.
1914	The Statistical Branch collected and published imports and exports statistics.
1925	The Statistical Branch was dissolved.
1930	The Statistical Branch was re-established to resume its previous duties: collection and publication of trade statistics.
1947	Simple figures on public finance, climate, population, public health, education etc. were collected by government departments as by-products of their routine work. No independent department was designed to handle the statistics before 1947. The Statistics Department was set up to organize a statistical system. Priority was given to cost-of-living surveys. A retail price index was published monthly. Other statistics collected from government departments and public bodies were published in the statistical supplement to the Hong Kong Government Gazette.
1948	The Government Statistician was gazetted as Commissioner of Registration. The Registration Branch took up the task of registering the population aged 12 and over. The Branch later became the Registration of Persons Office.
1952	The Statistics Department was unable to conduct an economic and social statistics development programme and was disbanded on December 31, 1951 and its functions transferred to the Statistical Office under the Commerce and Industry Department on January 1. The Office compiled trade statistics, retail price index and statistical supplements on a routine basis.
1959	A separate Census Department was set up with the appointment of K. M. A. Barnett as Commissioner, to organize the 1961 Census, the first since 1931.
1962	The Census Department was disbanded and the work of population projection was transferred to the Statistical Branch of the Commerce and Industry Department.
1963	K. M. A. Barnett was appointed Commissioner of Census and Statistical Planning under the supervision of Colonial Secretariat in December.
1967	The Statistical Branch of the Commerce and Industry Department and the Census and Statistical Planning Office of the Colonial Secretariat were merged in December to form the Census and Statistics Department. The Department consisted of three divisions: Headquarters; Economic Statistics (included the Research Section and Data Processing Section); and Social Statistics (comprised the Reticulation Section, Vital Statistics Section, and Miscellaneous Statistics/Publication Section). The Headquarters was in charge of the administrative and executive functions of the Department. The Economic Statistics Division collected, compiled and analyzed the trade statistics, price information and price index; conducted surveys on household expenditures; edited the monthly statistical supplement to the Government Gazette; and

supplied statistical information to international organizations. The Social Statistics Division dealt with vital statistics and censuses; advised other government departments on the method of collection and compilation of statistics; processed and analyzed the results.

1968   The Data Processing Section of the Economic Statistics Division was closed down in September, with its work largely handed over to the Organizational Surveys Unit.

1969   The Research Section of the Economic Statistics Division was reorganized to form a new Trade Research Section and a Statistician was appointed to supervise the various routines and organize new research exercises on external trade. Another new section, Economic Research Section, was set up to conduct limited research in the economic field other than external trade and consumer prices.

1971   On Novermber 30, the Governor-in-Council decided that the Department was to expand to undertake additional duties which included: revision and improvement of the existing consumer price index; collection of statistics of economic activities as a long term programme; the provision of advisory services to other government departments, in particular to the Finance and Economic Branches of the Colonial Secretariat.

1972   The National Income Section under the Economic Statistics Division was set up to estimate the gross domestic product. The Social Statistics Division was restructured into five sections: Demographic, Social and Housing Statistics, Geography, Consumer Price Index and Household Expenditure Survey, and General Statistics.

1974   The Department was reorganized into three operational divisions: Economic, Industry, Social and General. The Economic Division undertook trade and other economic researches; compiled national accounts and other financial statistics; and maintained the consumer price index. The Industry Division dealt with production and employment statistics in the manufacturing sector, censuses and surveys in other economic sectors, and trade statistics. The Social and General Division compiled demography, housing and population censuses, and other social statistics; conducted social surveys and provided technical services to other government departments.

1976   The Economic and Industry Divisions were combined to form the Economic and Industry Division.

1978   The Economic and Industry Division was renamed Economic Division; its duties remained unchanged. The Social and General Division was spilt into two — Social Division and General Division. Additional duties such as the oversight of the major statistical sections in the Housing Department, Medical and Health Department, Education Department, Social Welfare Department, Royal Hong Kong Police Force and Public Works Department were added to the Social Division. The General Division dealt with departmental administration, labour statistics, employment and wage surveys and the consumer price index. It also provided electronic data processing facilities for the Department, and technical services to other government departments.

1981   The Economic Division was spilt into two: Economic 'A' Division and Economic 'B' Division. The Economic 'A' Division collected and compiled trade statistics, price data, conducted economic censuses of trade and service sectors, and maintained the consumer price index. The Economic 'B' Division compiled national income estimates, and conducted economic censuses of the manufacturing and construction sectors.

1999   Economic Divisions 'A' and 'B' were modified into three: Economic Statistics Divisions 1, 2 and 3. Division 1 dealt with external trade statistics and price statistics. Division 2 was in charge of sectoral economic statistics such as manufacturing, construction, transport, business services, distributive trades, restaurants and hotels. Division 3 undertook national accounts statistics and balance of payments statistics. The Social Division was renamed Social Statistics Division and the General Division was renamed General Statistics Division.

2002   The structure of the Department remained unchanged. There were a total of five divisions: Economic Statistics Divisions 1 to 3, Social Statistics Division and General Statistics Division.

Sources:

1.   *Hong Kong — An Outline of Statistical Development*, Hong Kong, Government Printer, p.24; 1976, p.24, 1978, p.5, 1979, pp.1-2; 1981, pp.1-2; 1988, pp.1-2.
2.   *Hong Kong Annual Departmental Report by the Commissioner for Census and Statistics*, Hong Kong, Government Printer, 1968-1969, pp.1, 2, 5, 7, 14-18, 17; 1970-1971, pp.15-16, 1971-1972, pp.17-18, 1972-1973, pp.7-12.
3.   www.info.gov.hk/censtated/

	Census and Statistics Department — Changes in Directors		
Year	**Name of Department**	**Title**	**Name of Director**
1967-1969	Census and Statistics Department	Commissioner of Census and Statistics	Barnett, Kenneth Myer Arthur
1970-1973	Census and Statistics Department	Commissioner of Census and Statistics	Topley, Kenneth Wallis Joseph
1973-1978	Census and Statistics Department	Commissioner of Census and Statistics	Whitelegge, David Sherbrooke
1978-1986	Census and Statistics Department	Commissioner of Census and Statistics	Greenfield, Colin Charles
1986-1988	Census and Statistics Department	Commissioner of Census and Statistics	Butler, Richard
1988-1992	Census and Statistics Department	Commissioner of Census and Statistics	Mok, Ni-hung, Benjamin

Year	Name of Department	Title	Name of Director
1992-2002	Census and Statistics Department	Commissioner of Census and Statistics	Ho, Wing-huen, Frederick

Sources:

1. *Staff Biographies Hong Kong Government*, Hong Kong, Government Printer, 1974, 1976, 1978, 1982, 1984, 1986, 1988, 1990, 1993.
2. *Staff Biographies the Government of the Hong Kong Special Administrative Region*, Hong Kong, Government Printer, 1998, 2000.
3. *Staff List Hong Kong Government*, Hong Kong, Government Printer, 1968-1996.
4. *Staff List the Government of the Hong Kong Special Administrative Region*, Hong Kong, Government Printer, 1997-2000.
5. www.info.gov.hk/censtatd/

Revenue

Inland Revenue Department (1947-2002)

1946   A Taxation Committee to advise on measures to increase taxation revenue was appointed in September. The Committee proposed direct taxation as a necessary permanent measure.

1947   The Inland Revenue Ordinance of 1947 was passed and direct taxation was imposed as part of Hong Kong's normal fiscal system. The Inland Revenue Department under the Commissioner of Inland Revenue was set up on April 1 to carry out the provisions of the Inland Revenue Ordinance of 1947. Following the War Taxation Department's structure, the Department was organized into two Units. Unit 1 dealt with profits tax while Unit 2 dealt with personal assessment, salaries and annuities tax, interest tax and property tax. The Department had a General Division which handled general correspondence, departmental stores, equipment and collection of information on known and potential taxpayers.

1949   The Estate Duty Office ceased to be a separate entity and was amalgamated with the Inland Revenue Department with effect from April 1.

1952   A Committee was formed under the chairmanship of the Financial Secretary to consider amendments to the Inland Revenue Ordinance.

1955   The Inland Revenue (Amendment) Ordinance no. 36 of 1955 was approved on September 23 and came into effect on April 1, 1956. The Stamp Office of the Revenue Branch of the Treasury was transferred to the Inland Revenue Department.

1956   The Inland Revenue Department took over from the Treasury the collection of entertainments tax, bets and sweeps tax, dance halls tax and stamp duty.

1957	The Business Registration Office of the Commerce and Industry Department was transferred to the Inland Revenue Department. The Department was responsible for the collection of all revenue items described in the Annual Revenue Estimates as Internal Revenue. It was restructured into three units and one administrative headquarters. Unit 1 was in charge of the assessment of corporation profits tax and business profits tax. Unit 2 was responsible for the assessment of salaries tax, interest tax, tax under personal assessment and all queries and claims in connection with property tax; collection of earnings and profits tax except property tax which was assessed by and paid at the Treasury, and the collection of estate duty and all refunds and expenditure. Unit 3 dealt with the assessment and bets and sweeps tax, public dance halls tax and business registration fees. The Headquarters was responsible for the recruitment, disposition and control of staff, recording of inward and outward correspondence, legislation, tax appeals and general administration. The assessment of estate duty was handled by a separate section, under the direct control of the Commissioner of Inland Revenue.
1959	The Estate Duty Section became part of Unit 3.
1967	Unit 3 was responsible for the collection of hotel accommodation tax.
1973	The Commissioner's Unit was set up. It was responsible for legislation, handling objections and appeals, internal audit, public relations and liaison with other departments.
1976	The Department comprised the Headquarters and five other administrative units. The Headquarters was in charge of the general administration, finance, statistics, computerization and management studies, maintenance of the central index, approval of retirement schemes and of the establishment of charitable institutions or trusts of a public character, personal assessment and property tax assessment. Unit 1 was responsible for profits tax assessment. Unit 2 was in charge of salaries tax assessment. Unit 3 dealt with assessment and collection of stamp duty, estate duty, entertainments tax, betting duty and hotel accommodation tax; administration of the Business Registration Ordinance and the collection of business registration fees; collection of all earnings and profits tax, other than property tax not in default, and refunds on those taxes; the issue and control of tax reserve certificates; outdoor inspections, prosecutions and service of notices. Unit 4 investigated cases of suspected tax evasion. The Commissioner's Unit was responsible for estimates of tax revenue.
1979	The Commissioner's Unit handled complaints, forms control and deployment of staff.
1989	The assessment of interest tax was abolished with effect from April 1.
1990	Unit 4 was responsible for the prosecution of appropriate tax evasion cases.
2002	The structure of the Department was as follows: Headquarters Unit (concerned with taxpayer services, information systems, training and departmental administration); Unit 1 (responsible for corporation and partnership profits tax); Unit 2 (dealt with sole-proprietorship profits tax, property tax and personal assessment); Unit 3 (had the responsibility for revenue collection, inspection,

estate duty, stamp duty, Business Registration Ordinance administration and business registration fees); Unit 4 (in charge of field audits and investigations); and Commissioner's Unit (handled charitable donations and retirement schemes, complaints, appeals, technical research and internal audit).

Sources:

1. *Annual Report of the Commissioner of Inland Revenue*, Hong Kong Government, 1947-1949.
2. *Annual Review by Commissioner of Inland Revnue*, Hong Kong, Government Printer, 1991-1993.
3. *Hong Kong Annual Departmental Report by the Commissioner of Inland Revenue*, Hong Kong, Government Printer, 1951-1991.
4. www.info.gov.hk/ird/index.htm

Inland Revenue Department — Changes in Directors

Year	Name of Department	Title	Name of Director
1947-1951	Inland Revenue Department	Commissioner of Inland Revenue	Pudney, Eric William
1951-1958	Inland Revenue Department	Commissioner of Inland Revenue	Watson, William Frew
1958-1963	Inland Revenue Department	Commissioner of Inland Revenue	Drysdale, William James
1963-1972	Inland Revenue Department	Commissioner of Inland Revenue	Duffy, Arthur Daniel
1972-1975	Inland Revenue Department	Commissioner of Inland Revenue	Rainbow, Frank Evelyn
1975-1979	Inland Revenue Department	Commissioner of Inland Revenue	Giddy, Ronald Vincent
1979-1985	Inland Revenue Department	Commissioner of Inland Revenue	Ladd, Victor Alfred
1985-1997	Inland Revenue Department	Commissioner of Inland Revenue	Au Yeung, Fu, Anthony
1997-2000	Inland Revenue Department	Commissioner of Inland Revenue	Wong, Ho-sang
2000-2001	Inland Revenue Department	Commissioner of Inland Revenue	Sin Law, Yuk-lin, Agnes
2001-2002	Inland Revenue Department	Commissioner of Inland Revenue	Lau Mak, Yee-ming, Alice

Sources:
1. *The Hong Kong Civil Service List*, Hong Kong Government, 1947-1958.
2. *Staff Biographies Hong Kong Government*, Hong Kong, Government Printer, 1974, 1976, 1978, 1982, 1984, 1986, 1988, 1990, 1993.
3. *Staff Biographies the Government of the Hong Kong Special Administrative Region*, Hong Kong, Government Printer, 1998, 2000
4. *Staff List Hong Kong Government*, Hong Kong, Government Printer, 1959-1996.
5. *Staff List the Government of the Hong Kong Special Administrative Region*, Hong Kong, Government Printer, 1997-2000.
6. www.info.gov.hk/ird/index.htm

Rating Office (1945-1946)
Rating and Valuation Department (1947-2002)

1945	A Rating Office similar to the former Assessment Department was organized under the Briitish Military Administration after the Sino-Japanese War.
1946	The Assessment Department was re-established in August. The Stamp (Duty) (Amendment) Ordinance which levied an additional 10% on the enhanced value of land and buildings was enacted in October. The Department undertook the valuation and scrutiny of transactions for stamp duty purpose.
1947	The Assessment Department was transformed into the Rating and Valuation Department. The Rating Ordinance no. 6 of 1901 which empowered the collection of rates came into force again. The Landlord and Tenant Ordinance, which allowed certain increases in rent above pre-War standard rent, was enacted in May.
1952	The McNeill Committee on Rent Control was established. The Commissioner of Rating and Valuation was appointed a member and the Secretary of the Committee.
1953	The Rating and Valuation Department was responsible for the issuance of certificate of standard rent according to the Landlord and Tenant (Amendment) Ordinance.
1954	Ordinance no. 30 of 1954 brought rating in the New Territories in line with urban practice and removed the old exemptions such as schools and hospitals. The implementation was delayed until 1956.
1960	The first local Valuation Assistant (Tsang, Hoy-lun) qualified as a Chartered Surveyor. The Rating and Valuation Department resumed the duties of the Quartering Authority for negotiating and leasing premises for government purposes.
1962	Tsang, the first local Chartered Surveyor, was promoted to Rating and Valuation Surveyor. A new valuation list covering Hong Kong Island and the New Territories came into effect. Different charges were introduced for property tax, with special concessions for pre-War properties and exemption for residential owner-occupiers. The Tenancy (Notice of Termination) Ordinance imposed a measure of security for certain classes of tenancy by requiring the landlord to give a six-month notice of termination.
1973	The Department was divided into three major units: Headquarters; Rating (comprised the Hong Kong Division, Kowloon Division, New Kowloon and New Territories Division, and Special Properties Division); Valuation and Rent (which administered the Housing Estates Division, Leasing Division and Rent Control Division).
1974	The Tenancy Inquiry Bureau in charge of payments of compensation to tenants required to vacate from dangerous buildings were transferred from the Home Affairs Department to the Rating and Valuation Department. The New Kowloon and New Territories Division was spilt into two divisions: New Kowloon and New Territories.
1975	The estate duty valuation work for Hong Kong, Kowloon and New Territories was transferred from the Crown Lands and Survey Office of the Public Works

Department to the Rating and Valuation Department. The General Revaluation Division under the Rating Unit was established. Seven new rating areas in the New Territories were specified for rating: Yuen Long, Tai Po, Fanling, Sheung Shui, Tuen Mun, Sha Tin and Clear Water Bay. Amendments were made to the Rating Ordinance to exempt agricultural dwelling and village houses in the New Territories from rating.

1981   The Rating Ordinance was amended to ensure greater consistency in revaluation by introducing the valuation reference date concept, to extend the back-dating of interim valuations from 12 to 24 months, and to rationalize exemptions from payment and assessment. The Landlord and Tenant (Consolidation) Ordinance was amended. Part IV of the Landlord and Tenant (Consolidation) Ordinance was introduced.

1982   The Tenancy Tribunal was abolished in June. The technical functions of this Tribunal were transferred to the Department. The Rent Tribunal was abolished in October. The Department was responsible for reviewing rent increase certificates issued under Part II of the Landlord and Tenant (Consolidation) Ordinance.

1983   The Inland Revenue (Amendment) Ordinance of 1983 took effect; property tax was levied on actual income received. General rates percentage for the urban areas was increased to 5.5%.

1984   The rates were fixed at 5.5% for Hong Kong, New Kowloon and the mainland New Territories, and at 5.0% for the outlying islands.

1985   The Department assumed responsibility for stamp duty and estate duty valuation work in Yuen Long, Sheung Shui and Fanling.

1986   The Rating (Amendment) Ordinance of 1986 was passed. The rates percentage charge was fixed at 6.0% for all rated areas. The Department was organized into five units: Administration and Staff Development (which directed the Staff Development, Technical Secretariat and Administration Division); Appeals and Audit Unit; Computer Development Unit; Rating Unit (comprised the Rating Division and Special Properties Division); and Valuation Unit (which managed the Rent Control Division and Leasing Division).

1989   The grade of Rating and Valuation Surveyor was retitled Valuation Surveyor.

1990   A Stamp Duty (Amendment) Bill was introduced to curb property speculation. The Bill proposed to charge stamp duty on agreements for sale and purchase of residential properties.

1995   The Rating (Amendment) Ordinance was enacted; the main provisions of which included the abolition of half-refund of rates formerly allowed for vacant non-domestic premises, and the transfer of the billing and accounting functions relating to rates from the Director of Accounting Services to the Commissioner of Rating and Valuation. The Rating (Effective Date of Interim Valuation) Regulations took effect. These Regulations fixed the interim dates by reference to the occupation permit, letter of compliance, or consent to assign.

1997   The Government Rent (Assessment and Collection) Ordinance regulating the collection of government rent at 3% of the rateable value under Annex III to the Sino-British Joint Declaration came into force. The Department was responsible for the collection of this rent from approximately one million properties from June.

2001   The organization of the Department was as follows:

I.   Administration and Staff Development

1. Accounting and Billing Division
2. Administration Division
3. Support Services Division

II.   Rating Adviser

1. Computer Division

III.   Rating and Valuation

1. General Revaluation and Capital Valuation Division
2. New Territories Division
3. New Territories (Rural Properties) Division
4. Rating Division
5. Urban Division

IV.   Special Duties

1. Landlord and Tenant Services Division
2. Special Properties Division

2002   The structure remained the same, with a total of 11 divisions organized under four functional groups.

Sources:

1.   *Hong Kong Annual Departmental Report by the Commissioner, Rating and Valuation*, Hong Kong Government, 1954-1976.
2.   *Hong Kong Annual Report by the Commissioner, Rating and Valuation Department 1950-1951*, Hong Kong Governmnet, 1951, pp.1-4.
3.   *Hong Kong Annual Summary by the Commissioner of Rating and Valuation*, Hong Kong, Government Printer, 1981-1995.
4.   *Rating and Valuation Department Chronology and Events*, Hong Kong, Government Printer, 1997, pp.11-12, 18-29, 45-49, 59.
5.   Woodroffe, B.J.C., *The History of Rates in Hong Kong*, Hong Kong, Government Printer, 1983.
6.   www.info.gov.hk/rvd/content/index.htm

Rating and Valuation Department — Changes in Directors			
Year	Name of Department	Title	Name of Director
1947-1951	Rating and Valuation Department	Commissioner of Rating and Valuation	Ring, Julius
1951-1967	Rating and Valuation Department	Commissioner of Rating and Valuation	Shanks, Frederick
1967-1971	Rating and Valuation Department	Commissioner of Rating and Valuation	Cooke, Norman
1971-1984	Rating and Valuation Department	Commissioner of Rating and Valuation	Fry, Raymond Alfred
1984-1989	Rating and Valuation Department	Commissioner of Rating and Valuation	Blenkinsop, Gordon Penrhyn
1989-1997	Rating and Valuation Department	Commissioner of Rating and Valuation	Woodroffe, Barry Jonathan Clayton
1997-2002	Rating and Valuation Department	Commissioner of Rating and Valuation	Pang, Tsan-wing, Kenneth

Sources:
1.   *The Hong Kong Civil Service List,* Hong Kong Government, 1947-1958.
2.   *Rating and Valuation Department, Chronology of Events (1941-1997),* Hong Kong, Government Printer, 1997, Appendix C
3.   *Staff Biographies Hong Kong Government,* Hong Kong, Government Printer, 1974, 1976, 1978, 1982, 1984, 1986, 1988, 1990, 1993.
4.   *Staff Biographies the Government of the Hong Kong Special Administrative Region,* Hong Kong, Government Printer, 1998, 2000
5.   *Staff List Hong Kong Government,* Hong Kong, Government Printer, 1959-1996.
6.   *Staff List the Government of the Hong Kong Special Administrative Region,* Hong Kong, Government Printer, 1997-2000.
7.   www.info.gov.hk/rvd/content/index.htm

Property Division, Finance Branch (1989-1990)
Government Property Agency (1990-2002)

1989   The central executive arm which administered all government property matters — the Property Division — was created within the Finance Branch on July 19. The Property Division comprised four sections: Policy and Planning, Administration, Works and Management Services. It was responsible for formulating policies on site and property utilization; development of a comprehensive corporate plan; promotion of cost and value awareness among branches and departments; and compilation of management information for effective planning and decision-making.

1990   Following the reorganization of the management system of government properties, the Property Division of the Government Secretariat's Finance Branch, the Leasing Division of the Rating and Valuation Department, and part of the Property Management Section of the Buildings and Lands Department were merged to form the new Government Property Agency in April. The major duties of the Agency were to administer all government-owned and government-leased offices, quarters, and specialist accommodation, to develop and implement a comprehensive property plan for the economic use of government properties. Priorities were given to the identification of sites suitable for redevelopment or disposal, the introduction of appropriate commercial activities, the improvement of administration, and the examination of the spatial needs of government departments.

1992   The Agency was reorganized into four divisions: Administration and Management Services, Estate Management, Technical Services and Leasing. Apart from general administration work, the Administration and Management Services Division advised on departmental accommodation requirements and enhanced information technology services within the Agency. The Estate Management Division formulated measures to improve the design and management of government properties. The Technical Services Division monitored and facilitated planning and construction of government offices, buildings, and quarters; and provided technical advice on site utilization and building related activities of the Agency. The Leasing Division managed all leased offices, quarters and government specialist accommodation.

1993   The Leasing Division was abolished; a new division — Estate Development Division — was established.

1994   The Building Management Group of the Architectural Services Department was transferred to the Estate Development Division of the Government Property Agency. The new Building Management Section was responsible for the provision of cleaning and security services at government buildings.

1995   The Administration and Management Services Division was spilt into two: Management Services Division and Administrative Services Division. The Building Management Section was expanded and became Building Management Division.

1996   The Military Estate Division was established.

1997   Two new divisions — Special Duties Division and Legal Advisory Division — were established.

1998   The Estate Development Division was integrated into the newly established Site Utilization Division. Its main responsibilities were to ensure optimum utilization of government sites, to release under-utilized sites for re-development by the Government or for disposal through the land sale programmes, and to tender out government properties.

2000   The Acquisition, Allocation and Disposal of Offices and Quarters Division was set up to plan purchase, lease and allocate accommodation for government use; and to dispose of surplus quarters by lease or sale.

2002   The structure of the Agency was made up of seven divisions: Administrative Services (co-ordinated issues spanning different divisions and departmental administrative services); Acquisition, Allocation and Disposal (planned, purchased, leased and allocated accommodation for government use; disposed of surplus quarters by sale of lease); Legal Advisory (provided in-house legal advisory services on property matters); Management Services (formulated, implemented policies on space and furniture standards and advised on departmental requirements; developed, implemented and enhanced information technology services within the Agency); Property Management (provided building management services in government offices and quarters; undertook letting of surplus non-domestic government accommodation; safeguarded government interests in private developments); Site Utilization (ensured maximum utilization of government sites; released under-utilized sites for redevelopment by the Government or through the Land Sales Programme; tendered out government properties); Technical Services (monitored and facilitated planning and construction of government office buildings, fitting-out, maintenance and refurbishment programmes; provided technical advice on-site utilization and the Agency's building-related activities).

Sources:

1. *Hong Kong Government Telephone Directory*, Hong Kong, Government Printer, 1990-2000.
2. www.info.gov.hk/gpa/

	Government Property Agency — Changes in Directors		
Year	**Name of Department**	**Title**	**Name of Director**
1990-1991	Government Property Agency	Government Property Administrator	Mackley, Philip Robert Martin
1991-1997	Government Property Agency	Government Property Administrator	Wotherspoon, Ian
1997-2001	Government Property Agency	Government Property Administrator	Lai, Kwok-ying, Albert
2001-2002	Government Property Agency	Government Property Administrator	Kwan, Sik-ning, Maria

Sources:
1. *Staff Biographies Hong Kong Government*, Hong Kong, Government Printer, 1993.
2. *Staff Biographies the Government of the Hong Kong Speical Administrative Region*, Hong Kong, Government Printer, 1998, 2000.
3. *Staff List Hong Kong Government*, Hong Kong, Government Printer, 1990-1996
4. *Staff List the Government of the Hong Kong Special Administrative Region*, Hong Kong, Government Printer, 1997-2001.
5. www.info.gov.hk/gpa/

Registration

Companies Registry (1993-2002)

1993   The Companies Registry was formed as an independent government department on May 1. The Registry was run as a trading fund, selling or buying services from other government departments. It consisted of the General Support Services Division, Financial Services Division, Development Support Services Division, Legal Services Division, Customer Services Division, Administration and Registration Division (which directed the Administration Section, New Companies Section, General Registration Section, Overseas Companies Unit and Charges Section), Technical Support and Money Lenders Division (which administered the Computer Section, Microfilm and Public Search Section, and Money Lender Section). The Registry was in charge of general registration, incorporation of new companies, registration of charges, maintenance of information required to be submitted by companies and other organizations in Hong Kong and to make them available to the public. The Legal Services Division advised the Government on policy and legislative issues regarding company law and other related legislation; provided legal services which included enforcement of Registration Ordinance no. 290A and prosecutions, and rendering advice on legislation against fraudulent, unfit or defaulting directors and persons; allowed incorporation of qualified and properly registered public accountants in Hong Kong; afforded auditors statutory protection from liability arising through their reporting of fraud to the relevant authorities.

1995   The Administration and Registration Division was spilt into two divisions: Company Formation and Enforcement Division, and Registration Division. The Company Formation and Enforcement Division comprised two sections: Administration and New Companies. The Registration Division consisted of three sections: General Registration, Overseas Companies and Charges. The Technical Support and Money Lenders Division was renamed Public Research Division. The Microfilm and Public Search Section was split into two: Microfilm Section and Public Search Section.

1998   The Computer Section became the Computer Division.

1999   A Strategic Change Plan Study was carried out.

2002   The Registry was organized into five major parts: Company Law Reform Division, Legal Services Division, Business Manager, Development Manager and Registry Manager. The Prosecution Section was placed under the Legal Services Division. Under the Business Manager was the Financial Services Division. Under the Development Manager were the two divisions of Information Technology and Development. The Registry Manager had control of five divisions: Customer Services; Registration (Charges Section, Overseas Companies Section, General Registration Section); Company Formation and

Enforcement (New Companies Section, Administration Section), Public Search (Microfilm Section, Public Search Section, Money Lenders Section); General Support Services. There is also a Prosecution Section.

Sources:

1. *Companies Registry Report*, Hong Kong, Government Printer, 1993-1998.
2. www.info.gov.hk/cr/

Companies Registry			
Year	Name of Department	Title	Name of Director
1993-2002	Companies Registry	Registrar of Companies and General Manager, Companies Registry Trading Fund	Jones, Gordon William Ewing

Sources:
1. *Staff Biographies Hong Kong Government*, Hong Kong, Government Printer, 1993.
2. *Staff Biographies the Government of the Hong Kong Special Administrative Region*, Hong Kong, Government Printer, 1998, 2001.
3. *Staff List Hong Kong Government*, Hong Kong, Government Printer, 1993-1996.
4. *Staff List the Government of the Hong Kong Special Administrative Region*, Hong Kong, Government Printer, 1997-2000.
5. www.info.gov.hk/cr/

Land Office, Surveyor General's Office/Survey Department/ Public Works Department (1844-1890) Land Registry (1993-2002)

1844   To prevent secret and fraudulent conveyances in Hong Kong and to provide means whereby the title to real and immovable properties could be easily traced and ascertained, Ordinance no. 3 of 1844, which was responsible for the registration of deeds, was enacted. The Land Office, under the Surveyor General's Office, was responsible for the registration of deeds conveyances and the keeping of indexes of places and names in the registry book.

1867   The First Clerk of Surveyor General administered the Land Office which registered all transfers of landed properties, leases, rent-roll, and collected burial and monumental and deed registry fees.

1883   The Land Registry was set up under the Survey Department. It was under the control of the Land Officer and Official Receiver.

1912   The Land Officer and Official Receiver changed its title to Land Officer.

1930   The Crown Lands Office and the Surveys Office were combined to form the Crown Lands, Surveys and Valuation and Resumption Office.

1973   The Valuation Branch was set up.

1993   The Land Registry was operated on a self-financing basis. It comprised six divisions: General Support Services, Financial Services, Development Support Services, Urban, Technical Services - Reports on Title and Owners Incorporation, and New Territories Division. The Registry was responsible for the administration of the Land Registration Ordinance and Regulations by maintaining an up-to-date Land Register; provision of the Land Register and other land records to the public and government department and agencies.

1994   The Legal Division was set up. The Urban Division was renamed Urban Registration Division.

1995   Two new divisions were established: Imaging and Microfilm Division and Title Registration.

1996   The Imaging and Microfilm Division was abolished.

1999   Two new divisions were set up: Business Development Division and Change Management Division.

2000   The Registry consisted of nine divisions: Management and Customer Services, General Support Services, Financial Services, Business Development, Change Management, Legal Services, Urban Registration, Search and Technical Services, and New Territories Registries.

2001   The structure remained the same except for the addition of a unit of Information Technology Contract Project.

Sources:

1. *The Land Registry Trading Fund Hong Kong Annual Report*, Hong Kong, Government Printer, 1993-2001.
2. www.info.gov.hk/landreg/

Land Registry — Changes in Directors			
Year	Name of Department	Title	Name of Director
1993-1997	Land Registry	Land Registrar	Pang, Tsan-wing, Kenneth
1997-2001	Land Registry	Land Registrar	Cooper, Anthony Geoffrey
2001-2002	Land Registry	Land Registrar	Salkeld, Kim Anthony

Sources:
1. *Staff Biographies Hong Kong Government*, Hong Kong, Government Printer, 1993.
2. *Staff Biographies the Government of the Hong Kong Special Administrative Region*, Hong Kong, Government Printer, 1998, 2001.
3. *Staff List Hong Kong Government*, Hong Kong, Government Printer, 1959-1996.
4. *Staff List the Government of the Hong Kong Special Administrative Region*, Hong Kong, Government Printer, 1997-2000.
5. www.info.gov.hk/landreg/

Official Receiver's Office (1992-2002)

1992   The Official Receiver's Office was established as an independent department on June 1 to take over the functions of the Insolvency Division of the Registrar General's Department. This Registrar General's Department was different from the one that existed between 1844 and 1938 which was the predecessor of the Secretariat for Chinese Affairs. This Registrar General's Department was set up in 1952 to handle all registration matters. It was abolished in 1993.

1993   The Office consisted of four main divisions: Departmental Administration Division (directed the Chinese Language Section), Case Management Division (supervised the Case Management Section and Technical Section), Legal Services Division (administered the Litigation and Court Work Section; Advisory, Special Cases and Training Section; Registration, Prosecution and Policy Section), Financial Services Division (controlled the Accounting Investigations Section, Audit Section, Financial Management and Systems Section). The Departmental Administration Division provided general administration of the Department; dealt with translation and interpretation services; promoted the use of Chinese within the Department; and edited the departmental newsletters. The Case Management Division handled the major administration of all bankruptcy cases and compulsory winding up cases; carried out case investigation, realization of assets, dividend distribution and monitoring the funds held by liquidators. The Legal Services Division was in charge of litigation, court work, director disqualification, prosecution and legal advisory work. The Financial Services Division conducted financial investigations into insolvency cases and records; prepared accountant's report on the outcome of investigations; carried out regular checking on the companies Liquidation Account, the Official Receiver in Bankruptcy Account and the Bankruptcy Estates Account; co-ordinated the auditing of the accounts annually; liaised with policy bureaux for relevant legislative amendments on revised fees and charges; provided revenue collection services for insolvency transactions and kept records of receipts and payments.

1997   The Legal Services Division was divided into two parts: Legal Services Division 1 which comprised the Litigation and Court Work Section; Legal Services Division 2 which consisted of the Advisory, Special Cases and Training Section, Prosecution and Director Disqualification Section, and Individual Voluntary Arrangements Section.

1999   The Technical Section of the Case Management Division was replaced by Information Technology and Technical Section.

2000   The organization of the Office was as follows:

     I.   Departmental Administration Division
        1. Chinese Language Section
        2. Departmental Administration Unit

     II.   Case Management Division
        1. Case Management Section

III. Legal Services Division 1

  1. Litigation and Court Work Section

IV. Legal Services Division 2

  1. Advisory, Special Cases and Training Section

  2. Prosecution and Director Disqualification Section

V. Financial Services Division

  1. Audit Section

  2. Accounting Investigations Section

  3. Financial Management and Systems Section

2002   The organization structure of the Office remained the same.

Sources:

1. *Annual Departmental Report by the Official Receiver*, Hong Kong, Government Printer, 1993-1999.
2. *Hong Kong Government Telephone Directory*, Hong Kong, Government Printer, 1993.
3. www.info.gov.hk/oro/index.htm

Official Receiver's Office — Changes in Directors

Year	Name of Department	Title	Name of Director
1992-1999	Official Receiver's Office	Official Receiver	Hearder, Anthony Roblin
1999-2002	Official Receiver's Office	Official Receiver	O' Connell, Edward Thomas

Sources:
1. *Staff Biographies Hong Kong Government*, Hong Kong, Government Printer, 1993.
2. *Staff Biographies the Hong Kong Government of the Hong Kong Special Administrative Region*, Hong Kong, Government Printer, 1998, 2001.
3. *Staff List Hong Kong Government*, Hong Kong, Government Printer, 1992-1996.
4. *Staff List the Government of the Hong Kong Spcial Administrative Region*, Hong Kong, Government Printer, 1997-2000.
5. www.info.gov.hk/oro/index.htm

Services

Observatory (1883-1912)
Royal Observatory (1912-1997)
Hong Kong Observatory (1997-2002)

1879   The Royal Society suggested establishing a weather observatory in Hong Kong.

1883   The Observatory was established and William Doberck was appointed Government Astronomer. The Observatory was established with the twofold objectives of promoting general advancement of science and conferring practical benefits on shipping frequenting the China Sea. The operations included astronomical, time service and magnetic determinations. The major meteorological services concentrated on warning typhoons and tropical storms.

1884   Routine surface meteorological observations began; observations were made of atmospheric pressure, air temperature, wind speed and direction, cloud type and amount, direction of motion and rainfall amount. A "drum, ball and cone" system of symbols was employed to give information to the mariners in the harbour on the existence and approximate location of tropical cyclones.

1887   The title of the Government Astronomer was changed to Director of the Observatory.

1890   The annual cost of upkeep of the Observatory was HK$7,000. During this year, 40 stations of meteorological registers were kept onshore.

1895   Weather forecasts for the public were first published in the China Coast Meteorological Register in January.

1897   The storm signals invented by Admiral Fitzroy in 1861 were introduced in February.

1904   The universal time (Greenwich Mean Time) was adopted as the basis for Hong Kong time.

1906   The first rainfall outstation was set up in the police compound at Tai Po.

1912   The title change to "Royal Observatory" was sanctioned by King George V in June.

1915   Marine weather forecasts for ship were broadcast using radio telegraphy for the first time.

1916   Full 24-hour observations of the main meteorological elements began.

1917   The numbered signal system geared to the warning of wind conditions in Hong Kong was first introduced.

1918   A wireless time signal service began in September.

1921   The Observatory started operating one set of 3-component long-period seismographs to detect distant earthquakes and took upper air measurements with the use of pilot balloons.

1922   Lithographic operations for the production of the daily weather maps were adopted.

1930   Regular observation of upper air measurements were made twice daily — in the forenoon and afternoon.

1946   The Observatory resumed its duty in May. It was responsible for: surface meteorological observations; upper air observation; fleet meteorological service; typhoon warning service; seismological observation; publication of meteorological results; provision of meteorological service for merchant shipping and the general public; provision of flight documentation for departure flights.

1947   The Observatory was organized into two parts. The Administrative Headquarters consisted of Climatological and Instruments Section, and the Library and the Lithographic Press. The Kai Tak Meteorological Office was responsible for aviation forecasting at Kai Tak Airport.

1957   The Central Forecast Office was set up to supply all storm-warnings and forecasts and reports for the public and the press.

1964   The Observatory was restructured into three parts: Administration, Meteorological Division, Research and Climatology Division. The Meteorological Division administered the Marine Section/Communication Section. It provided meteorological services for aviation at the Aviation Forecast Office at Kai Tak Airport, and was in charge of the meteorological stations at Cheung Chau and Cape Collinson. The Marine/Communication Section provided marine weather service, liaised with merchant ships, and disseminated the basic and operational meteorological information provided by the Observatory to meet the requirements of aircraft, ships, and the general public. The Research and Climatology Division comprised the Instruments Section, Seismology/Astronomy/Time Service Section, Electronics/Radioactivity Section, and Hydrology Section. It was in charge of research work on Hong Kong rainfall. As one of the stations in the Worldwide Standardized Seismograph Network, the Seismology/Astronomy/Time Service Section provided time services, astronomy information and recorded earthquakes. The Electronics/Radioactivity Section took regular measurements of total beta-radioactivity of the atmosphere and rainfall and collected radioactivity samples at King's Park and the Observatory. The Hydrology Section collected basic hydrological data.

1965   The Geophysics Division was established to maintain the atomic time standard, operated network of tide stations and a wave recorder, monitored local distant earthquakes, compiled data and conducted investigations for engineering projects.

1966   The Observatory was restructured into two parts: Scientific Operations and Air Services; Administration and Training. The Scientific Operations and Air Services consisted of: Meteorological Services Division (included the sections of Marine, Central Weather Services, Aviation Weather, Communication); Research and Climatology Division (consisted of the sections of

Hydrometeorology, General Climatology, Upper-Air Climatology, Investigation, Records Library); Geophysics Division (comprised the sections of Upper-Air Sounding, Radioactivity, Satellite Meteorology, Electronic Services, Meteorological Instruments, Seismology, Astronomy, Time Service).

1973   The Computer Division was established.

1980   The Air Pollution Meteorology Research Unit was set up to conduct micro-meteorological surveys for the assessment of the air pollution dispersion potential in new development areas.

1984   An assessment of atmospheric transported conditions in the northwestern part of the New Territories and Victoria Harbour was carried out.

1988   The two branches of the Observatory were restructured. The Administration and Research Branch comprised seven divisions: Administration, Training, Computer, Research and Records, Physical Oceanography, Applied Meteorology Research, Special Projects. The Operation and Services Branch consisted of five divisions: Radiation Monitoring, Meteorological Services, Central Forecasting, Aviation Weather Services, Operation.

1993   The Observatory was reorganized into four branches. The Development, Research and Administration Branch consisted of the divisions of Development, Research and Administration. The Forecasting and Warning Services Branch comprised the divisions of Central Forecasting Office Operations, Radar Satellite and Instruments, Special Meteorological Services and Telecommunication. The Radiation Monitoring and Assessment Branch was made up of the divisions of Operation and System Development, Training and Emergency Preparedness, Assessment and Observational Network. The Aviation Meteorological Services Branch included two offices: Airport Meteorological Office (Kai Tak) and Airport Meteorological Office (Chek Lap Kok).

1997   The Royal Observatory changed its title to the Hong Kong Observatory.

2001   The four branches of the Observatory were restructured. The Development, Research and Administration Branch consisted of: Service Development; E-Government, Geophysics, Time and Port Meteorological Services; Short Climate Range Forecasting and Hydrometeorology; Climatological Services, Tropical Cyclone Research and Publication; Administration. The Forecasting and Warning Services Branch comprised: Central Forecasting Office 1, Central Forecasting Office 2, Forecast Development, and Information Technology and Telecommunication. The Radiation Monitoring and Assessment Branch included: Operation and System Development, Training and Exercise, Assessment and Observational Network, and Emergency Preparedness. The Aviation Meteorological Services Branch administered: Aviation Meteorological Data Processing, Windshear and Turbulence Detection, High Impact Weather, Aerodrome Meteorological Instrumentation, Weather Radar and Satellites, and Airport Meteorological Office.

2002   The structure of the Observatory has remained the same, except for the addition of a unit — System Development — to the Forecasting and Warning Services Branch.

Sources:

1. *Administration File: No. 41 Royal Observatory from Public Record Office*, Hong Kong, Government Printer.
2. *Annual Department Report by the Director Royal Observatory*, Hong Kong, Government Printer, 1947-1973.
3. Bell, Gordon, "Fifteen Years of Satellite Meteorology at Hong Kong", in *Weather*, 1981, vol.36, no.1, pp.1-9.
4. Dyson, Anthony, *From Time Ball to Atomic Clock*, Hong Kong, the Royal Observatory, 1983.
5. *Hong Kong Observatory*, Hong Kong, Government Printer, 1998-1999.
6. Information Services Department, *The Hong Kong Facts: Royal Observatory*, Hong Kong, Government Printer, 1988.
7. Lam, C.Y., Xianggang tianwentai shihua (History of the Hong Kong Observatory), *Qixiang zhishi* (Meteorology), no.3 1997, pp.2-5.
8. Malone, D.J., *History and General Organization of the Royal Observatory*, Hong Kong, Royal Observatory, Occasional Papers no. 34.
9. *Observations and Researches made at the Hong Kong Observatory in the Year 1884*, Hong Kong Governmet, 1985.
10. Royal Observatory: *The Hong Kong Time Service*, Hong Kong, Government Printer, February, 1987.
11. *Royal Observatory Hong Kong*, Hong Kong, Government Printer, 1986-1997.
12. Royal Observatory Hong Kong, *Hong Kong Public Weather Services*, Hong Kong, Government Printer, Oct, 1987.
13. "Report of the Director of the Observatory", *Hong Kong Administrative Reports*, Hong Kong, Government Printer 1909-1911.
14. "Report of the Director of the Observatory", *Hong Kong Sessional Papers*, Hong Kong, Noronha & Co., 1899-1907.
15. "Report of the Director of the Royal Observatory, Hong Kong", *Hong Kong Administration Reports*, Hong Kong, Government Printer, 1931-1939.
16. "Report of the Director of the Royal Observatory, Hong Kong", *Hong Kong Administrative Reports*, Hong Kong, Government Printer 1913-1930.
17. Report for 1884 from the Government Astronomer, *Hong Kong Sessional Papers*, Hong Kong, Noronha & Co, 1885, p.123.
18. Sham, P., "Centenary of the Royal Observatory, Hong Kong", in *WMO Bulletin*, 1983, vol. 32, no.4, pp.313-316.
19. Sham, P., "The Royal Observatory Hong Kong and its 105 Years of Meteorological Service", Conference Paper at the Commonwealth Meteorologists Conference, 1989.
20. Sham, P. and Lam, C.Y., Huangjia Xianggang tianwentai qixiang gongzuo de huigu ji zhangwang (A Review of the Royal Hong Kong Observatory), Zhongguo qixiang xuehui liushi zhounian dahui (Conference Paper for the 60th Conference on Meteorology of China), Nanjing, 13-20 Oct. 1984.
21. Starbuck, L., *A Brief General History of the Royal Observatory*, Hong Kong, Government Printer, 1951, p.1.
22. Starbuck, L., "A Condensed History of the Royal Observatory, Hong Kong" in *Marine Observer*, April 1953, pp.99-104.
23. www.hko.gov.hk/contentc.htm

Hong Kong Observatory — Changes in Names and Directors

Year	Name of Department	Title	Name of Director
1883-1887	Observatory	Government Astronomer	Doberck, William
1887-1907	Observatory	Director, Hong Kong Observatory	Doberck, William
1907-1912	Observatory	Director, Hong Kong Observatory	Figg, Frederick, George
1912-1932	Royal Observatory	Director, Royal Observatory	Claxton, Thomas Folkes
1932-1941	Royal Observatory	Director, Royal Observatory	Jeffries, Charles William
1941	Royal Observatory	Director, Royal Observatory	Evans, Benjamin Davies
1946-1956	Royal Observatory	Director, Royal Observatory	Heywood, Graham Scudamore Percival
1956-1965	Royal Observatory	Director, Royal Observatory	Watts, Ian Edward Mein
1965-1981	Royal Observatory	Director, Royal Observatory	Bell, Gordon John
1981-1983	Royal Observatory	Director, Royal Observatory	Peacock, John Edgar
1984-1995	Royal Observatory	Director, Royal Observatory	Sham, Pak, Patrick
1995-1996	Royal Observatory	Director, Royal Observatory	Lau, Chi-kwan, Robert
1996-1997	Royal Observatory	Director, Royal Observatory	Lam, Hung-kwan
1997-2002	Hong Kong Observatory	Director, Hong Kong Observatory	Lam, Hung-kwan

Sources:
1. *Hong Kong Blue Book,* Hong Kong, Noronha & Co., 1883-1940.
2. *The Hong Kong Civil Service List,* Hong Kong, Government, 1947-1958.
3. *Staff Biographies Hong Kong Government,* Hong Kong, Government Printer, 1974, 1976, 1978, 1982, 1984, 1986, 1988, 1990, 1993.
4. *Staff Biographies the Government of the Hong Kong Special Administrative Region,* Hong Kong, Government Printer, 1998, 2001.
5. *Staff List Hong Kong Government,* Hong Kong, Government Printer, 1959-1996.
6. *Staff List the Government of the Hong Kong Special Administrative Region,* Hong Kong, Government Printer, 1997-2000.
7. www.hko.gov.hk/contentc.htm

Chapter 7
Cultural Diffusion and Human Resoures

Roof-top School, 1964

The General Post Office, north face, 1968

Evolvement of Cultural Diffusion and Human Resources

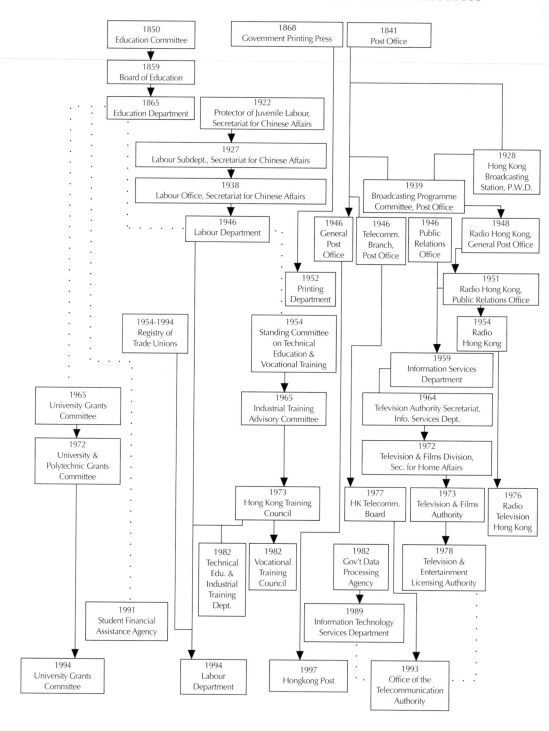

In this chapter, through tracing the history of administrative departments working on education, human resources and general information, we will examine how Western education systems were imported by the Education Department in the nineteenth century and how the new ideas and cultures were diffused by a series of new information institutions during the second half of the twentieth century. The cultural transformation from resistance to assimilation was rather slow in the nineteenth century, but had accelerated since the mid-twentieth century, with the assistance of the new mass media.

The early education policy was implemented in a rather passive way. It relied heavily on Western religious institutions, due to insufficient financial and human resources available to the Government. The premier educational bodies initiated by the Government, which included the Education Committee, set up in 1850, and replaced by the Board of Education in 1859, were chaired by the Bishop of Victoria and later by the missionary James Legge of the London Missionary Society. Only in 1865 did investigations on local educational institutions commence, when the Education Department was formally set up. Through the Education Department, the Government collected general data on school attendance and annual examination papers; it also provided financial support to government, district and grant schools during the late nineteenth and the early twentieth centuries.

The Education Department had been involved more actively in the promotion of Western education systems since the early twentieth century. In 1911, the Government established the first local university: The University of Hong Kong. In 1913, under the new Education Ordinance, schools in Hong Kong were classified into three groups: government schools; grant, private, subsidized schools; and technical institute. The Education Department stressed on improvements in teaching quality standardization through the centralization of examinations in 1935.

Financial assistance on education was extended to private and local schools after the Second World War. In the 1960s, the Government placed emphasis on the development of tertiary education. The second university — The Chinese University of Hong Kong — was established in 1963; and University Grants Committee was created in 1965 to advise on the development and funding of tertiary education institutions. The universalization of education became the first priority of education development in the 1980s. In September 1980, the nine-year compulsory education policy was implemented. In 1990, the Student Financial Assistance Agency was set up to administer several publicly funded financial assistance schemes and a number of scholarship schemes, in order to provide financial assistance in the form of grants and loans to full-time local students. More opportunities for fundamental learning and further studies in Hong Kong or abroad were made available to Hong Kong students.

Although the popularization of education was the Government's major objective, in the early days, inadequate attention was drawn to the correlation between education and training of the labour force. Established in 1946, the Labour Department was the successor of the Labour Office in the Secretariat for Chinese Affairs. Its previous duties concentrated mainly on the protection of workers' rights, improvement of working conditions and pay systems, especially the working conditions and overtime work situations for women and children.

Industrial and technology training only commenced in the 1960s. The Industrial Training Advisory Committee was set up in 1965 and evolved into the Hong Kong Training Council in 1973. It then became the Vocational Training Council in 1982. It advised the Governor on measures to establish a comprehensive system of technical education and industrial training; developed and operated schemes to train operatives, craftsmen, technicians and technologists; established and maintained technical institutes and industrial training centres.

The direct correlation between the job market and education was emphasized in 1983 by the restructure of the Education Branch into the Education and Manpower Branch. Apart from the Education Department and the newly established Technical Education and Industrial Training Department (1982), the new branch also oversaw the Labour Department, the Secretariat of the University and Polytechnic Grants Committee, and the Registry of Trade Unions. Governmental policies on all levels and types of education, industrial training, vocational training, labour matters and rehabilitation were now unified. The close relations between the Labour Department and the Education Department were emphasized; as was the interaction between educational development and labour market requirements.

The diffusion of culture also found a new channel in the 1920s. New knowledge and information were introduced to the public by a new telecommunication institution — Hong Kong Broadcasting Station — in 1928. This Station was transformed into Radio Hong Kong in 1948 and became an independent government department in 1954. It broadcast entertainment programmes as well as those for general information and education purposes.

The educational television programmes had become an important part of Radio Hong Kong Department since 1983. New cultural information was also transmitted to the general public through the mass media; the Public Relations Office was established in 1946 to liaise with the English and Chinese press and to release government notices and news to local and overseas press with the aim of encouraging communication between government departments and the public through the mass media.

To ensure quality and rapidity of transmission of the mass media, from the late 1970s onwards, a series of departments were established to provide supportive services to telecommunications developments in Hong Kong. The Government Data Processing Agency, formed in 1982, advised the Government on data processing matters, and provided a range of computer services within the Government. The Government Data Processing Agency evolved into the Information Technology Services Department in 1989. The Television and Entertainment Licensing Authority, set up in 1978, promoted government policies and provided public relations services. The Office of the Telecommunications Authority, established in 1993, was responsible for the promotion of a fair telecommunications industry and the issuance of licences for telecommunications services and equipment, as well as resolving interconnection disputes between competitive network providers.

The conveyance of culture from the traditional education format to the new presentation methodology through the telecommunications media has rapidly developed since the mid-twentieth century. The immense expansion of government departments mirrored the cultural transformation of Hong Kong society in the new era.

Human Resources

Education Committee (1850-1859)
Board of Education (1859-1865)
Education Department (1865-2002)

1850   An Education Committee was appointed.

1854   The Education Committee provided a grant of HK$5 per month to each of ten small schools.

1855   St. Andrew's School, the first public school, was established.

1856   The London Missionary Society founded an Anglo-Chinese college in Hong Kong.

1859   The Education Committee was replaced by the Board of Education. A Central School was formed by merging several small government schools. Stewart Frederick, first Headmaster of the Central School and Inspector of Schools, was appointed Chairman of the Board of Education.

1860   An unit dealing with educational affairs was established under the Inspector of Schools and was directly responsible to the Governor.

1865   The Board of Education was transformed into the Education Department.

1869   A Police School was set up to train policemen.

1872   Government financial support was given to a missionary school.

1882   Control of Queen's College (previously Central School) was released by the Education Department.

1893   The Inspector of Schools, Ernest John Eitel, closed eleven government schools.

1898   The Inspector of Schools compiled general educational statistics about school attendance, school fees, and results of annual examination.

1902   An Education Committee was appointed. The Inspector of Schools, Edward Alexander Irving, the Registrar General, Arthur Winbolt Brewin, and Ho Kai were nominated as members of the Committee. The Committee made recommendations to the Government on the existing education system. The Education Department provided financial support to three types of schools — government school (Queen's College), district schools (Anglo-Chinese district schools, vernacular district schools, Belilios Public School), and grant schools (English grant schools, Anglo-Chinese grant schools, vernacular grant schools).

1907   The Technical Institute was found.

1909   The title of the head of the Education Department was changed from Inspector of Schools to Director of Education.

1911   The University of Hong Kong was set up. The University comprised the faculties of arts, medicine and engineering. Students were admitted to the University based on the results of the university matriculation examination. The Board of Chinese Vernacular Primary Education was constituted in the same year to promote efficient Chinese vernacular education and collect funds to supplement government subsidies.

1913   The enforcement of the new Education Ordinance necessitated a different classification of schools into three groups. The first group was schools outside the Ordinance which included government schools, military and police schools, and excluded private schools. The second category was Controlled Schools which comprised grants schools, private schools and subsidized (New Territories) schools. The final type was the Technical Institute. The Education Department was responsible for the registration and supervision of schools.

1920   A Board of Education was established to assist the Director of Education in matters pertaining to the development and improvement of education. The Board members included the Director of Education, Senior Inspectors of English and Vernacular schools and nine members nominated by the Government.

1922   The grant and subsidy system was first implemented in the New Territories. A lump sum of HK$5 to HK$20 was given to the qualified schools quarterly. The Police School, formerly staffed by masters from the Education Department, was replaced by a Police Training School, and was placed under the complete control of the Police. The Board of Examiners was formed to hold examinations of the Hong Kong Cadets, Straits and Federated Malay States Cadets, and other examinees.

1935   The first school certificate examination was carried out under the control of the University of Hong Kong. The school certificate examination for Class 2 (the class next below the matriculation class) was under the control of the Education Department.

1938   The schools in Hong Kong were grouped under two categories: primary schools (included primary British schools, government district schools, primary vernacular schools and rural schools) and secondary schools (covered the central British schools, grant-in-aid schools, government secondary schools, Queen's College, King's College, Aberdeen Trade School, Junior Technical School, Belilios Public School, vernacular schools).

1939   The Training College was found in September.

1946   The Education Department was charged to rehabilitate and reconstruct the education system.

1947   The priority development plans of the Department included: the provision of visual aids to schools, recognition of London University degrees and diploma examinations, establishment of 50 government vernacular schools within 10 years, closure of undesirable private schools, and expansion of the rural training college.

1951   The Department provided school curricula.

1959   The Department was organized into three parts: Headquarters (directed the Accounts, Administration, Development, Examination Section, General, Inspectorate, Personnel, Registration); Hong Kong Suboffice; and Kowloon Suboffice.

1961   The Subsidized School Provident Fund Rules, the Grant School Provident Fund (Amendment) Rules, and the Amendments of Subsidy Code for Special Schools and Special Classes for Handicapped Children were enacted.

1962   The amendments of the Post-secondary Colleges Ordinance were enacted. They permitted greater flexibility in the constitutions of the colleges registered under the ordinance.

1963   The Chinese University of Hong Kong Ordinance was enacted. It allowed for the establishment of a second university in Hong Kong.

1968   The Department was structured into five divisions: Headquarters (included the Accounts, Aided Schools, Careers, Examinations, General, Inspectorate, Overseas Students and Scholarships, Registration); English Language Teaching Centre; Hong Kong Suboffice; Kowloon Suboffice; Research, Testing and Guidance Centre.

1969   The Department was restructured into six divisions: Administration, Educational Television, Further and Technical Education, Inspectorate, Primary and Secondary.

1970   The Government Schools Division was established.

1971   A new Education Ordinance 1971 was enacted to replace the old one. The Hong Kong Polytechnic Ordinance was published. The Development Division was set up.

1972   The Further and Technical Education Division was spilt into two divisions: Further Education Division and Technical Education Division.

1973   The Examination Division was formed.

1975   A Placement Service to help redundant teachers in primary education was set up. The School Social Work Scheme jointly run by the Education Department and the Social Welfare Department was implemented. An independent examination authority was proposed to the Legislative Council.

1977   The Department comprised ten divisions: Accounts, Administration, Further Education, Information and Public Relations, Music Administrator's Office, Planning and Building, Recreation and Sports Services, Registration, Schools, Technical Education.

1979   Two new divisions were established: Advisory Inspectorate Division and Services Division.

1983   The Music Administrator's Office was separated from the Education Department and the Recreation and Sports Services Division was abolished.

1986   The Technical Education Division was abolished and the Institute of Language in Education Division was set up.

1988   The Planning and Building Division was divided into Planning and Research Division, and Building and Systems Management Division.

1989   The Registration Division was abolished.

1997   Four divisions were disbanded during the year: Building and Systems Management, Further Education, Information and Public Relations, and Institute of Language in Education.

1999   Two new divisions were set up: Allocation and Support, Information Systems.

2000   The Department comprised nine divisions: Administration, Advisory Inspectorate, Finance, Information Systems, Planning and Research, School, School-based Management, Services and Special Duties.

2002   The Department had been restructured into three parts: Administration, Development and Education. Headed by a Senior Assistant Director, the Administration was mainly divided into three divisions: Administration, Finance and Infrastructure. The Deputy Director supervised the education work through three divisions: Planning and Research, Quality, School Administration and Support. Another Senior Assistant Director was in charge of the development plans of the Department through the Curriculum Development Institute and the School Development Division.

Sources:

1. "Education Department, Hong Kong Annual Report", *Hong Kong Administration Reports*, Hong Kong Government, 1938, pp.1, 7.
2. *The Government of the Hong Kong Special Administrative Region, Telephone Directory*, Hong Kong, Government Printer, 1997, 1999, 2000.
3. *Hong Kong Annual Report of the Director of Education*, Hong Kong Government, 1946-1951.
4. *Hong Kong Blue Book*, Hong Kong, Noronha & Co., 1844-1939.
5. *The Hong Kong Civil Service List*, Hong Kong, Local Printing Press, 1948, p.59.
6. *Hong Kong Education Department Annual Summary*, Hong Kong, Government Printer, 1955-1991.
7. *Hong Kong Government Gazette*, Hong Kong Government, 25 March, 1865; 20 June 1891, p. 495; 21 March 1891, p.197.
8. *Hong Kong Government Telephone Directory*, Hong Kong, Government Printer, 1964-1970.
9. "Report of the Director of Education" *Hong Kong Administrative Reports*, Hong Kong, Government Printer, 1909-1920.
10. "Report of the Inspector of Schools", *Hong Kong Sessional Papers*, Hong Kong, Noronha & Co., 1902, pp.371-376; 1903, p.13; 1904, p.37.
11. www.ed.gov.hk/

Education Department — Changes in Directors

Year	Name of Department	Title	Name of Director
1865-1878	Education Department	Inspector of Schools & Headmaster of Central School	Stewart, Frederick
1878-1897	Education Department	Inspector of Schools	Eitel, Ernest John
1897-1901	Education Department	Inspector of Schools	Brewin, Arthur Winbolt
1901-1909	Education Department	Inspector of Schools	Irving, Edward Alexander
1909-1924	Education Department	Director of Education	Irving, Edward Alexander

Year	Name of Department	Title	Name of Director
1924-1926	Education Department	Director of Education	Orme, Geoffrey Norman
1926-1933	Education Department	Director of Education	Wood, Alan Eustace
1933-1934	Education Department	Director of Education	Smith, Norman Lockhart
1934-1938	Education Department	Director of Education	Sayer, Geoffrey Robley
1938-1941	Education Department	Director of Education	Sollis, Clifford George
1946-1950	Education Department	Director of Education	Rowell, Thomas Richmond
1950-1961	Education Department	Director of Education	Crozier, Douglas James Smyth
1961-1964	Education Department	Director of Education	Donohue, Peter
1964-1969	Education Department	Director of Education	Gregg, William David
1969-1974	Education Department	Director of Education	Canning, John
1974-1980	Education Department	Director of Education	Topley, Kenneth Wallis Joseph
1980-1984	Education Department	Director of Education	Haye, Colvyn Hugh
1984-1987	Education Department	Director of Education	Leung, Man-kin
1987-1992	Education Department	Director of Education	Li, Yuet-ting
1992-1994	Education Department	Director of Education	Wong, Shing-wah, Dominic
1994-1996	Education Department	Director of Education	Lam, Woon-kwong
1996-1998	Education Department	Director of Education	Yu Lai, Ching-ping, Helen
1998-2000	Education Department	Director of Education	Law Fan, Chiu-fun, Fanny
2000-2002	Education Department	Director of Education	Cheung, Kin-chung

Sources:
1. *The Hong Kong Civil Service List*, Hong Kong Government, 1947-1958.
2. *Staff Biographies Hong Kong Government, Hong Kong, Government Printer, 1974, 1976, 1978, 1982, 1984, 1986, 1988, 1990, 1993.*
3. *Staff Biographies the Government of the Hong Kong Special Administrative Region*, Hong Kong, Government Printer, 1998, 2001.
4. *Staff List Hong Kong Government*, Hong Kong, Government Printer, 1959-1996.
5. *Staff List the Government of the Hong Kong Special Administrative Region*, Hong Kong, Government Printer, 1997-2000.
6. www.ed.gov.hk/

Student Financial Assistance Agency (1991-2002)

1990   The Student Assistance Agency comprised ten sections:

1.   The Accounts Section was in charge of general accounting functions.

2.   The Administration Section consisted of the General Registry and Typing Pool; it was responsible for the general administration of the Agency.

3.   The Fee Remission Section administered the Fee Remission Scheme to cater for needy Form 4-7 students attending government, aided, grant or assisted private schools; administered the Examination Fee Remission Scheme to give assistance to needy full-time Form 5-7 students by paying for the examination fees at the HKCEE and the HKALE.

4.   The Kindergarten Fee Remission Section provided parents in need with financial assistance.

5.   The Loan Repayment Section compiled student loan records for the purpose of loan repayment.

6.   The Scholarships, Grants and Loans Section administered the Student Finance Assistance Scheme; the Overseas Education Allowance Scheme and other funds derived from other organizations; and conducted the selection for the award of scholarships.

7.   The Scholarship Unit managed the UK/HK Scholarships Scheme to provide opportunities for outstanding local students for undergraduate studies in the UK; administered the Sir Edward Youde Memorial Fund to promote education and encourage researches.

8.   The Student Travel Subsidy Section provided travel subsidy to needy full time students, aged between 12 and 25, to cover part of the travelling expenses.

9.   The Tertiary Student Finance Section controlled the Local Student Finance Scheme to provide assistance in the form of grant and loan to full-time local students of the University and Polytechnic Grants Committee-funded institutions, who had resided in Hong Kong more than 3 years and were in financial need.

10.   The Textbook Assistance Section administered the means-tested School Textbook Assistance Scheme by providing financial assistance to needy parents for the purchase of textbooks and stationery for their children.

1993   A new section, Student Loan Section, was set up to administer the payment and repayment of loans and the maintenance of student loan accounts under the Local Student Finance Scheme, the UK/HK Governments Joint Funding Scheme, and the Student Finance Assistance Scheme.

1998   The Non-means Tested Loan Scheme Section was established.

1999   The Cross-net Travel Subsidy Section was formed.

2002   The Agency administers the following schemes: Local Student Finance Scheme, Non-means Tested Loan Schemes (3), Student Finance Assistance Scheme,

Financial Assistance Scheme for Post-Secondary Students, Senior Secondary
Fee Remission Scheme, Kindergarten Fee Remission Scheme, School Textbook
Assistance Scheme, Student Travel Subsidy Scheme, Cross-net Travel Subsidy
Scheme, Sir Edward Youde Memorial Fund Scholarship Schemes, Other
Scholarship Schemes. There is also an Office of the Continuing Education
Fund, and an Administration Support Section that undertakes general,
administrative, personnel, finance and accounting duties.

Sources:

1.　*The Government of the Hong Kong Special Administrative Region Telephone Directory*, Hong
　　Kong, Government Printer, 1998, 1999.
2.　*Hong Kong Government Telephone Directory*, Hong Kong, Government Printer, 1991, 1993.
3.　*Student Financial Assistance Agency Annual Report*, Hong Kong, Government Printer, 1992-
　　1996.
4.　www.info.gov.hk/sfaa/

Student Financial Assistance Agency — Changes in Directors

Year	Name of Department	Title	Name of Director
1990-1993	Student Financial Assistance Agency	Controller, Student Financial Assistance Agency	Willis Yau, Sheung-mui, Carrie
1993-1997	Student Financial Assistance Agency	Controller, Student Financial Assistance Agency	Wong, Wai-kin, Alfred
1997-2002	Student Financial Assistance Agency	Controller of Student Financial Assistance Agency	Willis, James Desmond

Sources:
1.　*Staff Biographies Hong Kong Government*, Hong Kong, Government Printer, 1990-1996.
2.　*Staff Biographies the Government of the Hong Kong Special Administrative Region*, Hong Kong, Government
　　Printer, 1998, 2001.
3.　*Staff List Hong Kong Government*, Hong Kong, Government Printer, 1990-1996.
4.　*Staff List the Government of the Hong Kong Special Administrative Region*, Hong Kong, Government Printer,
　　1997-2000.
5.　www.info.gov.hk/sfaa/

University Grants Committee Secretariat (1965-1972)
University and Polytechnic Grants Committee Secretariat (1972-1994)
University Grants Committee Secretariat (1994-2002)

1964　　Approval was given to suggestions to form a committee similar to the British
　　　　University Grants Committee by members of the Legislative Council to advise
　　　　the Hong Kong Government on the facilities, development and financial needs
　　　　of the Universities.

1965	The University Grants Committee (UGC) was formally appointed in October. A small government department, the UGC Secretariat, was established to provide secretariat support for the UGC. Without statutory powers, the UGC members were appointed by the Governor to advise the Government on the development and funding of the two universities — the Hong Kong University and the Chinese University of Hong Kong.
1969	The Secretariat aided the Joint Universities Committee, the Colonial Secretary and the Education Department to devise managerial routines, and administered government schemes on student grants and loans including the Local Student Finance Scheme.
1971	The UPGC Secretariat centralized the vetting of funding applications from the Hong Kong University and the Chinese University of Hong Kong.
1972	To include the Hong Kong Polytechnic within its purview, the University Grants Committee was retitled University and Polytechnic Grants Committee (UPGC).
1973	The UPGC Secretariat was organized into three administrative units: Accounts Section, Capital Projects, General and Student Finance.
1980	The General and Student Finance , acted as a member of the Joint Committee on student finance, formulated policy, and advised on the application of the Government's scheme of finance for students at the Hong Kong University, the Chinese University of Hong Kong, the Hong Kong Polytechnic and the Hong Kong Baptist College. It also recommended to the Government the total requirement for grants and loans for allocation years. A new section, Student Finance Section, was set up during the year to manage and control government schemes on student finance including the Local Student Finance Scheme.
1981	The Student Finance Section also provided financial support for students pursuing tertiary education in the UK.
1983	Hong Kong Baptist College was brought within the ambit of the UPGC.
1984	City Polytechnic of Hong Kong was included in the ambit of the UPGC.
1991	The Hong Kong University of Science and Technology and Lingnan College, were brought into the ambit of the UPGC. A Research Grants Committee was established. The UPGC Secretariat provided administrative and secretariat support to the UPGC, its subcommittees and the Research Grant Council; advised on the assessment and administration and monitored recurrent and capital grants made to the UPGC-funded institutions; and to liaise with the Government, tertiary institutions and other organizations on the development and funding of tertiary education.
1994	Following the adoption of university titles by the two polytechnics, Hong Kong Baptist College and Lingnan College, the UPGC reverted to its previous title of UGC in November.
1995	The Secretariat consisted of six sections: Capital, Departmental Administration, Finance, Policy, Research and Statistics.

2002   The Secretariat provided administrative support to the UGC which advised the Government on the development and funding of tertiary education. It also administered government grants, supported UGC's objectives of maintaining and improving the quality in the UGC-funded tertiary education institutions. The Secretariat comprised the five sections of Capital, Development, Finance, Quality and Research; and two administrative units — Departmental Administration Section and Statistician — directly under the Secretary-General of the Secretariat.

Sources:

1. *The Government of the Hong Kong Special Administraive Region, Telephone Directory*, Hong Kong, Government Printer, 2000.
2. *Hong Kong Government Telephone Directory*, Hong Kong, Government Printer, 1970, 1973, 1981, 1995.
3. *University and Polytechnic Grants Committee's Secretariat*, Hong Kong, Government Printer, 1980-1986.
4. *University Grants Committee of Hong Kong China, Reports,* Hong Kong, Government Printer, 1995-1998.
5. *University Grants Committee of Hong Kong, Reports*, Hong Kong, Government Printer, 1965-1968, 1968-1970, 1970-1972.

University Grants Committee Secretariat — Changes in Names and Directors			
Year	Name of Department	Title	Name of Director
1965-1972	University Grants Committee Secretariat	Secretary, University Grants Committee	Topley, Kenneth Wallis Joseph
1972-1973	University and Polytechnic Grants Committee Secretariat	Secretary, University Polytechnic Grants Committee	Bailey, Stanley Frank
1974-1980	University and Polytechnic Grants Committee Secretariat	Secretary, University and Polytechnic Grants Committee	Bailey, Stanley Frank
1981-1984	University and Polytechnic Grants Committee Secretariat	Secretary, University and Polytechnic Grants Committee	Bradley, William Michael
1985-1988	University and Polytechnic Grants Committee Secretariat	Secretary, University and Polytechnic Grants Committee	Frost, John Anthony
1989-1993	University and Polytechnic Grants Committee Secretariat	Secretary, University and Polytechnic Grants Committee	Spark, Leonard Francis
1993-1994	University and Polytechnic Grants Committee Secretariat	Secretary, University and Polytechnic Grants Committee	French, Nigel John
1994-1999	University Grants Committee Secretariat	Secretary-General, University Grants Committee	French, Nigel John
1999-2002	University Grants Committee Secretariat	Secretary-General, University Grants Committee	Cheung, Po-tak, Peter

Sources:
1. *Staff Biographies Hong Kong Government,* Hong Kong, Government Printer, 1976-1996.
2. *Staff Biographies the Government of the Hong Kong Special Administrative Region,* Hong Kong, Government Printer, 1997-2001.
3. *Staff List Hong Kong Government,* Hong Kong, Government Printer, 1965-1996.
4. *Staff List the Government of the Hong Kong Special Administrative Region,* Hong Kong, Government Printer, 1997-2000.
5. www.ugc.edu.hk/

Labour (Subdepartment), Secretariat for Chinese Affairs (1927-1938)
Labour Office, Secretariat for Chinese Affairs (1938-1946)
Labour Department (1946-2002)

1919   The Sanitary Board was empowered to make by-laws regarding the employment of children.

1921   A commission was appointed to inquire into the conditions and the legislation for the regulation of the industrial employment of children.

1922   The Industrial Employment of Children Ordinance no. 22 of 1922 provided for the appointment of a protector and inspectors of juvenile labour. The Secretary for Chinese Affairs became the Protector of Juvenile Labour.

1927   A Labour (Subdepartment) was set up within the Secretariat for Chinese Affairs to deal with guilds, labour disputes, and cost of living.

1937   The Secretary for Chinese Affairs transferred his role as Protector of Labour to the Chairman of the Urban Council or any person appointed by the Governor. The Urban Council was empowered to make by-laws in respect of industrial undertakings.

1938   A Labour Office was set up within the Secretariat for Chinese Affairs.

1946   A Labour Office was restructured into an independent Labour Department. The power of the registration and inspection of factories was transferred from the Protector of Labour (Chairman of the Urban Council) to the Labour Officer.

1948   All associations of workers or employers with certain defined objects were required by law to be registered in the Labour Office by the Registrar of Trade Unions, who was also the Commissioner of Labour.

1951   A Mines Unit was set up in the Labour Department for the supervision and control of mining operations, under the leadership of the Superintendent of Mines.

1958   The Department was organized into nine sections.

1. The Administration Section was in charge of the general organization, personnel maters, security, publication, and the co-ordination of the Department.

2. The Employment Liaison Office provided employment services to persons made redundant.

3. The Industrial Health Section dealt with the medical and rehabilitation aspects of workmen's compensation cases, investigation of occupational diseases and health hazards in industry.

4. The Industrial Relations Section handled industrial disputes and the promotion of joint consultation and improvements of industrial relations.

5. The Industrial Undertakings Section was responsible for giving advice on industrial policy and the maintenance of proper standards of safety, health and welfare in industry; and the day-to-day supervision of the labour inspectorate.

6. The Supervisory Training Section directed training of supervisors in the smaller industries.

7. The Trade Union Section advised individual trade unions on their organization, administration, and other problems, and undertook trade union education.

8. The Women and Young Persons, and Hours of Work Section dealt with industrial problems concerning women and young persons and enforced regulations relating to their working hours and working conditions.

9. The Workmen's Compensation and Emigrant Labour Section enforced the Workmen's Compensation Ordinance and supervised the recruitment of workers going overseas under contract.

1960   The number of sections was reduced from nine to eight by the amalgamation of the Employment Liaison Office and the Workmen's Compensation and Emigrant Labour Section into a new section known as the Employment and Compensation Section. It administered the Workmen's Compensation Ordinance of 1953, supervised the recruitment of workers going overseas under contract, and found alternative employment for redundant workers of government establishments.

1965   The Department was reorganized into five divisions: the Headquarters, Labour Relations and Development Division (which directed the Conciliation Section, Advisory Services Section, I.L.O. and Development Section), Employment Division (which supervised the Employment Services Section, Industrial Training Section, Labour Statistics Section), Industry Division (which comprised the Industrial Undertakings Section, Pressure Equipment Section, Protection of Women and Young Persons Section, Workmen's Compensation Section), and Industrial Health Division.

1968   All the sections were retitled units. The Headquarters was renamed Administration Division. The Labour Relations and Development Division was divided into the Labour Relations Division and the Development Division. The Labour Statistics and Surveys Unit was formed by the amalgamation of the Wages and Conditions of Service Unit and the Labour Statistics Unit. This Unit co-ordinated the work of surveying wages and conditions of employment and of collecting and compiling selected labour statistics.

1970   The Departmental Publicity Unit was formed to deal with all aspects of the Department's publicity and public relations.

1971   The Industrial Training Division comprising the Industrial Training Unit and the Apprenticeship Training Unit was established.

1976   The Industrial Training Division was restructured to become the Industrial Training Branch with the Training Council Division and the Apprenticeship Division. The Mines Department became part of the Labour Department and was renamed Mines Division. It consisted of the Mines and Quarries Unit and the Explosives Unit.

1977   The Employment Division was spilt into the Employment Services Division (consisting of the Local Employment Service, Overseas Employment Service) and the Employment Conditions Division (including the Youth Employment Advisory Service, and Women and Young Persons Unit).

1979   Comprising the Pressure Equipment Unit, the Factory Inspectorate Division (formerly Industrial Undertakings Unit) was set up to administer the Factories and Industrial Undertakings Ordinance, the Boilers and Pressure Receivers Ordinance and the regulations made under both Ordinances to protect safety, health and welfare of workers in industry; and to provide workers with industrial safety training. The Air Pollution Control Unit formerly under the Industrial Health Division became Air Pollution Control Division.

1980   The Workmen's Compensation Division was retitled Employees' Compensation Division. The Selective Placement Division was established to take over from the Job Placement Unit of the Social Welfare Department the responsibility of providing employment assistance to the physically handicapped.

1981   The Employment Services Division and the Employment Conditions Division were reorganized into three divisions: Employment Services Division, Women and Young Persons Division, and the Youth Employment Advisory Service and Overseas Employment Service Division. The Industrial Health Division was renamed Occupational Health Division.

1982   The Training Council and the Apprenticeship Divisions were merged with the Technical Education Division of the Education Department to form the Technical Education and Industrial Training Department. The Development Division and the Prosecutions and Training Division were reorganized into three divisions: Development, Prosecutions, and Staff Training and Development.

1983   The Department Publicity Unit was renamed Information and Public Relations Division.

1986   The Air Pollution Control Division was transferred to the Environmental Protection Department.

1988   The Youth Employment Advisory Service and Overseas Employment Service Division was renamed Careers Advisory and External Employment Services Division. The new division comprised the Careers Advisory Service, Foreign Domestic Helpers Service, External Employment Service, Employment Agencies Administration.

1991   The Women and Young Persons Division was renamed Labour Inspection Division. The Mines Division was transferred to the Geotechnical Control Office of the Civil Engineering Services Department.

1994   As a consequence of the merger of the Registry of Trade Unions with the Labour Department on April 1, the Labour Relations Division was restructured into two divisions: Labour Relations Divisions 1 and 2.

1996   The Department was reorganized into two branches: the Labour Administration Branch had the responsibilities for the groups of Employment Services, Labour Relations, Employees' Rights and Benefits, and Central Support Services; and the Occupational Safety and Health Branch which comprised eight divisions and was organized into the Occupational Safety Service (Operations Division, Support Services Division, Planning and Training Division, Legal Services Division, Boilers and Pressure Vessels Division), and the Occupational Health Service (Occupational Medicine Division, Occupational Hygiene (Operations) Division, Occupational Hygiene (Development) Division).

1997   The Occupational Safety and Health Ordinance enacted on May 23 extended the protection of safety and health at work to the non-industrial sectors. To take on the new responsibility, the Occupational Safety Service of the Occupational Safety and Health Branch of the Department was restructured into six divisions: Operations, Support Services, Legal Services, Boilers and Pressure Vessels, Information and Training, and Advisory and Development. The Occupational Hygiene (Development) Division of the Occupational Health

Service was divided into three regional divisions: Hong Kong/Kowloon, New Territories East, New Territories West.

1998   The Occupational Medicine Division of the Occupational Safety and Health Branch was divided into three subdivisions: Development, Hong Kong/Kowloon, New Territories.

2002   The structure of the Department remained largely unchanged with the Labour Administration Branch (Labour Relations, Employment Services, Employment Rights and Benefits, Departmental Support Services) and the Occupational Safety and Health Branch (Occupational Safety Service, Occupational Health Service) as its main functional administrative units. The main duties of the Department were to reinforce the well-being of workforce, and to promote safety and health for those at work. The Department provided employment services to meet changes and needs in the labour market; ensured legislation of safety and health for people at work was properly managed; improved and safeguarded employees' rights and benefits.

Sources:

1. *Annual Departmental Reports by Commissioner of Labour*, Hong Kong, Government Printer, 1951-1982, 1991.
2. *Annual Departmental Report by Commissioner for Labour and Commissioner of Mines*, Hong Kong, Government Printer, 1985-1990.
3. *The 50ᵗʰ Anniversary of the Labour Department 1946-1996*, Hong Kong, Government Printer, 1997.
4. *Hong Kong Annual Departmental Report by the Commissioner for Labour, Commissioner of Mines*, Hong Kong, Government Printer, 1983-1984.
5. *Hong Kong Annual Report of the Commissioner of Labour*, Hong Kong Government, 1946-1951.
6. "Hong Kong Civil Affairs Policy Directives, Labour policy", 8 Oct 1945, *Hong Kong Directives*, HKRS 211, D&S no.2/4.
7. *Labour Office Report*, Hong Kong, Government Printer, 1946-47, p.16; 1947-48, pp.2, 15, 26-27.
8. "Report by the Labour Officer on Labour and Labour Conditions in Hong Kong", *Hong Kong Sessional Papers*, Hong Kong, Noronha & Co., 1939, pp.120-122, 125.
9. *Report of the Commissioner for Labour*, Hong Kong, Government Priner, 1992-1999.

Labour Department — Changes in Names and Directors			
Year	Name of Department	Title	Name of Director
1938-1939	Labour Office, Secretariat for Chinese Affairs	Labour Officer	Butters, Henry Robert
1939-1940	Labour Office, Secretariat for Chinese Affairs	Labour Officer	North, Roland Arthur Charles
1940	Labour Office, Secretariat for Chinese Affairs	Labour Officer	Wynne-Jones, Edward Irvine
1940-1941	Labour Office, Secretariat for Chinese Affairs	Labour Officer	Hawkins, Brian Charles Keith

Year	Name of Department	Title	Name of Director
1945-1946	Labour Office, Secretariat for Chinese Affairs	Labour Officer	Hawkins, Brian Charles Keith
1946	Labour Office, Secretariat for Chinese Affairs	Labour Officer	MacFadyen, Quentin Allison Ashby
1946-1947	Labour Department	Labour Officer	Hawkins, Brian Charles Keith
1947-1955	Labour Department	Commissioner of Labour	Hawkins, Brian Charles Keith
1955-1959	Labour Department	Commissioner of Labour	Sedgwick, Patrick Cardinall Mason
1959-1960	Labour Department	Commissioner of Labour and Commissioner of Mines	Sedgwick, Patrick Cardinall Mason
1960	Labour Department	Commissioner of Labour and Commissioner of Mines	Hetherington, Robert Marshall
1960-1961	Labour Department	Commissioner of Labour and Commissioner of Mines	Sedgwick, Patrick Cardinall Mason
1961-1962	Labour Department	Commissioner of Labour and Commissioner of Mines	Hetherington, Robert Marshall
1962-1963	Labour Department	Commissioner of Labour and Commissioner of Mines	Sorby, Terence Dare
1963-1965	Labour Department	Commissioner of Labour and Commissioner of Mines	Sedgwick, Patrick Cardinall Mason
1965-1966	Labour Department	Commissioner of Labour and Commissioner of Mines	Alexander, David Richard Watson
1966-1971	Labour Department	Commissioner of Labour and Commissioner of Mines	Hetherington, Robert Marshall
1971-1973	Labour Department	Commissioner of Labour and Commissioner of Mines	Tsui, Ka-cheung
1973-1977	Labour Department	Commissioner of Labour and Commissioner of Mines	Price, Ian Robert
1977-1978	Labour Department	Commissioner of Labour and Commissioner of Mines	Williams, Peter Barry
1978-1983	Labour Department	Commissioner of Labour and Commissioner of Mines	Henderson, James Neil

Year	Name of Department	Title	Name of Director
1983-1986	Labour Department	Commissioner of Labour and Commissioner of Mines	Bridge, Ronald George Blacker
1986-1989	Labour Department	Commissioner of Labour and Commissioner of Mines	Hammond, Joseph Charles Anthony
1989-1991	Labour Department	Commissioner of Labour and Commissioner of Mines	Hammond, Joseph Charles Anthony
1991-1992	Labour Department	Commissioner of Labour	Chen, Darwin
1992-1994	Labour Department	Commissioner of Labour	Fok Lo, Shiu-ching
1994-1996	Labour Department	Commissioner of Labour	Ip, Shu-kwan, Stephen
1996-1999	Labour Department	Commissioner of Labour	Willis, Jacqueline Ann
1999-2000	Labour Department	Commissioner of Labour	Cheung, Kin-chung, Matthew
2000-2002	Labour Department	Commissioner of Labour	Tan Kam, Mi-wah, Pamela

Sources:
1. *The Hong Kong Civil Service List,* Hong Kong Government, 1947-1958.
2. *Staff Biographies Hong Kong Government, Hong Kong, Government Printer, 1974, 1976, 1978, 1982, 1984, 1986, 1988, 1990, 1993.*
3. *Staff Biographies the Government of the Hong Kong Special Administrative Region,* Hong Kong, Government Printer, 1998, 2001.
4. *Staff List Hong Kong Government,* Hong Kong, Government Printer, 1959-1996.
5. *Staff List the Government of the Hong Kong Special Administrative Region,* Hong Kong, Government Printer, 1997-2000.
6. www.labour.gov.hk/front.htm

Hong Kong Training Council (1973-1982)
Vocational Training Council (1982-2002)

1954   A Standing Committee on Technical Education and Vocational Training was appointed.

1965   The Industrial Training Advisory Committee (ITAC) was formed to replace the Standing Committee. The ITAC advised and examined on industrial training policies, and co-ordinated all aspects of industrial training affecting the main industries of Hong Kong.

1972   The ITAC was abolished on December 31.

1973   Pursuant to recommendations by the ITAC, the Hong Kong Training Council was appointed in October. The Council was to advise on measures necessary to ensure a comprehensive and appropriate training for industrial, commercial and service sectors; to exercise general direction and control over training boards and committees; and to advise on the allocation of government funds for industrial training purposes.

1974   The Hong Kong Training Council considered all proposals presented by the training boards and committees, having been fully investigated and evaluated by the Executive Committee. Ten industry training boards (Automobile Repairs and Servicing, Building and Civil Engineering, Clothing, Electrical, Electronics, Machine Shop and Metal Working, Plastics, Printing, Shipbuilding and Ship Repairs, Textile) were set up to deal with the manpower needs, job standards and training problems of the major industries. Five committees were created to deal with matters common to more than one industry: Apprenticeship, Instructor Training, Technical Training in Institutions, Translation and Vocational Training. Two ad hoc committees — Ad Hoc Committee on Training of Technologists and Ad Hoc Committee on Training in Commerce and the Services — were formed.

1979   To promote the development of training in commercial and service sectors, a new ad hoc committee — Ad Hoc Committee on Training in Industries — was set up in March to investigate the need for training boards and committee to cater for the training needs of industries not covered by the ten industry training boards and six commerce and services training boards (Acquaintance and Allied Fields; Banking; Hotel, Catering and Tourism; Insurance; Journalism; Wholesale/Retail and Import/Export Trades) were also established. The Ad Hoc Committee on Training in Commerce and the Services ceased its function from March 1. A Committee on Management and Supervisory Training of the Hong Kong Training Council was formed.

1982   Based on the foundation laid by the Hong Kong Training Council, the Vocational Training Council was established under the Vocational Training Council Ordinance. It advised the Governor on the measures required to ensure a comprehensive system of technical education and industrial training; developed and operated schemes for training operatives, craftsmen, technicians and technologists; established and maintained the technical institutes and industrial training centres. The Council supervised 19 training boards (Accountancy; Automobile Repairs and Servicing Industry; Banking; Building and Civil Engineering Industry; Clothing Industry; Electrical Industry; Electronics Industry; Hotel, Catering and Tourism; Insurance; Jewellery Industry; Journalism; Machine Shop and Metal Working Industry; Merchant Navy; Plastics Industry; Printing Industry; Shipbuilding and Ship Repairs Industry; Textile; Transport and Physical Distribution; Wholesale/Retail and Import/Export Trades) and six committees (Apprenticeship and Trade Testing; Electronic Data Processing; Management and Supervisory; Technical Education; Training of Technologists; Translation). The Training Council and the Apprenticeship Divisions of the Labour Department, and the Technical Education Division (excluding the Technical Teachers' College) of the Education Department were merged to form the Technical Education and Industrial

Training Department, which served as the executive arm of the Vocational Training Council. The Department was organized into four divisions and two sections: Departmental Administration Division, Finance and Supplies Division, Industrial Training Division, Technical Education Division, Estates Section, and Information and Public Relations Section.

1983   The Seamen's Training Temporary Centre was established at Little Sai Wan.

1984   The Management Development Centre of Hong Kong was set up for research, development, co-ordination and the promotion of management training.

1986   A new Committee on Precision Tooling Training was established.

1989   The Advertising, Public Relations and Publishing Training Board was formed.

1991   The Technical Education and Industrial Training Department was reorganized. Responsibility for vocational training of the disabled and administration of the statutory apprenticeship schemes was transferred to the Vocational Training Council. The function of disbursing subventions to the Council, previously handled by the Department, was passed to the Secretary for Education and Manpower.

1992   The Committee on Vocational Training for the Disabled was set up.

1996   The Council underwent a strategic and organizational review which was carried out by Segal Quince Wicksteed (Asia) Limited. The Committee on Information Technology was formed.

1997   In response to the recommendations by Segal Quince Wicksteed, major proposed reforms included: the creation of a single academic institution 'Hong Kong Institute of Vocational Education (IVE)' with a rationalization and unification of all courses; the revision of the Council's management structure and the training boards; the establishment of a Continuing Professional Development Centre and a Labour Market Analysis Unit; and a review of training effectiveness as part of total quality improvement.

1998   The Council experienced fundamental changes. It comprised eighteen training boards (Accountancy; Automobile; Banking and Finance Industry; Building and Civil Engineering; Electrical and Mechanical Services; Electronics and Telecommunications; Hotel, Catering and Tourism; Insurance; Maritime Services; Mass Communications; Metals; Plastics; Printing and Publishing; Real Estates Services; Security Services; Textile and Clothing; Transport and Physical Distribution; Wholesale/Retail and Import/Export Trades) and five general committees (Apprenticeship and Trade Testing; Information Technology Training; Management and Supervisory Training; Technologist Training; Vocational Training for People with a Disability).

1999   The former technical institutes and technical colleges of the Council were combined to form the Hong Kong Institute of Vocational Education (IVE). The entry requirements, design of courses, etc, were simplified under nine basic disciplines. The Council shifted its training emphasis from manufacturing to the services sector, with a concentration on IT, hospitality and financial services.

Vocational Training Council — Changes in Names and Directors			
Year	Name of Department	Title	Name of Director
1973-1975	Hong Kong Training Council	Chairman, Hong Kong Training Council	Ann, Tse-kai
1975-1982	Hong Kong Training Council	Chairman, Hong Kong Training Council	Tien, Yuan-hao, Francis
1982-1986	Vocational Training Council	Chairman, Vocational Training Council	Tien, Yuan-hao, Francis
1986-1988	Vocational Training Council	Chairman, Vocational Training Council	Chan, Kam-chuen
1989-1992	Vocational Training Council	Chairman, Vocational Training Council	Cheong, Kam-chuen, Stephen
1993-1994	Vocational Training Council	Chairman, Vocational Training Council	Cheng, Cheng-hsun, Graham
1995-1997	Vocational Training Council	Chairman, Vocational Training Council	Wong, Ping-wai, Samuel
1997	Vocational Training Council	Deputy Chairman, Vocational Training Council	Ng, Tat-lun
1998-2002	Vocational Training Council	Chairman, Vocational Training Council	Yeung, Kai-yin

Sources:
1. *Civil and Miscellaneous Lists Hong Kong Government,* Hong Kong Government, 1974, p.48.
2. *First Report of the Hong Kong Training Council, Oct 1973-March 1975,* Hong Kong, Government Printer, 1975.
3. *Fifth Report of the Hong Kong Training Council, April 1978-March 1979,* Hong Kong, Government Printer, 1979.
4. *Fourth Report of the Hong Kong Training Council, April 1977-March 1978,* Hong Kong, Government Printer, 1978.
5. *Hong Kong Annual Report,* Hong Kong, Government Printer, 1955, 1965.
6. *Second Report of the Hong Kong Training Council, April 1975-March 1976,* Hong Kong, Government Printer, 1976.
7. *Seventh Report of the Hong Kong Training Council, April 1980-March 1981,* Hong Kong, Government Printer, 1981.
8. *Sixth Report of the Hong Kong Training Council, April 1979-March 1980,* Hong Kong, Government Printer, 1980.
9. *Third Report of the Hong Kong Training Council, April 1976-March 1977,* Hong Kong, Government Printer, 1977.
10. *Vocation Training Council Annual Report,* Hong Kong, Government Printer, 1982-2001.
11. www.vtc.edu.hk/vtchome/main.jsp

2001   The Beauty Care Training Board and the Chinese Cuisine Training Institute Training Board were established.

2002   The Council attempted to provide a cost-effective and comprehensive system of vocational education and training to the community. Its policies were implemented by five functional committees (Standing, Administration, Estates, Finance, Training), twenty-one training boards (Accountancy; Automobile; Banking and Finance Industry; Beauty Care and Hairdressing; Building and Civil Engineering; Chinese Cuisine Training Institute; Electrical and

Mechanical Services; Electronics and Telecommunications; Hotel, Catering and Tourism; Import/Export/Wholesale Trades; Insurance; Maritime Services; Mass Communications; Metals; Plastics; Printing and Publishing; Real Estate Services; Retail Trade; Security Services; Textile and Clothing; Transport Logistics) and five general committees (Apprenticeship and Trade Testing; Information Technology Training and Development; Management and Supervisory Training; Technologist Training; Vocational Training for People with a Disability). The Hong Kong Institute of Vocational Education comprised nine campuses (Chai Wan, Haking Wong, Lee Wai Lee, Kwai Chung, Kwun Tong, Morrison Hill, Sha Tin, Tsing Yi and Tuen Mun); it provided internationally acceptable vocational education directly applicable to the requirements of Hong Kong employers and the community.

Sources:

1. *Hong Kong*, Hong Kong, Government Printer, 1965, p.23.
2. *Hong Kong Annual Report*, Hong Kong, Government, 1955, p.37.
3. *Report of the Hong Kong Training Council*, Hong Kong, Government Printer, 1973-1975, pp.1-29, 50-61; 1976-1977; 1978-1979, pp.1-2, 73, 76, 84.
4. *Vocational Training Council Annual Report*, Hong Kong Government Printer, 1982-1998.
5. www.vtc.edu.hk/vtchome/main.jsp

Registry of Trade Unions (1954-1994)

1948   The Trade Unions Ordinance of 1948 was enacted. The law regarding the registration and the internal administration of trade unions was enforced by the Commissioner of Labour, who was also the Registrar of Trade Unions.

1954   The Registry of Trade Unions became an independent department; H. J. Cruttwell, was appointed Registrar of Trade Unions.

1955   The Registry of the Trade Union was responsible for the registration of trade unions; the administration of the Trade Disputes Ordinance which affected registrations; and prosecutions of unions which violated the Ordinance.

1961   A new law, covering all matters relating to the registration of trade unions and the control of their internal administration, was enacted. Under the new Ordinance all registered unions were deemed to be corporate bodies for all purposes and were able to hold properties without further formality or the expenses of trust deeds.

1972   Trade unions were required to give the Registrar written notification within 14 days after the establishment or change of address, of every branch, business or charitable, cultural, educational or medical undertaking operated by them or in their registered names.

1975   The Registry was divided into three divisions. The first division gave guidance and advice to members of the public wishing to form trade unions and registered trade unions. The second division maintained a system to ensure compliance by registered trade unions with trade union law and to deal with post-registration matters. The third division compiled statistics and reported on local trade union movement.

1981   The Registry registered all trade unions in accordance with the Trade Unions Ordinance; processed and approved the rules of a trade union; examined trade unions' annual audited statements; monitored trade union activities; complied and studies statistics of trade unions; mediated internal disputes of trade unions; investigated complaints against malpractice of trade union officers; and helped trade union solve problems arising out of other Hong Kong legislation affecting trade unions.

1994   The Registry of Trade Unions was integrated with the Labour Department. A unit undertaking the registration function of trade unions was formed under the Labour Relations Division 2.

Sources:

1. *Annual Departmental Report by the Registrar of Trade Unions*, Hong Kong, Government Printer, 1954-1966; 1969-1987.
2. *Hong Kong Annual Departmental Report by the Commissioner of Registration*, Hong Kong, Government Printer, 1954-1971.
3. *Hong Kong Annual Departmental Report by the Director of Immigration 1977-1978*, Hong Kong, Government Printer, 1978.

Registry of Trade Unions — Changes in Directors

Year	Name of Department	Title	Name of Director
1954-1960	Registry of Trade Unions	Registrar of Trade Unions	Cruttwell, Humphrey John
1960-1969	Registry of Trade Unions	Registrar of Trade Unions	Hardy, Ralph James
1969-1973	Registry of Trade Unions	Registrar of Trade Unions	Allen, John Reginald
1973-1976	Registry of Trade Unions	Registrar of Trade Unions	Tsang, Tat-sing
1976-1978	Registry of Trade Unions	Registrar of Trade Unions	Yiu, Yan-nang
1978-1984	Registry of Trade Unions	Registrar of Trade Unions	Fung, Ping-cheung
1984-1985	Registry of Trade Unions	Registrar of Trade Unions	Lee, Sik-shiu
1985-1986	Registry of Trade Unions	Registrar of Trade Unions	Chan, Wing-kit, Alfred
1986-1987	Registry of Trade Unions	Registrar of Trade Unions	Mak, Sai-yiu
1987-1994	Registry of Trade Unions	Registrar of Trade Unions	To, Sau-hong

Sources:
1. *The Hong Kong Civil Service List*, Hong Kong Government, 1947-1958.
2. *Staff Biographies Hong Kong Government*, Hong Kong, Government Printer, 1974, 1976, 1978, 1982, 1984, 1986, 1988, 1990, 1993.
3. *Staff Biographies the Government of the Hong Kong Special Administrative Region*, Hong Kong, Government Printer, 1998, 2001.
4. *Staff List Hong Kong Government*, Hong Kong, Government Printer, 1959-1996.
5. *Staff List the Government of the Hong Kong Special Administrative Region*, Hong Kong, Government Printer, 1997-2000.

Information

Public Relations Office (1946-1959)
Information Services Department (1959-2002)

1946   After the Sino-Japanese War the Press Relations Office of the British Military Administration established a Public Relations Office to liaise between the English and the Chinese press and the Hong Kong Government. The Office also translated daily Chinese press, released government notices and news items and issued statements of government policy. The Office consisted of three units: Central Office of Information Films, Broadcasting Office, Reading Room.

1947   A new unit — Films Library — was created.

1949   The Office built up close linkages with Radio Hong Kong; the Public Relations Officer sat on the Radio Advisory Committee. The Office was responsible for film censorship.

1950   The reorganization of the Office began in autumn.

1951   Radio Hong Kong came under the administrative control and policy guidance of the Public Relations Office. The administrative and policy control of broadcasting passed from the Postmaster General to the Public Relations Officer.

1952   The reorganization of the Office was completed in 1952. Its major functions focused on the presentation and interpretation of Hong Kong's activities to citizens of Hong Kong and to the world through the mass media. The Office was restructured into two divisions: Broadcasting and Public Relations. The Broadcasting Division was responsible for the English and Chinese programme output. Radio Hong Kong was part of this Division. The Public Relations Division was composed of five sections: Accounts and Administration, Advertising, Film Censorship, Press, and Visual Display and Distribution.

1954   Radio Hong Kong was separated from the Office and became an independent department.

1958   The Publicity Section was set up under the Public Relations Division to improve the production of general publicity materials for use both in Hong Kong and overseas.

1959   The Public Relations Office was renamed Information Services Department and the title of the Public Relations Officer was changed to Director of Information Services with effect from June 19. The Department consisted of the Press Division (supervised the Radio News Room and Press Section) and the Publicity Division (directed the Films and Photography Section, Publications Section, Production Section, Film Censorship Section and Library). The Press Division was responsible for supplying news and information to the press in Hong Kong and overseas, and liaison between the press and government departments. The Publicity Division was responsible for the production, administration, and placement of all government advertising.

| 1960 | Four new sections were formed under the direction of the Publicity Division: Film Unit, Photographic Section, Distribution Section and Features Section. |

1960   Four new sections were formed under the direction of the Publicity Division: Film Unit, Photographic Section, Distribution Section and Features Section.

1963   The Television Progress Committee was set up to plan the implementation of policy on wireless television.

1965   Two new sections were formed under the Publicity Division. The Editorial Section produced newspaper and magazine feature materials for local and overseas publications. The Design and Display Section designed and produced advertisements for overseas newspaper supplements and processed publicity materials for government departments.

1966   The News Division was created to supply news and information to the press and to facilitate communications between government departments and the public through the mass information media.

1968   The Department was reorganized into three divisions and one bureau. The News Division offered information service to the local and overseas press with the aim of encouraging communication between government departments and the public through the mass information media. The Public Relations Division prepared a series of leaflets on government services and procedures to the public and maintained contact with Hong Kong people living overseas. The Publicity Division produced publicity materials for the mass media. The Police Public Information Bureau collected, collated and presented information connected with police actions and policy.

1971   The Technical Services Division (comprised the five sections of Design, Editorial, Films, Marketing and Photographic Service) was set up to provide production services to other divisions and departments and to co-ordinate major government publicity campaigns.

1983   The Department was reorganized into the Administration Division and three functional divisions. The Public Relations Division consisted of the Departmental Information and Public Relations units, Information Unit of Trade and Industry Branch, Information Unit of the Lands and Works Branch, Secretariat Press Office, Public Relations Subdivision, Media Relations Subdivision. The News Division contained the News Editorial and News Services Subdivisions. The Publicity Division comprised the Overseas Public Relations, Publishing, Promotion, and Creative Subdivisions.

1988   The Departmental Information and Public Relations Unit under the Public Relations Division was renamed Departmental Unit Subdivision. The Information Unit of Trade and Industry Branch was put under the Departmental Unit Subdivision. The Media Relations Subdivision was retitled Media Research Subdivision. The Overseas Public Relations Subdivision was transferred from the Publicity Division to the Public Relations Division.

1992   The Department was restructured into two branches. The Administration and Local Branch was composed of four divisions — Administration, News, Publicity, and Departmental Unit and Media Research. The Overseas Public Relations Branch consisted of the Overseas Public Relations Division and the Visits Division.

1993   The Department was reorganized into the Administration Division and four functional divisions: News and Media Research Division, Publicity Division, Overseas Public Relations Division and Visits Division. The News and Media Research Division decided on the most appropriate method of disseminating news and interpreting the policy and political implications of press releases; monitored media reports; advised senior officers on the presentation of news and arranged press conferences; and assessed media reactions to issues of interest to the Government. The Publicity Division recommended publicity objectives; controlled advertising and general publicity; advised government departments and voluntary bodies on general and specific publicity needs on the media to be employed and the availability of funds. The Oversea Public Relations Division monitored Hong Kong's overseas images; planned and organized systematic publicity programmes for projecting Hong Kong's image overseas; advised and implemented the Government's overseas public relations strategy and monitored its effectiveness. The Visits Division planned and co-ordinated the Government's outgoing and incoming visit programmes and monitored their effectiveness.

1995   The Public Relations Division, comprising the Secretariat Press Office and the Departmental Information and Public Relations Units, was established. The Departmental Information and Public Relations Units installed in government bureaux and departments were responsible for the flow of information to the news media and the promotion of a closer relationship between the Government and the public. These units were manned by Information Grade Officers seconded from the Information Services Department.

2002   The Department consisted of six divisions: Administration, Local Public Relations 1 and 2, Overseas Public Relations, Publicity, and Visits and Promotions outside Hong Kong. The Administration Division was responsible for general administration including human and financial resources management, accounting and supplies, information systems and technical support services. The Local Public Relations Divisions were responsible for local public relations matters. Under Local Public Relations Division 1 were 10 Secretariat Press Office teams and the relating department units. Under Local Public Relations Division 2 were the News and Media Research Subdivisions and three Secretariat Press Office teams and the relating department units. The Overseas Public Relations Division had three subdivisions: English Editorial Production Team, Information and Public Relations Units in Overseas Offices, and Overseas Public Relations. Comprising the four subdivisions of Promotions, Creative, Publishing and Internet Resource Centre, the Publicity Division was in charge of government publications, promotional campaigns, advertisements, creative and design work and government photography. The Visits and Promotions outside Hong Kong Division promoted a favourable image of Hong Kong abroad. It was divided into three subdivisions: Incoming Visits, International Visits and Conferences, International Promotions. There were also the Deputy Information Co-ordinator (who assisted the Information Co-ordinator to the Chief Executive of the SAR), the Press Secretary to the

Chief Secretary for Administration, and the Press Secretary to the Financial Secretary.

Sources:

1. *Annual Report of the Public Relations Officer*, Hong Kong, Government Printer, 1947-1949.
2. *Hong Kong Annual Departmental Report by the Director of Information Services*, Hong Kong, Government Printer, 1959-1972.
3. *Hong Kong Annual Departmental Report by the Public Relations Officer*, Hong Kong, Government, 1952-1958.
4. *Hong Kong Annual Report by the Public Relations Officer*, Hong Kong Government, Printer, 1950-1952.
5. *Hong Kong Civil Service List*, Hong Kong Government, 1949-1959.
6. Moss, Peter, *The 40th Anniversary of the Information Service Department*, Hong Kong, Government Printer, 1999.
7. www.isd/gov.hk/index.htm

Information Services Department — Changes in Names and Directors

Year	Name of Department	Title	Name of Director
1946-1947	Public Relations Office	Public Relations Officer	White, George
1947-1950	Public Relations Office	Public Relations Officer	Harmon, Walter Gordon
1950-1959	Public Relations Office	Public Relations Officer	Murray, John Lawrence
1959-1963	Information Services Department	Director of Information Services	Murray, John Lawrence
1963-1972	Information Services Department	Director of Information Services	Watt, Nigel John Vale
1972-1976	Information Services Department	Director of Information Services	Ford, David Robert
1976-1978	Information Services Department	Director of Information Services	Lai, Ming, Richard
1978-1979	Information Services Department	Director of Information Services	Slimming, John Desmond

Year	Name of Department	Title	Name of Director
1979	Information Services Department	Director of Information Services	Johnston, Bernard Renouf
1980-1984	Information Services Department	Director of Information Services	Sun, Yuan-chuang, Robert Strong
1984-1986	Information Services Department	Director of Information Services	Cheung, Man-yee
1986-1987	Information Services Department	Director of Information Services	Chan, Cho-chak, John
1987-1997	Information Services Department	Director of Information Services	Yau Lee, Che-yun, Irene
1997-2002	Information Services Department	Director of Information Services	Chan, Chun-yuen, Thomas
2002	Information Services Department	Director of Information Services	Choi, Ying-pik, Yvonne

Sources:
1. *The Hong Kong Civil Service List*, Hong Kong Government, 1947-1958.
2. Moss, Peter, *The 40th Anniversary of the Information Service Department*, Hong Kong, Government Printer, 1999.
3. *Staff Biographies Hong Kong Government*, Hong Kong, Government Printer, 1974, 1976, 1978, 1982,1984, 1986, 1988, 1990, 1993
4. *Staff Biographies the Government of the Hong Kong Special Administrative Region*, Hong Kong, Government Printer, 1998, 2001.
5. *Staff List Hong Kong Government*, Hong Kong, Government Printer, 1959-1996.
6. *Staff List the Government of the Hong Kong Special Administrative Region*, Hong Kong, Government Printer, 1997-2000.
7. www.isd.gov.hk/index.htm

Government Data Processing Agency (1982-1989)
Information Technology Services Department (1989-2002)

1982   The Data Processing Division of the Councils and Administration Branch became an independent organization — Government Data Division Processing Agency — with effect from April 1. The Agency advised the Government on data processing matters, operated and maintained a central computer bureau, provided a range of computer services within the Government and collaborated with the Civil Service Training Division for all aspects of computer services training.

1989   The Government Data Processing Agency was retitled Information Technology Services Department.

1996   The Director of the Information Technology Services was the Government's information technology (IT) adviser and service provider; the official government representative in most of the external information technology committees; and acted as member of advisory committees for departments of computer science of a number of tertiary institutes in Hong Kong. The Department advised the Government on the most efficient and cost effective use of IT, elevated computer literacy in the civil service, and organized a various types of training for government users. The Department was organized into five branches: Administration Branch, Departmental Services Branch 1, Departmental Services Branch 2, Management Consultancy Services Branch and Technical Services Branch.

1999   The Department was restructured into six branches: Corporate Services Branch, Departmental Services Branch 1, Departmental Services Branch 2, Departmental Services Branch 3, Infrastructure Services Branch, and Management and Community Services Branch. The Corporate Services Branch was responsible for the general and training administration, finance and accounts, human resource management, organization planning and development, stores procurements and administration, public relations and communications. The three Departmental Services Branches provided IT service management, system delivery and maintenance for common services and shared facilities; advised on the use of IT, assisted in formulating IT plans, and advised funding of IT projects. The Infrastructure Services Branch was responsible for IT infrastructure projects, ITSD network architecture, public key and security infrastructures, and information system structures. The Management and Community Services Branch assessed funding applications of computer projects; monitored expenditure of computer projects and post-implementation return; and advised on policy, programmes and partnerships for promotion of IT in the community.

2002   The Department was made up of five branches (Corporate Services Branch, E-government Projects Development Branches 1 and 2, Infrastructure and Security Branch, Technology and Sourcing Branch); and two divisions (Community Education and Industry Liaison Division, E-government Co-ordination Division).

Sources:

1. *Information Technology Services Department Service Overview*, Hong Kong, Government Printer, 1996, pp.1-15; 1999, pp.10-11.
2. www.itsd.gov.hk/itsd/index.htm

Information Technology Services Department — Changes in Names and Directors

Year	Name of Department	Title	Name of Director
1982-1986	Government Data Processing Agency	Data Processing Manager	Lau, Ka-men
1986-1989	Government Data Processing Agency	Data Processing Manager	Greenfield, Colin Charles
1989-1992	Information Technology Services Department	Director of Information Technology Services	Greenfield, Colin Charles
1992-2001	Information Technology Services Department	Director of Information Technology Services	Lau, Kam-hung
2001-2002	Information Technology Services Department	Director of Information Technology Services	Wong, Chi-kong, Alan

Sources:

1. *Staff Biographies Hong Kong Government*, Hong Kong, Government Printer, 1982-1996.
2. *Staff Biographies the Government of the Hong Kong Special Administrative Region*, Hong Kong, Government Printer, 1998, 2001.
3. *Staff List Hong Kong Government*, Hong Kong, Government Printer, 1982-1996.
4. *Staff List the Government of the Hong Kong Special Administrative Region*, Hong Kong, Government Printer, 1997-2000.
5. www.itsd.gov.hk/itsd/index.htm

Post Office (1841-1946)
General Post Office (1946-1997)
Hongkong Post (1997-2002)

1841   A. R. Johnston of the H. M. Commission at Macao was entrusted with postal duties by the Hong Kong Government and he ordered all mail for the expeditionary force to be forwarded to Hong Kong on June 22. The Post Office went into operation on August 25 under the direction of T. G. Fitzgibbon. He died on October 8 and his post was succeeded by D. Mullaly.

1842   Robert Edwards was appointed to take charge of the Office in Hong Kong after the permanent removal of British merchants from Macao. The Office was fully administered in Hong Kong.

1843   The Office was under the direct control of the British Government.

1844	T. J. Scales from the British Post Office was appointed Postmaster General of Hong Kong.
1847	A postal agency was established in Canton to handle mail.
1860	Control of the postal affairs of Hong Kong was passed formally from the Postmaster General of Great Britain to the colonial authorities in Victoria, Australia as of May 1. Eight postal agencies had been established in the treaty ports of China: Amoy, Canton, Foochow, Hankow, Hoihow, Shanghai, Swatow and Tientsin.
1861	Hong Kong issued postage stamps but they were British stamps.
1862	The Stamp Office was established to issue Colonial postage stamps.
1864	Use of Hong Kong stamps became compulsory.
1877	Hong Kong joined the Universal Postal Union as a British Overseas Territory.
1883	The Money Order Office was set up to issue postal notes and to handle transaction of money orders.
1890	The Tientsin postal agency was closed down and a new postal agency was set up in Ningpo.
1897	The Registration Branch was set up to register all correspondence.
1898	Several subbranches of the Office were set up such as the Western Branch in Praya West and the Tsim Sha Tsui Branch in Kowloon.
1904	The Dead Letter Office was established to deal with the unregistered letters. Letters without sender's address and name were destroyed as they could not be returned.
1905	The Registration Branch was renamed Registration and Parcels Branch. The Enquiry and Post Restante Branch went into operation to deal with the registered articles and parcels in the General Post Office.
1907	The Chinese Branch was created to collect Chinese registered articles and letters and to issue Postal Hong Licences.
1914	The Western Branch became the Sheung Wan District Branch and the Sai Ying Pun Branch was set up to meet the requirements of the University of Hong Kong and others.
1915	Two more subbranch post offices were opened in Wan Chai and in Yau Ma Tei. The Radio Telegraph Office was established and a radio telegraph station at Cape d'Aguilar was set up in July. The Office collected telegraph messages and was connected by telephone with the government and public telephone systems.
1916	The Chinese Branch was renamed Chinese Delivery Section. The Office signed a new parcel and mail agreement with the Commonwealth of Australia and Russia respectively. An agreement was entered into for the exchange of radio telegrams between Hong Kong and places in Indo-China through the wireless stations of Cape d'Aguilar and Kwong Tcheo Wan and Hanoi.
1920	A Money Order Agreement between Hong Kong and the Chinese Post Office was signed which provided for the exchange of money order transactions between China and foreign countries through the intermediary of Hong Kong.

1923	Courier services were instituted in Yuen Long, Tai Po Market and Tai Po Kau of the New Territory.
1925	The postal deliveries between Canton and Hong Kong were temporarily suspended due to a general strike in China against foreign powers.
1929	Subbranch post offices were established in Aberdeen and Stanley. Seventy-one traffic staff from the Public Works Department were transferred to the Office. Under the new arrangement, the Radio Telegraph Office was responsible for wireless administration and licensing. New postal services to Pakhoi, Chungshan, Kochow, Swabue, Toyshan, Kiukiang, Waichow, Suncheong and Shanghai were provided. A Wireless School was opened on June 4.
1932	The first experimental airmail flight was launched on November 4 to carry mail to Marseilles, France, by air and then to London by surface.
1933	The Kowloon Tong Subbranch and Yuen Long Subbranch post offices were opened.
1936	A regular service from London by Imperial Airways was inaugurated on March 26. The airmail services between Macao and San Francisco commenced on November 5 and provided Hong Kong with its first Pacific airmail services.
1942	The interrupted postal services were resumed in February. During the occupation period, postal services were chiefly concerned with local mail. The postal rates remained at the same level as 1941.
1945	The Office resumed its previous duties after the Sino-Japanese War.
1946	The Post Office was renamed General Post Office in 1946. The Office was organized into: Telecommunication Branch, Chinese Branch and Money Order Office. The Telecommunication Branch consisted of: Line Section, Radio Licensing and Inspection Office, Laboratory and Maintenance Section. The Line Section was responsible for the provision of radio services, line communications for government magneto telephone systems and apparatus for the railway signalling systems. The Radio Licensing and Inspection Office was responsible for wireless surveys and inspections on shipping, issue of broadcasting and receiving licences; prosecution of unlicensed and illegal receivers and transmitters; and provision of broadcasting transmissions. The Laboratory and Maintenance Section was responsible for repairs, adoptions and construction on equipment, including the maintenance of electro-medical equipment in all government hospitals. The Chinese Branch directed the Chinese Delivery Section and Money Order Office. The Chinese Delivery Section was responsible for the delivery of ordinary letters and articles as well as renting out post office boxes. The Money Order Office carried out exchange controls and administered the Trade Charge Money Order System.
1948	The wireless inspection function was transferred to the Cable and Wireless Limited, while the issuance of licences was still under the control of the Radio Licensing and Inspection Office. The Broadcasting Station under this Office was officially given the title of Radio Hong Kong.
1949	The British Army Post Office was set up to deal with the mail of the military forces stationed in Hong Kong.
1951	The Office was restructured into the Administration Office, Registration Branch, Parcels Branch, Radio Licensing and Inspection Branch, Chinese and

General Delivery Postmen's Sections, Money Order Office, Army Post Office and Radio Hong Kong.

1959   The Office was reorganized into three divisions: Accounts Division (comprised the Remittance Section, International Section, Stores and P. O. Boxes Section), Mail Division (consisted of the Airline and Shipping Section, Air Mail Section and Delivery Section), and the Wireless Division.

1961   The Airline and Shipping Section was replaced by Shipping Section.

1963   The Wireless Division was changed to Telecommunications Division. It was responsible for surveys and inspections of ship radio stations; examinations for competency in radiotelegraphy; issuance of licences; prosecution of unlawful possession of transmitting equipment and unlicensed broadcasting receivers under the Telecommunications Ordinance; provision of telex service, harbour-phone service, radiotelephone long distance service and ship/shore VHF radio-telephone service; and provision of technical advice to government departments on telecommunications matters.

1967   A Transit Mail Section under the Mail Division was set up.

1968   The Mail Division was renamed Postal Services Division and was divided into: Hong Kong Division, and Kowloon and New Territories Division.

1973   The Office was reorganized into five divisions: Administration/Headquarters, Planning and Systems, Accounts, Telecommunications, Postal Operations. The Administration/Headquarters Division was composed of the Overseas Services Section, International Section, Shipping Section and Internal Audit Section. The Planning and Systems Division controlled the Planning and System Section. The Accounts Division consisted of the Accounts Office (Main), Accounts Office (International Mail), Empty Bag Section, Government Telephone A/C Office, P. O. Boxes Section, Remittance Section and Stores. The Postal Operations Division comprised the Hong Kong Division and Kowloon Division.

1974   The Telecommunications Division was reorganized into three subdivisions: Advisory Services; Telephone, Radio and Electronics; Licensing and Inspection.

1977   The Telephone, Radio and Electronics Subdivision was renamed Operations Subdivision. The Licensing and Inspection subdivision was transformed into Regulatory Subdivision.

1980   The Telephone Traffic and Services Division under the Telecommunications Branch was set up. A new division — Overseas Services Section — was created under the Postal Services Branch. The Planning and Systems Division was integrated with the Postal Services Branch.

1981   The Frequency Management Division under the Telecommunications Branch was formed to monitor local radio-communications to ensure compliance with licensing conditions and radio frequency interference investigation purposes.

1982   A new division — Radio Spectrum Management Division — was created under the supervision of the Telecommunications Branch to facilitate assignments and annual radio licence renewals, to provide management statistics on spectrum usage and to assist in the detection of radio interference and the illegal use of radios.

1986   The Administration Branch was reorganized in four divisions: Administrative Services, Management Services, Postal Marketing, Accounts and Finance.

1987   Two new divisions were established under the Administrative Branch. They were the Mechanised Letter Sorting Division and the International Affairs Division.

1989   The Office was restructured into Postal Services Branches 1 and 2, and Telecommunications Branch. The Postal Services Branch I administered five divisions: Administrative Services, Accounts and Finance, Management, Mechanised Letter Sorting and Hong Kong Operations. The Postal Services Branch 2 controlled four divisions: Planning and Development, Postal Marketing, Kowloon Operations and New Territories Operations. The Telecommunications Branch supervised three divisions: Advisory and Planning, Spectrum Management and Regulatory.

1991   The Postal Services Branches 1 and 2 were reorganized into the Administration Branch and Postal Services Branch. The former branch supervised five divisions: Administrative Services, Accounts and Finance, Management Services, Postal Marketing, Planning and Development. The latter branch directed the four divisions of International Affairs and Operations Support, Hong Kong Operations, Kowloon Operations and New Territories Operations.

1992   The Telecommunications Branch was spilt into two branches. The Telecommunications Branch 1 was composed of two divisions: Policy and Legislation, Regulatory. The Telecommunications Branch 2 consisted of two divisions: Advisory and Planning, Spectrum Management.

1993   The Telecommunications Branch was detached from the Office to form the Office of the Telecommunications Authority to administer the Telecommunications Ordinance and the Telephone Ordinance. The Trading Fund Project Division was established under the Postal Services Branch to prepare the Office to operate on a self-financing basis.

1996   Two new divisions — Stamps and Philately, Information Technology — were set up under the Administration Branch. The Stamps and Philately Division issued special stamps, sold Hong Kong stamps to overseas, promoted local philatelic activities, organized seminars on stamp collecting and held stamps exhibitions. The Information Technology Division conducted research on new information technologies and formulated proposals to improve productivity and service standards.

1997   The Office consisted of three major functional branches — Corporate Development Branch, Business Development Branch and Postal Services Branch — and Financial Services Division. The Corporate Development Branch supervised four divisions: Human Resource Management and Administrative Services, Management Services, Planning, and Development and Information Technology. The Business Development Branch administered four divisions: Postal Marketing, Hybrid Mail and Retail Marketing, Customer Management, and Stamps and Philately. The Postal Services Branch controlled five divisions:

Operations, Hong Kong Operations, Kowloon Operations, New Territories Operations, and External Affairs and Operations Support.

1998 The Information System Planning Division was set up under the supervision of the Corporate Development Branch. The Customer Management Division of the Business Development Branch was renamed Customer Services and Sales Division. Three new divisions — Air Mail Centre Division, Operations Review and Overseas Mail Division, and External Affairs Division — went into operation under the control of the Postal Services Branch.

1999 The Electronic Services Division under the direction of the Business Development Branch was established.

2000 The Operations Review and Overseas Mail Division of the Postal Services Branch was abolished.

2002 The structure remained largely unchanged.

Sources:

1. *Annual Departmental Report by the Postmaster General*, Hong Kong, Government Printer, 1950-1952.
2. *Annual Report of the General Post Office*, Hong Kong, Government Printer, 1946-1947.
3. Bishop, George Thompson, *Hong Kong and the Treaty Ports: Postal History and Postal Markings*, London, Postal History Society, 1949.
4. *Hong Kong Annual Report of the Postmaster General*, Hong Kong, Government Printer, 1948-1995.
5. *Hong Kong Blue Book*, Hong Kong, Government Printer, 1844-1939.
6. *Hong Kong Government Gazette*, 21 April 1842; 29 November 1862; 31 January 1863.
7. *Hong Kong Post Office 1841-1991*, Hong Kong, Postmaster General, 1991.
8. *Hong Kong Post Office Annual Report*, Hong Kong, Government Printer, 1995-2000.
9. *Hong Kong Sessional Papers*, Hong Kong, Government Printer & Noronha, Co., 1885, 1898-1908.
10. "Postal", *Hong Kong Directives*, Hong Kong, Government Printer, 1945.
11. Proud, Edward B., *The Postal History of Hong Kong — 1841-1958*, Heathfield, 1989.
12. "Report of the Genreal Post Office, Hong Kong", *Hong Kong Administration Reports*, Hong Kong Government, 1931-1934.
13. "Report of the Post Office Department", *Hong Kong Administrative Reports, Hong Kong*, Government, 1909-1912.
14. "Report of the General Post Office, Hong Kong", *Hong Kong Administrive Reports*, 1913-1930.
15. "Report of the Postmaster General Hong Kong", *Hong Kong Administration Reports*, Hong Kong, Government Printer, 1935-1939.
16. *Report of the Postmaster General Hong Kong for the Year 1947/48*, Hong Kong, Government Printer.
17. Scamp, Lee C., *Postal Rate History of China and Hong Kong: The Pre-adhesive Period to the Beginning of Packet Service from Hong Kong (1800-1845)*, Houston, Nancol Enterprises, 1986.
18. www.hongkongpost.com/eng/main.htm

Hongkong Post — Changes in Names and Directors

Year	Name of Department	Title	Name of Director
1841	Post Office	Clerk in Charge	Fitzgibbon, T. G.
1841-1842	Post Office	Postmaster General	Mullaly, D
1842-1843	Post Office	Postmaster General	Edwards, Robert
1843-1844	Post Office	Postmaster General	Spring, Francis
1844-1845	Post Office	Postmaster General	Scales, Thomas Jackson
1845-1857	Post Office	Postmaster General	Hyland, Thomas
1857-1862	Post Office	Postmaster General	Chapman, William
1862-1875	Post Office	Postmaster General	Mitchell, Francis William
1875-1891	Post Office	Postmaster General	Lister, Alfred
1891-1896	Post Office	Postmaster General	Travers, Arthur Kennedy
1896-1899	Post Office	Postmaster General	Thomson, Alexander MacDonald
1899-1903	Post Office	Postmaster General	Hastings, William Charles Holland
1903-1908	Post Office	Postmaster General	Johnston, Lewis Audley Marsh
1908-1913	Post Office	Postmaster General	Messer, Charles McIlvaine
1913-1917	Post Office	Postmaster General	Wolfe, Edward Dudley Corscaden
1917-1924	Post Office	Postmaster General	Ross, Stewart Buckle Carne
1924-1928	Post Office	Postmaster General	Breen, Michael James
1928	Post Office	Postmaster General	Sayer, Geoffrey Robley
1928-1930	Post Office	Postmaster General	Smith, Norman Lockhart
1930-1931	Post Office	Postmaster General	Breen, Michael James
1931-1932	Post Office	Postmaster General	Hamilton, Eric William
1932-1933	Post Office	Postmaster General	Breen, Michael James
1933-1934	Post Office	Postmaster General	Carrie, William James
1934-1936	Post Office	Postmaster General	Breen, Michael James
1936	Post Office	Postmaster General	Butters, Henry Robert
1936-1940	Post Office	Postmaster General	Wynne-Jones, Edward Irvine
1940-1941	Post Office	Postmaster General	Forrest, Robert Andrew Dermod
1941	Post Office	Postmaster General	Wynne-Jones, Edward Irvine
1946-1948	General Post Office	Postmaster General	Wynne-Jones, Edward Irvine
1948-1950	General Post Office	Postmaster General	Lee, John Henny Burkhill

Year	Name of Department	Title	Name of Director
1950-1958	General Post Office	Postmaster General	Saville, Leonard Charles
1958-1968	General Post Office	Postmaster General	Crook, Alfred George
1968-1971	General Post Office	Postmaster General and Telecommunications Authority	Folwell, Cecil George
1971-1977	General Post Office	Postmaster General and Telecommunications Authority	Addi, Malki
1977-1980	General Post Office	Postmaster General and Telecommunications Authority	Bamford, David John Kyle
1980-1982	General Post Office	Postmaster General and Telecommunications Authority	Heathcote, Arthur Cyril
1982-1988	General Post Office	Postmaster General and Telecommunications Authority	Ardley, Hugh Gordon
1988-1989	General Post Office	Postmaster General and Telecommunications Authority	Siu, Kwing-chue, Gordon
1989-1992	General Post Office	Postmaster General and Telecommunications Authority	Wong, Sing-wah, Dominic
1992-1995	General Post Office	Postmaster General and Telecommunications Authority	Pagliari, Michelangelo
1995-1997	General Post Office	Postmaster General and General Manager of the Post Office Trading Fund	Footman, Robert Charles Law
1997-1998	Hongkong Post	Postmaster General and General Manager of the Post Office Trading Fund	Footman, Robert Charles Law
1998-2002	Hongkong Post	Postmaster General and General Manager of the Post Office Trading Fund	Luk, Ping-chuen

Sources:

1. *The History of Hong Kong Post Office*, Hong Kong, Postmaster General, 1991, p.66
2. *The Hong Kong Civil Service List*, Hong Kong Government, 1947-1958.
3. *Staff Biographies Hong Kong Government*, Hong Kong, Government Printer, 1974, 1976, 1978, 1982, 1984, 1986, 1988, 1990, 1993.
4. *Staff Biographies the Government of the Hong Kong Special Administrative Region*, Hong Kong, Government Printer, 1998, 2001.
5. *Staff List Hong Kong Government*, Hong Kong, Government Printer, 1959-1996.
6. *Staff List the Government of the Hong Kong Special Administrative Region*, Hong Kong, Government Printer, 1997-2000.
7. www.hongkongpost.com/eng/main.htm

Intellectual Property Department (1990-2002)

1990   The Intellectual Property Department was established in July by the transfer out of Trade Marks Registry and the Patents Registry from the Registrar General's Department. It consisted of a Departmental Administration Unit and five functional units — Law and Post-Registration, Policy Legislation, Trade Marks Registry, Patents Registry, and Examination and Operational Systems. The Department undertook responsibility for the registration of trade marks for goods and patents and other related matters from the Registrar General's Department. The Department provided effective systems for the registration of trade marks, patents and other forms of intellectual property and facilities to members of the public to search for trade marks and patents information; administered all existing and new legislation relating to intellectual property; promoted public awareness of benefits attached to the intellectual property rights and the part they played in industrial growth by facilitating the protection, dissemination and utilization of technical information; and participated in international intellectual property promotion activities.

1993   Two consultative documents on proposals for the reform of both trade marks and patents law were issued.

1994   The Law Reform Commission released its report on the reform of copyright and design.

1995   The Sino-British Joint Liaison Group agreed on the basis for the continued protection of all categories of intellectual property in Hong Kong after June 30, 1997.

1996   Criminal provisions were further extended to cover the making of infringing copies outside Hong Kong for export to Hong Kong.

1999   The Government allocated HK$17.3 million to the Intellectual Property Department to raise public awareness and respect for intellectual rights.

2002   The Department was organized into the following: Administration Unit, Development, Hearings, International Registration, Registration, Advisory, Registries (consisted of the Patents and Designs Registries, and Trade Marks Registry).

Sources:

1.   *Hong Kong*, Hong Kong, Government Printer, 1991-2000.
2.   www.info.gov.hk/ipd/eng/index.htm

Intellectual Property Department — Changes in Directors			
Year	Name of Department	Title	Name of Director
1990-1994	Intellectual Property Department	Director of Intellectual Property	Tai, Yuen-ying, Alice
1994-2002	Intellectual Property Department	Director of Intellectual Property	Selby, Stephen Richard

Sources:
1. *Staff Biographies Hong Kong Government*, Hong Kong, Government Printer, 1990, 1993.
2. *Staff Biographies the Government of the Hong Kong Special Administrative Region*, Hong Kong, Government Printer, 1998, 2001.
3. *Staff List Hong Kong Government*, Hong Kong, Government Printer, 1990-1996.
4. *Staff List the Government of the Hong Kong Special Administrative Region*, Hong Kong, Government Printer, 1997-2000.
5. www.info.gov.hk/ipd/eng/index.htm

Government Printing Press (1868-1952)
Printing Department (1952-2002)

1845   The government printing matters were handled by a private company, before the establishment of a printing department. Andrew Shortrede signed the first agreement with the Government to provide printing service in June. The contract remained in force until the late 1850s with some modifications of its terms.

1853   The Government intended to establish the Government Printing Press.

1859   The Government signed an agreement in similar terms to the first agreement with Delfino Noronha.

1868   Delfino Noronha became Noronha & Sons, official printer of the Hong Kong Government.

1879   Noronha & Co. was set up. It continued to serve as government printer.

1886   A Bill to regulate the printing of newspapers and books and the keeping of printing presses was passed.

1939   The bulk of the printing was done by prisoners in the Stanley Gaol and the rest by Noronha & Co. Occasionally odd jobs were tendered out to other commercial printers.

1952   The Printing Department was established in January, with the appointment of W. F. C. Jenner as the Government Printer. It supplied the needs of all other government departments and provided them with many and varied items of paper and stationery for efficient operation. Its major duties included the procurement of printing materials and service; printing of government forms, receipts, certificates, printed matters of all descriptions; posters, leaflets and other publicity materials;

syllabuses and bulletins used by the Education Department; production of security documents; sale and distribution of all publications.

1957   The control and issue of all paper stationery was transferred from the Stores Department to the Printing Department. The Department carried out repairs and maintenance work; for example, the reconditioning of old records and library books for various government departments.

1960   The Department was organized into three parts: General Administration, Letterpress Printing and Offset Printing. The General Administration comprised six sections: Accounts; Cost Accounts; Establishment; Inward and Outward Order; Publications; Stores and Supplies. The Letterpress Printing and Offset Printing were responsible for the printing production; the Offset Printing was also in charge of the security printing.

1969   The Planning and Production Unit was established to measure the productivity of all printing presses.

1971   Implication of bilingualism in government printing and publications was discussed in the Chinese Language Committee.

1974   The Planning and Production Unit was renamed Production Control Unit. It was responsible for the planning and specifying of all incoming work, optimum utilization of resources, co-ordination and direction of the three main production divisions, collection and analysis of production data and quality control.

1983   The Department comprised the Headquarters and eight divisions: General; Accounts; Stores and Procurement; Training and Development; Production Planning and Control; Origination; Printing; Finishing.

1985   The Department was restructured into the Administration Branch, Services Branch and Works Branch.

1995   The Department was divided into four major parts: Headquarters, Administration, Services, and Works.

2001   Under the direct control of the Government Printer, two divisions — Administration and Accounts — were in charge of the general administration of the office, human resource, financial management and accounting services of the Department. Other functional units included the Works Branch and the Services Branch; they were under the direction of the Assistant Printer. The Works Branch comprised three divisions: Origination, Printing and Finishing, Security. It was responsible for the overall supervision on printing, finishing, delivery and security printing. The Services Branch consisted of two divisions: Research and Development, Business and Customer Services. The Services Branch developed plans on business promotion, customer services and quality assurance. The Supplies Division, which handled all supplies and procurement matters, was also under the direct control of the Assistant Government Printer.

2002   The organization structure of the Department remained the same.

Sources:

1.   *Hong Kong Annual Departmental Report by the Government Printer*, Hong Kong, Government Printer, 1953-1954, 1957-1962, 1969-1972, 1974-1977.
2.   www.info.gov.hk/pd/content.index.htm

	Printing Department — Changes in Directors		
Year	Name of Department	Title	Name of Director
1952-1961	Printing Department	Government Printer	Jenner, William Frederick Cecil
1961-1970	Printing Department	Government Printer	Young, Stephen
1970-1978	Printing Department	Government Printer	Lee, Jack Ranyard
1978-1983	Printing Department	Government Printer	Rick, Dennis Robert
1983-1998	Printing Department	Government Printer	Myers, Harris
1998-2000	Printing Department	Government Printer	Tang, Kwok-bun, Benjamin
2000-2002	Printing Department	Government Printer	Tsui, Kwan-ping, David

Sources:

1. *The Hong Kong Civil Service List*, Hong Kong Government, 1952-1958.
2. *Staff Biographies Hong Kong Government*, Hong Kong, Government Printer, 1974, 1976, 1978, 1982, 1984, 1986, 1988, 1990, 1993.
3. *Staff Biographies the Government of the Hong Kong Special Administrative Region*, Hong Kong, Government Printer, 1998, 2001.
4. *Staff List Hong Kong Government*, Hong Kong, Government Printer, 1959-1996.
5. *Staff List the Government of the Hong Kong Special Administrative Region*, Hong Kong, Government Printer, 1997-2000.
6. www.info.gov.hk/pd/content.index.htm

Office of the Telecommunications Authority (1993-2002)

1946　　The Telecommunication Branch of the Post Office was responsible for the provision of telecommunications services, control of licensing of broadcasting transmission and maintenance of equipment for the Government.

1977　　The Hong Kong Telecommunications Board was set up in December to advise the Government on all matters affecting the operation of internal and external telecommunications services in Hong Kong and to ensure the maintenance of efficient communications. It also co-ordinated the civil and military telecommunications requirements, particularly with respect to the assignment of radio frequencies and sites.

1993　　The Office of the Telecommunications Authority was established on July 1 to assist the Telecommunications Authority and to take over the telecommunications services performed by the Telecommunications Branch of the Post Office and other government departments. The Office of the Telecommunications Authority was headed by the Director-General of Telecommunications who was concurrently appointed Telecommunications Authority under Section 5 of the Telecommunications Ordinance. His main duties included the promotion of a fair and competitive telecommunications industry in Hong Kong; protection of consumer interests through investigation of complaints and administration of price control arrangements; issuance and administration of licences for telecommunications services and equipment; and resolving interconnection disputes between competitive network operators. The Authority consisted of the Hong Kong Telecommunications Board and three functional branches: Regulatory Affairs Branch (supervised the Regulation Division, Economic and Legal Unit); Support Branch (comprised the Development Division, Administrative Services Division, Legislation and Planning Division); Operations Branch (consisted of the Advisory and Planning Division, Spectrum Management Division).

1994   Four advisory committees were created: Radio Spectrum Advisory Committee, Telecommunications Numbering Advisory Committee, Telecommunications Standards Advisory Committee, Telecommunications Users and Consumers Advisory Committee.

1995   Since June, the Office of the Telecommunications Authority had been operating on a trading fund basis, with its functions supported by income derived mainly from licence fees. The Office was required to achieve a reasonable rate of return and it tabled an annual operating report to the Legislative Council and published a corporate plan and an annual business plan, setting out it productivity improvements and investments plans. The Finance Division was created under the Support Branch in June to assist the general administration of the Trading Fund and to implement the new financial and accounting systems.

1996   The Regulatory Division under the Regulatory Affairs Branch was renamed Technical Regulation Division. The Economic and Legal Unit of the Regulatory Affairs Branch was retitled Economic Regulation Division.

1999   Following the termination of Cable and Wireless HKT's exclusive licence for external circuits and services, service-based competition in external telecommunications was introduced in January with the granting of licences for external telecommunications services. Full competition arrived in mobile telecommunications with the introduction of mobile number portability in March. The Complaint Committee on Junk Fax was formed in October to advise the Telecommunications Authority on significant cases of service suspension/termination, and amendments to the guidelines for senders of fax advertisements and the consumer education leaflets; and to monitor the general effectiveness of measures introduced to tackle the problem of junk fax.

2000   The Legislation and Planning Division of the Support Branch was transformed into a new Branch: Corporate Affairs Branch. It provided public enquiry services and dealt with consumer complaints. The In-Building System Section was set up within the Advisory and Planning Division of the Operations Branch to co-ordinate access of space in residential and commercial buildings and to conduct mediation of interconnection disputes.

2001   The Competition Affairs Branch was spun off in June from the Regulatory Affairs Branch to supervise work related to competition and economic studies; to ensure enforcement of fair competition of telecommunications services; and to advise the Government on broadcasting competition policy and on the implementation of broadcasting competition provisions in the Broadcasting Ordinance.

2002   The Office consisted of four branches: Competition Affairs Branch (Competition Sections 1, 2, 3 and 4); Operations Branch (Advisory and Planning Division and Spectrum Management Division); Regulatory Affairs Branch (Technical Regulation Division and Economic Regulation Division); Support Branch (Development Division, Administrative Services Division, Corporate Affairs Division and Finance Division). The Competition Affairs Branch managed the competition and economic studies and reinforced fair competition. The Operations Branch controlled Hong Kong's radio frequency spectrum and provided advisory and planning services to the public sector and technical support in the regulation of broadcasting services. The Regulatory Affairs Branch oversaw the regulation and licensing of public telecommunications services, enforced licensed conditions and administered the telecommunications numbering plan. The Support Branch was in charge of technical standard setting, international affairs, public relations and internal administration of the Office of the Telecommunications Authority.

Sources:

1. *Office of the Telecommunications Authority Annual Report*, Hong Kong, Government Printer, 1993-1995.
2. *Office of the Telecommunications Authority Trading Fund Report*, Hong Kong, Government Printer, 1995-2000.
3. www.ofta.gov.hk/

Office of the Telecommunications Authority — Changes in Directors

Year	Name of Department	Title	Name of Director
1993-1995	Office of the Telecommunications Authority	Director-General of Telecommunications	Arena, Alexander A.
1995-1997	Office of the Telecommunications Authority	Director-General of Telecommunications and General Manager, OFTA Trading Fund	Arena, Alexander A.
1997-2002	Office of the Telecommunications Authority	Director-General of Telecommunications and General Manager, OFTA Trading Fund	Wong, Sik-kei, Anthony

Sources:
1. *Staff Biographies Hong Kong Government*, Hong Kong, Government Printer, 1993,1996.
2. *Staff Biographies the Government of the Hong Kong Special Administrative Region*, Hong Kong, Government Printer, 1998, 2001.
3. *Staff List Hong Kong Government*, Hong Kong, Government Printer, 1993-1996.
4. *Staff List the Government of the Hong Kong Special Administrative Region*, Hong Kong, Government Printer, 1997-2001.
5. www.ofta.gov.hk/

Hong Kong Broadcasting Station, Public Works Department (1928-1948)
Radio Hong Kong, Post Office (1948-1951)
Radio Hong Kong, Public Relations Office (1951-1954)
Radio Hong Kong (1954-1976)
Radio Television Hong Kong (1976-2002)

1928	A government radio station was established at Victoria Peak. The broadcasting services were carried out by the Electrical and Wireless Telegraphy Office of the Public Works Department.
1929	Responsibilities for wireless traffic and operating staff were transferred from the Public Works Department to the Post Office, while installation and maintenance of wireless plants remained with the Public Works Department. The Hong Kong Broadcasting Programme Committee responsible for the organization of sound broadcasting was formed in September.
1939	The Postmaster General took control of the broadcasting services with the aid of the Broadcasting Programme Committee.
1941	The Station was closed down during the Japanese invasion.
1942	The Station was on air again under Japanese control.
1945	The daily English and Chinese transmission from ZBC were being broadcast in September under the British Military Administration.
1948	The Hong Kong Broadcasting Station was given the official title of Radio Hong Kong.
1949	Radio Hong Kong and the BBC in London were linked together by a two-way radio telephone circuit in April.
1951	Radio Hong Kong became a division of the Public Relations Office in April.
1954	Radio Hong Kong was separated from the Public Relations Office and became an independent department in April. It was responsible for the broadcast of the best available programmes not only for entertainment, but for information and education; it also collected the radio licence fees. Radio Hong Kong was organized into three sections: Administration, Chinese Programme and English Programme.
1956	The Legislative Council approved the introduction of all-day broadcasting in Chinese.
1957	All-day broadcasting in Chinese was introduced.
1960	Introduction of FM transmission.
1961	Programmes broadcast in stereo were demonstrated.
1970	A new government television unit — Radio Hong Kong Television (RHKTV) — was established in April. It began limited production in June 1971 and became fully operational in February 1972.
1971	Radio Hong Kong Television produced public affairs television programmes for transmission by the licensed commercial television stations.

1973	The Government decided that both the Chinese and English services should compile their own news bulletins without the aid of government information service. Radio Hong Kong had direct control of its own news output with effect from April.
1974	Two music channels — Radio 3 and Radio 4 — were created under the direction of the English Programme Section.
1976	Radio Hong Kong was renamed Radio Television Hong Kong, but its Chinese name remained unchanged. The Educational Television Division of the Education Department was merged with Radio Television Hong Kong and became the Educational Television Division in April.
1978	The Department was restructured into four divisions: Administration (comprised the Administration Section and Production Service Section), Radio (directed the Radio Programmes Section, News and Public Affairs Section), Television, and Engineering. The fifth channel under the English Programme Section was started as a joint venture with the BBC, to relay the segment of the BBC's World Service specifically intended for Southeast Asia.
1980	The Department provided a 24-hour broadcasting service on both English and Chinese channels.
1981	The Chinese channels consisted of three channels. Radio 1 focused on information, education and entertainment programmes. Radio 2 produced programmes for young listeners, outside broadcast programmes and promoted local music talents. Radio 5 provided an additional FM service of Chinese programmes such as Cantonese operas, provincial music, and programmes in Putonghua and Chiu Chow dialect.
1983	The Department was organized into a Departmental Administration Unit and four functional divisions of Educational Television, Production Services, Public Affairs Television and Radio.
1988	The Department was expanded, with a Departmental Administration Unit, a Central Information Unit and five functional divisions, which comprised the Cable and Wireless Engineering, Educational Television (Adult Education, School, Supplementary, and Youth and Children), Production Services (Art Services, Film Services, Film and Video Editing Services, Studio Services), Radio (Chinese Programme Service, English Programme Service), and Television (General Programmes, and Public and Current Affairs).
1994	With the assistance of the Computer Science Centre of the Chinese University of Hong Kong, the RTHK website was launched in December to provide new reports and a limited amount of television and radio programmes online.
2000	All radio channels and television programmes broadcast during the TV prime-time were webcast live.
2001	The Cable and Wireless Engineering Division had been abolished. Two new units were created — New Media Unit and Corporate Affairs Unit. The Corporate Affairs Unit supervised three subdivisions: Public Relations, Marketing and Sponsorship, and Programme Standards and Practices.

2002   RTHK was organized into four divisions (Radio, Television, Educational Television, Production Services) and three units (Departmental Administration, New Media, Corporate Affairs). Under the Radio Division were: Chinese Programme Service, English Programme Service, and News and Current Affairs. Under the Television Division were: Public and Current Affairs, General Programmes. Under the Educational Television Division were: School, Supplementary, Adult Education, Youth and Children, Documentary Special. Under the Production Services Divisions were: Film and Video Editing Services, Studio Services, Film Services, Art Services. The composition of the Corporate Affairs Unit had not changed.

Sources:

1.   *Annual Departmental Report* by *Controller of Broadcasting*, Hong Kong, Government Printer, 1954-1956.
2.   *Annual Departmental Reports by Director of Broadcasting*, Hong Kong, Government Printer, 1960-1976.
3.   *Hong Kong Government Telephone Directory*, Hong Kong Government Printer, 1978, p.185.
4.   Radio Television Hong Kong, *Sixty Years of Broadcasting in Hong Kong*, Hong Kong, Government Printer, 1988, pp.16-18, 41.
5.   "Report of the Director of Public Works", *Hong Kong Administrative Reports*, Hong Kong, Government Printer, 1928-1929.
6.   "Report of the General Post Office Hong Kong", *Hong Kong Administrative Reports*, Hong Kong Government, 1929, R8.
7.   RTHK — 50 Years Broadcasting in Hong Kong from 1928-1978, Hong Kong, Government Printer, 1978.
8.   www.rthk.org.hk/

Radio Television Hong Kong — Changes in Names and Directors

Year	Name of Department	Title	Name of Director
1954-1956	Radio Hong Kong	Controller of Broadcasting	Hindson, Curtis Lake
1956-1961	Radio Hong Kong	Controller of Broadcasting	Brooks, Donald Edgar
1961-1972	Radio Hong Kong	Director of Broadcasting	Brooks, Donald Edgar
1972-1976	Radio Hong Kong	Director of Broadcasting	Hawthorne, James Burns
1976-1978	Radio Television Hong Kong	Director of Broadcasting	Hawthorne, James Burns
1978-1982	Radio Television Hong Kong	Director of Broadcasting	Kerr, Donald John
1982-1985	Radio Television Hong Kong	Director of Broadcasting	Wilkinson, Charles Stuart
1986-1999	Radio Television Hong Kong	Director of Broadcasting	Cheung, Man-yee
1999-2002	Radio Television Hong Kong	Director of Broadcasting	Chu, Pui-hing

Sources:
1. *The Hong Kong Civil Service List*, Hong Kong Government, 1954-1958.
2. *Staff Biographies Hong Kong Government*, Hong Kong, Government Printer, 1974, 1976, 1978, 1982, 1984, 1986, 1988, 1990, 1993.
3. *Staff Biographies the Government of the Hong Kong Special Administrative Region*, Hong Kong, Government Printer, 1998, 2001.
4. *Staff List Hong Kong Government*, Hong Kong, Government Printer, 1959-1996.
5. *Staff List the Government of the Hong Kong Special Administrative Region*, Hong Kong, Government Printer, 1997-2001.
6. www.rthk.org.hk/

Television Authority Secretariat, Information Services Department (1964-1972)
Television and Films Division, Secretariat for Home Affairs (1972-1973)
Television and Films Authority, Government Secretariat (1973-1978)
Television and Entertainment Licensing Authority (1978-2002)

1964	Under the Television Ordinance no. 32 of 1964, the Director of Information Services was appointed the Television Authority for securing proper standards of broadcast television. The Television Authority Secretariat was established within the Information Services Department.
1967	A Television Board was appointed to advise the Television Authority in the exercise of its functions, to submit recommendations and proposals to the Governor-in-Council on matters affecting programme standards and the renewal or revocation of licences, and to conduct enquiries into the progress of television.
1972	The Television Authority Secretariat and the Film Censorship Unit were detached from the Information Services Department and became the Television and Films Division of the Secretariat for Home Affairs. The Commissioner for Television and Films was also the ex officio Chairman of the Television Advisory Board.
1973	The Television and Films Division was retitled Television and Films Authority. The Authority was directly under the Colonial Secretariat.
1978	The Television and Films Authority was renamed Television and Entertainment Licensing Authority. It was responsible for the regulation of station licences, the monitoring of the performance of television stations to ensure compliance with the terms and conditions of their licences, and the advertising and technical standard required.
1996	The Television and Entertainment Licensing Authority was under the Broadcasting, Culture and Sport Bureau. The Authority was organized into two major divisions: Broadcasting and Entertainment. Comprising the Broadcasting Subdivision and the Research and Development Subdivision, the Broadcasting Division was responsible for the maintenance of proper standards

of television and radio programmes transmitted from Hong Kong. The Entertainment Division had four subdivisions: Administration Subdivision, Film Subdivision, Entertainment Licensing Subdivision and Book Registration Office. It was responsible for the enforcement of the Film Censorship Ordinance and the Control of Obscene and Indecent Articles Ordinance.

1998   The Broadcasting Division was restructured into Compliance Subdivision, Standards and Research Subdivision and Broadcasting Registry. A Film Services Office was set up under the Entertainment Division to create, maintain a healthy development of the film industry and to promote Hong Kong films locally and abroad.

2002   The Authority consisted of the Broadcasting Division and the Entertainment Division. The Broadcasting Division was organized into three subdivisions: Broadcasting Registry, Compliance Subdivision, Standards and Research Subdivision. The Entertainment Division comprises: Administration Subdivision, Film Subdivision, Film Services Office, Licensing Subdivision. The Authority was in charge of broadcasting monitoring and regulation; film classification and film services; and entertainment licensing.

Sources:

1. *Hong Kong*, Hong Kong Government Printer, 1965, 1979, 1985.
2. *Hong Kong Annual Departmental Report by the Director of Information Services*, Hong Kong, Government Printer, 1964-1965, p.3; 1967-68, p.20.
3. *Hong Kong Annual Departmental Report by the Secretary for Home Affairs*, Hong Kong, Government Printer, 1972-73, p.25; 1973-74, p.1.
4. *Hong Kong Government Telephone Directory*, Hong Kong, Government Printer, 1998, p.544.
5. *Television and Entertainment Licensing Authority Annual Report*, Hong Kong, Government Printer, 1996-1998.
6. www.info.gov.hk/tela/index2.htm

Television and Entertainment Licensing Authority — Changes in Names and Directors

Year	Name of Department	Title	Name of Director
1973-1978	Television and Films Authority	Commissioner for Television and Films	Watt, Nigel John Vale
1978-1983	Television and Entertainment Licensing Authority	Commissioner for Television and Entertainment Licensing	Watt, Nigel John Vale
1983-1985	Television and Entertainment Licensing Authority	Commissioner for Television and Entertainment Licensing	Sun, Yuan-chuang, Robert Strong

Year	Name of Department	Title	Name of Director
1985-1987	Television and Entertainment Licensing Authority	Commissioner for Television and Entertainment Licensing	Kwok, Wai-hong, Harold
1987-1989	Television and Entertainment Licensing Authority	Commissioner for Television and Entertainment Licensing	Chen, Darwin
1989-1991	Television and Entertainment Licensing Authority	Commissioner for Television and Entertainment Licensing	Yam Kwan, Pui-ying, Lily
1992	Television and Entertainment Licensing Authority	Commissioner for Television and Entertainment Licensing	Sum, Mun-ling, E.
1992-1995	Television and Entertainment Licensing Authority	Commissioner for Television and Entertainment Licensing	Lau Ng, Wai-lan, Rita
1995-1996	Television and Entertainment Licensing Authority	Commissioner for Television and Entertainment Licensing	Cheung, Po-tak, Peter
1996-2002	Television and Entertainment Licensing Authority	Commissioner for Television and Entertainment Licensing	Chan, Yuk-tak, Eddy

Sources:
1. *Staff Biographies Hong Kong Government,* Hong Kong, Government Printer, 1974, 1976, 1978, 1982, 1984, 1986, 1988, 1990, 1993.
2. *Staff Biographies the Government of the Hong Kong Special Administrative Region,* Hong Kong, Government Printer, 1998, 2001.
3. *Staff List Hong Kong Government,* Hong Kong, Government Printer, 1959-1996.
4. *Staff List the Government of the Hong Kong Special Administrative Region,* Hong Kong, Government Printer, 1997-2000.
5. www.info.gov.hk/tela/index2.htm

Index